Persistence *of* Good Living

Global Change / Global Health

Cynthia T. Fowler and Elizabeth Anne Olson

Persistence

of

Good Living

*A'uwẽ Life Cycles and Well-Being
in the Central Brazilian Cerrados*

JAMES R. WELCH

THE UNIVERSITY OF
ARIZONA PRESS

TUCSON

The University of Arizona Press
www.uapress.arizona.edu

We respectfully acknowledge the University of Arizona is on the land and territories of Indigenous peoples. Today, Arizona is home to twenty-two federally recognized tribes, with Tucson being home to the O'odham and the Yaqui. Committed to diversity and inclusion, the University strives to build sustainable relationships with sovereign Native Nations and Indigenous communities through education offerings, partnerships, and community service.

ISBN-13: 978-0-8165-4734-0 (hardcover)
ISBN-13: 978-0-8165-5661-8 (paperback)
ISBN-13: 978-0-8165-4735-7 (OA ebook)

Cover design by Leigh McDonald
Cover photo by James R. Welch
Typeset by Sara Thaxton in 10/14 Minion Pro with Fournier MT Std, Constantia, and Diotima LT Std

An electronic version of this book is freely available, thanks to the support of the Wellcome Trust.

Library of Congress Cataloging-in-Publication Data
Names: Welch, James R., author.
Title: Persistence of good living : A'uwe life cycles and well-being in the central Brazilian cerrados / James R. Welch.
Description: Tucson : University of Arizona Press, 2023. | Series: Global change / global health | Includes bibliographical references and index.
Identifiers: LCCN 2022031523 (print) | LCCN 2022031524 (ebook) | ISBN 9780816547340 (hardcover) | ISBN 9780816547357 (ebook)
Subjects: LCSH: Xavante Indians—Brazil—Terra Indígena Pimentel Barbosa. | Xavante Indians—Brazil—Terra Indígena Pimentel Barbosa—Social life and customs.
Classification: LCC F2520.1.A4 W46 2023 (print) | LCC F2520.1.A4 (ebook) | DDC 305.898/4—dc23/eng/20221104
LC record available at https://lccn.loc.gov/2022031523
LC ebook record available at https://lccn.loc.gov/2022031524

This book is dedicated to deceased A'uwẽ friends and adoptive family who showed me abundant generosity of heart by treating me as kin and helping me feel at home among friends in their communities: Antônio Ru'wẽ'warazu'ata, Barbosa Sidowi, Bonfim Barotí, Darú Serenhimirami, Isabel Xavante, Marcos Sibró, Maria Sinhose'õ, Miriam Wautomõwáwã, Raimundo Serezabdi, Ronaldo Wa'atö, Samuel Sahutuwẽ, and Sereburã.

CONTENTS

ILLUSTRATIONS

Figures

Table

ABBREVIATIONS

FUNAI   National Indian Foundation (Fundação Nacional do Índio)
FUNASA   National Health Foundation (Fundação Nacional de Saúde)
SASI   Indigenous Healthcare Subsystem (Subsistema de Atenção à Saúde Indígena)
SESAI   Special Secretariat for Indigenous Health (Secretaria Especial de Saúde Indígena)
SPI   Indian Protection Service (Serviço de Proteção aos Índios)

ACKNOWLEDGMENTS

I am deeply grateful for the generous support of the A'uwẽ people at Pimentel Barbosa, Etênhiritipá (including both factions currently in dispute over control), Paraíso, Santa Vitória, and Sõrepré communities who shared their lives with me so that I might understand, record, and communicate what I learned from them. I deeply appreciate their trust in me to treat this knowledge with care, raising public awareness about their culture while respecting limitations to the circulation of some information. I have endeavored to honor these boundaries throughout this book, although any errors are my own and not due to failings of the A'uwẽ with whom I worked.

I am particularly appreciative of my adoptive parents, Valdo Pari'õwá and Aparecida Penherewé; my adoptive grandmothers, Iara Rẽzẽ and the late Maria Sinhose'õ; and my adoptive siblings, Lazinho Sõwa'õ, Eugênio Tsere'uté, Denoque Sadaps'o'owe, José Moreira Waciwadi Dariowa, Cidália Sinhoseheriwẽ, Dedé Sutupara, Valdinho Homodi'iwe, Hernan Soro'õ, and Portela Sere'ré, who shared their home with me during my first year of fieldwork (I lived in an annex built adjacent to their primary house).

Although the entire population now residing in the five communities mentioned above cared for my well-being and generously participated in my research, some people were particularly integral to my fieldwork experience and to the ideas presented in this book. In addition to my adoptive family, these included Adalto Serewaipó, Agostinho Tseretsu, Alceu Parawãtö, Angélica Wautomo'uptabi'õ, Antônio Ru'wẽ'warazu'ata, Barbosa Tsidowi Wai'adzatse', Caimi Wai'asse, Conceição Pezé, Darú Serenhimirami, Dalmacio Pinirawe, Edgar Wa'aro Wahone Xavante, Eduardo Serewedé, Elza Wautomoréi'õ, Francisco Sitomowê, Goiano Tserema'a Hipru, Iolanda Rẽzowé, Iraní Ro'o'si'mãrí, Jamiro Suwepté, José Paulo Seriuwarão Xavante, Josimar Ruru'e, Kouti Ruzane, Lincon Dure'we Xavante, Hipru Xavante, Marco Aurélio Serenho Ihi Xavante, Marcos Sibró, Maria Cristina Pehösi'õ, Neusa Wautomowazu, Paulo Supreteprã

Xavante, Raimunda Penhore, Raimundo Serezáohö, Roberto Huatá Wameru Otomopá, Romeu Híse, Ronaldo Wa'atö, Rubens Tob'uto, Samuel Sahutuwẽ, Sereburã, Tsuptó Buprewên Wa'iri Xavante, Vinícius Supreteprã, and Wahipó Ruzane Tebe Xavante. Some of these people are no longer with us today. I would also like to thank all members of the *êtẽpa* age set for graciously receiving me as their peer and including me in their social and ceremonial activities, as well as the *hötörã* age set for their tireless work mentoring us. Paulo Supreteprã Xavante and Tsuptó Buprewên Wa'iri Xavante interpreted interviews conducted with elders in their native language. Many others provided informal language support.

Every stage of this study benefited from insights and assistance from other scholars and colleagues. I share with them credit for all the book's accomplishments and none of its defects. I thank my PhD adviser, William Balée, for unfailing guidance, loyalty, brilliance, and inspiration. He is responsible for my learning to think like an anthropologist, for repeated reviews of earlier versions of this text, and for tirelessly encouraging me to publish this book and thereby register what he believed were its important results. I extend my deepest thanks Carlos E. A. Coimbra Jr. and Ricardo Ventura Santos for taking a leap of faith when I most needed it, inviting me to Brazil and lending me their constant academic and personal support over the years. Coimbra also introduced me to the Pimentel Barbosa community, reviewed earlier versions of this text, and allowed me to reproduce several of his photographs in this book. Santos also sponsored my early research in Brazil. Nancy M. Flowers offered her enthusiastic support, important insights regarding A'uwẽ society in the 1970s, and access to her census data, field notes, and photographs, which have since been donated to the Museu do Índio, Fundação Nacional do Índio (FUNAI), Rio de Janeiro. I also express my deepest gratitude to Laura Graham for her kind support over the years, timely ethnographic hints via email during my early research and subsequent conversations, and especially for providing essential feedback on the manuscript. Coimbra, Santos, Flowers, and Graham have exemplified the ethos of friendship, support, sharing, and collaboration that I found uniquely characterizes relations among the group of living anthropologists who worked with the A'uwẽ of Pimentel Barbosa. I have strived to extend this camaraderie to researchers from various disciplines who have followed me.

I am so grateful to Elizabeth Anne Olson and Cynthia T. Fowler, editors of the Global Change / Global Health monograph series, published by the University of Arizona Press, for their support, dedication, and expertise. Publication of this book would not have been possible without the professionalism, determination, and grace of Allyson Carter, senior editor at the University of Arizona Press. I also thank Kathryn Conrad, director of the University of Arizona Press, for accepting my proposal to publish this book under an open access license, a decision that led to the Press piloting a new open access project. Revisions benefited enormously from insightful and productive reviews by Beth A. Conklin and Seth W. Garfield. Copyeditor Melanie Mallon's meticulously excellent work contributed substantially by polishing and standardizing the final text.

Professor Eugênio Tsere'uté reviewed and corrected the orthography of native A'uwẽ terms used in the book, ensuring it consistently adheres to the writing system currently taught at elementary schools in the Pimentel Barbosa Indigenous Land.

Numerous colleagues and students accompanied me to A'uwẽ communities, providing support and companionship. Some of these include Aline A. Ferreira, Caio Bibiani, David Dowd, Hugo Genes, J. Rodolfo M. Lucena, Maurício V. Gomes de Oliveira, Noé Klabin, Rosanna Dent, and Rui Arantes.

I thank the staff at the Museu do Índio, FUNAI, for all their dedication and support over the years, including with logistics, multimedia resources, and library access, as well as graciously receiving my occasional A'uwẽ companions. FUNAI staff in Brasília and Mato Grosso state have issued permissions for my research numerous times, often going out of their way to handle them in a timely and personalized manner. Similarly, the Ethics Committee at the Escola Nacional de Saúde Pública, Fundação Oswaldo Cruz (FIOCRUZ) has tirelessly issued research permissions and resolved many problems on my behalf despite the unusual nature of my research in comparison to their usual portfolio.

This research was made possible with funding from diverse sources over the years: the Wellcome Trust (grant 203486/Z/16/Z), a Fulbright-Hays Doctoral Dissertation Abroad fellowship from the U.S. Department of Education (award no. P022A040016), the Anthropology Graduate Student Fund at Tulane University, the Department of Anthropology at Tulane University, Fundação Oswaldo Cruz (projects VPEIC-003-FIO-15 and PAPES V 0428), the Escola Nacional de Saúde Pública Sérgio Arouca (INOVA-ENSP), the Museu do Índio (Fundação Nacional do Índio), and the Conselho Nacional de Desenvolvimento Científico e Tecnológico (process numbers 500288/2009–7, 500072/2010–8, 475750/2012–8, 306099/2016–0, 307773/2019–1).

NOTES ON ORTHOGRAPHY
AND VERBAL TENSES

Native terms in the A'uwẽ (or Xavante) language conform to the orthography currently in use by A'uwẽ teachers at the Pimentel Barbosa Municipal School and the Etênhiritipá State Fundamental Education School, although any errors are my own. It is an orthography in transition, originally developed by missionary linguists (Hall, McLeod, and Mitchell 1987; Lachnitt 2003) based on dialects spoken in their immediate vicinities and later modified through its application and transmission by A'uwẽ teachers at Pimentel Barbosa and Etênhiritipá communities. The system as it is currently applied differs from versions in use in other A'uwẽ communities (most expressively by the elimination of the letters *t* and *d* from the phonemes *ts* and *dz*, respectively) and even from previous representations in publications coordinated by members of Pimentel Barbosa and Etênhiritipá communities.

I used past tenses to recall events, circumstances, and ongoing states from 2004 to 2022, the years in which I conducted fieldwork contributing to the contents of this ethnography. In doing so, I sought to communicate the vigor, resilience, and persistence of a living population that is proud of its cultural distinctiveness through this moment, as I finish writing. I expect it will continue to be just as alive and dignified into the future, although diverse historical transformations associated with internal colonialism and insertion in external sociocultural spheres will cause some of the details contained herein to change. This grammatical approach is intended to recognize that my observations and experiences do not equip me to characterize affairs in the future, whenever this book might be read. Past tenses cause some awkward constructions, especially when referring to ongoing traditions. As author, I was sometimes tempted to switch to present tenses to communicate ongoing continuity but refrained from doing so for the sake of consistency. Also, I chose to value the enduring quality of writing that, with time, could erroneously suggest the immutability of culture were present tenses used. Thus, the past tenses used in this book do not, in any way, suggest A'uwẽ people or culture have ended. Rather, they indicate that the material drawn on to prepare this text is bounded.

Persistence *of* Good Living

CHAPTER 1

Social Well-Being

People, Place, and Approach

Human Wellness in Ethnographic Perspective

This book presents results of long-term fieldwork in two principal Indigenous communities, Pimentel Barbosa and Etênhiritipá, pertaining to the A'uwẽ ethnic group (also known as Xavante or Shavante). It addresses age-related social organization that contributed to community well-being, which in turn intersected with cultural modes of using and caring for the local landscape under contemporary circumstances. The core of my approach is to explore how A'uwẽ human life cycles involved social relations, responsibilities, and events that anchored notions of how a good life should be lived against a backdrop of wholesale socioenvironmental change in recent decades.

Key aspects of life cycles that informed A'uwẽ concepts of well-being involved a sequence of informal age grades and two formal age group systems, one secular and one spiritual. Social relations viewed as "good" and "proper" at different phases of life cycles were also evident in forms of leadership and influence, heritable prerogative ownership, and notions of relatedness. These multiple systems of reckoning age identity provided alternative and interconnected frameworks for how a person at any stage of life might creatively engage with others responsibly and respectfully. They also oriented how people competently accessed landscape resources essential to the long-term social construction of well-being.

In this chapter, I first discuss how my ethnographic experience led me to a particular theoretical approach to social well-being and "country" (Butler et al. 2019), which I situate within anthropological literature on related concepts. In the second section, I introduce the A'uwẽ of Pimentel and Etênhiritipá communities, homes to most of the people who prepared me to write this book (recent community divisions brought the others to several newer communities), with comments about their connections to the local landscape. In the third section, I discuss my initial experience of meeting this population and being integrated into its social fabric through the explicit efforts of my hosts, reflecting on my approach to ethnographic fieldwork. Finally, I present the objectives and organization of the remainder of the book.

Well-being, a seemingly common-sense concept closely allied with health, defies attempts at definition, qualification, and quantification in transcultural perspective.[1] Rooted in the apparently simple condition of being well, it is a heterogeneous idea that provokes intriguing questions about its applicability to plural real-world circumstances, the role of disciplinary boundaries in framing its meanings, and how to reconcile myriad quantitative indicators that purport to capture its essential dimensions. Such a seemingly simple term provokes widely diverse academic interpretations in part because it involves multiple and often divergent facets that can be perceived in numerous ways and reach well beyond mainstream quality of life measures into other arenas, including social life as locally understood (Manning and Fleming 2019b).

The constellation of ideas coded with the term *well-being* come from various disciplines, including philosophy, psychology, economics, sociology, epidemiology, and public health. They include both "subjective" and "objective" definitions, which are distinguished by how they engage with individual perception versus external verifiability (Sumner 1996). They may also be distinguished by whether they are hedonic or eudaimonic, the former being closest to happiness and the latter indicating life lived fully and satisfyingly (Deci and Ryan 2008). Multiple pursuits to define and measure well-being are underway but have not neared their conclusion, in part because of disciplinary crosstalk but also because of its relevance to public policy, which requires ideas with identifiable links to resources and services within the public purview (Diener et al. 2009).

All academic fields contributing to well-being discussions have their own epistemological assumptions about appropriate methods for producing knowledge, most of which are very different from anthropology's. Among the unique contributions of ethnographic studies are robust and holistic approaches that prioritize the diversity of local understandings. Ethnographic approaches ask how different cultures engage their own concepts of wellness and what work others need to do to understand them. Thus, they tend to focus on aspects at the subjective, eudaimonic, and qualitative ends of the spectra. They also show greater interest in sociocultural than individualistic dimensions of well-being, while recognizing that these dimensions overlap and engage one another (Six 2007). Nevertheless, anthropological framings of well-being are considerably varied.

As Neil Thin (2009) pointed out, some earlier anthropological texts exhibited romanticized notions of Indigenous well-being as Neolithic, happy, joyful, peaceful, carefree, and simple (Lévi-Strauss 1955; Sahlins 1968; Thomas 1959; Turnbull 1961). Some contemporary anthropological writings that are not caught up in such idyllic representations nevertheless emphasize hedonic dimensions such as happiness (Mathews and Izquierdo 2009b), the "good life" (E. F. Fischer 2014), and conviviality (Overing and Passes 2000a). These perspectives seem to derive from the view that well-being is most closely allied with positive feelings and sentiments. For example, as Joanna Overing and Alan Passes (2000b) summarized, Amazonian societies tend to talk about how to live well, happily, tranquilly, lovingly, compassionately, and harmoniously. While this characterization might be ethnographically correct, it potentially oversimplifies cultural notions of wellness, which arguably involve more complexity through their proximity to altruism and adversity. For example, the Matsigenka in the Peruvian Amazon conceived of well-being as achieved through serving one's family and making sacrifices through sharing (Izquierdo 2009). Outside Amazonia, for the Aboriginal population at Murrin Bridge, New South Wales, representations of well-being focused on social relations through framing the benefits to others of selflessness and consideration for other people (Heil 2009). Thus, in many cultural contexts, notions of wellness presume adversity, call for selflessness, and attribute benefits to others. These formulations cast well-being in social rather than individualistic terms, predicating the happiness of others on one's own sacrifice. Connections between people are key to a comprehensive understanding of well-being (Anderson 1999).

Psychologists have argued that well-being is social and cultural as much as it is individual (Prilleltensky and Prilleltensky 2007). Similarly, within the field of public health, good health is understood as "not merely the absence of disease, but a state of complete physical, mental, spiritual and social well-being" (WHO 1948). My approach to A'uwẽ well-being is strongly inflected by the emphasis my hosts and consultants placed on certain aspects of social life as central to how a good life is lived. My reading of A'uwẽ thinking led me away from narrow quantitative indices intended for comparing individual wellness toward a broad interpretation of well-being as socially constructed and constituted. Consequently, I do not endeavor to explore the full range of ideas that potentially bore on A'uwẽ notions of well-being. Specifically, I do not emphasize formulations of physical, economic, emotional, or psychological well-being (Manning and Fleming 2019a). I also prioritize the contributions to well-being of interpersonal social relations rather than cosmological and ontological schemata that have been a major focus of anthropological thinking about Indigenous peoples in lowland South America in recent decades (M. M. J. Fischer 2018; Ramos 2012; Rival 2012). In this section, I use an ethnographic lens to explore A'uwẽ notions allied with the term *well-being* from a social perspective. I discuss how A'uwẽ perspectives led me to a particular anthropological formulation of social and environmental well-being that I find productive for understanding their specific case and promising for contributing to transdisciplinary and transcultural discussions about Indigenous peoples' health and healthcare.

In the following subsection, I introduce my late adoptive A'uwẽ grandfather Antônio (Ru'wẽ'warazu'ata), whose unique life and personality illustrate some of the dilemmas and solutions involved in assessing well-being from anthropological, public health, and other academic frameworks. I met Antônio as soon as I first arrived at Pimentel Barbosa in 2004 and came to know him by working with him in his gardens, accompanying him on hunts, and whiling the time away in conversations about any number of topics.

Antônio

Antônio was an agriculturist (figure 1), a hunter, a fisher, and often a collector of fruits, roles closely linked to his identity as a husband, father, and grandfather, who proudly cared for his family along with his two wives and his mother-in-law. Acquiring game meat and fish were mostly his domain as the senior male member of this small group of household caretakers. He was a determined and knowledgeable hunter, one of the last in the study communities to use a bow and arrows.

Antônio had not adopted the conservationist language acquired by several younger A'uwẽ men while living in metropolitan cities and engaging with national and international environmental conservation discourses (Graham 2002). Antônio worked on nearby ranches in the 1970s but had otherwise remained a resident of local A'uwẽ communities. His concern for the local environment was tangible and passionate, guided by his interest in obtaining resources from it over the long term. His understanding of how to preserve the landscape for the future was based on his life experience of extracting resources from it before, during, and after large-scale encroachment and circumscription by cattle and monoculture agricultural ranches. He spoke to me about the landscape prag-

Figure 1 Ru'wẽ'warazu'ata, or Antônio, clearing weeds in his garden plot, 2004.

matically, which communicated a strong sense of place, but without resorting to characterizations of it in animistic terms (Barletti 2016). In his own way, he expressed concern with what some Aboriginal people in Australia call caring for country (Fache and Moizo 2015), attentive to the integrity of his group's now circumscribed territory, which he understood as integral to the well-being of his relatives and community.

Among the first to invite me to accompany him for a day clearing weeds in his garden, he was also one of the first hunters to give me the opportunity to shadow him on group hunts, which were a special interest of mine (Welch 2014, 2015). On these hunts and during our conversations, Antônio demonstrated to me his deep knowledge of and concern for the landscape, as well as its incredible diversity of plants and animals. He considered a healthy and conserved landscape essential for extracting resources from their reduced territory in the present and future, and thereby maintaining what he characterized as traditional values involving provisioning one's family with wild and cultivated foods, sharing these foods with one's extended family and neighbors, and giving gifts of healthful foods at designated moments during some of life's most important ceremonial events.

Antônio and his wives, with the assistance of his mother-in-law, cared for their fourteen rowdy children with all the love, pride, and hard work one could imagine. In community ceremonial life, he performed an essential role as the elder owner and leader of the *tebé* (fish) ceremonies (*tepé'tede'wa*), which were an important component of the ceremonial complex that made up the initiation rites of girls and boys into novitiate adulthood (*danhono*) (figure 2). He also served as a post-officiant (*wai'a'rada*) during spiritual rituals, giving advice and critique to the younger individuals who were now responsible for carrying them out. He was the senior owner of a series of heritable prerogatives that he employed discretely for the benefit of his family and ceremonially for the community at large. I considered Antônio to exemplify social well-being in this A'uwẽ community.

Antônio (and other elders who paid me special attention over the years, many of whom are now deceased) looked after me in his own individual caring ways. His concern for me as a guest in the community was not exceptional for him (it was for me) and illustrated A'uwẽ capacities for creating special affective bonds with non-A'uwẽ who show an interest in their community and well-being. Among the ways they did this was by incorporating outsiders into adoptive families, and thereby exogamous moieties (halves of society who may only marry someone from the opposite half), as well as age sets (cohorts of individuals who participate in rites of passage as groups), and thereby age set moieties (halves of society determined by the alternation of sequential age sets). Such memberships oriented outsiders socially to the whole of society and gave A'uwẽ residents a basis for approaching them properly in socially proximate or distant ways, or with culturally appropriate affinity or antagonism.

Antônio's and others' interest in outsiders spoke to me about their concern with their families', communities', and ethnic group's welfare in a rapidly changing world of territorial circumscription, market insertion, transcultural engagement, biomedical healthcare services, and social media. By engaging outsiders like myself, these elders sought to enhance their community's sovereignty amid upheaval in diverse realms. This sovereignty derived from building knowledge and networks beyond the community that could reinforce internal sources of resilience. As mentioned elsewhere, in many ways we are "their" anthropologists rather than the other way around (Welch and Coimbra Jr. 2014).

Antônio died after several years of major paralysis resulting from a stroke. His last years of life were filled with deep emotion, as he tried but could no longer communicate well verbally with his loved ones and friends, including

Figure 2 Antônio weaving a ceremonial mantle in his role as elder owner of *tebé* (fish) ceremonies during rites of initiation into novitiate adulthood (*danhono*), 2006.

me. Although his family cared for him attentively, and close friends visited regularly, his wheelchair broke repeatedly, his clothes fell into a state of disrepair, and his evident desire to be close to other people went insufficiently attended as community life continued without his usual active participation. When his wheelchair worked, he spent much of his time in front of his house, where he could see the entire community plaza and all the activities that occurred there. When his wheelchair was broken, which was often, he spent most of his days in his kitchen annex behind the house (most houses have detached thatched kitchen annexes beside or behind the main house to protect the residence from kitchen fires), where he could enjoy the company of members of his extended family household and other visitors as they came and went.

His suffering could be easily interrupted with the pleasure of a friendly visit, a warm hand on his knee, a hug, or a cathartic cry with someone close. Antônio was ill, but he was also well in so many ways. His health was poor, but his depth of feeling and connection with others was rich and full until he died. Whereas some scientific or popular formulations of well-being might characterize him as disadvantaged, I understood his degree of wellness to be very high despite his stroke sequelae. This was because his A'uwẽ relatives and peers saw him as the same loving person who abundantly contributed to his family and community with all the responsibility and care that are expected of a husband, father, grandfather, elder, and ceremonial prerogative owner. In his final years, his person was defined not exclusively by his paralysis, but also by his lifelong successes, contributions, and affections.

Traditionalism and Social Well-Being

Antônio's example illustrates why I was led by my ethnographic data to focus on well-being as construed very openly, especially including many social aspects of wellness besides individual physical and mental health (Steckel 2016). Health is an important dimension of well-being. Yet, as Gordon Mathews and Carolina Izquierdo (2009a, 4) noted, "health and well-being may contradict one another." Antônio no doubt suffered in his final years, but he suffered within the fullness of a life lived robustly in connection with his family, community, non-A'uwẽ friends, and local landscape.

I am not the first to call for a broad ethnographic understanding of well-being. For example, Juan Pablo Sarmiento Barletti (2016) made a similar argument based on ethnographic research with the Ashaninka people in Peru, with particular focus on perceptions related to cosmological ontologies. Based on ethnographic work with the Matsigenka in Peru, Izquierdo (2005) sought to expand the notion of well-being to include cultural formulations of goodness and harmony, including spiritual realms, which may suffer even as biomedical measures improve. Ruth Panelli and Gail Tipa (2009) discussed Maori concepts of well-being involving sociocultural and environment dimensions integrated with spiritual elements. Because spiritual topics were closely held secrets among the A'uwẽ that cannot be shared with the public, and not having found ontological interpretations particularly ethnographically pertinent among the A'uwẽ, my contribution is to show how productive formulations of well-being can involve local social values of the kinds illustrated by Antônio's story, such as indulging affection and suffering together.

Within A'uwẽ communities, overwhelming support existed for the maintenance of certain challenging customary rites of passage, especially those related to two age group systems closely intertwined with social and ethnic identity, as I describe in chapter 3. Thus, most A'uwẽ supported cultural traditionalism in at least some contexts, even if younger people's attentions were not particularly directed toward the preservation of all other customs. I use the terms *traditionalism* and *traditionalist* to capture emergent A'uwẽ notions of contemporary advocacy of culture and customs considered "traditional" (*wahöimanazé*) within their culture (Graham 2005). I do not intend for these terms to imply religious conservatism specifically or to suggest any negative connotations such as antiprogressive thinking. Nor do I mean to suggest that culture was static, although some A'uwẽ perspectives of tradition involved ideas about an idealized past.

Multiple social configurations discussed in this book, such as those involving age sets and age groups, were important examples of culturally appropriate expressions of differentiation and rank contributing to a thoroughly plural social tapestry of contrasts between people that was fundamental to traditionalist perspectives of how a good life was lived. For example, my preinitiate male interviewees affirmed enthusiastically that their experience in the preinitiate house (*hö*) was unchanged from the time their male ancestors and grandparents had lived during youth with their secular age set mates under the supervision of their mentors in symbolic and social isolation from the rest of the community. They considered this continuity a source of great pride. Elder men tended to agree with these youths, asserting that the preinitiate experience, including residence in the preinitiate house under the indulgent guidance of their mentors, was a characteristically A'uwẽ format for constructing men from boys that remained unchanged through history. At other times and in other contexts, however, these same elders expressed that the preinitiate experience was now diminished and was likely of little value compared to their own era. Elder men conveyed similar ambivalence to me about the proper continuation and contemporary dilution of the spiritual age group system.

I interpreted these seemingly contradictory narratives as deriving from the simultaneous fallibility of the individuals engaged in these age group systems (especially protégés and their mentors) and the irreproachability of the social arrangements (mentorship relations derived from the intersection of formal age grades and age sets) perpetuated through the generations. Thus, the social configurations involved in mentorship remained intrinsically good (*wedi*) and beautiful (*īwe*), while the individuals involved in them may have fallen short of expectations. These irreproachable social arrangements are an excellent example of traditionalist values that were similarly shared by younger and older people. As I mention above, boys took great pride in asserting that their experiences in the preinitiate house were unchanged from the past. Notably, all boys opted to live with their secular age set peers away from home for up to about four years rather than stay at home, even though A'uwẽ notions of child autonomy (Idioriê 2019; Nunes 2011; Welch 2015) gave them the right to choose of their own accord. Also, female members of mentoring age sets were recently expressing new forms of agency by asserting their desire to participate in some formerly male-only secular age set ceremonies and to hold new ceremonies for female mentors and their female protégés (chapter 3). With females now participating in some such ceremonies, the enthusiasm to participate among youths of both genders was tremendous.

I understand the near universal enthusiasm to participate in age group system activities—especially diverse public ceremonies and rituals, as well as excursions into the cerrado by mentors and their protégés—as indication that these social arrangements were an expressive focus of A'uwẽ traditionalism, anchored in the interests of the entire population, including women and men of diverse ages. Furthermore, they were widely understood to represent the only proper and good way of creating men from boys, contributing substantively to notions of ethnic belonging. Thus, my ethnographic understanding is that these age group systems were examples of traditionalist social configurations amply believed to promote well-being among the population, both for those who participated publicly and those who helped prepare behind the scenes and watched.

By joining a coed secular age set and living in the all-male preinitiate house for years before advancing to novitiate adulthood, a boy was assuming his responsibility to do the internal and external work required to become a respectful and responsible adult, who provided for his family and participated appropriately in the community. By identifying with her secular age set, assisting preinitiates in thatching their shelter, holding ceremonial activities for her protégés, and participating in other ceremonies recently opened to females (figure 3), a woman was supporting her age set protégés and peers and contributing to the beauty of age set relations. By suffering with their protégés during public performances for many hours in the hot cerrado sun, coed mentors invigorated their protégés and contributed to their successful assumption of mentorship roles a decade down the line. By enduring and reciprocating the rivalry of their immediate elder age set, which belonged to the opposite age set moiety, age set peers participated in a culturally sanctioned form of antagonistic oversight that promoted their appreciation for respect and duty. In all these examples, social well-being was expressed through age group systems, persistent symbols of traditionalism amid dramatic transformations in the circumstances of life for the A'uwẽ.

Age group systems were not the only example of social well-being expressed through traditionalism. Other examples included weddings (and associated

Figure 3 Women participating in an age set singing performance (*danho're*) in the Pimentel Barbosa community, 2011.

wedding hunts), female knowledge regarding wild root vegetables (mostly roots and tubers), pregnancy and birthing practices, children's play activities, men's councils, and many more. What was unique about age group systems was the pervasive way they conditioned the human experience from childhood to old age, thereby providing social bearings for all but the youngest living individuals and, in the case of the spiritual age group system, women. Age group systems were ubiquitous aspects of daily social interaction through which meaning was constructed between individuals and groups of individuals (such as age sets and moieties).

Well-Being in Anthropological Perspective

According to John T. Haworth and Graham Hart (2007, 1), well-being

> has been viewed variously as happiness, satisfaction, enjoyment, contentment; and engagement and fulfilment, or a combination of these and other hedonic and eudaimonic factors. Well-being is also viewed as a process, something we do together, and as sense-making, rather than just a state of being. It is acknowledged that in life as a whole there will be periods of ill-being, and that these may add richness to life. It has also been recognized that well-being and the environment are intimately interconnected. Certainly, well-being is seen to be complex and multifaceted, and may take different forms.

Based on my ethnographic experience with the A'uwê, I identify with this characterization of well-being because it focuses on process and "sense-making," as well as interconnectedness with such factors as the environment. Antônio's sadness at the end of his life did not negate the fullness of his lifelong experience or cancel out his degree of contentment for having raised many children, hunted and gardened to provide them with food, and passed along privileged knowledge to them. It did not undo the rich pleasure he expressed when reconnecting with those who had shared his life of generosity and goodwill. It did not betray his community's respect for his years of ceremonial leadership and of caring for his ceremonial protégés. In these ways, Antônio exemplified several A'uwê ways of "well-living" and "well-dying" (McGillivray 2007, 29). He also illustrated the limitations of seeking an anthropological understanding of well-being rooted in the notion of happiness (Mathews and Izquierdo 2009a).

Based on these ethnographic observations, I seek to move beyond individualistic hedonic concepts of happiness, health, and wellness toward an understanding of A'uwẽ well-being as having involved social notions of quality and richness of community life. I focus on aspects of social life, such as age group systems, that my ethnographic research suggests many A'uwẽ understood to promote "the quality of their relationships with each other and the world, which, ideally, contribute to a deep and ensuring sense of intrinsic worth and existential certainty" (Eckersley 2011, 633).

Affiliated with social understandings of well-being is the issue of equality between individuals. For example, income, wealth, and gender disparities were shown to be key factors in determining subjective well-being in nation-states (Brulé and Suter 2019; Diener, Diener, and Diener 2009; Tesch-Römer, Motel-Klingebiel, and Tomasik 2008). Among the A'uwẽ, however, social equality was generally not expected and was not a value that contributed substantially to formulations of well-being. Within their society were clear inequities in status acquisition (see Werner 1981 for a similar account for the Mekrãgnoti subgroup of the Mebêngôkre or Kayapó). Furthermore, evidence from my research group suggests a recent emergence of differentiation in economic status and material wealth (Welch et al. 2009; Arantes et al. 2018). Indeed, despite cultural values prioritizing food reciprocity among neighbors and extended family members, contemporary A'uwẽ approached income and financial assets in a highly individualized manner, which permitted economic gaps between individuals and households, although these were hardly pronounced when compared to those present in larger and more socioeconomically diverse societies. These inequalities were anticipated by A'uwẽ social relations and were not mentioned to me as a source of unwellness.

Although other scholars have suggested that gender disparity continued among the A'uwẽ of Pimentel Barbosa (Graham 2014), gender inequality is challenging to ascertain given the imposition of non-A'uwẽ expectations of what gender equality should look like. Cultural assumptions regarding such behavioral cues as silence, averted gazes, exclusive responsibility for cooking and cleaning, and noninclusion in certain male social activities lead many non-A'uwẽ to identify male domination and female subordination. From my fragile vantage point as a non-A'uwẽ male, however, I would argue that A'uwẽ women had complementary social roles to men, being every bit as proactive and dominating in their preferred domains of influence as men were in theirs. Additionally, A'uwẽ women were actively asserting new forms of social autonomy as they became familiar with Brazilian gender norms (chapter 3). They did so with the widespread support of A'uwẽ men. Thus, as some aspects of gender differentiation had recently come to signify inequality and unwellness for A'uwẽ women, they found recourse by advocating for their own enfranchisement.

Immaterial wealth, usually in the form of social capital, has also been advanced as a key factor in the determination of well-being (Hamilton, Helliwell, and Woolcock 2016; Sixsmith and Boneham 2007). Some scholarship pointed to a complex dynamic whereby social capital is an interdependent but ultimately more stable predictor of hedonic well-being than income (Gleibs et al. 2013). Among the A'uwẽ, social capital as interpersonal networks based in trust and cooperation was not as open ended as it is in Western society. Rather, dependable social relationships were developed through such frameworks as age group organization and kinship, which provided people with largely predetermined social networks that reinforced themselves over time. Whereas age group organization was intrinsically equalizing by perpetually rotating people's social positions, A'uwẽ formulations of kinship promoted imbalanced genealogies. Thus, some groups of real and categorical siblings may have had relatively smaller or less well-off kin networks, while others may have benefited from extensive or comparatively affluent close consanguineal kin. These contrasts were understood by the A'uwẽ to affect well-being, especially as means to acquire resources through reciprocity in times of need and as sources of support and reinforcement in political affairs.

Also closely related to well-being is the concept of resilience, which has been defined as "the process of harnessing key resources to sustain well-being" (Panter-Brick 2014, 432). Proposed as an alternative paradigm to narratives of vulnerability, structural violence, and hardship (Almedom, Brensinger, and Adam 2010; Keck and Sakdapolrak 2013), resilience seeks to capture people's capabilities to overcome adversity and oppression. Social resilience refers to the transformative process by which social groups resist and rebuild in the face of major economic or political challenges. Cultural resilience involves the ability of whole communities or cultural systems to absorb disruption, reorganize, and change while maintaining important distinguishing characteristics, such as identity (Fleming and Ledogar 2008).

Resilience is an extremely relevant framework for understanding A'uwẽ agency in the pursuit of sociocultural well-being during decades of internal colonization (processes of colonization of a country's own people) associated with the appropriation of their territories, undermining of their sovereignty, and bureaucratization of their distinctiveness. This colonial enterprise began at least as early as the eighteenth century, when miners and cattle ranchers displaced them from their territories in the Província do Maranhão and the northern portion of the Província de Goyaz. It intensified with the establishment of enduring relations with Brazilian society in the 1940s and insertion into the market economy beginning in the 1970s. Throughout these events, A'uwẽ who now reside in Pimentel Barbosa and Etênhiritipá communities maintained their identity, key aspects of their social system, ceremonially pertinent dimensions of their food economy, men's spiritual practices, and many other cultural features they considered essential to who they were as a people. They did so by embracing changes that promoted their capacity to resist and adjust. For example, A'uwẽ women continued to prepare meals for their households, although they now did so most frequently with rice cooked in aluminum pots in the absence of wild root vegetables. Similarly, many men remained avid hunters in part because they replaced bows and arrows with rifles and adopted motorized transportation to transform the hunt into a single-day event compatible with contemporary work and school schedules. In the social realm, women no longer participated in traditional naming ceremonies, which they determined were disagreeable and caused unwellness, but now enthusiastically participated in formerly exclusively male age set ceremonies that reinforced their important role caring for their protégés in the secular age group system.

Among the A'uwẽ, resilience was an incomplete process that involved experimentation and continual discourse. I once asked a young adult male what features of A'uwẽ culture were important to preserving the essence of their cultural identity. He responded with this list: spiritual rituals (*wai'a*), proper haircuts (cut along a rigid horizontal line high above the eyebrows and ears, long in the back), plucked eyebrows and eyelashes, men's wooden ear plugs (*wedehu*), cotton neckties (*danho'rebzu'a*), log races (*uiwede*), singing performances (*danho're*), the men's council (*warã*), hunting (*aba*), fishing (*tepezo*), palm-thatched houses (but not necessarily the traditional round construction style), and defecating in the outdoors without latrines or toilets. Soon thereafter, however, this same young man began to cut his hair in a non-A'uwẽ style and to wear stainless steel ear plugs in his ears. Only after being shamed by his elders did he return to using the A'uwẽ haircut and ear plugs he had previously identified as culturally essential. Similarly, the Etênhiritipá community experimented with replacing game meat with fish in the ceremonial distribution held at the end of the quinquennial rites of initiation into novitiate adulthood (*danhono*) to decrease the event's environmental impact. The distribution of fish, however, was popularly judged nontraditional, ungratifying for recipients, and unconducive to cheerfulness. The community subsequently reverted to holding distributions of game meat.

Resilience also involved promoting community autonomy and self-sufficiency throughout a recent history of federal inputs and oversight. In practice this required cyclical rebounding in a boom-and-bust economy, including through renewed reliance on self-provisioning when financial resources were scarce (Santos et al. 1997). It also involved investment in seeking independent financial opportunities in cultural production and ecological conservation (Graham 2005). The A'uwẽ of Pimentel Barbosa also sought to leverage their independence by attentively developing relationships with an extensive network of national and international scholars (Dent 2016; Graham 2000; Welch and Coimbra Jr. 2014). Through this network, they documented and promoted their culture, investigated topics of general community concern, and established affective bonds of reciprocity with well-connected experts in diverse fields. In my experience, A'uwẽ valued these relationships as true friendships while attentively nourishing them so favors might be requested in times of need. For example, about a decade after completing my dissertation research, I received a call from a community leader requesting my assistance in volunteering to conduct a land demarcation study because the federal agency responsible for doing so, the National Indian Foundation (Fundação Nacional do Índio, or FUNAI), did not have available internal human resources. Thanks to indispensable collaboration and leadership by Ricardo Ventura Santos, Carlos E. A. Coimbra Jr., and Nancy M. Flowers over the course of two to three years, we were able to attend to this request, which culminated in the legal identification of a new A'uwẽ Indigenous land (Welch, Santos, et al. 2013). I understood our service to be part of the mutual obligations developed with researchers by the A'uwẽ as part of their resilience strategy.

Wellness, well-being, living well, and good living are but a few popular academic terms for the intersection of factors that contribute to quality of life. Too often these concepts are reduced to oversimplified indicators of vital statistics, food security, socioeconomic status, developmental indices, health conditions, access to public services, happiness, psychological satisfaction, or social capital, among others (although some studies seek considerable robustness in their use of such measures, e.g., Azzopardi et al. 2018). Each of these measures may reflect an important dimension of well-being (Godoy et al. 2005), but Antônio's example shows that quality of life is not easily reducible to any single factor or collection of numerical variables and should be understood as a complex process, incorporating the point of view (worldview) of the people of interest. Established quality of life indicators have been shown to be influenced by emic factors (those that are internal to a given culture), which standardized cross-cultural instruments do not contemplate (Jenaro et al. 2005; Schalock et al. 2005). The autonomy of Indigenous and other culturally distinct peoples to perceive well-being and its cultural determinants on their own terms and incorporating this diversity into research protocols and public policy are important steps in decolonizing healthcare (Manning and Fleming 2019a). Other limitations and biases of mainstream well-being scholarship have been addressed in reviews from public health and anthropological points of view (Carlisle and Hanlon 2008; Thin 2009).

An important endeavor to investigate cultural notions of public wealth or affluence as expressions of well-being was undertaken in the book *Images of Public Wealth or the Anatomy of Well-Being in Indigenous Amazonia*, edited by Fernando Santos-Granero (2015a). Although my emphasis here is not on public wealth, and the A'uwẽ are only Amazonian according to inclusive definitions, it is relevant to note that my findings regarding well-being do not coincide with those of most authors of this important book. For example, Santos-Granero (2015b, 28) generalized for the region: "Well-being attains its maximum expression in the sentiments of happiness, beauty, and rejoicing aroused by collective action." Beth A. Conklin (2015) asserted for the Wari' that collective well-being was related to the community's abundance of food, productivity, vitality, and ability to mobilize group activities and celebrations, as well as an ethos of caring for others. Among the Kisêdjê, well-being was about collective euphoria or rejoicing (Seeger 2015). Through well-organized large ceremonies, Kisêdjê people achieved the satisfaction of euphoria and a sense of public wealth, associated with a notion of living morally well or beautifully together. Although these accounts seem to emphasize social dimensions of well-being, they did so from a hedonic angle. In other words, they emphasized collective forms of happiness. In contrast, my findings led me to emphasize social aspects of living life fully and satisfyingly, including those that did not involve pleasure.

A central aspect of my ethnographic argument is that some A'uwẽ constructions of social well-being involved certain modes of strife, opposition, and hierarchy, which were also viewed as good and proper. This point was well captured by Cesar C. Gordon, who made a similar argument for the Xikrin subgroup of the Mebêngôkre (Kayapó), among whom differentiated social forms of resource and ceremonial goods ownership contributed to ethical and aesthetic concepts about what was "a good, beautiful and correct way life" (2016, 210). This author also suggested that among the Mebêngôkre, notions of well-being entailed the maintenance of pervasive social differentiation, which was linked to ceremonial and other kinds of property. The A'uwẽ case was similar, where the expectation for "good" social relations involved age-related ranking, distinct prerogative ownerships by kin groups, and differentiated social roles in diverse aspects of ceremonial and everyday social life. Gordon also expressed reservations about the universal applicability of the equivalence of conviviality and social well-being in Amazonia, which coincides well with my approach, whereby I highlight that A'uwẽ considered certain culturally appropriate and traditional forms of differentiation and ranking to be essential to living well.

Unfortunately, I did not directly ask Antônio how he understood quality of life or how he characterized his well-being. He did make comments to me over the years that suggest ways he might have answered that question. For example, between bursts of tears during an enduring hug while sitting at the side of his deceased daughter's body at her funerary mourning, he affirmed to me that I had earned my place in A'uwẽ life because I had suffered with the community. I had the sense he referred to the general suffering involved in living in his community with few of the comforts of city life, such as the hardship of pursuing game together without drinking water under the scorching sun in the sandpaper climate of the late dry season. I also understood him to be referring to the deeper social sufferings of community life, which in my experience included solitude and lack of privacy, along with the burdens of caring for my secular age group's protégés, enduring numerous demanding rites of passage and other ceremonies, as well as occasional interpersonal strife. Considering the circumstances of our hug, I also believed him to be referring to the suffering of losing loved ones, as this was not the first funeral I had attended during my fieldwork.

Sharing these sufferings brought us together through common experiences and, in that moment, specifically through mourning his daughter's death while embracing. I also understood him to be characterizing our friendship or adoptive kinship relationship as grandfather and grandson as based in something similar to Robert D. Putnam's (2000, 466) "thick trust," which is a basis for the strong bonds between close people that most contribute to social well-being. Examples such as this suggest the importance of robust A'uwẽ ideas like "suffering together" for peoples' perceptions of good living. This viewpoint brings to the forefront what is considered "'good' in the sense that it is meaningful and judged well by other people in accordance with social principles" (Thin 2009,

31). I agree with Thin's assertion that people tend to make meaningful distinctions between "feeling well" and "living a good life," the latter being of greater interest considering my ethnographic findings. Throughout my years working and sharing with A'uwẽ, the theme of producing desirable outcomes by suffering together has been recurrent, whereas I cannot recall a single instance of someone identifying their own happiness as an important value or goal. When people mentioned their own happiness or sadness, it usually was meant to express their approval or disapproval of others' social behavior. Thus, happiness indicated gratitude for being treated well and sadness pointed to feeling negatively affected by someone's lack of generosity or inconsideration.

I also agree with Isaac Prilleltensky and Ora Prilleltensky (2007, 57) that "contrary to prevalent notions that well-being is a personal issue, . . . it is also relational, organizational and communal." While individuals may experience or share aspects of well-being, it is as communities and societies that they collectively construct shared notions of well-being. This is not to say that people agree on everything, but rather, they have the potential to share meaning through common experiences and viewpoints. My A'uwẽ friends were a heterogeneous group of people who also agreed on many things, among them some aspects of what contributed to good living and satisfaction in life. Many of them explicitly recognized the distinction between individual and community values and understood that their representations of social wellness were influenced by different factors when speaking as community representatives as opposed to as individual residents. These stances may have differed slightly or substantially but did not imply contradiction. As I explore throughout this book, A'uwẽ culture afforded ample flexibility for individuals to shift stances and social positions contextually without experiencing incongruence. This characteristic of A'uwẽ social life is a central component of my approach to social well-being.

A'uwẽ social arrangements, such as age group organizations and agamous and exogamous moieties, were emblematic dimensions of how A'uwẽ understood their social values and identities. Furthermore, they were key components of traditionalism in contemporary A'uwẽ society, dovetailing with A'uwẽ notions of social wellness and good living. As an A'uwẽ Indigenous health agent, who worked assisting nurses at the community primary healthcare unit, told me, "Our main health problem is that we are weak because we no longer eat a traditional diet, no longer do traditional subsistence activities, and no longer value traditional rituals, all of which strengthen us physically and spiritually. Strength and resistance are increased by enduring physical hardship with our age set peers, which puts us in contact with strengthening spirits." The link between cultural traditionalism and well-being has been observed among Indigenous peoples elsewhere. For example, a study showed that among Aboriginal Australians, "attachment to traditional culture is found to be associated with enhanced outcomes across a range of socio-economic indicators" (Dockery 2010, 315). For the Matsigenka in Peru, "questions about general health, well-being, and happiness usually evoked stories about an idealized golden past" (Izquierdo 2005, 779). Among the A'uwẽ, social well-being depended on well-organized communities, which in turn required that individuals and families prioritized social behaviors and arrangements considered to be traditional. These arrangements did not negate individualism in A'uwẽ society. Nor did they deny the reality of internal community conflict and occasional divisions. Rather, they placed a burden on individuals to make thoughtful decisions considering traditional values for the sake of one's own and one's community's well-being.

Social and Environmental Wellness

Well-being is more than an internal state of being. One's environment may also contribute to one's wellness, happiness, and quality of life. This environment may be social and physical surroundings, including everything from physical housing and sanitation conditions to home or community life and one's greater urban or rural setting, including access to "natural" and cultural resources present in a local landscape (Adelson 2000). From an anthropological point of view, the kinds and dimensions of environments that may contribute to well-being differ from culture to culture and person to person. Whereas some studies emphasized social environments or ecologies, especially for their effects on child well-being (Earls and Carlson 2001), other studies emphasized how dimensions of the nonhuman landscape and ecology could affect diverse dimensions of social life quality (Laird, Wardell-Johnson, and Ragusaf 2014). Barletti provided a particularly insightful discussion of links between well-being and "place as a position from which to produce knowledge of the world and experience it" (2016, 44), which resonates well with A'uwẽ notions of ties between the local cerrado landscape and wellness. As Antônio illustrated, the well-being of his family and community was intimately related to his ability to access, furnish, and conserve local landscape resources such as game meat and fish.

The cerrado tropical savanna ecological landscape is not the only kind of environment one might address when discussing A'uwẽ well-being, but it is an often-overlooked dimension that was borne out in my research as central to well-being for many individuals and for communities more generally. Not only was the environment, understood as an anthropogenic landscape, a topic of frequent discussion regarding self-provisioning and sustainable resource use, but it was also considered a key link in communities' abilities to meet social needs for gifts of collected, hunted, or cultivated foods on certain ceremonial occasions, which were some of life's most important events. Game meat was given by grooms to brides' households to formalize their weddings. Collected wild root vegetables and maize (*Zea mays*) loaves were given by spiritual initiates to their spiritual singers, mentors who guided them in spiritual matters, during spiritual ceremonies. Furthermore, self-provisioning remained an important option for women and men to provide for their immediate families, support their parents-in-law, and engage in reciprocity with their extended families and neighbors. The link between environment, subsistence, and well-being among the A'uwẽ recalls the North American Cree, among whom well-being was less associated with health and disease and more closely aligned with the presence of game animals, food sovereignty, and maintenance of traditional values, including religious practices and native language use (Adelson 2000). In another example, Christopher Wolsko and colleagues (2006, 353) reported that "many participants expressed that this subsistence lifestyle is at the core of wellness for Yup'ik people [of southwestern Alaska], frequently referring to it as 'the lifestyle' or 'the way of life.'"

Previous literature on the connection between well-being and the environment has focused on several themes that I do not prioritize specifically for the A'uwẽ for being outside the scope of this book or discordant with A'uwẽ ways of engaging the environment. Some studies emphasized the role of environmental services, resources, and biodiversity on the economic quality or health of individuals' lives (e.g., Alfonso, Zorondo-Rodríguez, and Simonetti 2017; Dasgupta 2001; Ringold et al. 2013). Others pointed to a correspondence between climate change or degradation of local ecosystems and poor living and sanitation conditions, leading to poor human health (e.g., Billiot and Mitchell 2019; Green and Minchin 2014; Silva et al. 2005). Another line of research addressed connection to "nature" as a positive factor for the well-being of urban residents (e.g., Bell et al. 2018; Bieling et al. 2014; Dallimer et al. 2012; Luck et al. 2011; Russell et al. 2013; Watson 2013; White et al. 2019; Wolf et al. 2017). An especially productive line of reasoning was a proposed association between traditional ethnobiological and ethnomedicinal knowledge and wellness or well-being, which has been documented among diverse Indigenous, traditional, and local groups (Bignante 2015; Flint et al. 2011; Johnson 2017; Wolsko et al. 2006).

I find several other approaches to the well-being/environment nexus more useful for the A'uwẽ case. For example, Chantelle Richmond and co-authors (2005) identified reduced access to traditional territorial resources as one of three main factors affecting well-being among 'Namgis First Nation people. Studies of Aboriginal peoples in Australia and Torres Strait Islanders have focused on the complex relationships between people and "country," a notion that encompasses constructive and destructive aspects, including physical, emotional, social, and spiritual dimensions of landscape and health (Butler et al. 2019). Panelli and Tipa advocated for drawing on Indigenous perspectives to expand on the notion of foodscapes to better incorporate Indigenous perspectives of food as a nexus of diverse dimensions ("spiritual, physical, social, material, cultural, economic and political relationships") that contribute to "being alive well" (2009, 458). Other scholars argued for similarly integrative approaches (e.g., Sangha et al. 2015), including Burnette, Clark, and Rodning (2018, 369), who addressed "how subsistence living may contribute to well-being and resilience by promoting physical exercise, a healthy diet, and psychological health." In the A'uwẽ case, I would add to that list healthy social relations. My approach is consistent with the findings of Wolsko et al. (2006, 345), who found that for the Yup'ik, notions of wellness "emphasized the importance of living a traditional lifestyle, seeking creative solutions to manage drastic cultural change, and fostering connection within the communities and the native landscape."

My approach to well-being is different from but allied with the Indigenous concept of "living well" (in Portuguese, *o bem viver*) that appeared in public discourse in Latin America in the late 1990s and has become especially popularized in Brazil since being discussed in 2012 at the United Nations Conference on Sustainable Development, Rio+20, in Rio de Janeiro (Vanhulst and Beling 2013). One formulation of the concept was constructed on the Quechua notion of *sumak kawsay* (beautiful life), and partially incorporated into the 2008 Constitution of Ecuador as "Rights of Nature" (Acosta 2018). Like my own approach to well-being, this notion of living well is integrative in that it encompasses multiple dimensions of well-being, such as cultural identity, social life, and sustainable use of the environment. It differs from my theoretical orientation because it is intended to operate as a map for antiestablishment political action to achieve a decolonialized Indigenous form of noncommodified development after centuries of injustice and subjugation under capitalist globalism (Peredo

2019). Although I identify with some aspirational aspects of this multicultural and pluralistic philosophy for change, it transcends the objectives of this book, which are to identify how the A'uwẽ promoted well-being in everyday social life. In other words, my objectives here are ethnographic, not activist as embodied by the living well political agenda.

Considering social well-being as a process also suggests the importance of autonomy and sovereignty for making informed decisions in contexts of change, such as the A'uwẽ presently found themselves. The processes of change affecting the A'uwẽ were external, internal, and interconnected. They were rooted in deep to shallow time frames, operated from the most global to local scales, and recognized explicitly by adult A'uwẽ. Externally motivated changes that had occurred within the lifetimes of the women and men I met during my research ranged from the approximation of Brazilian national society; sedentarization and monetarization of communities; and inclusion in regional and global networks of scholars, service providers, artists, and friends. This incomplete list illustrates how change was ubiquitous, and its relationship to well-being was ambiguous. For example, many elders lamented the loss of their former mobility as trekkers but celebrated their ability to have many healthy children and grandchildren because of local access to basic healthcare services and a sedentary lifestyle.

Contemporary lifestyle changes (formal schooling, digital technologies, bilingualism, monetary income, biomedicine, etc.) may be read by some as improvements mitigating against unwellness. At the same time, maintenance of social and environmental traditionalism may be interpreted as a source of ethnobiological resilience and strength, and therefore a source of wellness. From an anthropological point of view, just as suffering does not contradict well-being, neither does environmental change, for it is often precisely when conservation is needed that communities rally to preserve it (Holt 2005). Furthermore, efforts to restore environmental autonomy and sovereignty can contribute positively to well-being by improving the social conditions of life.

Antônio demonstrated the irreducibility and ambiguous nature of well-being when individual health and the social experience of wellness might be at odds with one another (Mathews and Izquierdo 2009a). He also illustrated the intimate relationship between social dimensions of well-being and an environment undergoing transformation (Dasgupta 2001). The age group systems, with oppositional and hierarchical as well as fraternal and collective aspects, illustrate how social well-being was coconstructed by multiple segments of society that tended to prioritize traditionalism as expressed through certain conventional social roles and arrangements upheld as correct, beautiful, and respectful ways of living. Thus, from A'uwẽ perspectives, social relations of hierarchy and difference were integral to equality and collectivity, and all contributed through individual agency to social dimensions of wellness among community members. This local configuration of Indigenous perspectives regarding good living illustrates the processual aspect of collective social well-being, as individuals engaged one another and through their interactions constructed and reinforced shared notions of wellness.

My reading of A'uwẽ understandings of well-being directed me toward an analytical framework of social wellness as a heterogeneous process constructed by communities through shared understandings of forms of interpersonal and human-environmental relations, potentially involving both pleasure and strife, considered good and appropriate, being understood to accrue benefits for individuals, communities, and environments. This approach has the potential to rebalance debates about transcultural well-being indicators by redirecting attention to internal or emic societal contexts within and through which experiences of wellness and unwellness occur. This need has been well established for Aboriginal and Torres Strait Islander peoples, and similar principles likely apply to Indigenous and other traditional peoples elsewhere (Butler et al. 2019). It also has the potential to support community initiatives to increase well-being by strengthening its local cultural determinants, such as the social role of elders in an Indigenous community in Australia (Busija et al. 2020).

Underlying the ethnographic stories told earlier in this chapter is the reality that not all youths shared with their elders identical ideas about what behaviors were socially desirable and thereby contributed to living a good life. Younger women no longer abided being struck on their legs with wooden rods by their male mentors to test their strength. Younger contemporary fathers-in-law often invited their sons-in-law to disregard long-established A'uwẽ conventions of expressing respect through avoidance behavior. Youths tended to prefer to purchase store-bought foods rather than grow, collect, hunt, and fish local foods that were preferred by many elders as important to a healthful diet and most valued as gifts of reciprocity between relatives and neighbors. Nevertheless, certain cultural events anchored almost everyone's perspectives regarding traditionalism and its linkages to well-being.

For example, the excitement of weddings motivated even those youths who were most repelled by the idea of hunting to enthusiastically participate in large group hunting expeditions undertaken to acquire ample quantities of game meat for grooms to deliver as presents to the doorsteps of their parents-in-laws' houses. They thereby learned hunting techniques and gained the capacity to provide sustenance for their families. Even young agnostics regarding A'uwẽ spirituality participated in every spiritual ritual, a challenging task, to lend their peers support and solidarity. With time, and their advancement through the spiritual ranks, they tended to become believers in powerful spirits that inhabited the cerrado and to gain capacities to heal their family members of disease and injury. Rites of passage into novitiate adulthood were festive occasions in which the entire population participated in one way or another, including procuring and provisioning ceremonial gifts of sacred collected, hunted, and cultivated foods. They were occasions for previously unruly children to demonstrate respect for elders and commitment to their secular age set and age set moiety. These youths assumed such responsibilities with solemnity and dedication, striving to demonstrate to the community their intentions to be good daughters and sons, mentors, children-in-law, spouses, and parents. In each of these examples, the appeal of participating in certain community social events brought youths into closer alignment with their elders in their perspectives of how to live well. Although what A'uwẽ understood to be traditional may have changed through time, certain social expressions of traditionalism unified otherwise disparate points of view and brought people together in their understandings of well-being, laying the groundwork for resiliency.

In this section, I have sought to provide an ethnographic justification for a broader understanding of social aspects of well-being than is usually evident in mainstream multidisciplinary well-being literature. My argument addresses only a slice of the diverse considerations involved in a comprehensive treatment of well-being, which also include physical, mental, and spiritual dimensions, among others. Besides physical health, social configurations and relations, along with their linkages to the environment, were dimensions that my A'uwẽ family, friends, consultants, and interlocutors emphasized the most in their conversations with me, making them ethnographically salient dimensions in my research. They also stood out as the aspects of well-being that most reflected A'uwẽ emphasis on participation in local community, which was central to how they understood identity.

This framework requires that well-being be considered holistically within socioculturally distinct settings and encourages recognition of peoples' autonomy to understand health and well-being on their own terms and in relation to culturally relevant dimensions, including social life and local landscapes. It reinforces long-established but rarely adequately attended policy viewpoints that health involves diverse dimensions of well-being, including social wellness (WHO 1948). Academic and policy attention to this perspective of well-being will contribute to an alignment with diverse local sociocultural realities, opening of space for two-way intercultural dialogue, and thereby also to decolonialization of science and healthcare. A broad understanding of social well-being may also have concrete health effects in diverse transcultural contexts, beyond Indigenous and culturally distinct peoples illustrated by the A'uwẽ case. For many localized and virtual communities affected by adverse health events, such as COVID-19, forced migration, natural disaster, and economic crisis, restoring well-being requires more complex and holistic understandings of wellness to address nonphysical sequelae, including restoring community well-being.

The A'uwẽ of Pimentel Barbosa and Etênhiritipá Communities

A Cerrado People

Today, A'uwẽ are mostly residents of ten Indigenous lands (federally owned tracts possessed in usufruct by Indigenous peoples) recognized in Brazil, with a relatively small contingent residing in nearby towns and cities. With an overall population of approximately twenty-two thousand, they are among the ten largest ethnic groups in Brazil. Their lands are dispersed over a relatively large area in eastern Mato Grosso state in Central Brazil. The Pimentel Barbosa Indigenous Land (328,966 ha), home to the communities in which I conducted my research for this book, was situated along the Serra do Roncador (Snorer Mountains), bordering the Rio das Mortes (River of Deaths) within the Araguaia watershed, which drains into the Atlantic Ocean via the Tocantins River, with a small portion in the eastern edge of the Xingu River Basin, which drains into the Amazon River. I conducted my main research for this book in two local communities, Pimentel Barbosa (established in 1969) and Etênhiritipá (which divided from Pimentel Barbosa in 2006 and settled just a half kilometer away). I also maintained close relationships with three smaller communities that had separated from Pimentel in recent years, Paraíso, Santa Vitória, and Sõrepré, as well as a new unnamed community that was in the process of splitting from Etênhiritipá as I finished writing this book.

The cerrado ecoregion, or biome, is a highly threatened tropical savanna biodiversity hotspot (Myers et al. 2000; Oliveira and Marquis 2002; Ratter, Ribeiro, and Bridgewater 1997; Strassburg et al. 2017) covering more than two million hectares, approximately 24 percent of the total area of Brazil, mainly in the Central Brazilian Plateau. According to one estimate, of the approximately 10,000 plant species identified in the cerrado, about 4,400 were endemic (Klink and Machado 2005). This high level of endemism is partly attributable to several key ecological features of the cerrado. For example, fire proneness, seasonal dryness, and low soil fertility contributed to unique evolutionary adaptations, including a flora with more belowground than aerial biomass, an "upside-down forest" (Castro and Kauffman 1998).

The agricultural potential of the cerrado and its positive economic benefits for Brazil have been widely publicized for decades, at least since the mid-1970s (Abelson and Rowe 1987; Ferri 1976). By 2020, 45 percent of the cerrado ecoregion had been converted to human land use, of which 98 percent was under agribusiness management (MapBiomas 2021). Recent land conversion to soybean and sugarcane biofuel production in the cerrado resulted in large carbon imbalances (net carbon production) estimated to require seventeen to thirty-seven years to restore equilibrium (Fargione et al. 2008). In lieu of buffering the Amazon from further expansion of agricultural commodities and biofuels, in coming years, the cerrado region is prone to increasing pressures with associated climatic impacts (Davidson et al. 2012; Georgescu et al. 2013) and escalation of conflicts between agribusiness and Indigenous interests (Garfield 2001; Graham, Palmer, and Waiásse 2009; Welch, Santos, et al. 2013).

According to a recent application of Köppen's climate classification (Alvares et al. 2013), the Pimentel Barbosa Indigenous Land was in the tropical zone, with a dry winter, average temperatures greater than 24°C, and annual rainfall of 2,200 to 2,500 mm. Virtually all the rain fell during the wet season, typically from October/November to April/May. The cerrados are fire prone, and many of their endemic plants are adapted biologically and ecologically to periodic burning (Coutinho 1990; Ledru 2002; Ramos-Neto and Pivello 2000). Cerrado vegetation types, or "cerrados," are highly physiognomically and structurally varied, ranging from open to scrubby grasslands and woodlands to tall moist and dry forests (Eiten 1975; Oliveira and Marquis 2002; Oliveira-Filho and Ratter 2002; Ratter et al. 1973; Welch, Santos, et al. 2013). Despite the particularities of these sometimes highly divergent vegetation classes, the variation between them is "completely continuous in the sense that stands can be found in any region which may be ranged in a series from arboreal, through all grades of scrub and structural savanna, to (usually) pure grassland of the cerrado type" (Eiten

1972, 231). The cerrado shares a great deal in common with Amazon rainforest landscapes both botanically and zoologically, although its ecological processes are unique because of high seasonality, high belowground biomass, and pronounced fire proneness and adaptation (Castro and Kauffman 1998; Miranda, Bustamante, and Miranda 2002).

The A'uwẽ considered themselves a quintessentially cerrado people. Apart from references in oral histories to a very early coastal occupation, documentary and oral history evidence indicate that A'uwẽ have long lived, circulated, and migrated within this distinctive tropical savanna landscape (figure 4). They considered it to be their ancestral homeland. Even today, after considerable migration and dislocation in the twentieth century, all A'uwẽ communities are in cerrado regions. The historical mobility of the A'uwẽ people throughout considerable ranges of cerrado landscape in eighteenth-century Província do Maranhão and Província de Goyaz, as well as, later, Mato Grosso state (Baldus 1948; Freire 1951; Lopes da Silva 1992, 1999; Nimuendajú 2017; Ravagnani 1991), is especially striking because it was accomplished primarily on foot.[2] Although the region has some large and navigable rivers, A'uwẽ watercraft in the immediate precontact

Figure 4 Typical cerrado landscape in the Pimentel Barbosa Indigenous Land, 2005.

era in the Rio das Mortes region included floating logs and timber rafts but not canoes (Pohl 1837; Szaffka 1942). Contemporary A'uwẽ discourses regarding the value of extensive foot travel for health and well-being demonstrated that A'uwẽ values remained linked to the cerrado landscape.

Through their deep history as a cerrado people and their historical connection to the territories they had occupied since the early nineteenth century, when they were squeezed westward by encroaching non-Indigenous settlers, the people of Pimentel Barbosa and Etênhiritipá understood themselves to be of the cerrado spiritually and physically. Thus, one may speak about the human dimensions of environmental conservation in the sense that people were connected in myriad ways to local ecological integrity or functioning and territorial access, including political territorial rights. Human well-being depended in part on environmental well-being, which might be framed in terms of access to and conservation of landscape resources, biodiversity, and land cover within traditional territories. These dimensions contributed to the A'uwẽ's ability to provide for their basic human needs, such as food and shelter, sociocultural needs to perform certain ceremonies and rituals, and identity needs to engage in environmental activities or practices that contributed to their sense of ethnic uniqueness. A'uwẽ oral histories of migrations and community divisions contributed to a contemporary sense of place that factored into links between ecological landscape and community well-being. I explore some of these dynamics in the following pages, with a brief sketch of the two main communities I have lived in, visited, and studied over the years.

Pimentel Barbosa and Etênhiritipá

Along the banks of the Pimentel Barbosa River (or Riozinho, "Little River"), a tributary to the Rio das Mortes that feeds the Araguaia basin in Central Brazil, sat two adjacent arced, or semicircular, A'uwẽ communities with a total population of nearly a thousand people. When I first visited in 2004, this population resided in a single local community with two names. The A'uwẽ name Etênhiritipá signified the ancestral place where the community was located (and had been used at different times over generations as a residential community site and as a trekking camp). The community was also designated Pimentel Barbosa by non-A'uwẽ in memory of indigenist and federal employee Inspector Genésio Pimentel Barbosa, who was killed in 1941 during an A'uwẽ "pacification" effort undertaken by the Indian Protection Service (Serviço de Proteção aos Índios, SPI) (L. Souza 1953). Each of the two place names spoke to a different dimension of that community's shared deep history—the first to its immemorial association with the Central Brazilian cerrado ecoregion and the second to its more recent but enduring and sometimes mortal relationship with Brazilian national society (a mortality that continues today through conflicts with local landowners and government negligence in attending to Indigenous needs, as in the recent case of a botched SARS-CoV-2 intervention that inadequately prevented and treated cases of COVID-19 among Indigenous populations in Brazil).

In 2004, all residents who would split into two communities in 2006 (and later, into five, possibly six by the time this book goes to press) walked out the doors of their houses into the same central plaza (in a well-arranged community, A'uwẽ houses always form a round horseshoe or semicircle with their doors facing the center of the groomed plaza and the gap leading to the bank of a nearby river), with its shared view of a picturesque red stratified mesa. At that time, within the unity of their mutual past were also seeds of internal sociopolitical strife, some genealogically ancient and some newly forming, which ultimately resulted in the community's division two years later. In addition, innumerable formal and informal associations by A'uwẽ conventions united and separated different configurations of people in different ways, in different contexts, and at different times. In 2006, escalation of internal political conflict prompted just under half of the community residents to relocate to a new site a short walk away. That division resulted in the two adjacent communities having conflicting claims to the ancestral place name Etênhiritipá, with all its historical and moral authority, which previously applied to the locale now occupied by both communities.

Today, as one approaches from the southwest by the unpaved road that connects to interstate highway BR-158, the first community to come into view is the more recent of the two (figure 5). It was called Etênhiritipá by its residents, a name that was formalized through recognition by FUNAI and other governmental agencies despite it being contested by the neighboring community. The older community was located a short stretch farther along the dirt road, on the other side of a small cluster of buildings called the post, which included a schoolhouse and a primary healthcare unit. It was more commonly known by its non-A'uwẽ designation, Pimentel Barbosa, although elder residents insisted it also had historical claim to the name Etênhiritipá.

After fifteen years of separation, the two communities had their own identities and histories. They also shared many things in common. They both considered themselves the ancestral community of what had become nineteen

Figure 5 Aerial image of Pimentel (left) and Etênhiritipá (right) communities. Photo by Carlos E. A. Coimbra Jr., 2008.

distinct communities within the Pimentel Barbosa Indigenous Land, which had a total population of approximately 2,600 in 2022 (including a twentieth community that immigrated in 1985 from another Indigenous land). When the community's namesake, Inspector Pimentel Barbosa, was killed in 1941, ancestors and some of the oldest living members of both contemporary communities composed a single historical community residing at Arobonhipo'opá, located just within the northwest boundary of the present-day Pimentel Barbosa Indigenous Land (Lopes da Silva 1992; Sereburã et al. 1998; Welch, Santos, et al. 2013). Residents of both communities shared oral histories about their previous migrations westward from the far side of the Araguaia River to Wedezé and then to Sõrepré communities.[3] Even after their 2006 division, the two communities shared the pride of an oral history that identified them as the original People (A'uwẽ), descendants of the "first creators" (*höimana'uö*), creators of non-Indigenous (white) people (*warazu*), heirs to the cultural pride of the late precontact "mother community" Sõrepré, and architects of peaceful contact with the Brazilian government (Coimbra Jr. et al. 2002; Graham 1995; Lopes da Silva 1992; Welch, Santos, et al. 2013). The narrative of this book takes place at the sociospatial juncture of those houses, that plaza, and the trails, gardens, savannas and forests, communities, and towns that surrounded them.

A gratifying quality of the cerrado on the eastern flanks of the Serra do Roncador, where the Pimentel Barbosa Indigenous Land is located, is that its often low and scrubby vegetation allows many opportunities for panoramic views of the many low hills, ridges, and valleys that punctuate the landscape. The two communities, Pimentel Barbosa and Etênhiritipá, commanded impressive vistas that afforded residents continual visual reference to the surrounding landscape, with its abundant history, natural resources, and spiritual beings. Beyond the perimeters and gardens of those two communities, this landscape also contained other A'uwẽ communities and an irreparably complicated history derived from intrusion and displacement by non-Indigenous society, with its agribusinesses, roads, prisons, cities, governmental bodies, financial institutions, supermarkets, and so much more. Whereas in the 1970s the Pimentel Barbosa community was sandwiched in a small plot between multiple cattle ranches of non-Indigenous ownership (Coimbra Jr. et al. 2002; Graham 1995), today its Indigenous land is an island of primary and recuperating cerrado vegetation flanked by cattle ranches and monoculture farms, producing mainly soy, corn, and cotton, that threaten the region's ecological integrity (Welch, Brondízio, et al. 2013). These encroachments were not, however, visually apparent from within the communities. What was visible was the stunning surrounding topography, which bared few obvious marks of non-Indigenous activities, and the tidy arcs of houses that lined the perimeter of each community's meticulously weeded plaza. This history of circumscription and ecological change is a central backdrop to the social dynamics discussed in this book, because it was accompanied by generational changes in how people related to one another and the environment.

These histories of union and differentiation accompanied by sometimes ambivalent perspectives of persistence and transformation illustrate an encompassing pattern of sociocultural resilience amid staggering environmental transformations in recent centuries. Historical evidence suggests that the changes A'uwẽ experienced from eighteenth-century colonial conflict and displacement under the Portuguese Empire to twentieth-century tutelage and market insertion under the Brazilian government were encompassing. Thus, the apparent contemporary endurance of A'uwẽ age organization suggested it was linked to resilience and cultural values, including ethnic identity, cultural pride, and social well-being. A'uwẽ connection to place indicated that these perspectives and processes involved links among environment, social life, and wellness.

Prominent among the social dimensions that helped shape environmental access and conservation, as well as, more broadly, contributed to community well-being, were formulations of the human life cycle, which I explore in detail in the next two chapters. These included multiple systems of age grades, the stages of life through which all people pass during a lifetime, some of which operated in conjunction with age cohorts, usually called age sets. These age systems were consciously and conspicuously appreciated by A'uwẽ of Pimentel Barbosa and Etênhiritipá communities as essential aspects of social life, wellness, and ethnic identity. They were also central to how people engaged the cerrado landscape because they prominently shaped the social relations of resource access and conservation.

Fieldwork and Ethnographic Approaches

Introductions

In May 2004, I accompanied my colleague Carlos E. A. Coimbra Jr. to the Pimentel Barbosa community to discuss the possibility of conducting doctoral fieldwork regarding the nexus of age organization and environmental engagement. This was before the Etênhiritipá community split from the Pimentel Barbosa community in 2006. Thus, it then had a population of 535 people, which made it the largest local community within the Pimentel Barbosa Indigenous Land. By A'uwẽ custom, propositions to undertake research, such as my own, were usually presented in the morning or evening men's council (*warã*) so that they might be discussed in public, and a decision reached collectively, though a special kind of consensus. Although women did not participate directly in these meetings, they had other means of expressing their opinions, and men's council decisions were understood in A'uwẽ culture to express the will of the community (see chapter 4; Graham 1995). Unfortunately, I was unable to schedule my presentation in the men's council immediately after arriving. The council meetings on the evening we arrived and the following morning were not held because the community's men held a spiritual ritual (*wai'a*) from late afternoon through the following morning. The next day, the evening council was again not held because the men were resting from the spiritual ritual. Not until the third day of my visit was Coimbra able to introduce me to Chief

Tsuptó Buprewên Wa'iri Xavante and request an audience for me to present my research proposal at the men's council. Doing so was an experience for which I was little prepared.

I spoke in Portuguese, or my broken version of it, and Tsuptó translated for the others, most of whom were monolingual A'uwẽ speakers (since 2004 many more A'uwẽ women and men have become bilingual in A'uwẽ and Portuguese). Tsuptó allowed me to conclude my entire presentation before translating it from start to finish from memory. Afterward, multiple people stood to deliver speeches responding to my proposal while many others chattered simultaneously. Then the chief and vice-chief of the community, Tsuptó and Paulo Supreteprã Xavante, delivered particularly long speeches, and several follow-up questions were posed to me. Finally, a very elderly man, Sereburã, stood and delivered a speech of his own. Gradually, the background voices diminished somewhat, until just two people continued to speak at the same time as Sereburã. The three simultaneous speakers punctuated their deliveries with mutual affirmations, demonstrating that they were listening to one another as they spoke, consistent with Graham's (1995) account of A'uwẽ multivocal speech. When Sereburã sat down, the conversations ended. Tsuptó summarized for me that Sereburã and the elders had accepted my proposal, and he, as chief, would take whatever logistical steps were necessary to formalize that authorization. My nerves immediately settled with this encouraging news, and over the next few days, I began to engage with people in much more personable ways than was possible before they knew who I was and why I was there.

Social Incorporation and Ethnographic Perspectives

Approval of my project in the men's council immediately propelled me to a kind of celebrity status in the community, with many people competing for my time and attention through the kind desire to make sure I was well situated and, as I came to know later, in the hope that I (with my exogenous resources) would choose them as my adoptive family. Men of all ages went to great trouble to include me in their activities. Valdo, who later became my adoptive father (*ĩmama*), took me hunting on foot along a nearby creek lined with gallery forest. Preinitiates and their mentors invited me to visit the preinitiate house. Antônio, who later became my adoptive grandfather (*ĩ'rada*), took me to work with him in his garden, some eight kilometers from the community. I was also invited to participate in a spiritual ritual (*wai'a*) like the one that was being held the day I arrived in the community.

On the morning of this ritual, I was invited to a forest clearing, where men seated in a circle were repeatedly singing a song. While there, Valdo offered to prepare my accoutrements for the ritual. Flattered by the kind gesture, I readily agreed. At the time, I was ignorant that because fathers often prepare their sons' ritual ornaments, my acceptance of Valdo's offer marked him as my adoptive father (figure 6). That afternoon, I was asked if I would like to paint my body for the ritual with my older brother somewhere in the forest or meet my younger brother to paint with him in the forest clearing. Meeting at the clearing sounded simpler, so I agreed to paint with my younger brother. I did not realize at the time that those two brothers belonged to different spiritual age grades, and my choice to paint with my younger brother installed me in his group of spiritual initiates, approximately fifteen years behind my older brother's group of guards in the spiritual age grade progression. That inadvertent decision led me to have many years of firsthand experience of the youngest tier of the spiritual hierarchy and set me on course to complete the spiritual life cycle when I am approximately eighty-one, much older than is usual for A'uwẽ participants.

Figure 6 Photo of the author (*left*) with adoptive father Valdo Pari'õwá (*middle*) and brother Lazinho Sõwa'õ (*right*). Photo by Carlos E. A. Coimbra Jr., 2004.

After Valdo and his son painted me, tied special cords on my ankles and wrists, and bound a feathered cotton necktie around my neck, I was instructed to stand in a line of boys and young men at the upper margin of the forest clearing so our participation in the ritual could begin. After this phase of the spiritual ritual in the forest clearing had concluded, I was selected for inclusion in a small group of eight of the eldest initiates who were charged with singing and dancing around the community all night long. We were each handed a sacred cane arrow (*ti'ipê*) with a stripe of deep red pigment at its point and a fluff of raptor down feathers at its base. I was solemnly instructed to carry my arrow until sunrise, caring for it as though it were my own infant, never letting it touch the ground. Once again, I was ignorant that my inclusion in that group of eight at that phase of the ritual calendar distinguished me as an elder member (*ipredumrini*) of the initiate spiritual age grade and, simultaneously, as a member of the secular novitiate adult age grade (*dahí'wa* or *'ritei'wa*) and *êtẽpa* age set, whose members were mostly in their late teens (despite my age at the time, which was thirty-six). Fulfilling my ritual obligations that night without sleep or source of warmth was a challenge. Yet, the welcoming companionship of the seven other novitiate adult men chosen for the same task ensured my success. It also gave me an initial opportunity to experience what it meant to share in the camaraderie of age set membership.

Limitations and Insights

I returned to Pimentel Barbosa in November 2004 to begin fieldwork. Except for several short absences, I spent the next twelve months living in the only single-occupant house (*'ri*) in the community (figure 7), which functioned as an annex to Valdo and his wife Aparecida's house. My neighbor on the other side was Vice-Chief Paulo, who also offered me tremendous support with my research. His son Vinícius Supreteprã, also a member of my secular age set, was a constant companion and eager assistant. Valdo's entire family incorporated me into their lives, caring for my house as an extension of their own. His sons Denoque and Eugênio, the former of whom was a member of my secular age set, took great pains to include me in their affairs and provide me with continuous and much appreciated companionship. Since that first year of fieldwork, I have had the good fortune to continue visiting the community in numerous research capacities and to participate in ceremonial activities about once or twice per year. Over the years, I have visited the Pimentel Barbosa Indigenous Land about thirty-five times. I also have had the luxury of being able to maintain

Figure 7 Photo of the author's house under construction on the east side of the Pimentel Barbosa community, 2004.

regular contact with members of the community, initially using the intermittently serviceable public telephone located in the post and later using voice and video messaging services installed on peoples' smartphones and connected via unstable Wi-Fi in the schoolhouses.

My ethnographic approach was highly influenced by how I was received by the A'uwẽ at the Pimentel Barbosa community in 2004. I was incorporated into A'uwẽ society as a member of an exogamous moiety, a secular age set and associated age set moiety, and a spiritual age set and associated age set moiety. I was also incorporated into the community kinship system via my adoptive A'uwẽ parents. These insertions created for me a network of family and friends, as well as a series of social positions that both limited and expanded my access to certain aspects of society. For example, male members of the *êtẽpa* age set remain some of my closest friends today. Not only did they generously incorporate me into their ceremonial and social activities when I first arrived in the community, but they continued to be among the most dedicated of my A'uwẽ interlocutors and essential community contacts. Today, usually male members of the *êtẽpa* age set send regular messages and occasionally call me to the community to participate with them in important ceremonies.

In contrast, I have always had a comparatively hard time directly accessing women's perspectives and activities. Many of the prominent anthropological scholars of A'uwẽ society have been women. They include Regina A. P. Müller (1976), who wrote about body painting and visual arts; Claudia Menezes (1999), who examined the impacts of four decades of Salesian missionary intervention in A'uwẽ communities; Nancy M. Flowers (1983), who studied human ecology and changing economic systems; Aracy Lopes da Silva (1986), who addressed naming practices and formal friendship; Laura R. Graham (1995), who initially focused on the anthropological linguistics of men's ceremonial performances; and Angela Nunes (2002, 2011), who studied A'uwẽ children from an anthropological perspective. Two of these women, Flowers and Graham, conducted their principal fieldwork at the Pimentel Barbosa community, the same community that David Maybury-Lewis studied in the 1950s, when it was located at Wedezé, near São Domingos, and which I studied since the 2000s. Ironically, despite these exceptional contributions by women, most anthropological literature about the A'uwẽ, including that produced by these female scholars, is dominated by accounts of male aspects of society. Of the female scholars listed above, only Lopes da Silva dedicated substantial ethnographic attention to females, although Graham (2014) has also published on gender differences.[4]

This gender limitation has been experienced by all female and male ethnographers of A'uwẽ society with whom I have discussed the issue. In my experience, it was partly due to the prominent role men played in engaging with non-A'uwẽ visitors and the relative reticence expressed by women in the presence of new outsiders, which resulted in researchers' time and resources being dominated by men rather than by women. It was also the result of men's greater facility in spoken Portuguese, especially prior to the 2010s, when girls and women gained greater access to formal education with female A'uwẽ teachers. Additionally, certain male members of A'uwẽ society were rightful holders of the title "owners of non-Indigenous people" (*warazu'tede'wa*), which gave them the prerogative to act as ambassadors to anthropologists and other visitors. More generally, I also found men to consider outsiders of both genders to be male political business. At Pimentel Barbosa and Etênhiritipá, however, this seemed to be changing in recent years. I have observed an emergent but explicit effort of A'uwẽ women to seek the attention of ethnographers, documentary filmmakers (Flória 2009), and other researchers, so that the female dimensions of A'uwẽ life would also be communicated to the public.

My limitation to accessing women's perspectives was also due to my maleness, which situated me among A'uwẽ males rather than females in most social contexts. I engaged socially with women comparatively infrequently and usually, by their preference, as a novitiate adult man with a host of associated gender and age expectations. In other words, it was difficult to shed my gender and age social identities even for the sake of ethnographic work. Throughout this book, I recount various episodes of interactions with women, although they were often characterized by distant rather than close social dynamics. For example, my status from 2004 to 2006 as a novitiate adult created the preference that I remain in seclusion at home, as was expected of all male members of this age grade. Some community members lightheartedly discouraged me from visiting their households during the daytime. Despite recognizing that it was necessary for my research, certain women outside my adoptive household registered their disapproval of my regular visits during daylight and in full view of other households in antagonistic but humorous ways. For example, during one visit a woman held a urinating infant over my head. Other women splashed wet rice on the back of my neck and threw a watermelon rind at me. Still another shouted the accusation that I have the head of a tapir (*Tapirus terrestris*). The inappropriateness of novitiate men visiting other people's houses exemplified the diverse age-related configurations of social behavior that contributed to notions of social well-being in A'uwẽ society, which in this case were reinforced by antagonistic joking relations.

Additionally, a great portion of my time was consumed by my culturally appropriate participation in male activities, such as council meetings, spiritual rituals, hunting and fishing excursions, and secular age set socialization. These being the activities that were expected of me as a novitiate and mature adult man, I was constrained from spending comparable amounts of time in female social settings. My experience as a male fieldworker of certain social statuses in A'uwẽ social organization led me to garner a more detailed and personal understanding of male life than I was able to attain of female life.

I have had closer relationships with women, especially my adoptive mother, grandmothers, and aunts, although my richest data regarding women's points of view were gained through recorded interviews with bilingual translators. Such formal interviews permitted us some room to set aside our usual gender and other socially distancing relations to discuss a specific topic in greater depth than was possible in casual conversation.

As mentioned briefly above, a barrier for non-A'uwẽ researchers conducting ethnographic research with A'uwẽ women was that most women tended to be less bilingual than men in these communities, although this difference has reduced slightly over the last decade, as some younger women now (often reluctantly) speak or understand beginning- to intermediate-level Portuguese. Furthermore, even though at least two women in the Pimentel Barbosa community are now fully bilingual, they have thus far been unenthusiastic about collaborating as translators, partly due to lack of experience and partly because I am a man. In Paraíso, a community that split from Pimentel Barbosa in 2012, girls studied in town at the municipal primary school that served the general public, resulting in their total fluency in Portuguese at young ages. At Pimentel Barbosa, many middle-aged and elder men who had studied in regional cities or worked on local ranches when they were younger spoke Portuguese. Also, many of my male *êtẽpa* age set peers spoke Portuguese fluently or proficiently. Male members of other younger age sets who had opportunities to live in town, even for short periods, also tended to speak Portuguese with near fluency. This scenario encouraged the use of men as research consultants or as intermediaries during communication with women, although this limitation is likely to change over the next decade (cf. Graham 1990). In my case, my rudimentary ability to speak A'uwẽ was inadequate for conducting in-depth interviews on nuanced subjects, such as age organization, without the aid of a translator. The sum effect of these factors for me and, I suspect, for many ethnographers who had preceded me, was that female experiences tended to be accessed less frequently and indirectly via men, which rendered women's perspectives less visible.

Rather than considering these social associations a hinderance to my ethnographic work, I understand them to have been essential to my ability to understand certain viewpoints and frames of reference. As Steve Herbert (2000, 559) wrote, "it is only through the interrogation of one's subjective experience within a milieu, and the subjective reactions it engenders, that one can glean the meaning structures that motivate everyday agency." In at least one sense, my social position may have provided me with unusual access to certain aspects of female life, since being a "young" novitiate adult male when I began fieldwork provided me with knowledge of how women of diverse social statuses related to men of my particular age status. Additionally, the multidimensional nature of A'uwẽ social relations caused me to share many aspects of identity with some of the women I discuss in subsequent chapters. For example, although I did not share their femaleness, I did share with some females such qualities as age set and age grade membership, exogamous moiety, household residence, sibling-hood, and status as siblings-in-law. Also, entering the community as a novitiate adult gave me the opportunity to participate in transformations of activities and relationships as my age groups grew older over the course of the last eighteen years. Whereas I was once junior to many members of the community in various social configurations, I have had the experience of becoming gradually more senior and assuming social positions with increasing responsibilities.

Throughout this book, I explore A'uwẽ age organization, well-being, and en-vironmental engagement from a vantage point informed by the ethnographic perspectives these experiences afforded me. Consequently, some aspects of the book have an evident male bias. Nevertheless, I endeavor to present female topics and perspectives in as balanced a manner as possible based on sound ethnographic evidence available to me.

I am very aware of being an outsider to the group I studied and write about in this book. In many ways, I represent the colonial legacy that decimated their population in the early to mid-1900s; encouraged them to adopt deleterious foodways and personal habits, such as smoking; reduced their available ter-ritory to a small fraction of its traditional proportions in the 1970s; and later pressured them with government policies and interventions that were often counterproductive to their goals of improving health and well-being. I was born in Northern California in a region traditionally occupied by the Coast Miwok and did my postgraduate studies at Sonoma State University in Rohnert Park under adviser David Peri, a Bodega Miwok professor, and at Tulane University in New Orleans under adviser William Balée, a long-term specialist in Brazilian Indigenous ethnography and ethnobiology. Recently naturalized as a Brazilian citizen, I work for the Brazilian Ministry of Health and live in Rio de Janeiro in a neighborhood thought to have been historically occupied by the Tamoios many centuries ago. My employment symbolically approximates me even more to the national society and government that were responsible for bringing about radical changes in A'uwẽ social life, cultural practices, and economic dynamics over the course of the last half century.

At the same time, I believe the A'uwẽ saw my inclusion in their kinship and age organization, as well as my participation in the activities, rituals, and friend-ships these associations entailed, as a means of creating an affective bond with me that enabled and motivated me to publish faithfully about my experiences and observations. Perhaps part of their enthusiasm for incorporating me in their affairs so intimately derived from their positive regard for other anthropologists from the United States, especially Nancy M. Flowers and Laura R. Graham, whom they consider to be close friends and rigorous ethnographic conduits to the public. It also had to do with their deep faith in Brazilian anthropologist and biologist Carlos Coimbra Jr., who introduced me to the community, as scholar and friend. These associations were with outsiders who could be trusted with their guarded knowledge and who communicated effectively with the public about their affairs at a time (which is changing today) that community members lacked adequate literacy skills and academic training to do so themselves. Unlike when I first arrived in 2004, numerous A'uwẽ young adults from Pimentel Barbosa, Etênhiritipá, and other communities have already earned or are now obtaining university degrees, increasing the probability that unmediated A'uwẽ ethnographic authorship will become a reality soon. These circumstances do not erase the dangers of my publishing about a society that has suffered so much as victims of colonial legacy, to which I am inextricably linked through my personal identity as a non-Indigenous Brazilian American, an anthropologist, and an employee of the Brazilian federal government. I strive to mitigate this problem by being as faithful to my experience as possible and explicitly identifying inherent deficiencies and strengths resulting from my personal forms of engagement with the residents of these two communities.

Objectives and Organization

This book is primarily an ethnographic exploration of certain dimensions of social well-being in everyday A'uwẽ experience at the Pimentel Barbosa and Etênhiritipá communities. I draw on my experiences, observations, and peoples' representations of their social lives while recognizing my relationship to them. I strive for the most honest representation possible of what it meant to the people I worked with to be well socially. I found age organization to be a fundamental component of social well-being, and cerrado use and stewardship to be key dimensions of age organization and well-being. Thus, my secondary focus is on how people interacted with the local cerrado landscape in ways that contributed to social life and well-being.

A'uwẽ concepts of some age constructions they considered central to community wellness had aesthetically pleasing abstract components involving cyclical hierarchies that generate perpetual symmetries through highly regular rites of passage (quinquennial and quindecennial) for cohorts of youths. In addition to living according to these persistent traditionalist age formulations despite undergoing such dramatic social, economic, and environmental transformation over the last seventy-five years, A'uwẽ enjoyed speaking about them as models, as though their ideal expressions were almost geometric in nature. For many A'uwẽ, some proper social relations based on age that contributed to social well-being were pleasingly embraced as favorable means to enjoy camaraderie, prepare for the future, care for others, and remember the past. The age-based social formulations that A'uwẽ understood to promote community wellness are the primary focus of this book.

Social well-being also involved accessing wild resources and caring for the landscape, because many cherished activities that involved overt performance of age relations required foods, accoutrements, and substances that came from the cerrado. Sacred foods including wild root vegetables, maize (*nozö*) loaves, bread made from macaúba palm (*Acrocomia aculeata*) fruit pulp, and game meat were presented as ceremonial gifts to express respect and gratitude toward others at some of life's most important moments (Welch 2022a). Bodily ornamentation and grooming, fabrication of ceremonial objects, and formulating healthful remedies were essential to proper participation in social and ceremonial activities, in which most potential participants continued to partake enthusiastically. These foods and materials were derived from the cerrado, could only be accessed through intimate familiarity with the local landscape, and required caretaking to ensure their ongoing availability during an era of territorial circumscription and deforestation outside the Indigenous land. Using and caring for these cerrado resources were key components of good social living, although not all resources or self-provisioning activities enjoyed the same levels of interest among contemporary A'uwẽ. Current forms of environmental engagement involving accessing and caring for cerrado resources are a secondary theme in this book, addressed most thoroughly in chapter 6.

In the next chapter, I explore basic informal features of A'uwẽ age constructions that contributed to social well-being. These include the substance of infancy and consanguinity, as well as the informal life cycle. Informal age grades were the stages all people passed through on their journeys from the fetal stage through old age, being based on individualistic criteria associated with conception, growth, marriage, reproduction, and aging. Each of these stages of life was associated with its own patterns and expectations of behavior thought to contribute to social wellness and productive relationships with the environment. Informal age grades were not the only encompassing system for reckoning A'uwẽ life cycles and their associated implications for social and community well-being. Other systems are addressed in subsequent chapters. The informal age grades discussed in chapter 2 set the stage for discussing how their coexistence with other systems of age organization contributed to a plural social landscape of similarity and difference.

The formal secular age group system and the men's spiritual age group system are the focus of chapter 3. Females and males participated in the camaraderie of the formal secular age group system, which integrated age sets, age grades, and age set moieties with no overt spiritual purpose from the A'uwẽ perspective. The men's formal spiritual age group system, which also involved age sets, age grades, and age set moieties, was a secret society that promoted spiritual strength. The focus of this chapter is to communicate how these dimensions of human life cycles were understood among A'uwẽ and to comment on how these age statuses contributed to social well-being and environmental practice at different phases of life.

Next, in chapter 4, I discuss additional dimensions of age differentiation that also contributed to social well-being, including leadership, political influence, heritable prerogatives, political factionalism, notions of relatedness, and genealogical seniority. Many of these factors influenced how individuals, kin, and communities related to one another in ways that had the potential to avert conflict, discord, and even community divisions. When these forms of strife did occur, these factors provided resources for mitigating their impact and restoring good will.

In chapter 5, I reflect on the informal and formal age systems presented in chapters 2 and 3 and the age hierarchies discussed in chapter 4 to argue that the plurality of age organization in A'uwẽ society was associated with a particular social worldview, which included understanding of apparently contradictory pairs (for example, collectivity/individuality, symmetry/asymmetry, equality/inequality, and inclusion/exclusion) as congruent and mutually constitutive. Finally, I argue for the pervasiveness of heterarchy and contingency in A'uwẽ age organization. I then place my findings regarding A'uwẽ age organization in the context of previous literature regarding linguistically related Indigenous groups in Central Brazil, emphasizing how they relate to popular themes such as dual social organization.

In chapter 6, I return to the topic of environmental engagement, drawing together threads from previous chapters to discuss life cycles of interaction with the cerrado. I recall how different generations of A'uwẽ have had very different life experiences, ranging from being raised in the cerrado before ranchers developed their traditional territory to contemporary youths who preferred eating food from supermarkets. I discuss the transition from trekking and mobility to circumscription and sedentism to highlight how major environmental transformations affected different generations of A'uwẽ in dissimilar ways. After discussing A'uwẽ notions of environmental conservation, I explore three case studies illustrating the intersection of age organization and environmental engagement. These are women's collecting expeditions, age set fishing expeditions, and group hunting with fire. I argue that age identity and age organization were basic features in the tapestry of how the population interacted with the environment while grappling with ever-changing ecological, socioeconomic, and regional development circumstances.

In the final chapter, I explore social well-being in contemporary A'uwẽ society. I address three illustrative topics that help identify the complexities of A'uwẽ well-being and agency in recent times. The first of these is food security and reciprocity, which suggests that government assistance programs did little to mitigate food insecurity, while traditionalist forms of food sharing effectively reduced the frequency with which households suffered from the most severe form of food insecurity—not eating. The second topic is sedentism, primary healthcare units, schoolhouses, and electrification, which I address from the point of view that these governmental services fixed communities in place, with a mixture of results ranging from perceptions of increased to decreased wellness in diverse dimensions of life. The third is camaraderie, a privileged social bond that emerged through the relationship between mentors and their protégés, with its focus in the preinitiate house but lasting a lifetime. I argue that this form of camaraderie was a unique product of the secular age group system, which deserves special attention as a social anchor that permitted dimensions of traditionalism and well-being to persist under circumstances of extreme social and environmental change.

CHAPTER 2

Informal Life Cycles
of Good Living

A'uwẽ life cycles were diverse because A'uwẽ had multiple frameworks for understanding and naming the processes of transformation from infancy to advanced age. All A'uwẽ designated stages of life according to informal life cycles, which substantially differed for females and males. One or two formal life cycles called age group systems also differed depending on whether one was female or male. In this chapter I address gendered informal age grade sequences, their associated expectations for good social living, and comments regarding their significance for environmental engagement in contemporary context. The goal of this chapter is to set forth the most fundamental aspects of age identity among the A'uwẽ and their relationships to well-being as a foundation for discussion in subsequent chapters of the cultural importance of multiple systems of reckoning age for notions of social wellness.

Considered generally, outside the A'uwẽ context, passage through the human life cycle is accompanied by numerous psychological, physiological, social, and experiential changes. Although societies recognize and interpret these changes differently, notions of contrastive age are basic criteria for how social statuses change throughout a lifetime. In U.S. English, for example, an abundant set of contemporary terms are used informally and with low degrees of resolution to distinguish relative age. Some gender-neutral terms that suggest age include *infant, baby, child, kid, adolescent, youth, adult,* and *elder*. Male gender-specific terms include *boy, guy, fellow, lad, man,* and *gentleman*. Female terms include *girl, gal, lady, woman,* and *gentlewoman*. These terms are not mutually exclusive, and their application is contingent on many contextual and perspectival factors. For example, in English, a mother might say that her adolescent daughter is a

"beautiful woman" and yet call her adult daughter "my baby." Similarly, a po-
lite boy might be called a "gentleman," while irresponsible adult male behavior
might prompt the comment "boys will be boys." These are the kinds of informal
age grades I address in this chapter. I begin with a discussion of conception and
gestation among the A'uwẽ, the first stages of informal life cycles for both females and males, which has received precious little ethnographically grounded
attention despite its centrality to discussions of human substance and proper
social relations in lowland South America.

Substance of Infancy

Several of the basic principles of A'uwẽ social organization involved in notions
of social well-being were derived from cultural concepts regarding conception
and gestation of babies. A common theme in lowland South American societies'
ideas of how a fetus is formed is that different bodily aspects, such as blood,
flesh, or bones, are derived from either paternal or maternal substances (Seeger,
DaMatta, and Viveiros de Castro 2019). Thus, multiple paternal contributions
of semen by means of intercourse during pregnancy can physically create certain kinds of fetal mass (such as bones), besides establishing the possibility of
multiple (partible) paternity if the contributions are made by more than one
man (Beckerman and Valentine 2002; W. H. Crocker 1990). Partible paternity
is common among Indigenous groups throughout the region and is interpreted
differently according to each society's perspectives regarding the social acceptability of women having multiple sexual partners or engaging in extramarital
sexual relations.

For the A'uwẽ I interviewed, who were mostly in their late thirties to forties,
conception was viewed quite differently, as a singular event involving semen
from one biological father, although subsequent contributions of semen by the
father could help direct the development of the fetus in specific ways. Ongoing
contributions of semen were considered irrelevant to paternity or to the growth
(formation or enlargement) of fetal substance. Thus, the possibility of biological
paternal contributions by multiple men was explicitly denied by my interviewees. The increase in fetal mass that occurs throughout gestation was uniformly
attributed exclusively to maternal nourishment.

This contemporary understanding at the Pimentel Barbosa and Etênhiritipá
communities of a single conception event and exclusively maternal contributions to fetal mass may represent a historical change in beliefs due to engage-

ment with non-Indigenous peoples, although my interlocutors assured me it did not. According to Maybury-Lewis (1967, 63), "they [A'uwẽ] appear to view the fashioning of the child as a process induced by repeated copulation. . . . Shavante spoke of the father 'making his child' by repeated intercourse with its mother." Based on research among other A'uwẽ subgroups, Mariana Kawall Leal Ferreira (2015, 178) reported, "The Xavante theory of conception posits that a child is the product of the accumulated sperm in a woman's womb. Therefore, a child usually has multiple fathers and mothers, brothers and sisters, aunts and uncles, and so on." Thus, the historical A'uwẽ view of conception and formation of fetal substance through contributions of semen by different men may have been closer to the prevalent Amazonian pattern of partible paternity than my interviews attested. If so, there may have been a prior cultural model for a child receiving paternal support from more than one man understood to be biological fathers, which could have favorably affected a child's social well-being throughout life. If contemporary (but no longer universally accepted) notions of proper extramarital sexual relations were similar at that time, these fathers would have been real and categorical paternal uncles.[1] Nevertheless, even in the absence of a prevalent notion of partible paternity, such real and categorical paternal uncles treated their brother's children as though they were their own, for other reasons (see chapter 4). Thus, the potential social benefit of an understanding of multiple fatherhood for child well-being appeared to exist even in conjunction with a contemporary theory of singular conception.

Despite the contemporary A'uwẽ perspective that no more than one man and one woman biologically parented a child, the procreative role of neither was thought to end with conception. Parents might participate in a highly intentional process of fetal nurture during pregnancy until the child was thought to be sufficiently formed (see Maybury-Lewis 1967). During those formative months, a father might wear special painted ear plugs called "baby work" (*a'utézo rōmhöri*), often made by a father or grandfather with this guarded knowledge. These ear plugs were employed to stimulate pregnancy and influence the trajectory of the child's physical development toward maleness or femaleness, as desired by agreement between the parents. Doing this "work" for the benefit of the child is an example of how certain procreative activities can be considered to contribute to good living. After a mother perceived she was pregnant and communicated this to the father, he might continue to have intercourse with her while using baby work ear plugs to help complete its formation according to the desired sexual trajectory. His continued participation in this way was not required for a fetus to grow normally, and his additional contributions of semen were not thought to contribute to fetal substance (growing bigger). Rather, the ear plugs were believed to determine the sex of the child if used diligently for an adequate period of months during the early stages of gestation. Thus, baby work was understood to realize parents' desires for either female or male offspring.

In A'uwẽ society, although the male and female parental contributions to fetal formation and growth differed, the notion of bodily substance was framed exclusively in terms of blood (*dawapru*), derived from both mother and father. No interviewees differentiated between maternal or paternal derivations of different bodily aspects, including blood. Furthermore, the qualities of one's blood and body were said to derive in equal parts from mother and father. As one man told me, "Half of his body comes from the father and half from the mother, equally between the two. His eyes can look like the mother's or the father's. The nose can look like the mother's or the father's."

Nevertheless, for different reasons, the A'uwẽ explanation also resulted in greater emphasis being placed on the paternal aspect of fetal substance. Although a mother and father were thought to contribute equally to a child's blood, the father's was considered "stronger." Through its dominance, the father's blood had a greater influence over the child's body and identity. Thus, a child's bodily substance was derived in equal parts from mother and the father, but the paternal half exerted greater influence over the child's sociophysiological identity and determined its consanguinity. This formulation had important consequences for notions of relatedness, which correspondingly exhibited both patrilineal (traced through male descent lines) and bilateral (traced through both male and female descent lines) aspects. An overt expression of the patrilineal aspect was a system of two exogamous moieties, Tadpole (*porezaõno*) and Big Water (*öwawe*), which were said to be invariably transmitted from father to child by means of paternal blood (see Welch 2022b for a detailed argument that this system did not comprise three clans at Pimentel Barbosa and Etênhiritipá, as proposed by some previous scholars).[2] The mechanism by which children assumed their father's and not their mother's exogamous moiety affiliation was described to me in terms of a child's dominant paternal blood bringing with it ("pulling") their father's exogamous moiety. Marriage to or sexual relations with a member of the same patrilineal exogamous moiety was considered incestuous, and some people thought it contaminated the blood of resulting offspring. Thus, marrying into the opposite exogamous moiety was considered healthful and socially appropriate, important aspects of well-being.

Furthermore, belonging to such a moiety was viewed as pleasing and beneficial because it identified a person with proper social roles in the exercise of influence and casted them in jovial relations with their adversaries in the opposite moiety (see chapter 4).

Indicative of A'uwẽ notions of continuity between fetal and newborn babies, both were contemplated by the same word (*a'uté*). As is documented throughout Indigenous lowland South America, among the A'uwẽ, children were believed to share a very real, albeit invisible, connection to both parents during gestation and for some time after birth. The duration of this connection was understood heterogeneously, but most parents reported that it lasted until the child was sufficiently developed to be adequately resistant to certain kinds of diseases and burdens. Some understood it to last for weeks to months, while others thought it to end after several days because current healthcare services had substantially reduced the risk of child mortality and morbidity. This connection caused both mother's and father's food intake and other behaviors to have direct effects on their fragile fetus or newborn. Consuming certain proscribed foods (*dasai'pe*) or killing or touching certain game animals could cause the child to be stillborn, develop illnesses, suffer from developmental problems, or die. Conversely, eating prescribed foods could promote fetal or newborn healthfulness.[3] Although some parents no longer believed in or chose to ignore these food proscriptions and prescriptions, for many people they were important factors in how they went about caring for their babies in ways that promoted wellness. Practicing good parental food practices during this fragile stage of a baby's development affected entire households' self-provisioning activities, as they worked to procure a healthful diet comprising only foods that were considered beneficial for the baby when eaten by its parents.

Individualized Phases of Life

The A'uwẽ actively marked the role of age in social identity and experience in abundant ways. At the most general level, age was apparent in certain broadly applicable and relatively nonspecific terms, such as *ĩhöibaté* (young life/body) and *ĩhöiba'rada* (old life/body). Relative age was reflected somewhat more specifically in the kinship terminology, whereby some terms shifted according to whether the subject was younger or older than the speaker (see chapter 4). For example, siblings of the same gender referred to each other as either *ĩdub'rada* (older same-gender sibling) or *ĩno* (younger same-gender sibling).

Another set of categories that distinguished age with varying degrees of specificity in A'uwẽ society were age grades, the stages of life through which individuals or groups of individuals pass throughout the life cycle. Some terms belonged to a mostly gendered informal system comprising sometimes ambiguous or overlapping age classifications based on female or male developmental, individualistic, and subjective criteria, while other terms pertained to a formal system that operated for both women and men in conjunction with age sets (Bernardi 1985). In this section, I explore informal age grades, their influence on social experience at different stages of the life cycle, and linkages to well-being and environmental engagement. This formulation of the life cycle was accompanied by historically situated social expectations of age-appropriate behaviors that promoted community well-being and contributed to cerrado stewardship.

I found there to be two sequences of informal age grades, one female and one male. Only two terms in each were shared: child (a'uté) and elder (ĩhi). Otherwise, the female life cycle encompassed the informal age grades girl (ba'õno), adolescent (azarudu), childless wife (adabá), and married woman with child (ĩ'raré or araté).[4] Notably, pi'õ, a term popularized by Maybury-Lewis (1967) and used by anthropologists ever since for married woman with child, is in fact a vocative kinship term, not an informal age grade.

The male informal life cycle was more concise, including only boy (watebremĩ) and adolescent (ai'repudu) in addition to child (a'uté) and elder (ĩhi). The gap between male childhood or adolescence and elder status in the informal age grade system was accounted for by the exclusive use of formal age grade terms during these phases of life, as I discuss in the next section.[5]

An ancillary age-graded system within the vocative kinship terminology was frequently used for one's children and some bilateral nieces and nephews. Although the literature has tended to confuse these terms with the informal age grades identified above (which could be used to identify anyone in society irrespective of their kinship relationships with the speaker), their restricted application to certain kin differentiates them even though they refer to some of the same stages of life. This age-graded set of kinship terms was used only to address one's children and children of one's real and categorical brothers (see chapter 4). Thus, both female and male egos addressed their children, their brother's children, and all other children of their bilateral male cousins by a set of terms corresponding with their stage of life rather than by a single static term. These kinship terms for females were girl (otí), female adolescent (zarudu), childless wife (soimbá), and wife with child (pi'õ).[6] The kinship terms for males were boy (*bödi*), male adolescent (*'repudu*), preinitiate (*hö'wa*), and adult man (*aibö*). Thus, for example, a woman in the childless wife age grade (*adabá*) would be addressed as *soimbá* only by her parents and her parents' real and categorical male siblings. Because these age-graded terms were a part of the kinship terminology and not used by other kin or nonkin, they were not age grades in the sense developed in this chapter.

The term for child (*a'uté*) was the first age grade that could be considered informal because inclusion was defined by conception, an individualistic or subjective criterion (Bernardi 1985). According to my data, it was used for female and male infants (including the fetal stage) and children of all ages, until the onset of puberty.

Preadolescent girls were both children (*a'uté*) and girls (*ba'ono*), the former term used most to indicate young age irrespective of gender, and the latter used to indicate the female gender of a child (figure 8).[7] Similarly, preadolescent boys were both children (*a'uté*) and boys (*watebremí*), each term operating analogously to the equivalent female terms (figure 9).

A female ceased to be a girl (*ba'ono*) when she entered adolescence (*azarudu*), which began with puberty, as recognized by first enlargement of the breasts.[8] The onset of adolescence signaled her eligibility for marriage, which could occur soon thereafter. A'uwẽ females married at earlier ages than males (marriages as early as eleven years were not unusual among females around 2010 and probably more recently), who were only eligible for marriage after becoming novitiate adults (*'ritei'wa*), on average around age nineteen, but more commonly married as mature adults (*iprédu*), beginning at about twenty-four years old. The end of female adolescence was marked by her wedding ceremony (*dabasa*), in which her groom delivered a large quantity of game meat to her doorstep, and she subsequently presented herself by kneeling on a mat in front of her house. Through this ceremony, she became a childless wife (*adabá*). Usually, she had a first child not long thereafter, often within the first year of marriage, at which time she became a married woman with child (*ĩ'raré*). Upon reaching menopause, women became elders (*ĩhi*).

For males, boyhood (*watebremí*) might end when adolescence (*ai'repudu*) began, which was marked by fast growth spurts, deepening of the voice, and evidence of psychological changes thought to accompany the passage from childhood, including increased respectfulness of others and avoidance of typical child play activities.[9] Not all boys reached adolescence terminologically, however, because, while still boys (*watebremí*), they were inducted into the preini-

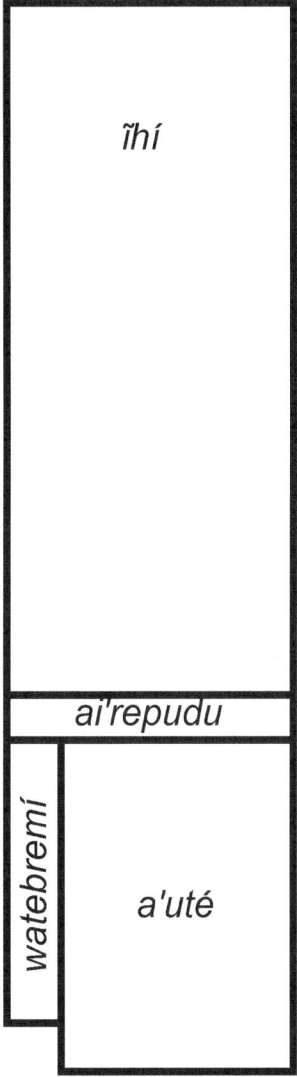

Figure 8 Diagram of female informal age grade system, chronologically from bottom up.

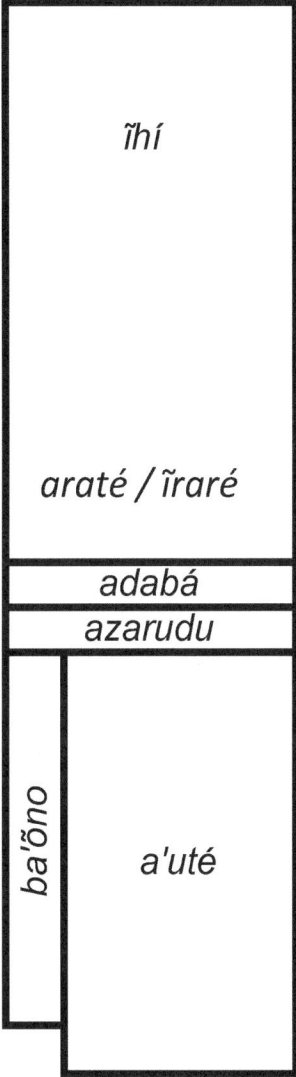

Figure 9 Diagram of male informal age grade system, chronologically from bottom up.

tiate house and thereby became preinitiates (*wapté*), which is the first formal age grade in the secular age group system (see next chapter). Thus, they skipped from being boys to being preinitiates, never passing through adolescence. Similarly, adolescence ended when an adolescent became a preinitiate. All young males became preinitiates during boyhood or adolescence. Adolescence was the last male informal age grade until old age because, during the intervening years, males occupied only formal age grades (beginning with preinitiation). Men became elders (*ihi*) when their hair turned gray, their skin became wrinkled, and they assumed the posture and stance of an elder, marked by such behaviors as carrying a walking stick.[10]

Children and Adolescents: A Time for Imitation

Transitions between informal age grades throughout a person's life cycle had diverse social implications. Infants including small/young children (*a'utépré*), small/young girls (*ba'õtõre*), and small/young boys (*watebremire*) required constant care and were not yet sufficiently independent to adventure far from home. The totality of their environment was therefore the domestic setting, as well as such locations in their mothers' daily routines as the primary healthcare unit and the river (to bathe and wash clothes). Infants who had not yet learned to walk were carried in covered baskets suspended with tumplines against their mothers' backs, usually wrapped in soft cloth bought in town. At these ages, children's well-being was the responsibility of caretakers, usually the women and older girls of the household, who ensured they were always fed, clean, protected from the elements, and in the company of others. For some time after children learned to walk, they remained dependent on caretakers for most of their needs.

By the time girls and boys were a little older, walking and talking proficiently, they were afforded a tremendous degree of liberty with the expectation that in time and of their own accord they would begin laying the educational groundwork for their eventual transitions into adulthood. This combination of childhood autonomy and expectations that they will learn (*rowaihu*) the skills needed to become adults of their own accord was a hallmark of A'uwẽ concepts regarding proper relations between parents and children that best contributed to the children's well-being. Specifically, parents' relations with their children were not directive. Rather, they were permissive, according to the logic that children should learn skills, responsibility, and respect through their autonomous experience and effort.

Many elders expressed to me their expectations that child play involve imitation (*danhizu*) of adults because they considered it to be the only worthwhile and effective means of preparing for A'uwẽ adulthood. Adults, for their part, should set an example (*dasi'sanho*) for young people to learn from and imitate. Direct and explicit teaching was not recognized as a valid form of parental behavior and was not considered to have the potential to promote effective learning and desirable behaviors among children. Thus, autonomy and imitation were considered by elders to be essential characteristics for children to grow up well. This approach to child rearing had implications for environmental engagement in contemporary times, as learning about the landscape and its ethnobiological resources depended on a child's voluntary manifestation of interest, attention, and practice in combination with available adult examples to observe and imitate.

Research on Indigenous peoples in Brazil has highlighted a tendency for children to learn informally as subjects of their own education according to principles of autonomy, self-determination, and permissiveness (Cohn 2002; Lopes da Silva and Nunes 2002; Schaden 1945; Tassinari 2014; Zoia and Peripolli 2010). As these scholars consistently described for numerous ethnic groups, childhood is often distinguished by a lack of formal instruction and free circulation in diverse social settings from which they may be restricted after reaching adulthood. Consistent with these conditions, child learning in such societies occurs through voluntary observation and imitation of adult behavior. A'uwẽ childhood was similarly described as an unrestrained and autonomous time in which children acted on their own initiative to re-create the social world around them (Nunes 2002, 2011). As Maria, an elderly grandmother, said with great sadness,

> Children have total liberty. One thing that they don't have today is imitation. In the past, children imitated their parents. Girls and boys formed groups and imitated family hunting trips. They roasted meat, hunted animals. It was training, a real rehearsal [for adulthood]. Imitating adults, that is how we learn. They made little houses and the "husband" would hunt little animals in the area behind the village. It was training for hunting. They also prepared for attacks and pretended to do [ritual] club fights. Then, they competed for best warrior by shooting arrows. Today they do not do this.

Girls, like boys, were expected to play at games that elders said should imitate adult life and serve as a prelude to assuming adult responsibilities. As the elder woman Iraní told me, "During the first year of life, you don't know anything. But as you grow, you begin understanding. We observe, pay attention to the adults. Being curious, we learn. We must not stop learning because as adults we have to look after ourselves."

I noticed substantial differences between girls and boys in their play behavior. In my observation, girls spent a great deal of time assisting adult women with diverse household chores such as preparing food, collecting water, and tending to infants. Girls but not boys constructed and played in miniature versions of traditional A'uwē domed houses sized to accommodate one or two children (figure 10), roasted small game over open fires, and pounded imaginary rice with improvised pestles. Boys often fashioned and played with toy bows and arrows, sometimes killing small lizards or birds (figure 11). I saw them dance and sing with clasped hands in circles, as adult men do (figure 12). They frequently held pretend club fights, using their arms and fists as substitutes for real clubs. Sometimes they would walk throughout the community challenging passersby, as though on scouting missions to protect an imagined territory. Importantly from an ethnobiological point of view, boyhood was also the time when males began to learn about animals, especially preferred game animals, by playing

Figure 10 Girls playing house, 2004.

Figure 11 Boy displaying lizard killed with play bow and arrows, 2005.

Figure 12 Boys playing at ceremonial dancing, 2004.

Figure 13 Boy playing with baby giant anteater, 2005.

with them as pets or as captured immature animals (figure 13). This dynamic was described as routine daily play, with immature animals serving as first opportunities for A'uwẽ children to learn their names, morphological characteristics, and behavioral traits (Carrara 2002). Children also played other games that elders did not mention as desirable, many of them derived from non-Indigenous play traditions or inspired by television. For example, typical boyhood games included knife-throwing contests, stilt walking, kite flying, slingshot shooting (which might be considered desirable if used to kill small edible birds and animals), and soccer (most of these activities were also occasional pastimes of preinitiates or younger adults). These diverse female and male child play behaviors suggest to me that they did imitate behaviors they observed among older people, which included new models of older peoples' behavior that did not fully comport with elders' expectations of desirable child's play. Thus, if elders were correct in alleging that contemporary changes in play activities suggested children were off track in their progress toward becoming adults capable of attending to the wellness of their future families, the greater problem would seem to be the behavioral models available for them to imitate rather than the social relations between children and their seniors.

Health studies (Ferreira et al. 2012; Welch et al. 2020) suggest that contemporary A'uwẽ children had inadequate access to healthy foods, with many suffering from chronic undernutrition. This unfavorable situation appears to have been derived partly from reduced access to healthful collected, hunted, fished, and gardened foods; partly by limited access to healthy but expensive industrial foods; and partly due to overemphasis on affordable rice prepared with ample cooking oil and salt as a staple food (see Coimbra Jr. et al. 2002; Graham 1995). This scenario is indicative of a lack of food sovereignty, in which consumers do not have control over food production and distribution systems. Lack of food sovereignty was a major concern of community leaders, who recognized its relationship to poor health, including cardiovascular diseases, diabetes, and hypertension. An important component of A'uwẽ food sovereignty in the past was access to landscape food resources. Whereas trekking was undertaken historically for the greater part of the year to obtain collected and hunted foods, recently fewer parents and other elder relatives of these affected children pursued these foods regularly. In addition to contemporary children having less access to these kinds of food diversity, A'uwẽ engage in less physical activity because of the discontinuance of trekking, acquisition of motorized vehicles, and introduction of televisions in most homes.

With the approach of adolescence, social gender differences became even more distinct, although both girls and boys tended to play less and adopt more respectful stances while in the presence of adults. Adolescent girls often continued living in the same household, socializing with mostly the same people, and performing similar routine domestic duties to those they imitated as children. Yet, for girls, a fundamental reorientation of social bearings accompanied adolescence in anticipation of marriage (see Maybury-Lewis 1967).

Whereas play was a distinguishing feature of younger boyhood, the approach of male adolescence carried the connotation of imminent induction into the preinitiate house. For boys, later childhood and adolescence involved a strong orientation toward life in the preinitiate house even before they resided there.

In my observation, male adolescence continued to be characterized by tremendous social liberty. There was a clear tendency, however, for male adolescents to distance themselves from their previous social circles of younger children and increasingly realign themselves based on their imminent status as preinitiates. For example, I noticed that adolescents often played near their future mentors in and around the evening men's council (*warā*), a social space usually avoided by children.

Results of health studies I conducted with colleagues and graduate students suggest that adolescence was marked by the first onset of several diet-related health conditions, some of which increased in prevalence during adulthood (especially overweight and obesity; Welch et al. 2020). The implications of these health findings for environmental engagement are like those mentioned above for childhood. Additionally, in the past, many female adolescents from ten to seventeen years of age were already collecting wild root vegetables, fruits, and hearts of palm with their elder female relatives. Many male adolescents in this age group were already preinitiates and had begun hunting with their mentors. During my research I observed very few girls of this age joining collecting excursions and no boys accompanying their mentors while hunting. Thus, recently, this age group was not yet learning basic subsistence techniques and related traditional ecological knowledge. This scenario suggests that fewer people engaged in these activities or that they began them later in life, which potentially contributed to lack of food sovereignty. As I discuss in chapter 7, among the main reasons for this recent decrease in participation in routine subsistence activities was monetarization of economies and increased sedentarism.

Wives, Mothers, and Providers

Although the childless wife informal age grade (*adabá*) was frequently brief, it constituted an important social transition in a woman's life. Her wedding ceremony concluded when she presented herself in the plaza to have her cotton necklaces, meticulously prepared for the occasion by her ceremonial father (*danhorebzu'wa*), removed from her neck by a younger real or categorical sister (figure 14). For a young bride, the event marked her transition from adolescent to childless wife. Also on that day, her husband typically took up residence in her house (unless she was a second, third, or fourth wife, or he was a novitiate adult). Generally, the two knew each other relatively well by then because he had paid her and her parents nightly visits, covertly under cover of darkness,

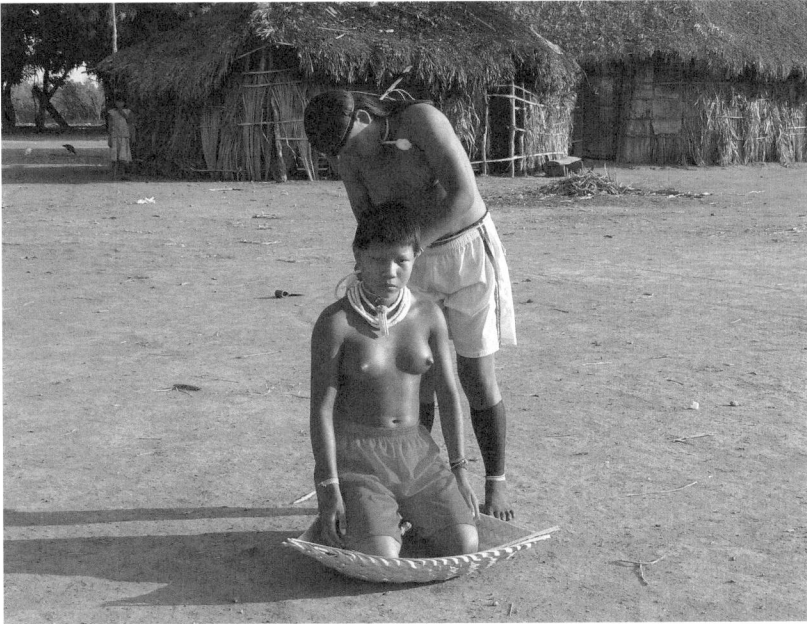

Figure 14 Bride kneeling during her wedding ceremony as a young real or categorical sister removes necklaces from her neck, 2005.

for some time to give him and his bride's household the opportunity to become familiar with one another, facilitate their mutual accommodation in advance of his moving in with them after marriage, and afford the young couple time to develop an affective relationship (see Graham 1995). This preparation was considered essential for the formation of stable caring relationships between future spouses (*damro*) who previously did not know one another.

Unlike in some other A'uwẽ communities that have reportedly discontinued the practice, at Pimentel Barbosa and Etênhiritipá all first marriages between young brides and grooms continued to be arranged by their parents (subsequent marriages might be arranged directly by prospective parents-in-law and their prospective son-in-law). The preference for this form of marriage was consistent with the understanding that marriage united extended families, not just individuals, and therefore had broad social repercussions potentially affecting all residents in a community. Therefore, well-arranged marriages promoted social well-being among the married couple, their extended families, and the entire community. Most people saw them not as a violation of individual rights, but rather as a means of promoting enduring beneficial relationships. Nevertheless, exceptionally, young people might not consent to marry a chosen spouse. In the only example of such a case I observed, the intended bride's parents respected her decision not to marry and after a time successfully sought another young man she found acceptable. Her decision did have social repercussions, including the abrupt relocation of the intended groom's household to another community and the consequent cancellation of her brother's marriage to his sister (sibling exchange).

A young woman's household responsibilities did not significantly change with her new status as a childless wife or her subsequent status as married woman with child (*i'raré*). She was expected to cook and care for her husband and children, independently of usual assistance and contributions by her real and categorical mothers and grandmothers. Yet, it was her commitment to fulfilling those responsibilities for the well-being of her new husband and young children that initially earned her the approval of interested elders. Typical female domestic service included such diverse activities as caring for young children, choosing which groceries to purchase, collecting, distributing foods among relatives and neighbors, carrying food and water from one place to another, cooking, housekeeping, washing clothes, preparing cotton string for ceremonial use, and making beaded accessories. Traditionalist perspectives placed additional expectations on them, including that they perform gardening tasks and collect firewood, fruits, hearts of palm, and wild root vegetables. They also processed manioc for consumption as a cooked root vegetable and as toasted manioc meal (*farinha*). All these roles were considered by traditionalist perspectives to contribute to the health and well-being of their families.

Many women preferred to perform some tasks more than others, and it was not unusual for sisters to trade or schedule responsibilities according to their preferences. I have also observed wives instructing their husbands to pay professionals to do chores they disliked, such as hulling rice. As of 2019, when I conducted a collaborative study of household food economies (Welch and Coimbra Jr. 2022), many younger women indicated that they preferred not to engage in these subsistence activities, opting instead to spend their income, usually Bolsa Família (Family Allowance), a governmental social assistance program for mothers with young children that ended in 2021, on purchased industrialized foods. This change from the past corresponded with widespread agreement among many people of all ages that they eat less food produced or acquired within the Indigenous land, opting instead to eat food from supermarkets in towns neighboring the land. Nevertheless, I observed several novitiate adult women accompany their female elders during collecting excursions to learn how to identify and collect wild foods (see chapter 6). This minority of young women expressed great enthusiasm during these short trips into the cerrado and fallow gardens, suggesting that they appreciated the importance of providing healthful traditional foods to their families in addition to store-bought foods. I do not suggest that these women cared more about the well-being of their families than women who did not collect frequently, but rather that some young women not only associated dietary traditionalism with healthfulness and wellness, but also were actively taking measures to ensure that their families benefited from this relationship.

One task seemed to me especially emblematic of contemporary cultural tensions surrounding women's traditionalist service responsibilities. This was the female task of collecting wild root vegetables from the cerrado. When Maybury-Lewis conducted his fieldwork in the 1950s, maize was a highly valued food, but the caloric basis of the diet was wild root vegetables, mainly in the *Dioscorea* genus, collected by women (Flowers 2014; Maybury-Lewis 1967; Welch, Santos, et al. 2013). In my observation, wild root vegetables were sought and consumed much less in recent decades than Maybury-Lewis described for the 1950s, even though they remained highly valued as an unusually healthful food item and as a traditional gift item in certain ritual contexts (Welch 2022a). According to both women and men, husbands had the primary responsibility of hunting for game meat, another food item considered exceptionally healthful, and wives had the responsibility of gathering wild root vegetables (figure 15). Just as elder women complained that contemporary men did not acquire sufficient game meat for their families, elder men maintained that women collected wild root vegetables too infrequently. My observations also suggest that elder females considered wild root vegetable collecting and conservation important for the well-being of their households and extended families (as healthful healing foods) and of participants in spiritual rituals and secular rites of passage (as sacred gifts given by protégés to their mentors) (Welch 2022a). Elder females frequently expressed lament regarding increasing lack of familiarity with wild root vegetables among their younger female relatives. I discuss dynamics related to decreased wild root vegetable collecting by women in contemporary times and their efforts to promote the stewardship of these plant resources in greater detail in chapter 6.

Coresident women cooked over the same open fire in their cooking annex (less frequently over a propane gas stove), but married women with children

Figure 15 Women returning from a wild root vegetable collecting excursion, 2005.

could separate their cooking resources and efforts from the others, preparing their food in a separate pot for their nuclear families. Nevertheless, sharing food was constant, and no one in a household went hungry while someone else had food in their pot. Whereas some women preferred to exercise exclusive control over their domains, others opted to consult, cooperate, or collaborate with their husbands. It is my tentative opinion that these forms of female service contributed to the construction of female domains of social influence rather than constraining them in subordinate relationships. I advance this position recognizing that A'uwẽ women's perspectives of gender roles were transforming, and their viewpoints regarding female service might be quite different in the future.

Another valued role of young wives was childbearing. Children and grandchildren were adored by their parents and grandparents, and contemporary parents often expressed that they valued having many children, which exemplified healthy, happy families. Some elders told me, however, that in the past, parents did not desire as many children. According to elders, in the past, young women did not have children as early because men treated them with greater respect (*danhisé*). As Maria explained,

From my point of view people used to be more respectful towards women. In the past, a man always respected women, even his sister, by turning his back to her in deference. That was beautiful. Men learned this in the preinitiate house. In the past, women were alerted to not abide sexual aggression by men. Our mothers oriented us to take care of ourselves, and we did not accept sex. Men were respectful, which is difficult to make happen. Today it is different. Young men do not obey and do not have respect.

Additionally, according to the eldest individuals I interviewed, an ample interbirth interval of several years was preferred in the past because of the challenges of life that affected parenthood at that time, such as trekking and warfare. Using demographic reference data for 1999–2004 collected by L. G. Souza (2008), Bibiani (2018) showed a reduction in the total fertility rate by about 20 percent from 1999 to 2011. This elevated change may suggest that some women opted to have fewer children since I first investigated the topic or other dynamics affecting interbirth spacing or family size have shifted in recent decades.

In my observation, the care of a young child was a collective affair, involving numerous female members of an extended family for the sake of their mutual interest in ensuring the health and wellness of their shared kin. Within a household, women of multiple generations cared for children. It was extremely common for a child to be attended by their real and categorical grandmothers, mothers, sisters, and other female relatives. Often, a mother would leave a child in the care of these relatives while she spent multiple days at distant gardens, especially during planting or harvest time. This was made possible by the cultural practice of allomaternal nursing, which is nursing of a child by women other than the mother. Typically, maternal aunts (who were categorical mothers) and grandmothers would nurse a child in the absence of their mother. Grandmothers nursing children was a common practice even when they were postmenopausal, which is entirely possible physiologically. This mutual care of children by closely related women was an important and valued dimension of the female domestic experience. Some younger mothers rejected allomaternal nursing, however, possibly because until 2015, it was formally discouraged by the Special Secretariat for Indigenous Health, and nurses routinely intervened when the practice was detected. This public health policy was based on the possibility of disease (e.g., hepatitis B and HIV) transmission to the child without regard to other local factors, such as the unavailability of infant formula. The policy remains polemical with regard to Indigenous peoples.

Whereas women's social well-being appeared to exhibit ample resilience, health indicators suggest that other aspects of their physical wellness warrant concern. Standing out among health conditions during womanhood (over seventeen years of age) were elevated frequencies of overweight, obesity, and substantially increased risk of metabolic complications (Welch et al. 2020). These findings show that dietary health continued to deteriorate after adolescence, roughly when many women married and began to have children. This scenario was largely attributable to transformed diets, which included large proportions of rice, sugars, cooking oil, and many other industrialized and ultraprocessed foods (Welch et al. 2009). A substantial portion of young women did not engage in collecting activities, many did not garden to produce foods, and many relied almost exclusively on purchased foods. Thus, besides altering the quality of their diets, these changes and other factors, such as presence of a television, contributed to substantially reduced physical activity levels (Lucena et al. 2016). The combination of chronic undernutrition in childhood and excess weight in adulthood was a double burden of malnutrition, which tends to afflict poorer world populations (Popkin, Corvalan, and Grummer-Strawn 2020). Furthermore, there was a risk of a generational gap in transmission of traditional ecological knowledge as a result of the lack of participation in collecting activities among younger women.

Elders, Guardians of Ethnobiological Knowledge

Women had even greater social influence as elders than as younger wives with children. Elder status carried the connotations of advanced age, wisdom, and respectability. Not only was advanced age alone thought to make women deserving of respect, but elder women often had large numbers of grandchildren, both real and categorical, who adored them. The range of social influence commanded by such elder women was grippingly apparent at their funerals, when seemingly countless individuals from even distant communities and Indigenous lands came to mourn their passing. The social influence that such women had was often less explicit than that of elder males, who held court at the men's council, but it was nonetheless apparent in the esteem with which they were regarded by large segments of society.

For males, becoming elders represented a final transition beyond the abundant subordinate social roles that accompanied the greater part of the male life cycle.[11] Whereas much of mature manhood involved innumerable social constraints relative to one's seniors, as elders, men were afforded the greatest social autonomy and influence as heads of households, extended family founders, and political leaders. Being free of the constraints of most forms of social subordination, however, did not imply freedom from responsibility or accountability. It was precisely because of their sanction to lead that elders were expected to answer to the will of the community with impartiality and equity. Theirs was the right to direct community decisions but only insofar as they did not contradict community consensus. Politically successful elders heeded a lifetime of learning to respect others through their experiences as subordinate protégés, housebound novitiate adult sons, respectful young sons-in-law, and junior council members. As elders they thereby came to appreciate the value of reconciling one's opinions with those of the community for the sake of generalized contentment and social amenability.

Cultural and ecological knowledge in general was the privileged domain of elders, and the older a person was, the more privileged their knowledge. Elders were considered guardians of traditional knowledge and experts in many domains, such as ceremonialism, oral history, subsistence, and craft production. Among the correlates of elder status was a special role in the A'uwẽ epistemology of health and knowledge. According to A'uwẽ elders, their society never had an equivalent social role to shaman (in Portuguese, *pajé* or *xamã*). This assertion is not to say that there were no healers, but rather that no individuals assumed specialized social roles as shamanic healers for entire communities. For the A'uwẽ, all elders were healers who attended to members of their own families. In other words, females and males sought some kinds of healing from such men as fathers, grandfathers, and patrilineal uncles (and less usually elder women), while women sought expertise in reproductive health from such female kin as their mothers, grandmothers, and maternal aunts. Thus, all elders were guardians of health and healing knowledge.

Similarly, elders were considered most knowledgeable about the environment, including plants and animals. Elder status itself qualified an individual to speak about topics that might be characterized as biodiversity, ethnobiology, ethnoecology, and self-provisioning. Often, younger individuals I knew to be extremely knowledgeable about these topics declined to opine about them if it was possible to defer to an elder (see Graham 1995 for similar examples). Seeking responses to the same questions from multiple people, as when using such ethnobiological methods as consensus analysis or pile sorts, often resulted in younger people declining to participate based on the argument that only elders should respond. Even when I asked more than one elder, it was not uncommon for one person to defer to an even older person because of their presumptive greater environmental knowledge. Although these may have been avoidance strategies, individuals who agreed to participate thoroughly enjoyed the activities in part because they could display their considerable knowledge to me and other observers.

In my experience, many elders were among the people most actively involved in performing subsistence activities. In the home of my adoptive parents lived two grandmothers, the mother and maternal aunt of my mother. Maria, now deceased, and Iara were born before permanent contact was established with the SPI and after the population had left the ancestral community Sõrepré, probably in the 1920s or 1930s. Early in my research at the Pimentel Barbosa community, I noticed Maria and Iara constantly working around the house, caring for children, sweeping the floors and raking the grounds outside, and cooking food over an open fire. When we began construction of my house next door, Maria and Iara, at approximately seventy or eighty years of age, were the first to climb the large mango trees (*Mangifera indica*) to remove obstructing limbs with axes. As time went on, I also noticed that they frequently disappeared for hours at a time, returning with large carrying baskets full of firewood, fruits, manioc, wild root vegetables, and all sorts of other foods. When they returned with wild cerrado fruits, they would set the basket on the floor of the house to share them with the children.

Other elders in different households were similarly engaged in performing subsistence activities that younger people did with less frequency. Women performed such activities as gardening, collecting, cooking, and cotton spinning. Men were often involved in hunting, fishing, clearing and maintaining gardens, and producing ceremonial accoutrements. During my initial years of research, elder men who hunted often did so with bow and arrows, which were no longer used by younger individuals with access to firearms. Elders were also among the most prolific of hunters, rarely returning to the community without a large game animal suspended on their backs. I am unaware of any individuals continuing to hunt with bow and arrows, as none of the elders who did so are still with us.

As Antônio illustrates in chapter 1, elders also had their own notions of cerrado resource conservation, which did not necessarily map neatly onto principles of international conservation discourse. For A'uwẽ elders, certain landscape resources, most notably game meat and wild root vegetables, were essential for successfully conducting important ceremonial activities. Considering A'uwẽ settlement on small Indigenous lands compared to their vast historical territory, the relevant conservation question for these elders was what must be done to ensure that hunting and collecting continued to be productive in the long term (Welch 2014). In other words, how could they ensure their sustainability or that they would continue "forever"? They were considerably less interested in the question of whether hunting and collecting should be continued in the future, although evidence-free ethnic shaming from rural neighbors, allies of the anti-Indigenous agribusiness caucus, and even some ecology scholars suggested that they should be halted altogether to avoid or mitigate environmental destruction (Welch and Coimbra Jr. 2021; Welch, Brondízio, and Coimbra Jr. 2022).

Elders were also among the most fervent proponents of using political advocacy to pursue the demarcation of additional Indigenous lands for A'uwẽ use, because they recognized, based on their personal experiences, that the size of the current Pimentel Barbosa Indigenous Land would be inadequate for future ceremonial group hunting and collecting needs considering the increasing size of the resident population. Although I continue this conversation in more depth in chapter 6, it is important to note here that the Pimentel Barbosa Indigenous Land remained a green island with negligible deforestation (0.6 percent) amid highly degraded agribusiness properties, allowing significant regeneration of land cover previously removed by ranchers and serving as a refuge for cerrado wildlife (Welch, Brondízio, et al. 2013; Welch, Santos, et al. 2013).

Elders, mothers and wives, adolescents and children, and even infants and unborn children illustrate how A'uwẽ of different stages of life, or informal age grades, experienced life as autonomous individuals engaged with cultural frameworks of norms and expectations that changed as one progressed through the life cycle. Furthermore, these informal age grades had implications for social well-being and environmental practice. Unborn children and very young infants were seen as dependent, fragile, and malleable. Development of their sexual attributes could be directed through copulation while the male partner wore special ear plugs. Their good health required numerous behavioral and dietary precautions by both the mother and the father until the most dangerous stage had passed, including limitations on what animal foods they could eat, touch, or hunt. Children and adolescents were given ample autonomy but nevertheless expected to voluntarily observe and imitate productive adult behavior, especially self-provisioning activities, to lay the groundwork for their eventual transformation into responsible adults. Wives and mothers similarly had ample autonomy to determine their own conduct but were evaluated by others, especially elders, according to their productive caring for family, including collecting valued healthful wild foods, processing and cooking food, and caring for the home. These various traditionalist expectations of peoples' behavior at different stages of life, despite a pervasive morality of personal autonomy, contributed to notions of how a good and responsible social life was lived. People did not need to conform to these expectations, but doing so was thought to promote wellness within families and communities.

CHAPTER 3

Age Group Systems and the Formalization of Social Relations

Secular Age Group System

In addition to understanding the life cycle in terms of informal age grades, A'uwẽ did so in terms of formal age group systems, which structure the human life cycle in relatively few societies.[1] Alfred R. Radcliffe-Brown (1929, 21) defined age grades as "recognized divisions of the life of an individual as he passes from infancy to old age," although he also made the important point that in some societies, a special relationship exists between age sets (cohorts) and age grades (phases). Bernardi (1985, 2) made the relevant distinction that only formal age grades are "institutionalized in relationship with age classes." In societies with such systems, age hierarchies are formalized in terms of distinct age sets (cohorts) that pass through fixed age grades (ranks) (Bernardi 1985; Prins 1953; Stewart 1977). An analogy is U.S. university structure, in which cohorts called *classes* (e.g., the class of 2023) pass through a series of ranks called *years* (i.e., frosh, sophomore, junior, and senior). Such structural arrangements have been called age group systems, age set systems, and age class systems (Bernardi 1952, 1985; Prins 1953; Stewart 1977).

In this book I use *age group system* for formal systems of age sets in conjunction with age grades and reserve *age set system* and *age grade system* for the respective subsystems exclusively comprising age sets and age grades, respectively, which together may compose an age group system. Age set systems and age grade systems may also exist independently of each other. Although I do not employ it here, I consider *age class system* to be synonymous with *age set system*, with both referring specifically to systems of age cohorts irrespective of their possible articulation with age grades.

Age group systems are best known from Africa and North America (Stewart 1977). The A'uwẽ are a rare and largely unrecognized example of a society with age group systems in South America. In my research, I found formal age group systems were extremely important to how A'uwẽ identified themselves, related to one another, and conceived of their social positions in society (for other authors who have mentioned the social importance of age grades and age sets, see Coimbra Jr. et al. 2002; Giaccaria and Heide 1984; Graham 1995; Lopes da Silva 1986; Maybury-Lewis 1967). I submit that A'uwẽ age organization, including age group systems, remains a relevant anthropological topic and deserves reevaluation considering contemporary ethnographic circumstances. I address it here because my field experience indicated that diverse formulations of age were extremely pertinent to A'uwẽ values and experiences of well-being and provide an effective lens into interrelated ethnographic issues, such as environmental engagement. In this chapter, I explore how these relevant life cycle systems operated ideally and in practice, thereby contributing to how people understood good social living, with attention being given to how these systems helped shape people's interactions with the environment throughout life cycles.

Frank Henderson Stewart (1977) specified that a person may not occupy two formal age grades at the same time because they are discrete ranks that members of age sets pass through according to public and collective criteria, leaving no doubt about which one a person belongs to at any given time. Furthermore, Stewart adopted the convention that any stage of life that precedes age set inauguration is not a formal age grade. Said another way, individuals may not occupy formal age grades until they do so as members of age sets. The age grades discussed in the previous chapter were informal in part because they did not operate in conjunction with age sets.

In this section, I discuss the secular age group system that entailed the greater part of the human life cycle. I call it secular because from the A'uwẽ perspective, it did not have an overtly spiritual focus, in contrast to the spiritual age group system (presented later in this chapter), which did. The named age sets contributing to this system were configured in a repeating series of eight: nozö'u, aba-re'u, sada'ro, anhanarowa, hötörã, ai'rere, êtẽpa, and tirowa (table 1). The formal secular age grades these age sets occupied during the life cycle were preinitiate (wapté), initiand (heroi'wa), novitiate adult (dahí'wa or 'ritei'wa), and mature adult (iprédu).[2] Although most of my consultants considered the terms 'ritei'wa and dahí'wa synonymous, I found that they had slightly different meanings. Whereas 'ritei'wa referred exclusively to those who participated in noni sprinting

Table 1 Secular age set names and associated terms

Sequence	Age set name	Associated term(s)	Gloss of associated term(s)
1	*nozö'u*	*nozö*	Traditional maize
2	*abare'u*	*abare*	Pequi fruit (*Caryocar brasiliense*)
3	*sada'ro*	*dazada'ro*	(Bad) breath or sun
4	*anhanarowa*	*anhana*	Feces
5	*hötörã*	*hötörã*	Oscar fish (*Astronotus* spp.)
6	*ai'rere*	*ai'rere*	Guariroba palm (*Syagrus oleracea*)
7	*êtēpa*	*êtēpa*	Scarce stone (used as mortar or pestle)
8	*tirowa*	*ti* or *ti'a*	Arrow or tick (arachnid), respectively

races during the sequence of ceremonial events that made up the secular rites of passage into adulthood (*danhono*), *dahí'wa* applied to all women and men, irrespective of their participation in *noni* sprinting races, beginning with their mutual participation in the subsequent *wamnhono* mask ceremony, near the end of the secular rites of passage into adulthood. Nevertheless, novitiate women and men identified with both terms. This finding is incongruent with previous scholarship asserting that the *'ritei'wa* age grade pertained only to males (Lopes da Silva 1986; Maybury-Lewis 1967).

I continue this section by discussing secular age sets as they shaped both female and male formulations of social life. I then introduce a privileged social bond, camaraderie, arising through preinitiate and mentorship experiences, and its pervasive implications for this age group system and A'uwẽ sociality (I continue the discussion of camaraderie and well-being in chapter 7). I discuss how age set moieties were perpetuated through the repetition of fraternal relationships between protégés and mentors, positioning individuals within a complex social fabric of similarity and difference that was simultaneously symmetrical and hierarchical. Finally, I discuss how this age group system involved a spatial geometry and had implications for life cycles of wellness and environmental engagement.

Female and Male Participation in Age Sets

Secular age sets (*da'usú za'ra*) were the most specific form of age ranking for the greater part of the life cycle. They were also in many respects the most socially salient, by which I mean that they were the most talked about in daily social life and conditioned how people related to one another in a highly conscious and nuanced manner. In my field experience, age sets were how people usually reckoned age in everyday circumstances, much as they were when Maybury-Lewis (1967) conducted research in the same community in the 1950s and 1960s. Although I found that birthdates were used for birth certificates and medical records, they were famously inaccurate by months or years and were commonly forgotten. Instead, age was most often framed in terms of lifelong membership in named secular age sets. Everyone in society would belong to an age set, except for a few individuals with severe developmental disabilities. Membership in a particular age set placed each person in explicit age juxtaposition to the rest of society and operated in conjunction with other aspects of social identity, such as informal age status, gender, and kinship, as a basis for how people related to one another socially and how they engaged with the local environment.

Lopes da Silva (1986) observed that females were affiliated with age sets "by extension" from the male system, because females belonged to the same age sets as males yet did not participate in the collective age set experience of living in the preinitiate house. Although I appreciate her impression that female participation was not as involved as male's, I also found enthusiastic support for the notion that age sets were no less salient for females than for males. Although females continued living at home while boys of similar ages lived in the preinitiate house, females also came to meaningfully identify with their age sets through interaction in the social arenas that made up the female experience. From an early age, female age set peers identified socially with one another and with their male age set mates. For example, among the most marked forms of early female age set sociality were competitive games between age sets. During log races (*uiwede*) and wrestling matches (*wa'i*), male and female age set mates formed blocs of solidarity that rooted for each other's teams with intense enthusiasm. Boys and girls shared in each other's shame of defeat and defended each other against derision by members of opposing age sets. Another explicit expression of female age set solidarity was in domestic discourse, which involved a seemingly constant exchange of teasing remarks that reflected allegiances and rivalries deriving from age set membership, among other social dynamics. During my visits I observed volleyball matches with teams composed of men or women from the same age set. Women had important roles in the final phases of age set initiation rites. Since approximately 2010, female mentors routinely participated with men and boys in daytime dance ceremonies (*rowete danho're*).[3] Even more recently, female mentors proudly began holding their own ceremonial activities to mark their protégés' induction into a recently inaugurated age set and thereby asserted female privilege to participate fully as members of age sets. This four-day sequence of activities included three log races, a wrestling match, and a day of singing around the community. Thus, recently, age set membership was more relevant than ever for female mentors and protégés. Such participation demonstrates that understandings of good living were in transition but in ways that reinforced cultural resilience amid the backdrop of pervasive sociocultural, economic, and environmental change.

Each new age set was inaugurated when, at the conclusion of the approx-imately quinquennial initiation rites into novitiate adulthood, a ceremony (*dazahihöri*) was held in which the newly designated novitiate adults (*dahí'wa* or *'ritei'wa*) cut the back of the hair of boys and girls who were selected for in-clusion by their parents (cf. Giaccaria and Heide 1984; Maybury-Lewis 1967). Theirs was the age set that the novitiate adults, their immediate age set seniors, would call "younger age set" (*sinhö'ra*) for the coming five or so years in rec-ognition of the asymmetrical and rivalrous relationship between them. That ceremony not only inaugurated the new age set, but also provisionally marked selected girls and boys as its lifelong members. Their final membership was conditioned on their participation in induction rites that would install them in the age set and designate boys as new residents in the preinitiate house. The boys' induction rites (*wapté röiwïhã*) were solemn but had elements of humor, with the new preinitiates' mentors often dressing in costume, such as women's underclothing (figure 16). Male participation in preinitiate induction rites was what marked their passage into the preinitiate age grade. Because females were not inducted into the preinitiate house, they did not become members of the preinitiate age grade. In five years, during the next initiation rites into novitiate adulthood (*danhono*), those same boys and girls, members of the same age set, participated in a sequence of ceremonies that marked women's and men's mu-tual advancement to the novitiate adult age grade (*dahí'wa* or *'ritei'wa*). Thus, females and males pertain equally to the formal age grade system, although males enter as preinitiates and females enter as novitiate adults.

"Our Traditions": Mentors and Protégés
Preinitiate houses were constructed about one to two years, and sometimes more, after the previous one was dismantled. They were built just beyond the end of the open arc of residences in time for the first group of inductees to move in, no earlier. Boys might be inducted into the preinitiate house in as few as two to as many as five staggered groups, depending on the number of boys and other

Figure 16 Preinitiate induction rites (*wapté rõiwĩhã*) for a group of boys who thereby began their tenure as preinitiates (*wapté*) and residents in the preinitiate house (*hö*), 2004.

scheduling issues. Most parents identified chronological age and stature as the primary factors in their decisions about when their sons would be inducted in the preinitiate house. Most people denied that the physical onset of adolescence or the psychological development that tends to accompany adolescence was a major factor. Nevertheless, in most cases, boys who had recently reached adolescence tended to be included in the next scheduled group of inductees. Also factoring into such decisions was the number of children of similar ages in an extended family, since having many children in the same age set concentrated the burden of ritual preparations for parents and other relatives. Furthermore, consideration was given to the distribution of siblings between age sets, since it was considered a beautiful and beneficial form of rivalry for brothers or sisters to compete against each other in competitions between adjacent age sets, such as log races (*uiwede*) and wrestling matches (*wa'i*).

The first group to be inducted was called "first penis sheath" (*īrõ'rada*) because assuming preinitiate coresident status historically involved adopting the practice of wearing a penis sheath (*īrō*), the only article of adult male clothing used at the time (Maybury-Lewis 1967). The members of this first induction group came to be known as their age set's eldest members. It was from among their ranks that age set leaders were chosen, and adults expected them to set good examples for their younger age set peers. If they entered in three groups, the second was called "middle penis sheath" (*dawawa'īrō*) and the third, "last penis sheath" (*īrō'té*) (see Graham 1995). If they entered in just two groups, middle penis sheath was omitted. Should a fourth group be inducted, which is not very usual, it was called *hödawa'u'hā*. Sometimes, at the very last moment, parents would decide to add a son to an age set immediately before it exited the preinitiate house, so that he would be initiated into novitiate adulthood with them. In this event, such a boy would be called *ubranhowahā*, which indicated that he was inducted alone, immediately preceding the initiation rites. Such boys resided in the preinitiate house for very short periods, as little as a few days. Although such late induction into the preinitiate house reduced the amount of time a boy spent in coresidence with his peers and mentors, this disadvantage was offset by the perceived benefit of his membership in the age set with which he would be most compatible and therefore enjoy the most fruitful bonds of camaraderie for the rest of his life. Coresidence in the preinitiate house physically located members of this secular age set slightly apart from the community, just beyond the last house in the community arc of residences, while symbolically and socially isolating them by limiting their free circulation in the community and restricting visits to their parents' homes to short nighttime stops and moments of special need, such as when suffering from illness or injury.

All of an age set's induction groups graduated together, shortly before a new group of female and male children and adolescents were ceremonially identified for inclusion in the next age set during an age set inauguration ceremony. By that time, the first contingent of boys to be inducted into the preinitiate house may have lived together for about three to four years, whereas the subsequent groups may have lived with them for about two years or less. Preinitiate houses were dismantled after they were vacated during the rites of initiation into novitiate adulthood (*danhono*).

Mentors (*danhohui'wa*) were members of the second anterior (older) age set to have resided in the preinitiate house before its current occupants.[4] They were therefore on average about ten years older than their preinitiate protégés (*höwa nōri*). Under mentors' guidance, preinitiates were said to be involved in the process of becoming responsible adults. From the A'uwẽ perspective, this was the only correct configuration for educating boys of this age, not only because mentors were thought to have already learned everything necessary for assuming this role, through their experiences as protégés and as novitiate adults, but also because the mentor-protégé relationship was considered a good and productive foundation for much of male adult sociality. Consequently, most elders were largely excluded from the process of youth education. For example, it was often considered inappropriate for elders to directly meddle in preinitiate affairs. They infrequently went to the preinitiate house of their own initiative, preferring to go at the request of the boys' mentors or during ceremonial activities. The social relationship between mentors and their protégés was an essential part of the age group system both structurally and experientially. Thus, it was intimately associated with how preinitiate males learned to become adults and thereby eventually contribute of their own initiative to the well-being of their age set associates, families, and communities.

Although induction into the preinitiate house was a public and collective event, being a preinitiate coresident was seen as both a personal and a collective process of transformation. As one mature adult told me, living in the preinitiate house was about learning to think like an adult by "opening your mind" (*da'rã si sãmra dahã*). The boys were encouraged to behave themselves, which included keeping quiet, sticking together, and minding their own business. They painted their bodies for song performances with almost uniform designs, the same ones their mentors used as preinitiates, and their mentors before them. They walked in view of the public community in single file lines with nearly identical postures, in order of height and alternate exogamous moiety identity, just as preinitiates had walked for generations before them. It was through these expressions of behavioral conformity that boys transformed themselves into conscientious adults who contributed to the wellness of their families and communities. In my observation, these sedate objectives did not get in the way of preinitiate youths having fun while living together away from their families and women. Indeed, the preinitiate house was usually a playful space, with kids incessantly joking with each other and playing games, albeit out of view of the rest of the community. Thus, their responsible and conforming behavior was often maintained for the benefit of others besides themselves and their mentors.

The strong A'uwẽ morality of preinitiate collectivity (Graham 1995; Maybury-Lewis 1967) also encompassed a strong philosophy of individuality, even during the formative preinitiate house experience. Preinitiate education was based equally on the premise that group unity facilitated individual learning and the assumption that the group was characterized by internal difference. On the one hand, preinitiates shared a single social identity, occupied the same residence, underwent similar educational experiences, and collaborated as a unified team. On the other hand, they also belonged to distinct staggered induction groups, separate households, and opposite exogamous moieties. They were also divided into separate associations based on individual formal friendships and mentorship relationships, as well as occupying unequal positions in an internal age set leadership hierarchy. Furthermore, they were recognized as having varied individual competencies and personal characteristics. Some of these differences were reflected in slight alterations to their body paint designs during song performances that publicly marked them as unique within the unity of preinitiate collective conformity. The coresident educational experience built on both age set collectivity and diversity to produce socially competent adult members of society with the capacity to display unity when required and individualism when called for.

The preinitiate age grade was emblematic of male notions of traditionalism and good living specifically because it was widely recognized by men to be the primary socially orienting event in their lives and in the lives of all men, past and present. Novitiate men, mature men, elder men, and male ancestors alike were thought to share the experience of having left their natal households to join an age set of peers under the affectionate guidance of their mentors. That shared experience more than any other gave A'uwẽ men a sense of historical continuity (Graham 1995). Every male member of every generation could be identified by where and when he was a preinitiate. Preinitiates of all ages were thought to have been inducted into the preinitiate house through the same rites of passage and to have been held to the same program of personal development while there. In this sense, the preinitiate age grade symbolized tradition and historical continuity more specifically than any other age grade, including that of elders.

In many contexts, elders also characterized the preinitiate experience as not only what transformed boys into men, but also what made them A'uwẽ. It was counted among the most valued features of men's culture and among what they believed distinguished them from non-Indigenous peoples and, just as important, from other Indigenous peoples. It made not only men from boys, but more specifically, A'uwẽ men from A'uwẽ boys. Both youths and elders agreed that the preinitiate experience had continued in the same format since time immemorial, serving for them as a strong symbol of historical continuity and a counterbalance to perceptions that contemporary life was associated with the disintegration of traditional values regarding social well-being in A'uwẽ society. When elders spoke about the preinitiate house and the age set system elaborated through it, they uncompromisingly asserted that they were perfectly part of "our traditions" (*wahöimanazé*) and are therefore inherently irreproachable.

In the past, according to recollections of living elders, male preinitiate protégés accompanied their mentors hunting and collecting materials for ceremonial accoutrements. The preinitiate experience was therefore boys' first exposure to many of the subsistence activities that would be expected of them as adults, such as tracking animals (*abaze pra'rĩ*), identifying useful plants, and articulating temporary residence at base camps. It was also when they first learned the territory, place names, and the locations of landscape resources. These excursions were also opportunities to hear stories about historical events in diverse locations throughout the territory (Basso 1996). Thus, as preinitiates, young people first came to know their landscape and its resources, thereby familiarizing themselves with its ethnobiological features. This practice continued, in my experience, but not as frequently, and with more emphasis on fishing and collecting than on hunting. In fact, the preinitiates I have known over the years did not hunt at all with their mentors until the year before their graduation to novitiate adulthood, during a large ceremonial hunt known as the mentors' hunt (*uiwede zada'rã*) (Welch 2015). It was therefore relatively late in their young lives that they began to gain knowledge of hunting skills, especially those associated with group hunting and the use of fire to flush game animals out of the brush. Nevertheless, contemporary preinitiates, almost exclusively through their fishing and collecting excursions under the supervision of their mentors, were exposed to the local cerrado landscape and learned fundamental skills of self-provisioning and landscape stewardship. These opportunities profoundly influenced how preinitiates accessed and managed landscape resources for the rest of their lives, because the permissive relationship between mentors and their protégés provided an unparalleled social setting to learn skills and knowledge they could be expected to utilize as adults.

Age Set Moiety Indulgence and Antagonism

The close relationship between male mentors and their protégés continued after residence in the preinitiate house, with every second group of preinitiate coresidents joining an intergenerational chain of mentors and protégés connected through intimate bonds of friendship and respect. All members of such an age set moiety shared a morality of intimate loyalty irrespective of their relative ages.

Together they formed a single group of mutual interest and concern, protecting one another's guarded information from the rest of the community and thereby safeguarding their untarnished public image. They were all on the same side and designated each other "our secular age set side" or "people on our secular age set side" (*waza'runiwĩmhã*). They also commonly called each other by a series of terms that generically indicated same-sidedness (us, as opposed to them), and might be used for members of one's age set side, or any number of other associations. Examples are "our side" (*waniwĩmhã*) and "people on our side" (*wahöiba niwĩmhã*).[5]

If the members of this chain of alternate age sets considered themselves to be on the same side, who did they consider to be on the other side? These were their rivals, consisting of the adjacent chain of alternate age sets, also spanning the range from youth to elders, but offset by one step. In other words, adjacent age sets belonged to opposite sides or agamous moieties and alternate age sets belonged to the same side or agamous moiety. Members of the first side called these rivals "the other secular age set side" or "people on the other secular age set side" (*höamoniwĩmhã*) (Graham 1995; Lopes da Silva 1986; Maybury-Lewis 1967). They might also call those people by a series of terms that indicate other-sidedness generically, such as "their side" (*õniwimhã*) and "people on their side" (*õhã höabaniwimhã*) (Graham 1995; Lopes da Silva 1986).

It was the prerogative of the next oldest age set in the opposite age set moiety to promote preinitiate good behavior by punishing transgressions. According to A'uwẽ scholar Michael Rã'wa Tsa'e'omo'wa (2021, 32), "The collective education [of preinitiates] is always monitored by the novitiate adults, who are also responsible for the care of these adolescents." Feelings of rivalry extended along the chain of mentors and protégés on each side, creating an oppositional stance between them. As Lopes da Silva (1986) noted, adjacent age set members often jokingly demeaned one another, attributing to each other the opposite of virile qualities: cowardice, weakness, powerlessness, slowness, and clumsiness.

Intergenerational age set rivalries might also blend good-natured humiliation with social lessons. For example, popular age set pranks intended to teach younger individuals in the other age set moiety to mind their own business involved rubbing white-lipped peccary (*Tayassu pecari*) urine on the victim's legs or making him smell dried peccary feces. In addition to being grotesque and effective tools for public humiliation, each was believed to promote valued skills in the victim. Peccary urine applied to the legs was thought to make one a tireless runner, while smelling peccary feces was believed to improve one's ability to detect their scent, which is useful for hunting. Thus, in more ways than one, such age set jokes were intended to leverage the adversarial social relationship of moiety opposition for the sake of stimulating the good and appropriate development of youths.

Age set rivalry was nowhere as explicit as in certain competitive games. Log races (*uiwede*) are an elegant example of the strong oppositional aesthetic of age set moieties (figure 17). A'uwẽ enthusiastically competed with one another in relay races in which heavy log sections cut from buriti (*Mauritia flexuosa*) palm trunks were shouldered by runners in short sprints along a five-kilometer path. Men's and, less frequently, women's races were held throughout the rainy season and on certain other auspicious occasions, mobilizing entire communities to passionately watch, root for their allied team, and even assist when their team was behind. Competing teams were always members of rivalrous adjacent secular age sets and thereby involved an age increment of approximately five years on average between them. Thus, a younger and less experienced team competed against an older and stronger team, creating a structural inequality between them that was understood to promote the betterment of the younger group by

Figure 17 Women's log race (*uiwede*) between adjacent secular age sets *tirowa* and *êtẽpa*, 2014.

Figure 18 Male members of *ai'rere* age set ceremoniously leaving the community to compete in a log race against members of *êtẽpa* age set, 2014.

challenging them to exert themselves and thereby gain physical strength that would improve their performance through time.

These races were billed as competitions between women or men of two specific age sets, novitiate adults and their immediate seniors, preinitiates' mentors, but members of many other age sets also participated in support of their same-moiety allies. In the hot afternoon sun, the two principal competing age sets made conspicuous exits from the community, walking single file in dignified flourishes through the plaza and down the road to the west (figure 18). They were followed by a busy migration of members of other age sets, from children to mature adults, some on foot, others on bicycle, and a few in trucks and on motorcycles. This crowd included spectators, but many would also run in the race in support of their sides' age set.

In effect, these races were not only between two primary age sets but also between their age set moieties, whereby all same-side members were comrades, sharing in their primary age set's responsibilities, successes, and defeats. The primary age sets' reputations as successful depended on contributions by their entire side and vice versa. An age set's win was a win for the whole moiety, and a loss was the whole moiety's loss.

These configurations of fraternity and rivalry between secular age sets grouped into age set moieties composed a morality of camaraderie and competition, which contributed to a social fabric of how people were thought to properly relate. Groups of mentors and protégés taught and protected one another, while members of opposite-moiety age sets watched vigil over one another and encouraged good behavior through antagonistic feedback. Both cases were imbued with cultural understandings of betterment—encouraging good and proper behavior by one's juniors, behavior that society judged as constructive for individuals and for society at large. Fraternity and rivalry were different configurations of respectful relations understood to produce capable and responsible adults from boys and young men.

When A'uwẽ people talked about secular age set moieties, they invoked a pervasive social distinction accompanied by a host of symbolic oppositional implications. The notion of sides, however, also referred to something more tangible. About every five years, when a new preinitiate house was constructed for the boys in the youngest age set, it was physically relocated to the opposite side of the community (figure 19). With the location of the preinitiate house alternating from one side to the other with each age set, all age sets in the same age set moiety occupied the preinitiate house when it was, literally, on the same side of the community (cf. Graham 1995, 93). Thus, when people said "our side" (*waza'runiwĩmhã*) and "the other side" (*hö'amoniwĩmhã*), they referred not only to the figurative opposition between the two age set moieties, but also, more specifically, to the physical position of the preinitiate house, a spatial reference that was wrapped up in their very social identities.

From this arrangement emerged the beginnings of a sort of spatial geometry of secular age set sociality. A'uwẽ horseshoe or semicircular communities were usually oriented with the open side facing an adjacent river, which was the community's primary source of water. A'uwẽ designated the two age set moieties, both literally and figuratively, as "left side" (*danhimi'e*) and "right side" (*danhimire*), with the opening to the river as the point of reference. This distinction was based on the physical location of the preinitiate house during its alternate occupations by age sets of each moiety. As shown in table 1, age sets were named according to a predetermined cyclical sequence of eight names. Although the names were applied in sequence, they alternated between the age sets residing on the left side and right side of the Pimentel Barbosa and Etênhiritipá commu-

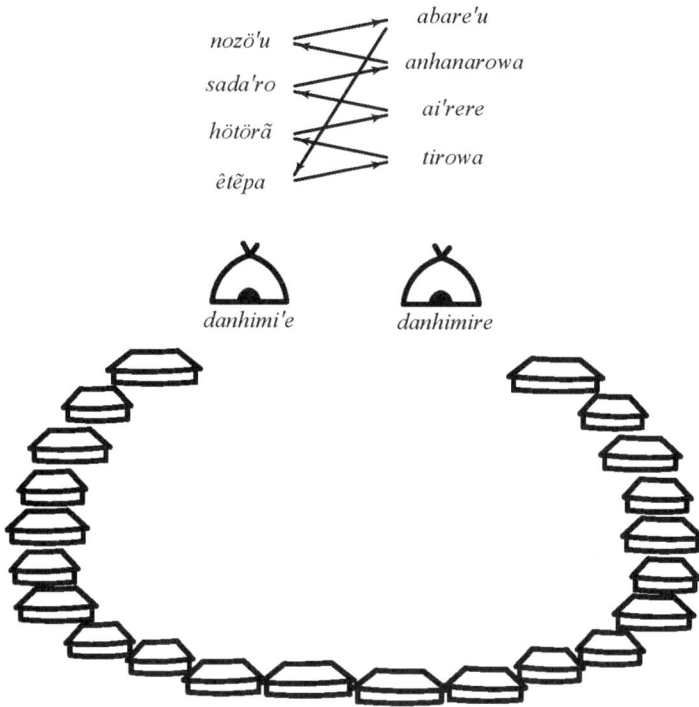

Figure 19 Stylized sociospatial model of community and preinitiate house (*hö*), which alternated between left and right side with each age set.

nities, such that four age set names perpetually pertained to each side. Thus, age sets inaugurated into the preinitiate house on the right side were, in continuous sequence, *tirowa*, *ai'rere*, *anhanarowa*, and *abare'u*. The four age sets that cycled on the left side were, in turn, *êtẽpa*, *hötörã*, *sada'ro*, and *nozö'u*. After about forty years (five years for each of eight age sets), the names repeated. Interestingly, according to some elders, the left/right location of the preinitiate house is subordinated to an east/west distinction, whereby the age set moiety comprising *tirowa*, *ai'rere*, *anhanarowa*, and *abare'u* was always located on the east side of the community, and the *êtẽpa*, *hötörã*, *sada'ro*, and *nozö'u* sequence on the west side. Thus, the left/right distinction might be inverted between communities, in accordance with their orientation relative to the river and the cardinal directions. This account of age set orientation according to the cardinal directions was not initially remembered by some of my interviewees, required some group discussion to settle, and does not seem to comport with the orientation of preinitiate houses in all current and historical communities, suggesting that it is not as salient as the left/right distinction, which factored more prominently in people's speech. The union of the symbolic and spatial opposition between left and right with the cyclical sequence of eight age set names generated a complex set of social relationships that were simultaneously synchronic, diachronic, symmetrical, and hierarchical in ways that bore importantly on how people engaged one another in daily social life.

Although secular age set names repeated, age set identity did not. The younger of two age sets carrying the same name was not a continuation or reincarnation of the elder. Carrying the same age set name did not imply more than a passing sense of unity, which was overshadowed by the important link between them as members of the same age set moiety. Consequently, there was a need to distinguish between senior and junior age sets that carried the same name and had living members. This was accomplished by appending the suffix -'*rada* (first or old) to elder age set names. For example, members of the age set called *tirowa'rada* occupied the preinitiate house eight cycles, or approximately four decades, before the younger *tirowa* age set. During my initial fieldwork, four age sets with living members carried the -'*rada* designation: *tirowa'rada*, *ētēpa'rada*, *ai'rere'rada*, and *anhanarowa'rada*. The sequences of allied age sets on each side were situated within a never-ending chain from elders to youth, bonded with camaraderie and fraternity through their relations to one another as mentors and protégés.

This repetition of secular age set names lent the two age set moieties corporate continuity, in the sense given by Radcliffe-Brown (1935) following Maine (1931). According to their formulations, the notion of corporateness implies both organizational perpetuity and continuity of rights and duties over persons or things. Some scholars place near exclusive emphasis on possession of real property as a criterion of corporateness (e.g., Verdon and Jorion 1981). That interpretation is not consistent with Radcliffe-Brown's formulation of "perpetual corporate succession," considered independently from his application of the idea to the specific case of unilinear descent groups, which emphasized rights over persons (1952, 31):

> Where inheritance of private property may be said not to exist or to be of minimal importance, there are problems of succession in the widest sense of the term. The term "succession" will here be taken as referring to the transmission of rights in general. A right exists in, and is definable in terms of, recognized

social usage. A right may be that of an individual or a collection of individuals. It may be defined as a measure of control that a person, or a collection of persons, has over the acts of some person or persons, said to be thereby made liable to the performance of a duty.

Also, "By an estate is here meant a collection of rights (whether over persons or things), with the implied duties, the unity of which is constituted . . . by the fact that they are . . . the rights of a defined group (the corporation) which maintains a continuity of possession" (Radcliffe-Brown 1935, 288). For Claude Lévi-Strauss (1984, 193), "corporate group" was akin to "moral person," implying ownership of property, which might be real property, titles, or prerogatives. In the A'uwẽ case, the corporateness of age set moieties derived from the perpetual extension of social privilege and responsibility downward through the alternating sequence of mentors and protégés. That privilege included possession of a symbolic claim to place, either the right or left side of the community, rights of social vigilance over alternate groups of other-side preinitiate boys, and the responsibility to sponsor same-side preinitiates. That sense of secular moiety corporateness involved the association of each with four age set names, but it did not result in each age set name deriving its own sense of corporate identity. In other words, the repetition of age set names generated corporate age set moieties but not corporate age sets.

The ordering of secular age sets within an age set moiety was at once synchronically hierarchical, because at any given time, each age set was either subordinate or senior to every other age set, and diachronically symmetrical, because each age set would eventually pass through the entire sequence from protégés to seniors. An analogous relationship existed between age set moieties, which also might be considered synchronically hierarchical, because at any given time, each age set moiety was either allied with or estranged from the current set of preinitiate coresidents with all their ceremonial importance, and diachronically equal, because each age set moiety passed through those phases of alliance and estrangement in alternation.

Because A'uwẽ consciously formulated the social geometry of secular age sets in terms of a spatial reality with a temporal dimension, the model I presented of left and right age set sidedness may be considered close to how the A'uwẽ themselves understood these social constructions (for a similar observation, see Maybury-Lewis 1967). It is incumbent to repeat here my strong conviction that A'uwẽ people conceived of these social organizations in highly structural terms and that describing them in such a manner does justice to A'uwẽ perspectives regarding age and the human life cycle. The structural patterning of age organizations, including the informal age grade system and the two formal age group systems, as well as their intersections and interactions, were consciously known to A'uwẽ and contributed to their notions of good traditional living. For example, rumors that other, distant communities failed to uphold one or another feature of this complex social geometry of secular age provoked disappointment that its residents had abandoned traditionalist values and contributed to affirmations that only the communities of the Pimentel Barbosa Indigenous Land maintained patently A'uwẽ ways of proper living.

Novitiates, Unseen Adults

After living in the preinitiate house for up to about four years, boys began a very involved ceremonial process of becoming novitiate adults that often lasted more than six months. These secular initiation rites exhibited considerable cultural conservation in social form, logic, and meaning despite the pervasiveness of contemporary sociocultural change (Tsa'ẽ'omo'wa 2021). An endurance exercise (*dasiwaté*), held around March and lasting several weeks, involved the boys entering the river for considerable intervals throughout each day and night, vigorously splashing the surface of the water to produce synchronized plumes of water (figure 20). The beginning of the water-splashing exercises also marked a terminological change for males from preinitiation (*wapté*) to initiand (*heroi'wa*). Females did not pertain to the initiand age grade because they did not participate in the water-splashing exercises. The initiand phase extended until the end of the sequence of ceremonies that began with ear piercing (*daporezapú*) and ended with a wrestling match (*wa'i*) some five days later. This wrestling match marked the end of initiand status and the beginning of a transition to novitiate adulthood (*dahí'wa* or *'ritei'wa*), a liminal phase in which no specific term properly applies.

The brief initiand phase of the male life cycle is notable not only for its busy schedule of preinitiate ceremonial activities, but also for involving a qualitative shift in the social relationship between preinitiates and their mentors. When boys relocated to the river to splash water, mentors actively adopted the perspective that they must express respect for the boys differently than they did while overseeing the coresidence experience. Having begun the water-splashing rite, the boys were considered to have adopted a more adult-like social posture. At the same time, boys came to be recognized as potential sons-in-law,

Figure 20 Ceremonial "water splashers" (*watei'wa*) during initiand age grade (*heroi'wa*) before initiation into novitiate adulthood, 2011.

since during the initiand phase, preinitiates might be the subjects of marriage negotiations between their mentors and parents. At this time, many mentors had young daughters, for whom their preinitiate protégés were considered ideal marriage candidates, provided they pertained to the opposite exogamous moiety. Whereas protégés and mentors shared intimate social proximity, sons-in-law and fathers-in-law treated each other with respectful deference and social distance. During the initiand age grade, when mentors were uncertain as to the identities of their future sons-in-law, they tended to treat all protégés with the respectful distance that was appropriate for sons-in-law. For example, mentors largely avoided the riverbank where the boys camped while splashing the water and did not attend many of the boys' other ceremonial activities. Conversely, the protégés tended to act more timidly around their mentors during this phase for the same reasons, which speaks to their respect for potential fathers-in-law.

Those preliminary negotiations were often concluded before the end of the preinitiation rites later in the same year, during which a public ceremony was held to identify the young girls who had been promised in marriage to boys as they entered novitiate adulthood. These arrangements were demonstrated by a mother carrying her young daughter to the intended husband, who lay on a woven mat next to his age set peers under blankets to conceal his identity, and briefly placing her on the mat next to the young man. The accord did not signify that the two future spouses were engaged or "girlfriend" and "boyfriend" to one another. It was a promise that must be confirmed with a gift of a maize loaf presented privately to the parents of the young man when the girl reached adolescence. The public ceremony whereby young girls and boys on the cusp of novitiate adulthood were promised in marriage once again provoked changes in how many boys and their mentors related to one another. Once the marriage arrangements were made, mentors and protégés who would not become in-laws might return to the former social intimacy of their mentorship relationship.

For young men, becoming a novitiate adult was accompanied by the end of coresidence with their preinitiate age set peers and a return to their natal households. Returning to one's parents' home after years of preinitiate coresidence demanded major behavioral changes of novitiate adults and cast them in new social positions relative to the rest of the adult community. As preinitiates, they were both the youngest members of the formal age hierarchy and very much a focal point of community attentions. The daily, seasonal, annual, and quinquennial rhythms of the entire community revolved substantially around the preinitiate house and its occupants. New novitiate men, in contrast, were comparatively marginal, being relegated to what is arguably a more socially isolating stage of the male life cycle than the symbolic seclusion of preinitiation. They were excluded from the preinitiate house, not yet involved in marriage and fatherhood (this happened for many young men during their initial years as mature adults), and still largely external to community political affairs. Invisibility and seclusion were important values for novitiate men, as they are discouraged from walking openly in the community and from visiting other houses. With few explicit social responsibilities, however, they were afforded ample liberty to pursue personal interests, provided they did not draw too much attention to themselves. Given this new freedom, they became particularly vulnerable to traditionalist accusations of being lazy, making mischief, and lacking work values. Interestingly, novitiate men often agreed with such characterizations, recognizing, for example, that they were avid users of smartphones and often experimented with their bodily aesthetics to mimic non-A'uwẽ clothing, hairstyles, and ear plugs. Thus, whereas the preinitiation age grade was explicitly emblematic of historical continuity through its involvement in the traditional coresident educational process, novitiate manhood largely symbolized its converse, historical change.

During their years as novitiate adults, male age set peers remained extremely cohesive despite living apart. They continued meeting regularly to go on excursions into the cerrado, sing, play sports, and socialize together. They remained one another's primary peers and comrades. Nevertheless, being dislodged from the preinitiate house and dispersed between natal households fragmented the group and led them gradually to turn their attentions elsewhere. As other scholars have suggested, this shift represented a relative decline in age set cohesion (Graham 1995; Maybury-Lewis 1967). It also represented the beginning of the novitiate adults' inclusion in other collectivities that would become more important later in life. While at home, a novitiate adult man might become more aware of what it meant to share in his father's privileged knowledge, gradually adopting it as part of his individual identity. Such guarded information might include plant remedies, powerful woods for ear plugs, and other proprietary ethnobiological and ceremonial information his father likely intended to share only with his sons. He might become an active listener in his father's political affairs and come to recognize the importance of lending his father political support. Being a novitiate adult living in one's father's household was an important opportunity for a young man to learn what it meant to be his father's adult son before beginning life as a married man, a son-in-law, and a father. These aspects of his return to his natal household between preinitiation and mature adulthood helped solidify his loyalty to his father and his solidarity with his brothers, fundamental social orientations that fortified his most reliable social support network before his residential relocation to his parents-in-law's house after marriage and becoming a mature adult.

Perhaps one of the most important aspects of being a novitiate adult male was to be considered sexually mature. As preinitiates, boys frequently talked about girls but were prohibited from engaging in social or sexual activity with them. As one boy told me, the worst part of being a preinitiate was not being allowed to talk to girls. As newly initiated adults, however, novitiate men might for the first time have socially sanctioned sexual relations with certain real or categorical sisters-in-law. Real and categorical older brothers might consent to their wives engaging in such relations should they wish, although they also might do so without his knowledge or permission. Some men conveyed that brothers should be proud of fathering each other's children, which was an expression of male sibling unity and culturally appropriate intimacy between sisters-in-law

94 || *Chapter 3*

and brothers-in-law. Nonetheless, I found that many contemporary wives and husbands preferred to keep such paternity unspoken even if the husband consented to the relations.

Some men first marry during the novitiate age grade, although usually not for several years. As might be expected, many novitiate men had keen interest in sexual relations, to which they dedicated a notable portion of their attention (cf. Maybury-Lewis 1967). Furthermore, the entire adult population took great interest in the progress of their developing marital relationships, an expression of good living with implications for the social well-being of extended families and entire communities.

After a tentative public commitment had been made between the parents of a potential bride and a boy on the cusp of novitiate adulthood, and once that bride was an adolescent and therefore old enough to marry, her parents would signal their interest in initiating the first active phase of their relationship by delivering a maize bread loaf to the young man's parents at night. If his parents accepted the loaf, the accord was sealed. In some cases of which I am aware, this happened during the young man's third or fourth year in the novitiate adult age grade, but for many young men, it did not happen until after they were mature adults (*iprédu*). Once the maize loaf was accepted, the two were considered boyfriend or fiancé (*piõsiwe*) and girlfriend or fiancée (*dasiwẽ*). Also, from that moment forward, the real and categorical fathers of the bride and groom began calling each other in-laws (*wasiní*) and ceased to interact socially as expressions of interfamilial respect and commitment. Once it was established that the two were fiancé and fiancée, the young man began visiting his future wife by night. Graham (1995, 66–74) provided a detailed account of one such young man's nighttime visits (*barana si'iné*) to the household she lived in. For A'uwẽ, nighttime visits were thought of like dating in that they allowed the couple to get to know each other for the first time and gradually facilitate his incorporation into her household.

Even after marriage, novitiate adult men continued to live in their natal households and visit their wives only at night. This behavior conformed to the social expectation that members of their age grade remain out of sight in the community and not be seen visiting other people's households. Even though it was common knowledge that they visited their wives at night, they should not be seen doing it. In this context, secrecy was fictitious but nevertheless expected as an expression of respect and deference. Under the cover of dark, they took back routes around the community and quietly sneaked in the door. More recently, with an increase in the use of motorcycles by young men, they still avoided crossing the community plaza, although the sound of the motor gave them away.

The process by which some novitiate adult men at Pimentel Barbosa and Etênhiritipá became committed to their future wives and eventually married largely followed the plans made for them by their parents. The community was acutely aware that their marital practices differed from those of non-Indigenous Brazilian society and even of some other A'uwẽ communities, where arranged marriages are said to be less common. Yet, novitiate men rarely expressed dissatisfaction with their elders' expectations of them in this respect. In my observation, they mostly welcomed the marriage choices made for them and, through the process of visiting their brides at night, came to cherish them with all the intimacy of young love.

Male novitiate health continued to be affected by the intense focus on ceremonial activities that characterized this stage of life. Even more so than during preinitiation, ceremonial singing and competitions were a high priority for novitiate men, who paid considerable attention to their physical well-being by means of strengthening activities such as performance rehearsals, observing food proscriptions and prescriptions, applying plant medicines to recently cut (or "scarified") legs, wearing special amulets, and participating in excursions to the cerrado with their mentors to fish or collect ceremonial materials. Considering that their status as novitiate males corresponded with license to be sexually active, this age grade might also be characterized as the pinnacle of male vanity. These young men concerned themselves with their health, beauty, grooming, clothing, and overall appearance of vitality and strength. They wished to be admired by women and by the community generally for their attractiveness, good ceremonial form, and success at physical competitions, including ceremonial matches such as log races as well as soccer matches. Women of this age grade were usually married, mothering children, and comparatively less involved in ceremonial presentations and competitions. Although they did dance in some ceremonies and run log races, they did so less frequently than novitiate men. I suspect their greater health concern at this stage of life was reproductive health, although I do not have data on this dimension because of its privileged nature, whereby women refrained from sharing with men their specialized knowledge of promoting health during pregnancy and birth (see chapter 4).

For women, the relevance of novitiate adulthood for environmental engagement was overshadowed by their parallel informal statuses as adolescents (*azarudu*), young childless wives (*adabá*), and married women with children (*ĩ'raré*). To the degree that they approached married life and became wives and mothers during novitiate adulthood, expectations of their proper involvement in subsistence activities changed.

During my most recent visits, men in the novitiate adult age grade participated in group subsistence activities with regularity. They continued to hold age set fishing trips for the benefit of their families (their natal families or, if married, their in-laws) as well as their mentors, who accompanied them on these excursions. These trips were held with some frequency, in part because they were used as opportunities to rehearse their song repertoires for subsequent performances in the community. They also provided welcome social venues to spend time with their age set peers and mentors during a phase of life that was otherwise characterized by home seclusion and a great deal of isolation from their friends (age set peers and mentors) outside their natal households. These young men also participated almost without exception in group hunts, many of which employed fire to flush game out of the brush. These too were welcome opportunities to socialize with their age set peers, who usually stuck together during the hunts. They also eagerly participated in group hunts because most were held in conjunction with ceremonial events of consequence for themselves, their friends, or their families, such as weddings and rites of initiation. Participating in such ceremonial group hunts was a means to contribute to these important life moments, as well as to the ample distribution of game meat that followed successful hunts. Thus, novitiate men had more opportunities than they did as preinitiates to learn to hunt, which included learning the landscape, landscape names, hunting practices, as well as such associated skills as how to butcher animals, identify edible fruits and other foods, and identify and collect ceremonial accoutrements. Participating in each of these subsistence activities promoted the social and physical well-being of participants by preparing them for a lifetime of provisioning for their families and passing along their knowledge and skills to their protégés. It also contributed to the well-being of the recipients of their efforts, those who received pieces of game meat, by sustaining them with high quality protein foods and encouraging among them a sense of festivity and happiness.

Some novitiate men also began to hunt individually, which they did not do as preinitiates. I noticed this pattern especially in the few cases of men who married earlier than their age set peers, as young novitiate adults (not all novitiate men adopted individual hunting after marrying). I suspect these young hunters decided to take up individual hunting upon confronting the expectation to provide for their new wives, infant children, and parents-in-law before they had access to monetary resources through employment. In other words, to satisfy the expectation by their wives and in-laws that they provide food for their families, they opted to learn individual hunting, which would allow them to meet traditionalist expectations of providing healthful foods in addition to fish (game meat is generally more appreciated than fish). They thereby satisfied familial expectations that they contribute to the wellness of their new families. These few individuals began of their own initiative to borrow firearms from relatives and go alone into the cerrado to hunt large game animals, which required a different set of skills from group hunting. Some were unsuccessful at first but came to have greater success with time. Some but not all preferred to hunt by motorcycle rather than on foot. Several eventually came to be known as excellent hunters, while most of their age set peers still had limited experience with individual hunting. Others picked up the practice later, after becoming mature men, but were able to catch up in terms of skills and now are highly respected as successful hunters.

For most young men, becoming a novitiate adult marked a major social reorientation from the collectivity of living among age set peers in the preinitiate house back to the privacy and seclusion of family life. As novitiate adult men now living at home, they maintained the collective age set spirit through evening meetings, covert song rehearsals, collective excursions into the cerrado, and a host of other group engagements that punctuated the usual monotony of their days at home. With time, their attentions turned toward their future spouses and in-laws in anticipation of advancement to mature manhood (*iprédu*) approximately five years after being initiated into novitiate adulthood.[6]

Responsibilities of Mature Adulthood

Passage from novitiate to mature adulthood did not occur simultaneously with the conclusion of initiation rites into novitiate adulthood. Rather, it happened through distinct rites (*dasi'tó*), which included a footrace (*sa'uri*), held separately for women and men during the days to months after preinitiates concluded their initiation into novitiate adulthood (Graham 1995). Thus, recruitment into the mature adult age grade occurred collectively for all same-gender members of an age set.

For mature adult women in the formal secular age grade system, the informal age grade motherhood (*i'raré*) might have been a more salient classification because of its ample implications for female social influence. Also, although women participated in formal age set activities in an increasing variety of ways, they did not have the liberty to participate in all the age set activities that their male counterparts partook in. Much of what went on in the preinitiate house, between male mentors and their protégés, and within secular age set moieties was considered male prerogative. Nevertheless, formal mature adult status was far from irrelevant for women because it delineated certain kinds of salient social relationships in unambiguous ways. For example, becoming a mature adult woman implied assuming her role as a mentor to female protégés and reinforced her antagonistic stance toward novitiate adults. These relationships were far from incidental to the female experience, being routine topics of conversation and sources of amusement among female kin.

For men, mature adulthood differed from earlier stages in the life cycle in many respects, but there were perhaps two aspects that most transformed the experience of its newest members. The first involved the incorporation of young mature men in their wives' households immediately after marriage according to a strong pattern of uxorilocal postmarital residence. The second was their inclusion in the dawn and dusk men's council meetings. Those two correlates of mature adult status brought about major changes in young men's social positions relative to the rest of society. The first made them junior in-laws and, potentially, future heads of household in new residential hierarchies. The second set them at the periphery of a political arena in which they would eventually become senior members. Thus, achieving mature adult status in the formal age grade system positioned them as seniors relative to much of society but also relegated them to junior status within new domestic settings and the political arena. It also gave them new opportunities to deepen and widen their social networks and thereby gradually transition out of the subordinate roles that had hitherto characterized their social position in the community. I discuss several dimensions of men's experiences of uxorilocal residence below. Their participation in men's council meetings is discussed in chapter 4.

Although men could marry as novitiate adults, they could not move into their brides' homes until mature adulthood. Some male age set peers married later than others because their intended wives reached adolescence and therefore became eligible for marriage later. With fewer domestic commitments, these men might spend more time with their protégés in the preinitiate house.

I encountered a somewhat less strict pattern of uxorilocality than was reported by Maybury-Lewis (1967) and Graham (1995). Intercommunity marriages, which were less common, were almost always followed by virilocal residence (moving into the husband's parents' household). Intracommunity marriages, on the other hand, were usually but not always followed by uxorilocal residence, at least for a time. Although several men lived with their parents-in-law indefinitely, most young husbands lived uxorilocally for no more than several years. When they decided to move out, sons-in-law and their wives frequently constructed their own separate houses adjacent to those of his parents-in-law, and women of both houses continued to share the same kitchen annex.[7] In such cases, movement between the two houses was unconstrained, and their residents often gathered in front of the houses to socialize in the evenings, suggesting they remained socially close. Arguably, although they no longer resided under the same roof, the two houses and their shared kitchen annex continued to operate as a single domestic group or extended family residence. Despite these contemporary specificities, uxorilocality remained a paradigmatic cultural model of proper household composition among the A'uwẽ. A strong pattern of uxorilocal residence was observed in almost all intracommunity marriages for at least several years, and much longer if shared kitchens are considered indicative of domestic groups. As a cultural pattern and social value, uxorilocal residence enjoyed favor as a factor in good living in part because it reinforced the ideal that sons-in-law should demonstrate respect (*danhisé*) by contributing to the ongoing sustenance of their parents-in-law.

A potential exception to the pattern of uxorilocal residence illustrates the salience of the social expectation that sons-in-law contribute to the well-being of their parents-in-law by provisioning them with food. During a conversation with me about food reciprocity, a fifty-year-old man who lived adjacent to his parents-in-law (by two of his three wives) and shared a kitchen annex with them informed me he intended to move his house to a location on the far opposite side of the community. When I asked why, he replied that he was tired of supporting his parents-in-law and hoped they would ask for food less frequently if he was not located next door. He believed that the farther away he moved, the less he would be expected to share his food with them. Despite his comment, ten years later he remained in his house next to his parents-in-law and continued to contribute to their sustenance regularly with a share of his groceries, game yield, and garden produce. Although the sentiment expressed in his earlier comment may appear selfish, it was not exceptional in the sense that many spouses expressed feelings of burden by expectations that they share considerable portions of their food with parents-in-law, siblings-in-law, and nonresident children.

These examples of hardship, however, also contributed to a broadly appreciated social dynamic that mitigated hunger during episodes of food shortages and contributed to food system resilience through pervasive and enduring networks of interdependence (see chapter 7). Thus, uxorilocal residence and its associated expectation that sons-in-law provide for their parents-in-law was a forceful cultural model of how community well-being was promoted by expressing respect for others even when doing so required enduring hardship.

Environmental engagement by mature adults varied considerably, in part because of the great range of chronological ages it entailed. Whereas elders were considered guardians of traditional ecological knowledge, many young mature adults explicitly lacked interest in performing traditionalist subsistence activities when food could be readily purchased at the supermarkets in towns about seventy kilometers from the Indigenous land. There were exceptions, however, as illustrated by relatively small numbers of young mature women who were eager to accompany their elders on collecting excursions and several young mature men who had already learned to hunt alone with the assistance of firearms and motorcycles. Also, many young mature women participated in collecting firewood as well as harvesting and processing manioc, rice, maize, and other garden products. Large numbers of young mature men participated in group hunts held for weddings or rites of passage to support their friends and relatives for whom the hunts were held (Welch 2014). Both young adult women and men often enjoyed fishing, which they considered more pleasurable than other kinds of cerrado excursions, such as collecting and hunting (see chapter 6 for additional discussion of these environmental dynamics).

Mature adults were also responsible for practicing land stewardship to ensure cerrado resources were available in future years and for future generations. Environmental stewardship was debated extensively in men's council meetings, especially when some event occurred that was considered to be at odds with their contemporary conservation principles. For example, if a hunting fire was ignited at too short an interval for the location, council discussion would debate the error in detail to discourage its repetition. Similarly, if a wild root vegetable–collecting ground was overharvested by a large group of women, the mistake and its consequences would be discussed at length in council meetings. Through word of mouth, these messages would be communicated to women throughout the community (Graham 1993, 1995).[8] Women had their own mechanisms for group discussion of such critical conservation issues, which usually involved domestic discussion in the absence of men accompanied by visits by women to other residences, where they reported on what had been deliberated elsewhere. Cerrado stewardship by mature adults appeared to have been a relatively new phenomenon associated with increased awareness about potential impacts of practicing traditional subsistence activities with a growing population inside a circumscribed Indigenous land. As hunting and collecting fell into widespread disfavor among mature adults who had financial income and preferred to purchase food at supermarkets, the subsistence activities with the greatest potential to negatively affect the landscape were group hunting with fire and collecting wild root vegetables for ceremonial purposes. Yet, as many elders told me over nearly two decades, game animals were abundant as a result of underhunting, and wild root vegetables were only scarce near communities, where they were accessed most easily on foot.

The informal age grade system and the secular age group system for both females and males are diagrammed in figures 21 and 22. These representations are not meant to imply rigid correspondence between any informal and formal age grades. Rather, because informal age grades were based on individualistic and subjective criteria, the divisions between them in these diagrams should be understood as variable in accordance with the personal experience of each male or female. Similarly, the vertical dimensions of the age grade boxes are not scaled to their respective durations. For example, *azarudu* (female adolescent), *adabá* (childless wife), and *ai'repudu* (male adolescent) were potentially very brief age grades despite the standardized height of their boxes. The purpose of these diagrams is to facilitate conceptualization of the informal age grade and secular age group systems as coexistent and interdependent.

Men's Spiritual Age Group System

Maybury-Lewis (1967, 1979b) was responsible for calling attention to the A'uwẽ as an unusual example of an Indigenous group in lowland South America with a formal age group system, which was the secular system I described in the previous section. The men's secret spiritual society also operated as an age group system, making the A'uwẽ a highly unusual case of a society with two distinct age group systems (Welch 2010).[9] Both systems were characterized by age sets that passed through a series of formal age grades by means of public rites of passage accompanied by age set moieties produced through the alternation of sequential age sets. Thus, this spiritual system marked social age in an analogous format to the secular system, although in a categorically different domain of social relations. This finding deserves special note because it suggests that the

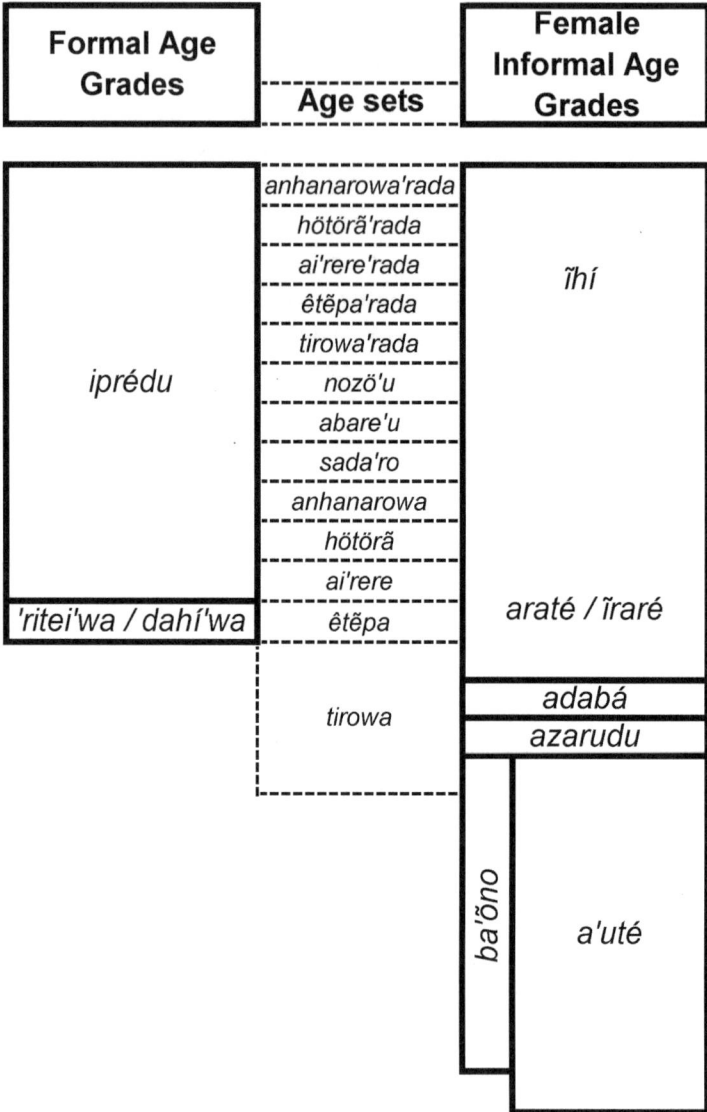

Formal Age Grades	Age sets	Female Informal Age Grades
iprédu	anhanarowa'rada	ĩhí
	hötörã'rada	
	ai'rere'rada	
	êtẽpa'rada	
	tirowa'rada	
	nozö'u	
	abare'u	
	sada'ro	
	anhanarowa	
	hötörã	
	ai'rere	araté / ĩraré
'ritei'wa / dahí'wa	êtẽpa	
	tirowa	adabá
		azarudu
	ba'õno	a'uté

Figure 21 Diagram of female life cycle, including the informal age grade system and the secular age group system, configured for 2005.

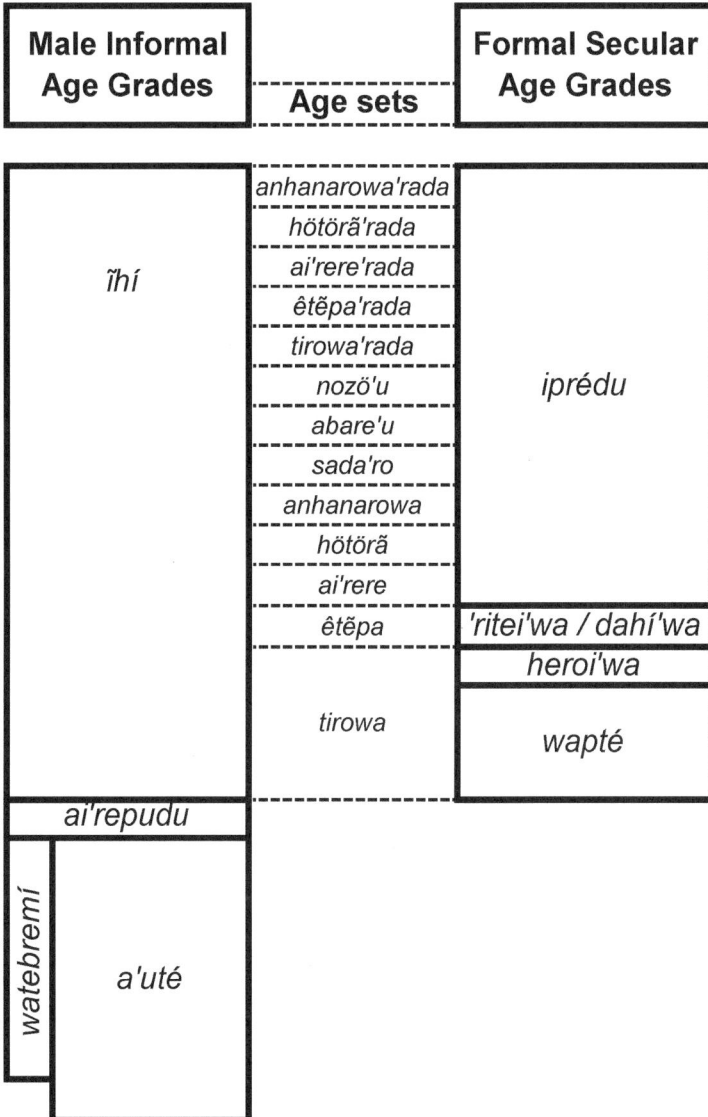

Male Informal Age Grades	Age sets	Formal Secular Age Grades
ĩhí	anhanarowa'rada	*iprédu*
	hötörã'rada	
	ai'rere'rada	
	êtĕpa'rada	
	tirowa'rada	
	nozö'u	
	abare'u	
	sada'ro	
	anhanarowa	
	hötörã	
	ai'rere	
	êtĕpa	'ritei'wa / dahí'wa
		heroi'wa
	tirowa	*wapté*
ai'repudu		
watebremí *a'uté*		

Figure 22 Diagram of male life cycle, including the informal age grade system and the secular age group system, configured for 2005.

pattern of moieties generated through hierarchical alternation of age sets was a characteristically A'uwẽ social formulation in multiple fields of social relations. I also argue that popular A'uwẽ perspectives gave credit to this social construction for contributing to the persistence of social well-being in difficult contemporary times of broad transformation of human and nonhuman surroundings.

Strength Through Hardship

Males dedicated tremendous effort toward the goal of acquiring spiritual power, which was the pinnacle of good living for most traditionalist A'uwẽ men. They were initiated into the male spiritual age group system at as young as eighteen months or so or as late as approximately seventeen years of age, because the spiritual initiation rites (*darini*) were held only about every fifteen years. I entered the spiritual age group system unceremoniously as an initiate (*waiãra*) in 2004, one year after the last set of initiation rites had been held. In 2018, I participated in the subsequent set of initiation rites as a guard (*damaʼaiʼaʼwa*), the next age grade in the spiritual sequence. This was one of the most physically and mentally challenging endeavors I have ever undertaken, even though I thought I was in adequate physical shape beforehand. All initiated men camped in a tall palm leaf enclosure outside the community toward the river. The uninitiated boys slept in the community plaza, unable to bathe for the entire twenty-three days of the ceremonies. My group was awoken at precisely 3:00 a.m. each morning by one of our spiritual guards riding his motorcycle in circles just inches from our feet. We slowly arose, some waiting until a guard pulled their blankets off, went to the river to take a bath, and then began painting our bodies and affixing ceremonial accoutrements in preparation for heading up to the community plaza to begin our daily activities. Waking very early and taking a bath in the predawn morning were considered healthful activities for members of our spiritual age grade, besides having the benefit of allowing us ample time to eat a light breakfast snack after preparing our bodies and minds for the day's taxing activities.

As the sun began to rise the first day, we sprinted to the community and began performing ritualized threatening stomping gestures in front of the initiands, who were always divided into two groups based on spiritual moiety membership as rattle owners (*umrẽʼtedeʼwa*) or wood owners (*wedehöriʼwa*). After several minutes, my partner Rubens Tobʼuto, a younger member of my group who was also being promoted to guard status and with whom I did everything during these rites, called me to join him in looking for missing children in their houses. Although the initiands were supposed to sleep in the plaza, the youngest children often went home at night and slept in until after we showed up to en-force their ritual performance. Rubens led me to the house of an approximately eighteen-month-old child who was in bed. He cried profusely as Rubens pulled him out of his bed, delivered him to his mother to put on his A'uwẽ cotton necktie and place his ceremonial club in his arms, and held his hand while leading him to the plaza where, in tears, he joined his initiand peers, who were singing in place with clubs or striding while shaking rattles. We then went to the house of another missing child, where Rubens had me perform the duties of removing the crying child from his bed and leading him to the center of the plaza. This became our morning routine, pulling crying children from their beds and leading them to the plaza. As their guards, our behavior toward these children was appropriate to our antagonistic posture of enforcement intended to ensure the boys properly performed the duties necessary for them to acquire spiritual power. As an anthropologist, I found it an uncomfortable task, but one I was nevertheless required to perform, or my own guards would punish me for neglecting my duties.

After collecting missing children, we returned to the monotonous task of performing ritualized stomping gestures in front of the initiands, which we did in the full blazing sun until late afternoon each day. This was our main activity for this phase of the rituals, repeatedly pounding our feet on the ground and swinging our arms in feigned anger in front of the initiands from morning to afternoon. Our duties were occasionally interrupted when initiands required regrouping because they had scattered or requested to relieve themselves in the cerrado, which they were only allowed to do under our supervision. In the late morning and afternoon, women and girls would storm into our circle to deliver gourds and plastic bottles of water to the initiands. We ran to intercept them and splash their water receptacles on the ground to prevent initiands from quenching their thirst. Our guards watched vigil over us, exercising their authority when we ran the three-hundred-meter distance from the plaza to our camping enclosure by arbitrarily taking away our food and water, sending us back into the sun before stopping to rest, and in my case taking away my shoes and flip-flops so I would suffer the pain of stomping barefoot on the hot gravely soil. By the end of the first week, my legs and feet were in such pain I could no longer give chase to women who charged us carrying water for the initiands.

Eventually the hours and then the days began to blur together as though we were in trance, and I was surprised that an entire day could pass in what seemed like just an hour or two. After some fifteen days of this routine, the itinerary changed, and we held a series of different spiritual rituals, completing the entire sequence in twenty-three days. These duties were expected to test our limits and thereby develop our physical and spiritual strength. They were considered excellent hardships that would produce valuable benefits for us and the community in the form of spiritual capacities that could be further developed as new initiates and guards during spiritual rituals (*wai'a*). They exemplified in a highest form what it meant to promote well-being through suffering.

Secrecy

I participated in my first spiritual ritual during my initial site visit, just a few days after my study had been approved in the men's council in 2004. I interpreted the invitation to participate as symbolic expression of admittance into the community and as a tangible gesture of good faith. In the first place, it demonstrated their willingness to incorporate me into their affairs and assume the additional responsibilities of supervising an ignorant participant, which included manufacturing ritual adornments for me, painting me, guiding me, correcting my errors, and answering my questions. In the second place, it signaled that the community was ready to take a first step toward trusting me with sensitive information, since spiritual content is the most closely guarded information in male A'uwẽ society. As they expressed to me very clearly before I participated in that first spiritual ritual, I would witness and learn certain things that I was prohibited from sharing with anyone, including A'uwẽ women and the non-A'uwẽ public. On numerous occasions before becoming a guard in 2018, including the spiritual ritual during my first visit, I was selected for the grueling task of carrying a special sacred cane arrow (*ti'ipê*) while singing and dancing from late afternoon to after sunrise the following day (figure 23). Participating in that role exposed me to privileged aspects of spiritual rituals, which I was carefully instructed to protect.

Secrecy was a trademark of the A'uwẽ social experience, and nowhere was it as important as in spiritual matters. Females were excluded from male spiritual rituals as a matter of male imperative. There are records, oral histories, and personal recollections of women being included in spiritual rituals as a consequence of grave misbehavior, including men sharing privileged spiritual content with a wife (e.g., Giaccaria and Heide 1984). My interlocutors, including elder women who were included in spiritual rituals (*wai'a sipi'õ*) in past decades, emphasized that the practice had been discontinued. Therefore, as a matter of

Figure 23 The author and fellow spiritual initiates (*wai'āra*) carrying sacred cane arrows (*ti'ipê*) at night during spiritual ritual (*wai'a*). Photo by Carlos E. A. Coimbra Jr., 2005.

contemporary principle and practice, women did not pertain to A'uwẽ spiritual practice, which may therefore be considered a men's secret society.

Men protected their guarded spiritual knowledge from female acquisition because, as one elder man explained, "Theft of a secret not only gives its power to the thief but takes that power away from its owner." Men did not want women to take their spiritual power from them. The gender partition in spiritual ritual affairs was especially evident during an interview I conducted with an elderly woman, the late Conceição Pezé, using a mature man as translator. As a follow-up question to a discussion about her disillusionment with contemporary community life, I asked what aspects of her society made her the proudest. The translator warned me that the question was inappropriate because as a woman, Conceição could not discuss men's spiritual rituals. I requested that he communicate the question anyway because I wanted to allow her to decide if men's spiritual rituals or other aspects of A'uwẽ society make her the proudest. Conceição replied,

Women do not have the right to speak about rituals. I may not even say anything about them. I do not understand rituals, not at all. What a shame that I cannot talk about them! All I know is that the men sing and dance. I only know this. As for the spiritual ritual, we women cannot watch. I don't know what happens during it. The only rituals I participated in when I was younger were in imitation of the elder men when the men went hunting. Women did rituals by imitating men, but only for fun. Each age group of women ran a log race, sang. It was imitation for the sake of happiness. But I think that the rituals the men do are good. They make us happy, lift our spirits. During the men's rituals, even though we stay in our houses, women become happy. If they stop, we will become sad. This rule is very difficult; many things are prohibited for women.

I do not know whether he formulated the question in a way that led her to respond that male spirituality makes her the proudest. Yet the interview demonstrated unequivocally that women do not feel at liberty to discuss this topic that at least men consider the apex of A'uwẽ culture.

Responsibility During Rituals

A form of spiritual ritual that was commonly performed during my fieldwork began in a forest clearing between the community and nearby river. Women were not allowed in this clearing, even though the activities that occurred there were not, strictly speaking, considered privileged. A'uwẽ women did not witness what men did there, but they might hear about it afterward or view it in photographs. Spiritual singers (*zö'ra'si'wa*) arrived in the early morning to reveal and sing the original song selected for this occasion. Painted, adorned, and with palpably focused states of mind, they greeted the early morning light sitting in a small circle around a smoldering fire. At their backs, planted in the ground, stood sturdy war clubs from which hung small bundles of personal items. Singers shook their rattles vigorously, incessantly, while forcefully singing the day's song. Spiritual initiates (*wai'āra*) arrived in midafternoon to prepare themselves by painting their bodies, grooming their hair, and tying special fiber straps (*abarudu*) around their wrists and ankles.

After initiates were fully prepared, and the spiritual singers (*zö'ra'si'wa*) resumed their mesmerizing pulse of song while sitting in a circle at the center of the clearing (figure 24), the ritual continued. Initiates stood in a long arced line around the upper half of the clearing. The younger and shorter boys stood toward the ends of this arc of initiates, while the taller and older ones stood in

Figure 24 Spiritual singers (*zö'ra'si'wa*) during spiritual ritual (*wai'a*), 2005.

the middle. They stood motionless and expressionless while small groups of two to six spiritual guards (*dama'ai'a'wa*) made repeated passes in front of them, in which they swung their arms in stylized shows of aggression and stomped their feet forcefully against the ground and sometimes on initiates' feet as punishment for spiritual transgressions (figure 25). All the while, spiritual post-officiants (*wai'a'rada*) sat at the far periphery of the clearing, talking among themselves and gleefully heckling the participants.

After the foot-stomping procession, senior initiates (*wai'ãra ipredumrini*) remained in a line at the edge of the clearing, while junior initiates (*wai'ãra a'uté'rene*) returned to the community. The singers stood at the center of the clearing while one of their members holding a war club in his left hand and a rattle in the right hand looked over the senior initiates, shifting his gaze from one of them to another and then back again. He then raised his rattle and pointed it squarely at one of the senior initiates, thereby calling him forward to the center of the clearing. He did this some six to eight times, calling as many senior initiates forward and thereby drafting them to the solemn chore of singing and dancing around the community the entire night, from dusk until after sunrise,

Figure 25 Spiritual guards (*dama'ai'a'wa*) stomping near feet of spiritual initiates (*wai'āra*) during spiritual ritual (*wai'a*), 2005.

carrying sacred cane arrows. Very occasionally an initiate refused his call. Although doing so was considered somewhat irresponsible, the seriousness of the task required that one not accept if he doubted his resolve or capacity to complete it properly.

Subsequently, the entire contingent of male spiritual participants and elders returned to the community plaza, where all the women were inside their houses with doors and windows (openings in the thatching) closed. All participating men began singing around the community, forming an enormous arc that moved from house to house. After singing at the first house, the group of elder initiates selected to carry cane arrows ran from around the plaza to a hidden location in the cerrado, where secret activities were held away from eyes and ears of women and uninitiated males. They returned carrying the sacred cane arrows fletched with avian down and laced with poison pigments. Meanwhile, the other initiates, guards, and singers continued singing around the community. As the sun began to descend, and the first round of public singing was complete, initiates returned to their houses briefly to collect food items prepared

Figure 26 Spiritual guards (*dama'ai'a'wa*) collecting food items delivered to piles by spiritual initiates (*wai'āra*) during spiritual ritual (*wai'a*), 2005.

by their mothers, aunts, and grandmothers and delivered them to the singers in the center of the plaza. The singers retrieved these maize loafs, cooked wild root vegetables, bottles of soda, and other treats from two piles, one for each exogamous moiety, sharing them with their elders and consuming them amid animated conversation (figure 26).

The cane arrow carriers continued singing throughout the night, which could be quite cold during the dry season in the region of the Serra do Roncador, Mato Grosso. Most singers, guards, and post-officiants retired to their homes to enjoy several hours of sleep. Even most initiates went home to rest up for the continuation of the ritual the following morning. Yet, the cane arrow carriers were not usually left completely alone. There were often several guards about to make sure they upheld their responsibilities, maintained the rhythm of their song, continued the seemingly endless rounds around the community with only minimal time to rest, and stayed away from such comforts as coffee or the warming fire that burned in the middle of the plaza. If one of the chosen cane arrow carriers could not complete his duties through to sunrise as a result of illness, injury, or fatigue, the guards verified the legitimacy of his problem before waking up an alternate senior initiate, who was required to take his place and carry his sacred arrow for the remainder of the night. Also often present were a few spirited post-officiants who remained near the fire in the throes of cheerful nighttime conversations, and occasionally additional initiates who wished to offer support to their spiritual age set mates chosen to carry arrows during the darkest and coldest hours of the night. At times, when the strains of cold and lack of sleep caused the initiates to forget the song, a guard or singer returned to the plaza to help them recuperate the performance. Eerie sounds, which only occurred during spiritual rituals, sometimes emanated from the cerrado near the community and suggested the veiled presence of other entities in the vicinity.

At the first detectible signs of morning light, the small circle of initiates was gradually rejoined by the men who slept during the night. One by one, initiates, guards, and singers stepped back into the arc and added their rested and forceful voices to the growing chorus. Once the sun was up, the last round of singing was concluded, and the sacred cane arrows were retrieved from their carriers. Often, in the cold early morning, arrow-catching competitions marked the end of the ritual. Guards in hiding behind the ring of houses shot long ceremonial arrows in tall arches into the community plaza. These arrows could be longer than two meters from hardwood foreshaft to bamboo base and featured showy feather fletching interspersed with strips of snakeskin and two tufts of hair at the base. Initiates rushed to grab them in the air before they hit the ground, a dangerous activity but one that carried the reward of a gratifying public cheer (figure 27). Then, once again, initiates returned home to fetch food items for distribution to the singers.

Forty-Five Years of Service

The stark differences between ritual roles of initiates, guards, singers, and post-officiants were associated with the formal age grade system that informed all aspects of A'uwẽ spirituality. Their contrastive roles spoke to the hierarchical and symmetrical aspects of the system, whereby rank was qualified by moiety association such that hierarchy between same-moiety allies fostered social proximity and between opposite moiety produced distance and punitiveness. As it was in the secular age group system, this spiritual age group system involving age set moieties was understood to be the perfect social arrangement for stimulating proper progress and improvement among youths. The unity of

Figure 27 Spiritual initiates (*wai'āra*) competing to catch a cere-monial arrow shot over houses by spiritual guards (*dama'ai'a'wa*) at conclusion of spiritual ritual (*wai'a*), 2005.

permissive orientation with adversarial vigilance created the ideal conditions for their acquisition of desirable traits and capacity to promote well-being among kin and community. In this case that capacity derived from spiritual receptivity, strength, and force.

External to this system was the category of boys who had not yet been ritually initiated into the spiritual system (*wautoptu*). Spiritual initiates (*wai'āra*) were those young males who were initiated during the most recent spiritual initiation rites and were the youngest participants in spiritual ceremonies. The difficult task of carrying sacred arrows while singing all night was assigned only to senior members of the initiate age grade (*wai'āra ipredumrini*), who were novitiate or mature adults in the secular age group system. Children, adolescents, and preinitiates in the secular system were junior members of the initiate age grade (*wai'āra a'uté'rene*). Over the course of the fifteen-year term that young males occupied the initiate spiritual age grade, they gradually passed from spiritual age grade juniority to seniority as they become secular novitiate adults.

Status as a spiritual initiate might influence young males' health status. As described above, being an elder member of this age grade meant one might be called on to perform the physically demanding task of singing all night while carrying special arrows. This activity was understood to promote physical and spiritual health in part by exercising one's resilience in the face of physical exhaustion, lack of sleep, and cold temperatures. Initiation into the spiritual initiate age grade and advancement of initiates to the guard age grade during the spiritual rites of passage (*darini*) were especially acute processes of health promotion through challenging physical trials and suffering.

The next spiritual age grade in ascending order was that of guards, or soldiers (*damaʾaiʾawa*). This grade was also divided into junior (*aʾutéʾrene*) and senior (*ipredumrini*) designations, although in their case the designation was said to be fixed, without promotion as they became older in the secular age group system. Guards had the explicit juridical authority to enforce on initiates certain rules of behavior. Of greatest importance was the rule of spiritual secrecy from females and non-Aʾuwẽ, violation of which was said to carry grave penalties. In the context of spiritual rituals, guards watched over spiritual initiates as enforcers. They punished dietary transgressions with foot stomping and enforced good ritual performance while restricting access to common comforts. According to Valmir Serewaõmowê (2014, 74), "This is how the ceremony is, the guards impose respect, command the norms of the ritual." Illustrative of their authority over initiates were the bows and arrows they carried and frequently deployed with jabbing motions against misbehaving initiates. Thus, guards, consistent with the militaristic nomenclature of their status, assumed an overtly antagonistic stance toward initiates but arguably to encourage their spiritual betterment. Guards also had primary responsibility for obtaining diverse ethnobiological materials from the cerrado and using them for privileged functions and to manufacture several important objects for use during the rituals, such as sacred cane arrows. Details of these important forms of engagement with the environment that derived from the spiritual age group system were closely held information that cannot be recorded in this book.[10] It is important to note, however, that they had great repercussions for how some spiritual guards related to the landscape during this phase of life because they perpetually sought scarce resources, some of which could only be obtained by traveling to distant locations within their traditional territory, spending considerable amounts of time in the cerrado, or cultivating trade relationships with Indigenous residents of other communities and Indigenous lands.

Actively leading the spiritual ceremonies were singers (*zöʾraʾsiʾwa*), the next senior spiritual age grade. Despite the impressive visual and auditory potency of their singing performances, the primary work of singers seemed to be internal. Whereas guards administered to initiates antagonistically, singers were their closest spiritual allies and private spiritual mentors. Under the guidance of their mentors, initiates began to learn about how to acquire spiritual force.

Although singers did not suffer the physical trials described above for initiates and guards, they engaged in other activities of a spiritual nature that promoted well-being in different ways. These activities and their associated internal work were closely guarded.

The most senior spiritual age grade was that of post-officiants (*wai'a'rada*), who were initiated into the spiritual system before the third most recent spiritual initiation rites. Post-officiants had no formal role to play in spiritual rituals. As A'uwẽ men of all ages told me, post-officiants were extraneous to spiritual activities. Their attendance was optional, and their participation limited to the sidelines. They were considered something like spiritual retirees, having left that work in the hands of well-prepared younger individuals. Yet, post-officiants who chose to attend could participate indirectly. They remained attentive, especially to younger initiates, whom they often helped groom and dress before spiritual rituals. Also, although post-officiants watched spiritual ceremonies from the sidelines, they did so vocally, heckling poor performances to motivate improvement among initiates, guards, and singers. Accordingly, post-officiants remained senior authorities in spiritual rituals despite being formally excluded as active participants. With an initiation interval of about fifteen years, the entire succession from initiate to post-officiant status took approximately forty-five years. Depending on the age at which a young male was first initiated into the spiritual hierarchy, attaining post-officiant status might occur relatively late in life.

Contrasting Modes of Promoting Wellness

The oppositional stance of guards toward initiates found stark contrast in the very different sort of relationship that existed between singers and initiates. Being the next oldest age set in the initiates' spiritual age set moiety, singers were their indulgent mentors. They were considered both responsible for and together with (*dasiré*) members of the initiate spiritual age grade. In private spaces and in hushed voices, singers counseled initiates in privileged aspects of A'uwẽ spirituality. Shared between them was a sense of mutual concern and absolute trust, a morality of secrecy and solidarity regarding spiritual matters. This morality was considered good and proper, contributing to the spiritual well-being of initiates. Notably, singers indulged initiates in keeping secret their violations of the dietary restrictions imposed by guards. The threat of discovery was predicated on getting caught, and alternate spiritual age sets were united by a morality of mutual secrecy, exemplifying the solidarity between allied spiritual age sets. Thus, singers' interest in initiates' spiritual development was of a categorically different nature than that of guards.

Unlike secular age sets, spiritual age sets were not named. Consequently, the cyclical aspect of eight rotating secular age set names had no parallel in the spiritual system. Also, men tended to discuss spiritual matters in oblique terms and beyond the auditory range of other people, with the result that spiritual age sets were somewhat invisible in the context of everyday life. Despite being unnamed and infrequently mentioned in public, spiritual age sets were explicitly recognized social groups in the same sense as secular age sets. I make that assertion based not only on observation, but also on conversations with spiritual participants in which they explicitly described the system in terms of cohorts that passed between age grades and were allocated in alternation between two opposing sides or moieties. In this context, A'uwẽ individuals used specific terms to refer to one's own spiritual age set moiety (*wasiré wai'a*) and its complement (*wai'a amo*). They also spoke of the structural parallel between the spiritual and secular age grade systems, noting that the operation of alternation was similar in both, despite the content of the spiritual domain not being comparable to that of the secular domain.

The social solidarity between singers and initiates also extended to alternate spiritual age sets such that every second spiritual age set in the initiation sequence was linked by a sense of mutual identity and a bond of sociospiritual unity. Alternate spiritual age sets were allies, in that specific context, and were bound by a code of mutual duty. Members of the same spiritual moieties helped one another, shared with one another, and trusted one another.

Whereas members of alternate spiritual age sets were comrades, members of adjacent sets were adversaries, as illustrated most explicitly by the social dynamic between guards and initiates. Through the repetitive allocation of age sets between opposing moieties, alternate age sets were joined in separate and opposed chains of solidarity. The two groups were implicated in a bifurcation of spiritual practice rooted in an ethos of distrust and constraint. Members of opposite spiritual moieties should not, and in my experience did not, exchange spiritual knowledge outside prescribed settings, such as the quindecinnial initiation rites (*darini*), during which some collaboration between moieties was considered appropriate. Operating in secrecy from one another, opposing spiritual moieties maintained their own, independent agendas of spiritual action. This oppositional configuration was understood to be the proper means for challenging younger spiritual age sets and thereby encourage their spiritual learning and advancement. It was therefore an important underpinning to notions of good living in the male spiritual realm.

For males, segregation of the educational process between moieties in both the secular and spiritual age group systems was not coincidental. Both systems entail the principle that one's same-side elders were one's allies and role models, while opposite-side elders were adversaries and watchmen. They were also both based on the bifurcation of respect relationships between indulgent and antagonistic models. Furthermore, they both involved the belief that the dual social roles of mentors and watchmen and the alternation of age sets that produced them were part of and necessary for the continuation of traditional culture (*wahöimanazé*), which was integral to well-being for the community and the individuals that compose it.

The spiritual system entailed the plurality of equality and hierarchy in much the same manner as the secular age group system. Spiritual rank involved the presumptive influence of spiritual maturity according to two contrastive configurations, one collegial and one authoritative. In both cases, however, the pedagogical theory was one of encouraging betterment among youths. Whether through indulgent comradeship or adversarial enforcement, the universal expectation was that youths attained spiritual competence. Although in this text I do not discuss the content of A'uwẽ spiritual knowledge, it is important to note that knowledge alone did not transmit spiritual capacity. Equally important was bodily and spiritual fortification through hardship. By enduring suffering, fatigue, and distress, one developed the strength and resolve required to attract the attentions of powerful spiritual entities and benefited from engaging them. For young A'uwẽ males, the spiritual process was arduous. It demanded the resoluteness of spiritual participants, a vigorously maintained traditionalist value that was imparted in contemporary context through age organization.

The spiritual age group system constituted a separate domain from the secular age group system and was an additional dimension in the matrix of age contingencies in A'uwẽ society. Among males, the various hierarchies of secular age sets, secular age grades, and informal age grades were all juxtaposed with a distinct spiritual age hierarchy such that myriad relationships of equality or difference might exist between the same individuals. Although ideologically distinct, the spiritual age group system was not isolated in the day-to-day male experience because it factored into all social relations by establishing interpersonal boundaries and liberties. Because solidarity or separation in the spiritual age group system might or might not coincide with alliance or rivalry in the secular age group system, social modes of interaction varied between people and between contexts. Similarly, seniority or juniority in one domain might not correspond with rank in another. Furthermore, those configurations of age identity and difference coexisted with abundant other forms of social identity. In chapter 5, I explore in greater depth how the plural nature of A'uwẽ age organization, despite its highly structured nature, contributed to pervasively contingent formulations of social identity that created fertile ground for individual creativity and agency. I also discuss these multiple constructions of age relations within the context of previous literature regarding the A'uwẽ and other Indigenous groups that are linguistically related.

CHAPTER 4

Seniority and Leadership

Construction of Political Harmony

The relationships between age, life cycles, and social influence were apparent in abundant social contexts and imbued with notions of respect, proper relations between people, and community wellness promotion. In daily interactions in their homes, gardens, preinitiate houses, communities, cerrados, or towns, A'uwẽ social interaction involved various arrangements of influence, privilege, responsibility, and authority based in multiple age hierarchies and other systems of social ranking and difference. A social context that is especially relevant to discussions of social influence is politics, which also implicated age in complex arrangements of similarity and difference. Just as plural age hierarchies created multiplex relationships between social actors, they also did so between political actors. Yet, age was only one among many social factors that mutually affected the contours of political influence. In this chapter, I address leadership and process in the political arena to demonstrate that how people went about constructing meaning through social life involved not only the age systems already presented in this book, but also a host of other configurations of social seniority and inequality, such as those deriving from heritable prerogatives and genealogy. Inequality in the A'uwẽ case did not imply injustice, but rather established kinds of respectful subordination considered proper and good that situated and distinguished individuals relative to one another throughout their life cycles. These forms of social differentiation were another layer in the A'uwẽ social tapestry that reinforced social traditionalism as a factor in good living today. This chapter focuses on aspects of social well-being related to different formulations of seniority that contributed to leadership. I return to the discussion of environmental practice and well-being in chapters 6 and 7.

Return to Venerable Forms of Leadership

According to Maybury-Lewis (1967), in the mid-twentieth century, community leaders were not formally installed and had no explicit authority. Rather, chiefly designations merely recognized where power already lay, acknowledging those especially prestigious leaders whose powers of influence derived from the ability to speak for their factions, facilitate agreement within the community, and thereby promote a sense of consensus. Becoming this kind of chief, according to Maybury-Lewis, required that one have the support of his political faction and that this faction be dominant in the community. Chiefly status endured only if one retained prestige among a dominant faction and thereby maintained one's influence over public opinion. Although men potentially competed for chieftaincy, there could be as many chiefs as there were exceptionally prestigious men who enjoyed the support of a dominant faction.

In contrast to that historical account, in 2004, there were two formally recognized leaders with the explicit authority to conduct external relations on behalf of the community. Tsuptó was chief (*damaʾdöʾöʾwa*), and Paulo was vice-chief. Both Tsuptó and Paulo were relatively young, well educated, fluent Portuguese speakers, and had extensive familiarity with national Brazilian society, having lived and studied in large cities (see Franca 2007; Graham 1995). They represented a brand of community leader that emerged after Maybury-Lewis conducted his fieldwork because of the relatively recent importance of interfacing with external social and political spheres. According to my most recent information, the Etênhiritipá community had a chief and vice-chief, although Pimentel Barbosa was without vice-chief after a recent community fission. Yet, chiefly elders continued to exert influence much as described by Maybury-Lewis for the 1950s, except, perhaps, for his emphasis on leadership being derived from factional dominance.

Interviews with Tsuptó, Paulo, and other influential elders provided important insights into how contemporary leaders understood the historical transformations in political process that occurred between the era Maybury-Lewis referred to and the present. According to Tsuptó, oral tradition told that the A'uwẽ were a politically united people for much of history, with the influence of leadership being coordinated through the forum of the men's council (*warã*). The splintering of the A'uwẽ people into geographically dispersed and politically autonomous subgroups, each with its own leaders, occurred when internal conflict turned segments of the population against one another during the occupation of the ancestral community Sõrepré, estimated to have been in the late nineteenth century (Lopes da Silva 1992; Welch, Santos, et al. 2013). Those events eventually led to overt conflict and the ultimate division of the A'uwẽ population into different subgroups and communities. Thus, although Sõrepré community was often characterized by A'uwẽ oral historians as the historical pinnacle of their society, where the population was large, reaching into the thousands, and remained united in a single location for decades, it was also the location were social strife severed the population into splinter groups that would permanently separate, initiated long-lasting feuds between kin groups, and turned A'uwẽ leadership forms toward a more authoritative model.[1] The history of conflict at the Sõrepré community was therefore also notable for contributing to a marked decline in community well-being.

In 2004, then vice-chief Paulo spoke of the important shift in leadership organization that occurred following Sõrepré, emphasizing the former plurality of leadership, whereby chieftainship was shared by respected elder males who built consensus in dialogue with the entire men's counsel. According to Paulo, however, the internal conflict that began at Sõrepré precipitated authoritative forms of leadership, whereby single leaders manipulated the community and directed the benefits of their positions to their close relatives. According to this report, for decades thereafter, leadership became more about individual influence and much less of a cooperative process, which he considered a corruptive influence contributing to the deterioration of community wellness.

Tsuptó, Paulo, and other contemporary leaders at Pimentel Barbosa and Etênhiritipá represented themselves as engaged in the work of reversing those undesirable leadership patterns that followed the heyday at Sõrepré by promoting peaceful methods of dispute resolution and prioritizing the well-being of the whole community over personal or kin group interests. One way they did so was by deemphasizing the importance of their contemporary formal leadership positions in favor of traditionalist versions of leadership based on the idea of multiple informal leaders whose status derived from a combination of genealogy, seniority, personal capacity, and prestige. Such informal leaders were designated by the synonymous terms *danhim'apito* or *danhim'hö'a*, but also were simply recognized as mature adults (*iprédu*) or elders (*ĩhi*). There were no A'uwẽ designations that translated as "community owner" or "community master," as has been documented in other Amazonian societies (Fausto 2008). This A'uwẽ formulation led Tsuptó and Paulo to defer to prominent elders who sat at the center of the men's council and commanded the respect of the entire community. Thus, despite the relatively recent innovation of younger and formally recognized leaders authorized to make certain kinds of decisions on behalf of the community, real power remained with multiple elder leaders who used their influence to coordinate decision making through consensus. Advocates of this recent recuperation of more traditionalist and plural leadership styles among the elders in the men's council, and the absence of a singular authoritative chief, viewed it as an important change since the aftermath of Sõrepré with tangible benefits for the population's social, psychological, and physical well-being.

Both Maybury-Lewis (1967) and Graham (1995) identified leaders as those who conventionally spoke first and last in the men's council. During my early research, those roles were nearly always filled by the late Sereburã, then one of the eldest, most respected, and charismatic men in the community—also notably Tsuptó's father's brother. When Sereburã stood to open council discussion, he usually introduced subjects that had already captured the attention of the community and set into motion the task of discussing solutions. In his closing remarks, he often summarized the preceding discussions, provided his opinions considering other people's comments, and reiterated any decisions that had been reached or that he detected were evident in the discourse. Usually, decisions were not reached in a single meeting, as topics of discussion were addressed in multiple meetings over the course of days, weeks, or months. In one sense, Sereburã seemingly spoke the mind of the community. In another sense, his words transformed disparate voices into unified resolution. Sereburã's methods illustrate Maybury-Lewis's (1967) and Graham's (1995) accounts of influence deriving from prestige, and prestige from the ability to facilitate collective decision making. Sereburã's political influence in the community was at that time unchallenged, and yet his voice was not only the voice of an individual. Sereburã spoke in dialogue with the community, with other senior leaders, and with his close friends and kin. He spoke as a member of the mature adult secular age grade (*iprédu*), as an informal elder, and as a member of the senior *ai'rere'rada* age set. He also spoke as a male, a member of the *porezaõno* exogamous moiety, a senior owner of several heritable prerogatives, the grandson of important historical leaders, and a real or categorical father to many younger men in the community. Sereburã's political influence derived from that robust confluence of social factors with his magnetic personality, practiced eloquence, lifelong leadership preparation, and willingness to respect the collective will. The maintenance of his prestige according to traditionalist standards under rapidly changing historical circumstances also depended on his willingness to lead alongside young bilingual individuals in new chiefly political roles. As Sereburã once said to me, "Tsuptó is chief out there [outside the community]. Sereburã knows nothing about non-A'uwẽ. But here in the village I am leader. In the village I am chief."

Sereburã's example illustrates the relationship between political influence and process and provides a point of departure for discussing the mutual importance of multiple systems for reckoning age, seniority, and rank for how prestige was allocated in the political arena. Integral to that political arena was the men's council, where Sereburã downplayed any divisive aspects of his political and social affiliations to facilitate the will of the community. The men's council was a deliberative space where the ideals of consensus and participation usually overrode the narrowed interests of individuals, families, and factions, and therefore where the best interests of the entire community should be considered. As Graham argued, the plurality of men's council discourse counteracted the oppositional forces of political factions (Graham 1995). During council meetings, numerous men spoke simultaneously, expressing both agreement and disagreement, thereby submerging their individuality to a cacophony of collectivity. However so, men's council conventions simultaneously promoted influence structures that prioritized maleness, seniority, membership in the Tadpole exogamous moiety, and genealogical privilege.

Interruptions to Political Unity

Among the many divisive aspects of the political process, factionalism is the most widely recognized, having been a major theme in Maybury-Lewis's (1967) scholarship regarding the A'uwẽ, where it was described as a ubiquitous dimension of social organization and something of an eternal competition for supremacy between kin groups. I have argued elsewhere that my more recent ethnographic data indicated that kinship-based political factionalism was not a generalized template for a pervasive division of society into political allies and adversaries (Welch 2022b).[2] As I argue in this book, my understanding of A'uwẽ social organization foregrounds the plurality of different configurations of equality and difference in such a manner that no single hierarchical arrangement took absolute precedence over others. A'uwẽ were no more politically factional than they were many other less divisive or conflictual things. Thus, from my point of view, it is erroneous and a disservice to the A'uwẽ to characterize their worldview as fundamentally rooted in discord between factions.

In this section I address factional political discord not as a singularly prominent dimension of A'uwẽ social organization, but rather as an interruption to the pursuit of political unity. Episodes of conflict between clearly delineated factions were unusual and undesirable, having the potential to significantly reduce social well-being for extended periods. Factionalism has been characterized as central to politics because esteemed leaders earned their prestige through their endeavors as members of factions, retained such influence through the continued support of their factions, and all the while asserted the interests of their factions through behind-the-scenes politicking (Graham 1995; Maybury-Lewis 1967). As I came to understand it in the 2000s and 2010s, factional politics was a complex phenomenon involving transitory alliances for limited purposes, diverse formulations of genealogical relatedness, and multiple systems of social hierarchy. Not all political disagreement was aligned with factions. Rarely was a community clearly segregated into delineated factions. Many people avoided publicly choosing one faction over another until forced to do so by an imminent community division.

In the usual course of political life, political influence within a forum that privileged a morality of consensus permitted certain segments of society to enjoy ideological hegemony. Relatively few influential leaders and their patrilineal associations, bilateral kin networks, and political viewpoints became points of reference for the entire community, despite all its internal heterogeneity. This form of leadership was based in prestige and consent. It was evidence of political accord, which is considered good for the entire community.

Periodically, when political tensions reached breaking points, the unifying forces of participatory politics failed, and divisions between key actors were plainly exposed. At such moments of political breakdown, previously subordinate voices might consolidate into explicit opposition, and community leaders might seek to resolve their differences through dispute rather than consensus. This course of action set them on the path to a community division because it was hard to reverse course after political conflict had become overt. When opposing groups initially differentiated themselves as factions, their support networks might be limited to close kin and allies, while others abstained from taking sides. Community divisions might occur before or after conflict escalated to the point of generalized social polarization. When it escalated, factional leaders sought support and reinforcement from within the community and elsewhere, motivating more people to align themselves publicly. When a faction moved to another location, establishing a new community, before conflict escalated, people might decide to join them earlier or later without contributing to a climate of discord.

This fissioning process is not new. A'uwẽ oral history described a complex series of divisions and reunions since the historical occupation of the Sõrepré community. With each such division, the collective memory of political relations gained an additional layer of complexity, providing another historical motivation, genealogical argument, or ideological justification for contemporary political prerogatives or disputes. Thus, each new political crisis involved a combination of recent and historical factors with the potential to escalate the timbre of disagreement as they gained play in political discourse.

This historical and contemporary process of community division was largely responsible for the multiplication of communities within the Pimentel Barbosa Indigenous Land. Whereas in the past, community divisions could result in relocation of subordinate factions to new sites at considerable distances from a mother community, recently people were constrained by the boundaries of the federally recognized land. Additionally, recently established communities had tended to be near the very small town Matinha on a federal highway (BR-158) flanking the western border of the Indigenous land. This pattern was likely due to the advantages of proximal access to the highway by motor vehicle, and thereby shorter distances to the nearest towns with banks and supermarkets. A recent concentration of communities in the portions of the land most affected by invasions by ranchers in the 1970s therefore have histories of severe deforestation. In comparison, the portions of the land least deforested by historical ranchers (near the northern and eastern borders) did not have communities in the 2000s and 2010s. This geographic distribution had potential consequences for collecting, hunting, and gardening, which might suffer in the vicinities of the new communities because of continuing impacts of past vegetation removal and cattle pastures planted with invasive grasses.

The departures of Paraíso, Santa Vitória, and Sõrepré communities from Pimentel Barbosa were largely congenial. In contrast, my impression of factional processes during the 2005–2006 division of the Pimentel Barbosa community and the 2021–2022 division of Etênhiritipá (still incomplete as of the finalization of this text) was of immense tension and insecurity among members of opposing factions. I heard allies accuse their opponents of contemporary and historical injustices. I listened to stories of siblings who stopped speaking to one another and other kin who claimed to have disowned each other. Difficult choices were made as people took sides, discontinued friendships, broke marriage promises, and moved residences. Yet, through it all, I perceived that how people negotiated those tortuous ruptures was strongly influenced by how they fit into the fabric of A'uwẽ sociality. They made those decisions individually and idiosyncratically but all the while as members of age groups, kin networks, and genders. Just as Serebrurã administered political consensus as a member of various social collectivities, each member of society navigated the terrain of political crisis as a member of multiple social bodies and statuses. In the remainder of this section, I trace the interaction of such social factors in the political sphere by looking at configurations of leadership and influence as an additional age hierarchy based in seniority.

Preludes to Male Leadership

Explicit political participation was reserved for mature male adults through their inclusion in the men's council, but the practice of leadership began much earlier for boys. As discussed in chapter 3, each secular age set was internally stratified by relative age and individualized through specific leadership positions during preinitiation. Such designations were made by parents and adult relatives according to various criteria ranging from perceptions of relative age, kinship relations, and personal characteristics such as leadership potential, including discipline, sporting competence, body size, and physical beauty. Selection as age set elders or leaders was accompanied by expectations of exemplary behavior and assumption of responsibility for one's peers. Thus, even at early ages, the capacity for having differentiated social influence was associated with various individual and genealogical factors, the majority of which were beyond a boys' immediate control and might contribute to exceptional prestige later in life. Furthermore, these distinctions helped to establish at an early age that social inequality was congruent with the morality of collectivity, unity, and conformity that also accompanied secular age set membership. Preinitiate differentiation prepared youths for the adult political process because it required them to adopt mature social perspectives such as deferring to those with senior rank, respecting other people's domains of influence and authority, and subordinating individual to group agendas.

When an age set reached the novitiate adult age grade, its leadership dynamics become somewhat more structured. No longer residing in the preinitiate house, novitiate adult men held evening council meetings (*warã*) in the community plaza to the side of the mature adult men's council. Observing the aesthetic of left- and right-side secular age set moiety alternation, the position of each novitiate men's council relative to the mature adult men's council recalled the location of its now dismantled preinitiate house: an age set whose preinitiate house was on the left side of the community held its council to the left of the adult men's council, and vice versa (Graham 1995). During their initial years as novitiates, members of an age set had few decisions to make and therefore little to discuss in their nightly council meetings. When I was a novitiate adult, my age set peers usually spent that time in informal conversation followed by a round of singing performances. They began by singing the night's song while standing in their council space and facing the current preinitiate house on the opposite side of the community (figure 28). They then sang around the community in front of residences while the mature adult men conducted their evening council meeting, always starting on the same side as the current preinitiate house and finishing on the side of their own preinitiate house.

After completing my initial year of fieldwork, I returned to the Pimentel Barbosa community in 2006 and was present immediately before the novitiate adults would be promoted to full mature adult status during the approximately quinquennial secular initiation rites (*danhono*). During that visit, I observed a

Figure 28 Novitiate men (*'ritei'wa*) performing a song during their evening council (*warã*), held to one side of the centrally located mature men's council, 2005.

Figure 29 The author participating in a circular novitiate men's evening council (*warã*). Photo by Carlos E. A. Coimbra Jr., 2005.

striking difference in how the novitiate men went about their age set business. They seemed to take greater interest in organizing age set activities and had adopted a more formal format for nightly council meetings. They now consistently imitated the circular form and presentation style of mature adult men's council meetings (figure 29). One by one, young men stood in front of their peers to present their reports and opinions about topics of import, while respected individuals sought through their opening and closing comments to crystallize the plurality of voices into collective decisions. Those meetings provided first opportunities for young men to practice adult political oration (Graham 1995).

Upon reaching the mature adult secular age grade (*iprédu*), all males enjoyed the right to participate in the men's council, giving the political process a presumption of collectivity. Indeed, addressing a topic in a council meeting implied that everyone had the opportunity to speak out and that any decisions reflected the will of the community. The collectivity of the council, however, was accompanied by systems of internal stratification that differentiated the allocation of influence and access to voice among its members. Four important factors that influenced disparities in the men's council were relative age, exogamous moiety membership, heritable prerogative ownerships, and genealogical seniority. I address these factors in the remainder of this chapter.

Just as secular age set membership was a most salient means of reckoning age in daily life, so it was in the men's council. The newest participants in the council were members of the most recent age set to have entered mature adulthood (*iprédu*) and served as mentors (*danhohui'wa*) to the preinitiates (*wapté*) that currently occupied the preinitiate house. By social convention, members of this youngest mature adult age set mostly limited their participation in council meetings to listening and occasionally making background comments. They positioned themselves spatially around the periphery of the council circle and rarely stood to deliver a formal address, except, for example, when reporting to their elders about their preinitiate protégés and their activities as mentors. Being a member of the youngest age set in the adult men's council was an opportunity to observe and imitate one's elders in preparation for future leadership. Yet, juniority in the men's council also muted one's voice because silence was considered the proper and respectful form of self-expression by younger mature adults. Thus, relative age tended to tilt the scales of men's council consensus in favor of older mature adults who were not constrained by expectations that they exhibit respectful silence.

Political Influence Among Women and Men

Reaching motherhood involved establishing a sphere of female influence that began at home but gradually reached well beyond with the proliferation of her children and grandchildren. Like male influence, female influence was exercised independently from but often in dialogue with her spouse and other close opposite-gender kin. Mothers were neither victims nor objects of male prerogative, but rather active decision makers in their chosen domains who might coordinate with their husbands and other important men (see chapter 7).

Usually, only male members of older age sets who had the benefit of years of peripheral participation in council meetings presumed to stand to advocate for a position and thereby sway the decision-making process. Thus, political influence in the men's council came with seniority. Yet, many factors influenced who was considered senior. Seniority in terms of secular age set membership was an important factor. All other things being equal, members of older secular age sets were thought to deserve more respect, deference, and political influence than members of younger age sets. Political influence also came with personal prestige, which depended on one's genealogy, seniority within his age set, and personal merits. Thus, it was likely that the child of a respected leader, an age set elder, or someone with a strong personality and recognized competitive skills would be more vocal and have more influence in the men's council.

Maybury-Lewis (1967) wrote that the five eldest age sets were the most active speakers in the men's council in 1958–1962. In 2005, members of the seven eldest age sets spoke most frequently. Nonetheless, not all members of these eldest age sets had the inclination to deliver influential speeches. One of the least vocal individuals was the late Darú, a member of the eldest age set and thus one of the two eldest males in the community. Darú was widely respected for his extensive knowledge of the past, kind nature, and exceptional skill with handicrafts. He characterized himself, however, as someone who preferred to work rather than speak and was usually silent during council meetings. In contrast, the late Barbosa, a categorical brother of the late Sereburã and among the most vocal of men's council seniors, belonged to the fourth eldest age set and was therefore a considerably junior relative to Darú. Barbosa was an extroverted man with practiced oratory skills. He followed Sereburã as informal community leader despite his relative youth among senior mature men. When Sereburã stopped attending council meetings because of declining health in about 2011, Barbosa assumed the role of opening and closing discussion with formal speeches intended to facilitate consensus and decision making.

In 2019, most elders who formerly led the men's councils in the Pimentel Barbosa and Etênhiritipá communities during my years of research were deceased, creating a leadership vacuum with the potential to disrupt consensus building and conflict resolution. Slightly younger elders were assuming leadership roles, but without the practiced expertise of such leaders as Sereburã and Barbosa. Sometimes there were long silences in the men's council before someone would take the initiative to give an opening or closing speech. Sometimes no one did so, and the conversation proceeded informally, without the benefit of a skilled orator to facilitate consensus. I suspect this gap will be temporary, with current leaders growing into their new roles, gaining respect, and assuming responsibility for leading council meetings. Until they do so, the communities may be disadvantaged in their pursuit of sustained political unity and potentially at greater risk of political discord that negatively influences community well-being.

The morning and evening men's councils were almost without exception male forums for discussing public affairs of interest to the whole community. During these meetings, women were often preparing meals, caring for children, or engaging in conversation with their female kin in front of their houses. In

the Pimentel Barbosa community, louder men's council discourse was potentially audible to women sitting in front of several residences situated closer than
others to the center of the community plaza, or by women who happened to
be crossing the plaza returning from the river or visiting other households.
This meant that particularly animated speeches might be heard by women and
spread by word of mouth from one household to another. When men wished
to keep their discussions unheard by women, they tightened the circle of men
and carefully spoke in hushed voices. Otherwise, they expected women to be
informed, either directly or indirectly, of their deliberations. Upon returning to
their residences, men might share with their wives and other female kin some
of what was discussed to keep them informed and to hear their opinions (Graham 1995). Women discussed these matters among themselves at home and
while working in gardens and in the cerrados, thereby indirectly participating
in men's council deliberations. Graham (1995) also reported two occasions in
which women joined the men's council because they were particularly interested
in the topic, seating themselves behind the men after the meetings had already
begun and discussing matters quietly among themselves without making formal
addresses to the entire council.

Women's discursive influence was also apparent when elder females delivered speeches in public spaces with similar practiced eloquence to elder men
speaking in the men's council. I had opportunity to observe women's formal
discourse on diverse occasions. For example, I regularly conducted group interviews about topics of interest for my research. When I did so, it was common
for potential interviewees of younger ages to insist that the only legitimate interviewees were elders, who knew more and could speak more authoritatively
about the given topic. Consequently, I held numerous group interviews with
elders. These elders preferred to meet for interviews with only members of their
gender. When I interviewed women in groups, they strictly adhered to the A'uwẽ
formulation of community meetings whereby influential individuals delivered
formal speeches in sequence, rather than engaging in informal back-and-forth
conversation. I also observed women give formal speeches when we made video
recordings of them for a land demarcation study for FUNAI and cultural documentation projects sponsored by the Museu do Índio in Rio de Janeiro, all of
which were to be curated by the museum as part of its permanent digital collection. On these occasions, the importance of creating enduring audiovisual
registers of their messages seemed to prompt them to deliver formal speeches
(for a critique of the ideology of video technology as permanent, see Graham

2016). Thus, in my interviews, many elder women delivered eloquent speeches while standing in front of other women or in front of a video camera and on-lookers. Although I am not a linguist, it appeared to me that they did so according to similar conventions as men in their council meetings (cf. Graham 1995). I therefore conclude that influential elder women, like their male counterparts, cultivated their discourse skills through observation and imitation throughout their lives despite not participating directly in men's council meetings.

Although men's council meetings and women's formal discourse addressed such diverse topics as to defy generalization, it is pertinent to note that recurrent topics included access to and conservation of the local cerrado landscape. In men's council meetings, a few of the many environmental issues discussed with regularity were preinitiate and novitiate adult excursions into the cerrado to fish and collect materials for ceremonial accoutrements with their mentors, group hunting excursions including those employing fire to flush out game, efforts to secure federal governmental support for recognition of traditional territories as Indigenous lands, planting community rice fields, men's fishing excursions, and women's collecting excursions. During such discussions, men frequently raised the issue of overseeing younger participants who did not yet have adequate experience in the cerrado to operate autonomously without risking their safety or environmental wellness. These two concerns appeared to be relatively new in men's council discourse, deriving from contemporary concerns that preinitiates, novitiate adults, and even younger mature adults were not as well prepared today as they were in the past for undertaking subsistence activities in the cerrado without supervision. Furthermore, they seemed directly related to emergent perspectives among influential mature adults that some subsistence activities had the potential to ecologically overburden their now limited Indigenous lands if not carefully planned and executed in accordance with A'uwẽ traditional ecological knowledge and in ways that distribute their impacts both spatially and temporally to allow appropriate regeneration (Leeuwenberg and Robinson 2000; Welch 2014, 2015; Welch, Brondízio, et al. 2013).

Exogamous Moieties and Heritable Prerogatives

Another aspect of political influence was exogamous moiety membership, which was a pervasive social distinction with ramifications throughout social life. As discussed in chapter 2, exogamous moiety membership was inherited patrilineally, with children of Tadpole (*porezaʾõno*) fathers being Tadpole and children of Big Water (*öwawe*) fathers being Big Water. One of the most important expressions of this moiety affiliation was its role in regulating marriage, with unions between members of the same moiety being considered incestuous and thought by many to be disrespectful and to contaminate the blood of any children. Although I heard reports that some other A'uwẽ communities no longer marry according to moiety affiliation, at Pimentel Barbosa and Etênhiritipá, it remains a primary factor in spouse selection. I encountered only one intramoiety marriage at Pimentel Barbosa and Etênhiritipá, which was held in some disesteem by others. Nevertheless, I did not perceive that this couple was overtly disrespected as individuals or treated differently than other couples. To the contrary, they were highly respected influential elder members of the community. Several individuals confirmed that people did not talk about it publicly out of deference to the children, whose blood was privately thought by some people to be unclean.

Exogamous moiety affiliation derived from the idea that the essence of fetal substance, blood (*dawapru*), derived equally from both mother and father, but because male blood was considered stronger than female blood, a child gained its father's moiety identity, which was immutable. It was an intrinsic aspect of one's physical and social identity that affected one's insertion into the fabric of society in innumerable ways.

Rights and Responsibilities of Exogamous Moiety Membership

I found exogamous moiety affiliation to be accompanied by a series of rights and responsibilities that directly influenced the political process. According to Paulo, then vice-chief of the Pimentel Barbosa community and a member of the Big Water moiety, "We are the servants of the Tadpole moiety. We defend them and sweep up after them." In another context, Supreteprã Xavante (2015, 99) explained that the Big Water moiety guaranteed security in the military aspect of the community, while the Tadpole moiety administered the political aspect, with control over internal politics of the communities. In my observation, regarding community leadership, the Tadpole moiety had ultimate decision-making authority, with the right to appoint official leaders from among its ranks. Under the contemporary structure of formal chieftainship, Tadpole individuals might be chiefs and Big Water individuals vice-chiefs. In 2005, then vice-chief Paulo told me that the Tadpole moiety leadership prerogative did not preclude the possibility of Big Water moiety members being appointed as primary chiefs and Tadpole people being vice-chiefs under unusual circumstances. He explained that Tadpole elders could decide to temporarily loan that prerogative to the Big Water moiety should it be in the best interest of the community, for example, if a Big Water individual was best qualified. Interestingly, that came to pass in 2007, when the Tadpole chief of the Etênhiritipá community (recently separated from the Pimentel Barbosa community) died. At that time, the Tadpole elders at Etênhiritipá appointed Paulo, formerly vice-chief, as chief. They also appointed as his new vice-chief a younger Tadpole individual, Caimi Wai'asse. This temporary arrangement held until several years later, when a member of the Tadpole moiety assumed the position of chief and a different Big Water individual was appointed vice-chief. This differentiation of formal community leadership positions (chief and vice-chief) according to their exogamous moieties was a contemporary innovation anchored in political traditionalism, whereby existing moiety characteristics were translated and adapted to fit today's political needs. As an instance of resilience whereby contemporary circumstances were interpreted through the lens of cultural traditionalism, it is also an example of how new forms of political organization can exemplify notions of good living.

Under the informal process of men's council leadership coordinated by chiefly elders, Tadpole individuals were understood to have prerogatives of facilitation and diplomacy as well as the responsibility to hear and respect the opinions of Big Water individuals. Effectively, this configuration amounted to a hierarchical ranking of the two moieties, with Big Water in subordinate position to Tadpole. Moiety ranking appears to be a common feature throughout Indigenous South America (Lévi-Strauss 1944). Thus, other configurations of age hierarchy and seniority may be subverted by one's exogamous moiety ranking, affecting how two individuals interact in formal settings, such as the men's council, and informal settings, such as during a private conversation.

The symbolic relationship between the Tadpole and Big Water moieties may be inferred from the mythic oral history of two formal friends (*da'amo*) who, as preinitiates (*wapté*), created the world's animals (Giaccaria and Heide 1984; Graham 1995; Sereburã et al. 1998). Formal friends (who called each other *ï'amo*) always pertained to opposite exogamous moieties in expression of an aesthetic of complementarity between the two. In this case, the Tadpole friend repeatedly asked his Big Water friend, "What shall we create now?" The Big Water friend always replied, "You choose!" The Tadpole friend would then choose an animal and, by naming it, bring it into being. In that dynamic, the power of creation resided in the pair of friends acting together but depended on the Tadpole friend acting as initiator, decider, and doer. In contrast, the Big Water friend acted as supporter, agreer, and observer.

The usual social dynamics between members of the two moieties may be described as complementary and competitive. In daily social interactions outside the men's council, members of the two exogamous moieties enthusiastically treated each other with esteemed and pleasurable competitive jocosity. Similarly to the demeaning joking that characterized banter between members of opposite secular age set moieties, opposite exogamous moiety playful derision usually focused on the strength (*siptede* or *danhiptede*) of one's own moiety and the weakness (*sib'uware*) of the other, causing them to lose friendly competitions, such as hunting fire races (see chapter 6), *noni* sprinting races, efforts to remain awake all night during spiritual rituals and water-splashing exercises during the initiand phase of secular age set initiation rites, and any informal situation where opposite exogamous moiety members challenged one another to playful tests of their respective fortitude. Such good-natured competition and reciprocal gibe were celebrated as healthy and inspiriting social expressions of the culturally appropriate complementary yet adversarial relations between these moieties. They reinforced the social relevance of exogamous moiety membership beyond marriage selection and contributed to cultural resilience by strengthening its salience at a historical moment of considerable sociocultural transformation.

In the context of the men's council, the proper political role of Big Water was to listen to Tadpole proposals, voice agreement or opposition as required, and then allow the Tadpole moiety to act in its rightful role as primary decision makers. With the Tadpole moiety obliged to consider Big Water opinions, and the Big Water moiety allowed to complain and object when this did not occur, this traditionalist form of decision making approximated an A'uwẽ version of consensus and was considered socially proper and good. Big Water had ample agency and influence in this dynamic. With two council meetings per day, the Big Water moiety had abundant opportunities to present their opinions and point out when their advice should be or should have been followed.

Heritable Prerogatives and Political Influence

Heritable prerogatives were vigorously maintained and protected by their owners and widely valued as deserved individual dignities worthy of respect. According to Giaccaria and Heide (1984, 122), "All of these 'authorities' [ownerships] have an action that we would call particularly trusted advisors: their judgment prevails over that of men and elders of the same group, their advice is heard with respect and put into practice; if it should happen that one of these individuals has a particularly strong and numerous family, and has particularly gifted people, such as an orator, then his influence comes to be imposed over other groups within the village." All the eldest individuals who owned a particular prerogative were considered senior. Because genealogically distant individuals could be owners of the same prerogatives, there could be multiple senior owners in a single community and many more in other communities. Despite there being multiple elder owners of each prerogative, each was an autonomous owner and ultimate authority regarding their knowledge domains within their local spheres of social influence. They freely exercised the prerogatives owned by them and their younger kin, advising their community on matters they were exceptionally qualified to speak to as senior owners. Each had the independent right and responsibility to pass such prerogative knowledge to next of kin or other designees while still alive. Prerogative ownership thereby influenced political affairs by introducing an additional dimension of age seniority within topical domains of general community interest. Although heritable prerogatives influenced political processes, they did not operate as "patrilineages" that ultimately determined dualistic consanguineal factional associations, as proposed by previous scholars (Maybury-Lewis 1967; Welch 2022b).[3]

Heritable prerogative ownerships were private (owned by individuals who possessed the knowledge), exclusive (protected from nonowners), and hierarchical (senior owners exercised control), but dovetailed coherently with cultural ideals of collective consensus-based community decision making. For example, the political silencing of respectful young mature adults did not diminish the perceived collectivity of decisions made in the men's council. Similarly, heritable prerogative ownerships were understood to contribute in good ways to participatory political discourse even though they overshadowed other viewpoints. They involved a form of authority gained through deference and agreement.

Differently from other forms of political prestige, that which derived from closely guarded prerogative ownership was earned by means of less public, less visible processes. This kind of influence was derived from knowledge that was acquired and often exercised in private and was based on muted and potentially unverified reputation, with only minor dimensions being publicly known through their performance in highly visible settings. The shroud of covertness that protected many heritable prerogatives discouraged their theft by nonowners and stimulated amplification through gossip as others imagined and discussed them and their senior owners.

An example of how senior owners exercised their heritable proprietary knowledge and used it to influence the political process can be found in white-lipped peccary ownership (*uhö'tede'wa*). My adoptive mother's brother Roberto Huatá Wameru Otomopá was a senior white-lipped peccary owner. As an owner of this prerogative, he explained, he located these game animals by dreaming so that he and other hunters could find them the next day. He considered himself such an avid dreamer that he frequently awoke knowing where hunters could find large white-lipped peccary bands and where smaller bands were located that should not be hunted to protect their numbers. Roberto hunted alone much of the time, but when he dreamed a large band was nearby, he informed other men at the morning men's council, encouraging them to give pursuit. In this manner he influenced council discussion and thereby gained prestige as an opinion leader. His heritable prerogative thereby contributed to his influence in the men's council.

Examples of heritable prerogatives that I heard about ranged from technological skills to supernatural practices. At one extreme was the art of pottery, which was a female proprietary knowledge domain that had been abruptly discontinued with the introduction of aluminum pots many decades ago. Although in the Pimentel Barbosa Indigenous Land, only one owner of that knowledge remained alive in 2022, she had not yet passed it on to her daughters, granddaughters, or other appropriate recipients. I was told that when pottery making was actively practiced, pottery owners enclosed their work area with a brush barrier to ensure that nonowners could not watch. When other women desired pots, they would place orders with these women. At the other end of the spectrum was male proprietary knowledge of the proper use of certain naturally occurring sacred substances that pierced the veil separating the physical and spiritual dimensions, allowing a person to directly see the spiritual world. Although female pottery manufacture and male spiritual vision were quite divergent kinds of knowledge, the principles of their ownership and transmission were very similar. They both involved socially sanctioned secrecy, authority held by elders, and presumed parallel inheritance with the possibility of adaptation in accordance with a senior knowledge holders' wishes (they might choose to give their prerogative to a friend in repayment for an exceptional service, loan it to a substitute in the absence of an appropriate lineal recipient, or even transmit it to an opposite-gender child).

Sorcery (*abzé* or *simi'ö*) is especially relevant to the topics of political influence and heritable prerogatives. Considering heritable prerogatives were subject to gossip because their secrets were closely guarded, sorcerous knowledge was even more so. Because there were no shaman specialists among the A'uwẽ, anyone with knowledge of curing techniques, especially elders, performed spiritual massage and prepared remedies for their extended family members. In exceptional cases, treatment of last resort for grave illness involved applying shamanistic techniques collectively during a special kind of sacred ritual (*wai'a*), whereby men performed sucking magic simultaneously as a group (Welch 2010). None of these men were considered shaman specialists even though they collectively acted as shamanistic healers during this single ritual. Differently than family healers and participants in male spiritual healing rituals, owners of sorcery (*simi'ö'tede'wa*) owned proprietary knowledge about how to poison people using secret plant substances (Welch 2022b).

A'uwẽ evaluated others' sorcerous capabilities through supposition and insinuation because very little verifiable information was available to them. Presumed sorcerous capacities were practiced covertly, causing reputations as powerful sorcerers to be earned indirectly and the political influence they facilitated to be muted and veiled under normal circumstances. When political circumstances were amiable, and political discord was minimal, sorcerous potentialities could reinforce undertones of deference or distrust in political forums. When the political mood was tense, and people were motivated to examine a social landscape in which factional opposition was causing polarization, discussion of sorcery became magnified. Threats led to accusations, which provoked retaliations. At such times, underlying currents of distrust deriving from reputations of sorcery knowledge ownership became overt by leveraging rumors of genealogical links to ancestral sorcery knowledge owners. Through this process, previously latent political influence became actualized.

I heard many sorcery accusations and threats during my fieldwork. In some cases, accusations followed circumstantial evidence, such as physical proximity between an adversarial adult and one's child followed by the death of the child. In other cases, accusations were based mainly on patrilineal associations with reputations of heritable prerogatives. For example, one man accused another of supernatural maleficence because his deceased father was suspected of having killed an entire community with sorcery. In another example, a man expressed fear for his life because he suspected retaliation after being accused of murder by a family known to have powerful knowledge ownerships. In these and other cases, suspicions of sorcery knowledge ownership were transformed into verbal action as people sought to discredit opponents, incite fear, and justify aggression within contexts of factional conflict involving imminent or recent community divisions. Accordingly, sorcery discourse leveraged the ambiguity of heritable prerogative prestige as a strategy in political conflict, thereby transforming previously silent political powers into real forms of influence. These sorcery accusations amplified the already acrimonious relations between factions, thereby contributing to the social unwellness of a community embroiled in unnerving conflict.

Over the years, relations substantially calmed after the Etênhiritipá community divided from the Pimentel Barbosa community in 2006. Nevertheless, accusations of sorcery between them persisted. For example, in about 2016 the water tank at Etênhiritipá stopped pumping and was not fixed by public health services for over a year. During this time, women from Etênhiritipá collected water from the tank at Pimentel Barbosa. Some women from Etênhiritipá, however, told me they disliked this arrangement because they feared people from Pimentel Barbosa would take advantage of the opportunity to poison the water with sorcerous substances.

Political prestige and influence, whether derived from practiced leadership skills, exogamous moiety membership, or heritable prerogative ownerships were inseparable from relative age and seniority. Based on these examples, it is tempting to characterize A'uwẽ communities as gerontocracies, where elders exerted considerable political influence. Yet, I believe doing so would exaggerate the mechanisms of silencing younger adults and would devalue the importance of newer forms of political leadership that often placed younger men with intercultural experience in formal positions of chieftaincy or vice-chieftaincy to complement traditionalist formulations of plural elder leaders who exerted influence according to cultural concepts of consensus. These contemporary forms of leadership exhibited social wellness and resilience by promoting the persistence of traditionalist formulations of influence involving seniority and structured consensus through the incorporation of innovative forms of leadership that drew on A'uwẽ social models to attend to contemporary demands for younger political leaders.

Notions of Relatedness

In the previous section, I discussed some of the ways age hierarchies conditioned how people negotiated seniority, influence, and power in the political arena. I seek to show that the political process involved not only those age hierarchies presented in previous chapters (age grades and age group systems), but also other means of reckoning social seniority and identity (political prestige, exogamous moieties, and heritable prerogative seniority). Those relationships highlight multiple ways that the social construction of influence implicated notions of relatedness. Thus, those who exercised political influence did so through a matrix of social relationships that affected what it meant to be older/younger, senior/junior, or dominant/subordinate. In this section, I explore the kinship terminology and associated perspectives to illustrate diverse ways relative age affected how people understood relatedness and to set the stage for a discussion in the subsequent section of genealogical seniority and its implications for political processes.

Kinship offers an important window into A'uwẽ notions of relatedness for three main reasons. In the first place, in their daily social interactions, A'uwẽ viewed one another through the lenses of kinship and age systems, uniformly calling one another by kinship or age system terms rather than personal names, which were considered impolite. Just as age systems were living frameworks for defining one's relationships with other people, so were kinship terminologies. In the second place, A'uwẽ viewpoints and behaviors relative to kin showed a high correspondence with relationship logics evident in the kinship terminology. As a result, understanding kin terms people used for one another helps conceptualize the contrastive ways they related to one another socially. In the third place, A'uwẽ kinship systems were highly structured, complex, and contingent in ways that gave people more ways to play with the rules than to break the rules (Valentine 2017). This does not mean they were "fluid," but rather means that they were so nuanced and contingent that they provided people with multiple options to construe their relationships with most other people in society. A'uwẽ considered all members of their communities to be some kind of kin, but they prioritized the use of kinship terms that reflected the bonds they found most relevant, desirable, or respectful at any given time.

Real and Categorical Parents

To orient oneself within the A'uwẽ kinship terminology, it is first important to understand some basic marriage principles that found clear expression in the first ascending generation. The A'uwẽ kinship terminology had abundant examples of consanguineal-affinal equations (terms that apply to both consanguineal kin and in-laws) and a corresponding logic of sibling exchange (marriage arrangements whereby two or more sets of siblings marry one another) in certain generations (figures 30 and 31). For example, in the first ascending generation of the vocative terminology, *ĩtebe* was used for father's sister and mother's brother's wife; *ĩmama* was used for father, father's brother, and mother's sister's husband; *dati'ö* was used for mother, mother's sister, and father's brother's wife; and *ĩmawapté* was used for mother's brother and father's sister's husband. Thus, as was the case in many actual marriages I documented, the terminology suggests paternal uncle married maternal aunt, and paternal aunt married maternal uncle. Although these terminological consanguineal-affinal equations were maintained even in the absence of actual sibling exchanges, it was very common for father's brother to marry mother's sister and for mother's brother to marry father's sister. These types of marriage arrangements based on the principle of sibling exchange were often negotiated after a first marriage was successful and the son-in-law became well integrated into his parents-in-law's household. In many such cases, the parents-in-law wished to offer a second child for marriage to a sibling of the first son-in-law because they were already known by the parents-in-law to be a good fit.

Many men had especially intimate paternal relationships with their sisters' children. As Maybury-Lewis observed, a mother's brother and his sister's children often called one another friends, gave each other choice foods during distributions, and entered name bestowal relationships (Maybury-Lewis 1967). Such men treated their sister's children with similar indulgence to fathers. As discussed in detail by Lopes da Silva (1986), a special social bond was established between a woman's children and one of her brothers (real or classificatory) when, during their childhood, he painted them, adorned them with cotton necklaces, and sent them to their parents' house carrying large maize loaves (figure 32). This ritual was performed by just one of her brothers for each child, often the same brother for all her children. Through that ritual, the mother's brother became their ceremonial father (*danhorebzu'wa*), and they became his ceremonial children (*ta'rebzu*). The social dynamic between ceremonial parents and their ceremonial children was especially intimate, an example of a joking relationship (Lopes da Silva 1986), reflecting the same paternalism characteristic of other real and classificatory parents and their children. He continued to play a very important role in their lives, including bestowing names on his ceremonial sons and sponsoring marriages (*dabasa*) for his ceremonial daughters.

Ceremonial fatherhood (*danhorebzu'wa*) and childhood were accompanied by a host of changes to the kinship terms they used for one another. Using

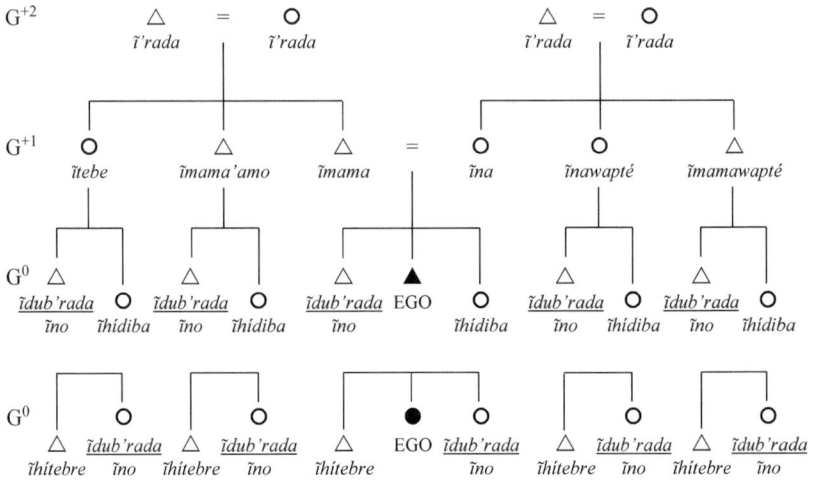

		male
		female
		male ego
		female ego
G		Generation
		filiation
		siblingship

<u>older sibling</u>
younger sibling

Consanguineal-affinal terminological equations in G^{+1}:

ĩtebe	Father's sister and mother's brother's wife
ĩmama'amo	Father's brother and mother's sister's husband
ĩnawapté	Mother's sister and father's brother's wife
ĩmamawapté	Mother's brother and father's sister's husband

Obs.: Includes ego's and two ascending generations. G^0 is repeated for male and female egos.

Figure 30 A'uwẽ referential kinship terminology.

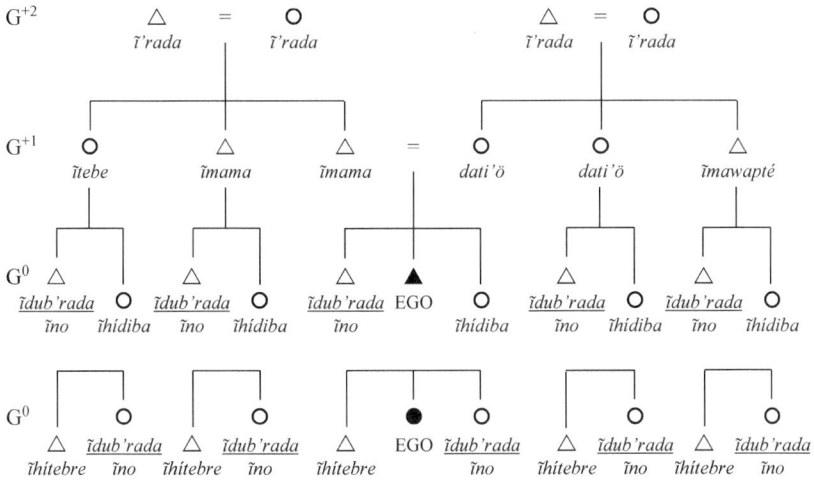

G^{+2} △ = ○   △ = ○
     ĩ'rada   *ĩ'rada*   *ĩ'rada*   *ĩ'rada*

G^{+1} ○   △   △ = ○   ○   △
   ĩtebe   *ĩmama*   *ĩmama*   *dati'ö*   *dati'ö*   *ĩmawapté*

G^0 △   ○   △   ○   △   ▲   ○   △   ○   △   ○
ĩdub'rada   *ĩdub'rada*   *ĩdub'rada* EGO   *ĩdub'rada*   *ĩdub'rada*
ĩno   *ĩhĩdiba*   *ĩno*   *ĩhĩdiba*   *ĩno*   *ĩhĩdiba*   *ĩno*   *ĩhĩdiba*   *ĩno*   *ĩhĩdiba*

G^0 ○   ○   ● ○   ○   ○
  △ *ĩdub'rada* △ *ĩdub'rada* △ EGO *ĩdub'rada* △ *ĩdub'rada* △ *ĩdub'rada*
ĩhĩtebre *ĩno* *ĩhĩtebre* *ĩno* *ĩhĩtebre*   *ĩno* *ĩhĩtebre* *ĩno* *ĩhĩtebre* *ĩno*

△   male

○   female

▲   male ego

●   female ego

G   Generation

| filiation

—   siblingship

<u>older sibling</u>
younger sibling

Consanguineal-affinal terminological equations in G^{+1}:

ĩtebe	Father's sister and mother's brother's wife
ĩmama	Father, father's brother, and mother's sister's husband
dati'ö	Mother, mother's sister, and father's brother's wife
ĩmawapté	Mother's brother and father's sister's husband

Obs.: Includes ego's and two ascending generations. G^0 is repeated for male and female egos.

Figure 31 A'uwẽ adult vocative kinship terminology.

Figure 32 Children (*ta'rebzu*) carrying ceremonial maize loaves across the community plaza after being ritually painted by their ceremonial father (*danhorebzu'wa*), 2005.

the referential terminology as an example, after childhood, ceremonial children stopped calling their ceremonial parents by the terms for mother's brother (*īmamawapté*) and father's sister (*ītebe*). Ceremonial sons began referring to them as ceremonial parent (*aimana*), while ceremonial daughters called him father (*īmama*) and her mother (*īna*). At the same time, he ceased to call them by the term for preadult ceremonial children (*ta'rebzu*) in favor of the term for adult ceremonial children (*simana*). These terminological shifts provoked corresponding changes in how other close kin referred to one another. For example, spouses of ceremonial children might call the ceremonial parents by the term for parent-in-law (*īmaprewa*), and fathers might call their children's ceremonial parents by the special term *sorebzu'wa* rather than brother-in-law terms.

Lopes da Silva (1986), characterized ceremonial parenthood as the consanguinization of categorical affines, such that individuals in the opposite exogamous moiety came to consider one another same-moiety members. Although I would argue that they were already considered consanguines according to a bilateral dimension of A'uwẽ notions of relatedness, her insight highlights that mothers' brothers and fathers' sisters could play intimate parental roles. Children therefore might grow up with a great deal of social access to and familiarity with the homes of their paternal aunts and maternal uncles, and therefore also their cross-cousins.

Real and Categorical Siblings

The preference for marriage exchanges evident in the first ascending generation did not extend to the ego's generation. In fact, according to many of my consultants, marriage was proscribed between both cross-cousins and parallel cousins (cross-cousins are linked by parents of different genders, while parallel cousins are linked by parents of the same gender). Nonetheless, one mature man with considerable insight into the kinship system explained that marriage between first-degree cross-cousins was not proscribed because they belong to opposite exogamous moieties. According to him, such marriages were very infrequent but might be arranged if parents believed it to be in the best interest of the individuals and families involved. For example, siblings might wish for their children to marry to strengthen their blood or because political relations with other families were less favorable. Nevertheless, in practice such first cousin unions were rare. I found only one example of first-degree cross-cousin marriage in a sample of 253 marriages (0.4 percent) in the mid-2000s, while Maybury-Lewis (1967) found no examples in the 1950s and 1960s. Thus, the logic of marriage between groups of siblings in the first ascending generation did not result in a pattern of first-degree cross-cousin marriage in the ego's generation.

Another explanation I heard for not marrying first-degree cousins was that one could not marry anyone they called a sibling or considered close bilateral kin (*wasi'höiba*), which included one's close same-moiety kin and one's first-degree cross-cousins. In contrast to the first ascending generation, in which uncles and aunts were distinguished terminologically by crossness, same-generation cousins were not similarly distinguished. Rather, they all received the same terms used for real siblings (which were inflected for the gender of the speaker and the relative age of the sibling).

Thus, in the ego's generation, the A'uwẽ terminology was generational, which means all real siblings and first-degree cousins were represented by the same kinship terms and were therefore understood to be real and categorical siblings. The generational aspect in the ego's generation was consistent with the tendency to avoid marriage with any of one's parallel and cross-cousins and derived logically from the A'uwẽ formulation of consanguinity. As discussed in chapter 2, a child received its substance, or blood (*dawapru*), equally from both parents, although male blood was believed to be stronger. That formulation lent consanguinity two aspects, one patrilineal and one bilateral. The patrilineal aspect was manifested most overtly in the two exogamous moieties, Tadpole (*porezaõno*) and Big Water (*öwawe*). Although one received substance equally from father and mother, because father's blood was stronger, one always inherited their father's and not their mother's moiety affiliation. Marriage between members of the same moiety was considered inappropriate. The bilateral aspect was most explicit in the generational aspect of the ego in the kinship terminology, whereby all one's parallel and cross-cousins were considered categorical siblings. Cross-cousins were siblings insofar as they share mother's blood, but they were not siblings to the extent they did not share father's dominant blood. When the two notions of consanguinity are considered together, A'uwẽ marriage "rules" seem to be nearly complex or semicomplex (Lévi-Strauss 1965, 1969) or "non-prescriptive" (Viveiros de Castro 1995), whereby spouses ideally should not be members of one's patrilineal exogamous moiety or one's first-degree cross-cousins. The coexistence of binary and cognatic aspects in Gê kinship terminologies was anticipated by Gordon (1996) based on Eduardo Viveiros de Castro's (1993) analysis of Dravidian systems in Amazonia.

Important differences between those two aspects of consanguinity are their relative strength and temporal aspect. Because male blood was dominant, patrilineal consanguinity was more substantial than matrilineal consanguinity. That distinction helps explain the noted ambiguity regarding the acceptability of cross-cousin marriage, whereby some but not all individuals considered it acceptable even though it was rare. Important in this context are comments by many individuals that parallel cousins were "real" (*uptabi*) siblings, but cross-cousins were not, even though they were called by the same terms in the kinship terminology. Interviews revealed that cross-cousins were considered kin, and marriage to them was often thought to be inappropriate, but they were not considered kin of the same close order as parallel cousins. Such assessments follow from similar comments that father's brother and mother's sister were "real" parents, while mother's brother and father's sister were not, distinctions that were well reflected in the referential kinship terminology.

Another consequence of the dominance of male blood is that consanguinity was understood to be bilateral for several generations, but decreasingly so. The distinction in the ego's generation between parallel cousins as "real" siblings and cross-cousins as something else indicates that consanguinity, while bilateral in the ego's generation, was more patrilineal than matrilineal. Similarly, the matrilineal aspect nearly vanished in the first descending generation. According to all my interlocutors, any opposite-moiety children of cross-cousins might marry because their blood is sufficiently differentiated. Interestingly, there is also evidence that bilateral consanguinity was recognized at that level even though marriage was allowed. Although some individuals identified such marriages as neither better nor worse than other marriages, others identified them as preferable for the sake of avoiding political conflict because all parties to the marriage were related. The ubiquitousness of consanguinity was also expressed by one older adult male, who told me that irrespective of moiety affiliation or genealogical distance, "we are all related; everyone one might marry is some kind of kin."

Although marriage between cross-cousins was not attested as a preference terminologically or in practice, single-generation sibling exchange was again suggested in the ego's generation. For example, brother terms (for example, *īdub'rada* and *īno* for older and younger brothers of a male ego, respectively, in the vocative terminology) also applied to wife's sister's husband. Sister terms (for example, *īhídiba* for sisters of a male ego in the vocative terminology) also applied to wife's brother's wife. Also, brother's wife was the same term as wife's sister (for example, *īsidána* in the vocative terminology for a male ego). These equations were consistent with A'uwẽ practices of multiple marriages between sets of siblings in a single generation. In other words, a brother and a sister married a brother and a sister, or two brothers married two sisters, but rarely did any of their children marry one another.

Bifurcate Generational System

Given the characteristics described above, I classify the A'uwẽ vocative terminological configuration as bifurcate generational (Dole 1969) or the Mackenzie Basin type (Spier 1925). Due to the generational feature, this contemporary terminology cannot be classified as Iroquois (or Dakota) as proposed by Maybury-

Lewis (1967). The defining features of bifurcate generational systems are the extension of parent terms to one's parents' same-gender siblings, separate terms for one's mother's brother and father's sister, and one set of sibling terms for all one's bilateral cousins (mother's brother's child, mother's sister's child, father's brother's child, and father's sister's child). In the A'uwẽ case, this classification reflected important features of how people construed relatedness. It was not a two-section system because consanguinity was extended bilaterally in the ego's generation. Thus, marriage exchanges were not repeated in subsequent generations. Also, consanguinity had an egocentric (cognatic) aspect, and patrilineality was not reflected terminologically in all generations. One's same-generation categorical siblings were, in this sense, a kindred, being shared only by one's actual siblings (mother's child or father's child).

It is important to note that the generational logic continued into the first descending generation. Using the vocative terminology for a female or male speaker as an example, all children of real and categorical brothers were called by a single set of terms, mentioned in chapter 2, that changed in accordance with their life cycle stage (daughters: *otí* [girl], *zarudu* [female adolescent], *soimbá* [childless wife], and *pi'õ* [wife with child]; sons: *bödi* [boy], *'repudu* [male adolescent], *hö'wa* [preinitiate], and *aibö* [adult man]). All children of real and categorical sisters were called *ĩrapté*. Accentuating the generational logic in this first descending generation, all spouses in the first descending generation, regardless of the gender of the sibling connecting them to the ego, were called either *saihí* for wives or *ĩza'amo* for husbands (interestingly, *ĩza'amo* was also used for husbands of real and categorical sisters in the ego's generation). Thus, the crossness apparent in the first ascending generation was not continued in either the ego's generation or the first descending generation. For this reason, the A'uwẽ kinship terminology cannot be considered Dravidian, which requires, among other factors, a terminological logic of cross-cousin marriage (Trautmann 1981).

Relative Age

An essential aspect of the kinship terminology was the pervasive and conditional role of relative age, which corresponded with very real contrasts in how people related to one another according to their respective age identities. The generational aspect described above is one example. Also, separate terms were used for older and younger same-gender siblings (*ĩdub'rada* and *ĩno*, respectively). Additionally, as discussed below, one's mother's brother and one's father's sister might perform ceremonial roles that caused extensive terminological changes after childhood. Other examples are to be found in the substitution of age group terms for kinship terms during certain phases of life. For example, same-gender siblings in adjacent age sets tended to not call each other by sibling terms during their youth. Rather, before an age set attained mature adulthood, its members called all members of the next oldest age set, including siblings, *īhi'wa* and might be called by them *sinhõ'ra* until achieving novitiate adulthood. Similarly, the term *sinhõ'ra* was used for same-gender siblings in the next young-est age set (opposite age set moiety) while they were adolescents (*ai'repudu*) or preinitiates (*wapté*). Subsequently, these individuals often resumed use of sibling terms *īdub'rada* or *īno*. These examples illustrate the contingent nature of the kinship terminology, whereby the designations used for other people shifted through life as their multiple relationships to one another underwent transformations. As one man explained, "These things always change. You never know what's coming and all the terms can change" when, for example, people join adjacent age sets. The importance of age is also apparent in several age-specific terms that implicated simultaneously age, kinship, and friendship. For example, the term *wasirewarõ* might be used for members of the ego's secular age set who were in the ego's exogamous moiety or whom the ego considered particularly intimate friends. That term said as much about age set intimacy as about patrilineal relatedness. Similarly, *wasirewāhõno* might be used for members of the ego's secular age set who were also in the ego's exogamous moiety, socially very close to the ego, or first-degree cousins to the ego. That term also spoke to age set intimacy and close kinship, but construed relatedness bilaterally.

This brief account of the A'uwẽ kinship system touches on just a few notions of relatedness that were particularly salient for how people referred to one another respectfully and engaged in proper social dynamics that contributed to healthy relationships with others. Some of these principles were related to marriage possibilities and proscriptions, usually within the context of who were considered consanguineal kin. Formulations of consanguineal kinship, especially as it relates to fathers, real and categorical siblings, and real or categorical children, are important for understanding how people made decisions, often under challenging circumstances, in the political arena. When political strife was acute, people often could not make decisions about whom to support or how to treat one another based on the criterion of what would promote community wellness. Rather, they were limited to choosing courses of action that were perceived to advance more restricted interests. Nevertheless, they did so according to other sets of values that include multiple configurations of social

relations considered to exemplify good living. Among these were the age relations considered to be beautiful.

Genealogical Seniority in the Political Enterprise

Community Divided

In mid-2005, I began perceiving particularly strong undercurrents of political
tension at the Pimentel Barbosa community, with at least four distinct topics
of disagreement. The first three were resource sharing, leadership, and economic development. Meanwhile, although I was not aware of it at the time,
a fourth debate emerged regarding who would be the ceremonial ear piercer
(*daporezapu'u'wa*) for the group of preinitiates to be initiated into novitiate
adulthood in late 2006 (the *tirowa* age set). Established custom called for a single
piercer to be chosen from among the children of owners of the heritable prerogative master of ear piercers (*daporezapu'u'wa'tede'wa*). The decision for someone
to be piercer was made by the elder heritable prerogative holder(s). Two individuals were being promoted as candidates for the job by their respective fathers
and supporters, each claiming the right based on ancestral precedent.

Ignorant of that debate and after months of prodding by my A'uwẽ friends
and adoptive family members, I decided in July 2005 to have my ears pierced. I
was a male member of the novitiate adult age grade (*dahí'wa* or *'ritei'wa*), a status
that was inscribed on the body in a most essential manner through the piercing
of one's ears (figures 33 and 34). Pierced ears, and the practice of wearing special
wood plugs in them, signaled that one had been initiated into adulthood and
was equipped to dream songs by communicating with the ancestors (Graham
1995). Lacking pierced ears, I was a novitiate adult in name only, a status that was
occasionally ridiculed or questioned by my age set moiety rivals. The decision
to have my ears pierced involved a desire on my part to respect the wishes of my
A'uwẽ hosts and to assume more completely my status as novitiate adult. The
piercing process was simple. One Friday morning in July during the early morning men's council, I expressed my interest to be pierced. The men responded
with a loud clamor of support punctuated by laughter, a brief discussion, and the
departure of several messengers to fetch sleeping men and request the retrieval
of piercing equipment.

My impression was of broad support for the idea in a public forum. I did not
perceive any disagreement as to how my piercing would be executed. I was later
told that the preference was that I be pierced by the ceremonial piercer from

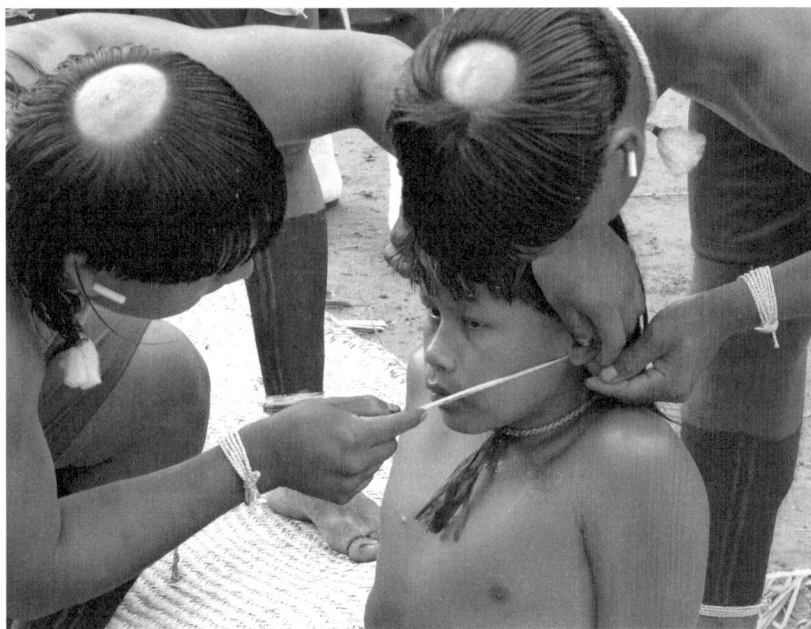

Figure 33 Boy having his ears pierced in anticipation of his passage to novitiate adulthood (*'ritei'wa*), 2011.

Figure 34 The late elder Hipru Xavante wearing traditional A'uwẽ ear plugs, 2005.

the previous age set initiation rites, when my age set (*êtẽpa*) had been pierced and initiated into adulthood. Unfortunately, that individual was traveling and therefore unavailable. It was decided that I would be pierced by one of the two contenders for the position of ceremonial ear piercer in the upcoming age set initiation rites. This young man had never pierced before, so an elder man who had been piercer many years before gave him careful instructions and oversaw the process. Sereburã stood at my back with his hands on my shoulders and cried a mourning song (*dawawa*) (see Graham 1995) while the young piercer moistened the puma (*Puma concolor*; *asada* in A'uwẽ) leg bone awl with saliva and then, for each side in turn, aligned it against my cheekbone and thrust it through my ear lobe. Temporary reed ear plugs covered in urucum (*Bixa orellana*) salve were inserted in my freshly pierced ears. With that, the event was finished, and people gradually left to go about their business for the day.

Not until January 2006, when I returned after a short absence, did I hear that the events of that morning had precipitated a grave dispute that was polarizing the community. Close kin and supporters of the candidate for the position of ear piercer who did not pierce my ears accused their opponents of subversively stealing the ceremonial ear-piercing role by having their candidate pierce my ears without consulting them. Furthermore, they accused members of the Tadpole exogamous moiety of meddling in the business of the Big Water moiety and, more specifically, of the owners of the ear-piercer heritable prerogative, by facilitating that decision and participating in the piercing event that morning in July. I was very surprised by these accusations because it seemed improbable that none of the men who supported their ear-piercing candidate was present in the morning men's council the day my ears were pierced.

Some people attributed the political tension to these events, characterizing it as originating inside the Big Water moiety, being essentially a longstanding multigenerational dispute between two families that came to a head over the issue of who from among their ranks would be ceremonial piercer. Other people characterized it as a disagreement derived from the other three sources of tension mentioned at the beginning of this section.

Between January and July of the same year, tensions escalated to the point that an effective community split took place. Initially, the decision was made to employ two ear piercers, one for each of the two interested Big Water kin groups and their allies. That decision motivated the two groups to hold separate age set initiation rites, each with its own piercer and its own contingent of ceremonial positions. Other community functions split, and the discord developed into a full factional dispute. For example, two men's council meetings were held each morning and evening, the two Indigenous health agents attended only members of their own factions in the primary healthcare unit, and members of rival factions refused to sit in automobiles together. In July, I encountered several people from the faction that would relocate in the local FUNAI office to inform the local agent that they were declaring themselves independent from the Pimentel Barbosa community, would henceforth be known as the Etênhiritipá community, and would be led by Chief Samuel Sahutuwẽ and Vice-Chief Paulo Supreteprã. That stage of the separation was, perhaps, the most intense, with rampant incidents of physical altercations between members of opposing factions, accusations of politically motivated murder and sorcery, and death threats. There was no longer social space for people to remain neutral, so household members, spouses, close kin, and intimate friends went through the painful process of deciding in which community and in what household they would reside. In late 2006, Chief Samuel's new community physically moved, relocating about a half kilometer away, where it could access shared resources, such as the community primary healthcare unit. As I write this book, many years later, circumstances have improved considerably. As recently as 2022 I learned of visits and open communication between men of the two communities and observed women visiting kin in the other community. Yet, each community goes about its business autonomously and pursues its own strategy of economic development. The households and kin groups that were ruptured by the separation have reconstituted themselves within their new social environments.

I feel a great deal of ambivalence about my role in the dispute that contributed to the community separation. I regret that the circumstances of my ear piercing provided reason for the long-held antagonisms between rival kin groups within the Big Water moiety to transform into open opposition and for the previously simmering debate about economic development to coalesce into a fully fledged community division. Even more, I lament that the ensuing events required previously united households, extended families, and age set peers to break from one another. I know I could not have anticipated these events and believe that had the choice of my ear piercer not helped precipitate the conflict, some other event or events would have done so soon thereafter. That view is maintained by all my A'uwẽ contacts on both sides of the division, who express that I was an unsuspecting pawn in political affairs beyond my control.

Patrifilial Loyalty and Sibling Solidarity

The events described above involved a totality of social phenomena. Through the experiences, opinions, decisions, and actions of the people involved, they engaged the full gamut of sociocultural beliefs and practices, with all their internal variability. Furthermore, the experience of those events was deeply individualized for those involved. Consequently, attempting to reduce them to a social model of factionalism would oversimplify the whole affair and diverge substantially from how A'uwẽ view the process. My objective in this section is not to distill from those political events a limited set of predictive or explanatory factors. Rather, in keeping with the objectives of this book, I seek to explore how age organizations contributed to social well-being. I highlight a pair of social relationships, patrifilial loyalty between fathers and children and sibling solidarity that bound patrilateral and bilateral kin of the same generation. Those two axes of fidelity promoted a highly dynamic field of social relations involving notions of genealogical seniority and unity in addition to the diverse and irreducible multitude of sociocultural factors that contributed to the social experience. I argue that those two axes were salient aspects of A'uwẽ sociality—among many others—that fundamentally bore on the political enterprise (in its best and worst moments).

In January 2006, when I first became aware of major escalation of political tensions at the Pimentel Barbosa community, the factional division that threatened to divide the community was still largely in flux. Although key proponents on each side had vocally and unambiguously established their alignments, most mature adult men reserved judgment, at least publicly. Many younger individuals avoided taking sides in deference to their parents, who had not yet aligned themselves. According to many elder individuals at that time, their eventual affiliations would be based on the issues they perceived were involved, which centered on the four sources of tension mentioned above.

By January 2006, I knew of twelve men who had openly voiced their support of one side or the other. Among those early deciders, 75 percent were members of the Big Water moiety, suggesting the dispute was at that time more divisive within than between exogamous moieties. Furthermore, 67 percent of Big Water moiety early deciders supported the faction led by a Tadpole moiety leader rather than the faction led by a member of their own moiety, indicating that there was not a tendency for people to support the community leader pertaining to their exogamous moieties. By June 2006, all but one head of household had publicly affiliated themselves with one of the two factions, although I found there to be a great deal of uncertainty remaining among younger individuals who were not heads of households. Moiety affiliation did not significantly influence political alliance, with equal proportions of members of both exogamous moieties supporting the two factions. These observations, which show that moiety distribution was balanced between and within political factions, run contrary to Maybury-Lewis's (1967) thesis that patrilineal exogamous moiety membership and factional affiliation were ideologically analogous (Welch 2022b).

By this time, I observed people were less interested in discussing the four substantive issues that had previously been important in their evaluations of the conflict. Instead, I found kin relations had become important factors in how people negotiated the political landscape and ultimately aligned themselves as the community divided.

Among the most frequently invoked theories of political solidarity that were expressed to me beginning in June 2006 was "family," construed in those contexts as close same-moiety siblings including one's real siblings and first-degree parallel cousins (*wasisinawa*) or close bilateral kin including one's close same-moiety kin and one's first-degree cross-cousins (*wasi'höiba*). For example, formal and informal leaders on both sides of the dispute frequently threatened that they had numerically and tactically strong kin in other A'uwē communities who were keeping close tabs on the political situation at the Pimentel Barbosa community and would, if necessary, come to their aid to provide reinforcement. Such references to close kin in other communities were especially evident immediately after the physical separation of the two communities, when concern was focused on administrative control of shared resources, such as the primary healthcare unit. Both sides operated under the assumption that the larger of the two communities would gain the bureaucratic upper hand in managing those facilities. By March 2007, after the physical relocation was complete, several households of close kin of factional leaders had already relocated from neighboring communities to Pimentel Barbosa and Etênhiritipá. I also heard abundant discussion of others who were on call to do the same should it be necessary to tip the population balance between them. Notions of solidarity between close same-moiety siblings (*wasisinawa*) and close bilateral kin (*wasi'höiba*) were central to how individuals, married couples, and extended family households aligned themselves politically and, ultimately, decided where to reside after the community separation.

Perhaps an even more important factor was what I call patrifilial loyalty. This term is not to be confused with Meyer Fortes's "filial piety," which implied a sentiment with reverential overtones that tended to be extended to ancestors (Fortes 1959, 18; 1961, 174). Patrifilial loyalty was the commitment of a child, usually a son, to support his father socially and politically and reside in his community, where this support was most beneficial. Patrifilial loyalty might also extend to one's categorical fathers (father's brothers) and potentially even one's mother's brother who served as ceremonial father, but under the pressures of divisive factional politics, loyalty to one's real father appeared to be paramount. In March 2007, after the two communities split, 98 percent of married males with living real fathers lived with them in the same community. In other words, virtually all sons remained politically and residentially unified with their real fathers. This statistic suggests that virtually all married females whose parents and parents-in-law chose to live in different communities opted to live with their husbands in their fathers-in-law's communities. Thus, nearly all women faced with this decision chose to live apart from their parents rather than separate from their husbands, who remained with their real fathers (or mothers chose to live apart from their daughters). Nonetheless, some young unpregnant and childless married women did exercise their prerogative to live with their parents and end their marriages with husbands who decided to live in the other community.

Another relationship that was important for how people sided in the community division was sibling solidarity. Independently from their respective loyalties to their fathers, real and categorical siblings shared close social bonds. Although sibling solidarity might be extended to all bilateral categorical siblings through the principles of bilateral consanguinity and close bilateral kinship (*wasi'höiba*), it was especially salient among close same-moiety real and classificatory siblings (*wasisinawa*). I am reminded of a conversation with my adoptive brother Denoque and our father, Valdo, in which Denoque called me his "brother" in Portuguese and Valdo corrected him, saying he should call me by the Portuguese word for "friend." Denoque objected, arguing that I was his adopted brother, not just a friend. Valdo insisted that the A'uwẽ word for brother would be correct, but the closest translation in Portuguese was friend, because A'uwẽ brothers are all close friends. Groups of real and same-moiety categorical brothers were extremely close in the usual routine of life and during the factional dispute.

During the community separation, however, sibling solidarity was strongest when there were living real or categorical fathers to bind them. Some close same-moiety siblings whose fathers were deceased aligned themselves with opposite factions in the separation. In some cases, even the most intimate of real brothers moved apart from one another and some stopped speaking to each other for several years. In these cases, the brothers aligned themselves with other close same-moiety siblings (*wasisinawa*), close bilateral kin (*wasi'höiba*), or with their spouses' allies according to their own priorities. For example, a married couple once disagreed about whether to move to another community after it separated from Pimentel Barbosa. The wife wished to move to be with her brother in the other community, while the husband wanted to remain in Pimentel Barbosa, where he had categorical brothers. Unable to agree, she moved to her brother's community on her own, and her husband remained behind for about three weeks before deciding to acquiesce to be with his wife. Subsequently, all their real children moved to the new community to be with their parents and their mother's brother. Thus, sibling solidarity was a strong social bond but might not be sufficient to withstand competing forces in factional separations unless combined with patrifilial loyalty.

According to oral histories, sets of influential brothers with no living fathers have opposed one another in past political disagreements, implicating their descendants in disunity for generations to come. An important example of such an oral history begins with Apöwẽ, a renowned leader of the population I studied from before the SPI contact era (1940s) until the 1970s. Most written accounts of Apöwẽ cast him as a strong leader who, despite having achieved power by killing his political opponents, was widely respected by his people (Flowers 1983; Graham 1995; Maybury-Lewis 1967). That view was maintained by many of his actual grandchildren and their political supporters, including the leadership of other communities, which previously split from the Pimentel Barbosa community and remained estranged. In contrast, according to influential individuals at the Pimentel Barbosa community, Apöwẽ was a despotic leader who defied the morality of collective decision making in the men's council by using authoritarian and coercive strategies, often murder, to force people to comply with his political program (cf. Dent 2020). These oral historians recalled that contrasting viewpoints were present during Apöwẽ's life, when their own ancestors, who were close same-moiety categorical siblings to Apöwẽ, disagreed with his ruthless strategies and advocated for cooperative leadership and peaceful methods of conflict resolution. These contrasting versions of the oral history suggest that a disagreement between close categorical brothers in the absence of patrifilial loyalty to a living father may sustain estrangement between their patrilineal descendants for generations.

Affinal Obeisance

Whereas patrilineal relatedness seems especially important for the A'uwẽ formulation of genealogical hierarchy (seniority) that I call patrifilial loyalty, kinship-based intergenerational ranking was also evident between parents-in-law (*damaprewa*) and their children-in-law (female: *dazani'wa*; male: *dazaõmo*). Whereas the bond of patrifilial loyalty was one of intimate solidarity, the bond that united intergenerational in-laws was characterized by distant respect (*danhisé*). Many A'uwẽ, especially elders, believed reserved deference between sons-in-law and parents-in-law an important expression of traditionalist notions of good living. According to Graham, young sons-in-law and their parents-in-law showed their mutual respect through avoidance behavior, including absolute absence of direct speech (Graham 1995).[4] She characterized it as a "muting" of the son-in-law and accounted for it as a means of minimizing the potential for conflict between an established residential family and a new coresident husband, who might have different political alliances. This traditionalist formulation of shame, respect, and separation as a beautiful form of social interaction between in-laws was similar to that described for the Xikrin subgroup of the Mebêngôkre (Gordon 2016). Although such relationships were overtly formal and distant, they also had the potential to mature into strong sociopolitical alliances.

According to my data, in addition to reciprocal avoidance behavior, this relationship manifested in a perception by both parties that the son-in-law should contribute to the sustenance of his parents-in-law (laboring in their garden, contributing game meat and fish, and purchasing food) without expectation of return. This obligation preceded marriage and continued throughout life, whether or not the son-in-law resided in the parents-in-law's house according to the pattern of uxorilocal residence. It contrasted with the typical relationship between a young man and his own parents, which entailed the liberty to consume their food without reciprocating with contributions of food, work, or money. I characterize the traditionalist social orientation of sons-in-law relative to parents-in-law as affinal obeisance to distinguish it from the more intimate and entitled character of patrifilial loyalty. Affinal obeisance afforded parents-in-law considerable influence over sons-in-law and figured importantly into many young married men's social realities.

After some years, once a new A'uwẽ couple had developed an intimate spousal relationship and given birth to several of their own children, relations between parents-in-law and sons-in-law often remained respectfully formal but more relaxed. Among contemporary A'uwẽ, many younger parents-in-law were dropping their expectations of this form of respect relationship, opting instead to engage with their sons-in-law more casually from the beginning, without avoidance behavior. They considered these forms of respectful constraints on the relationship between parents-in-law and son-in-law to be overly burdensome and unproductive. Thus, notions of what comprised a healthy affinal social relationship were undergoing substantial changes in recent years. Such changes should not be understood as loss of culture because these same individuals were strong advocates of maintaining traditional A'uwẽ social relations in other forms and contexts. Social and cultural resilience involves making innumerous choices about adjusting some viewpoints and practices to permit the conservation of others under contemporary circumstances. These decisions affect social relations, economic conditions, foodways, spiritual practices, pastimes, health, and many other dimensions of daily life that bear on well-being. The choice by some parents-in-law to relax some of the behavioral and social constrictions traditionally placed on sons-in-law was a reinterpretation of what constituted good and proper social relations, but not an indication that these sons-in-law now disrespected their parents-in-law or no longer behaved or identified as A'uwẽ.

The genealogical configurations of patrifilial loyalty and affinal obeisance, along with leadership seniority and heritable prerogative seniority, did not influence political process in a strict manner. Rather, they were a few among many age-related ideological factors that influenced how people went about the business of social interaction. Some others included the age systems discussed in this book, which together made up an intricately complex landscape of seniority and juniority, rivalry and alliance, that people engaged in personally and in contextually appropriate ways as they navigated political life. These configurations were considered traditional, and most of them enjoyed widespread popular support as essential factors in the persistence of social well-being in communities and the maintenance of A'uwẽ identity in the present era of radical sociocultural change. These divergent principles created a "particular structural positioning of differential elements" (Gordon 2016, 214) that enabled people to navigate community harmony and discord in creative ways by engaging with multiple social frameworks considered beautiful and proper.

CHAPTER 5

Age Organization in Perspective

Plurality, Agency, and Heterarchy

Theoretical Framing of Age Constructions

I begin this chapter with a discussion of key features of A'uwẽ age organization based on my ethnographic reading of informal age grades, the secular age group system, the male spiritual age group system, and other forms of seniority. I then discuss these age constructions considering previous literature focusing on culturally and linguistically related Indigenous groups in Central Brazil. My primary focus is the A'uwẽ social experience, considered broadly, as it involved social *structure, organization,* and *practice.* I consider social structures to be abstract and relatively persistent relationship formations that link people and contribute to their social statuses in society. That formulation loosely follows Lévi-Strauss (1963) and is similar to what Radcliffe-Brown (1952) called "structural form." In contrast, social organization, as I use the term here, refers to patterned relations between people that emerge from their observable interactions, which suggest individual agency and potential for change (Firth 1951). I apply the notions of social structure and organization in such a way as to anticipate that they overlap with and engage other dimensions such as social relations, behavior, roles, values, ideologies, and institutions (Lévi-Strauss 1963; Parsons 1951; Radcliffe-Brown 1940, 1952). Furthermore, I consider social structure to be inextricably linked to individual experience, and therefore to such anthropological concepts as practice, action, praxis, personhood, and transformation (Bourdieu 1977; Fuchs 2001; Giddens 1979; Harris 1989; Ortner 1984).

Recognition of those dynamic interconnections informed my research approach and is evident in how I present my data in this book. I use the social experience, considered individually and collectively, as an investigative approach to ascertain social configurations and to evaluate how people engaged and understood them under changing historical circumstances. I attempt to assess the pragmatic import of social structure and organization vis-à-vis close scrutiny of individual expression, with all its inherent inconsistencies and contradictions. How people apply, conform to, resist, and modify paradigmatic formations indicate their social meanings and demonstrate the potential that they are simultaneously encompassing and multifarious.

Ethnographically, there are many avenues for investigating social life. A'uwẽ ceremonialism beautifully captured some of the more overt and intriguing aspects of A'uwẽ culture from an external point of view. These iconic displays were profoundly aesthetic, affective, and arduous. Not only did they compellingly illustrate through body adornment and performance some of the formal structures of A'uwẽ social life, but they were also dramatic and photogenic, making them ideal ethnographic, literary, and audiovisual subjects.

For these and other good reasons, many sociocultural anthropologists have paid close attention to ceremonial expression in A'uwẽ society. Maybury-Lewis (1967) painstakingly documented A'uwẽ rituals as evidence of the society's symbolic social structures. Müller (1976, 1992) systematically cataloged ceremonial body decoration as an ethnographic window into the organization of A'uwẽ society. Lopes da Silva (1986) addressed ceremonial name transmission and formal friendship to critically analyze the nature of A'uwẽ social organization. Graham (1995, 2005, 2016) studied how A'uwẽ ritual performances involved agency, identity, and politics of representation.

In this chapter, I also discuss ceremonialism as one of many productive ethnographic windows into social structure, organization, and practice. I do so with special attention to how people related to one another in ceremonial and everyday interactions according to their own circumstances and values. I choose to examine everyday expression because it was an arena where the informality of life illustrated some of the more nuanced aspects of social life at the dynamic interface between social structure and practice. My analytic approach derives principally from my field experience with the A'uwẽ, in which I encountered the age structures and organizations that compose human life cycles to be so overt and tangible, being expressed abundantly in routine discourse and behavior, that I could not escape considering them to be relevant factors in social reality. Among the A'uwẽ, social structure and organization were explicitly evident in paradigmatic perspectives regarding proper social relations, which were understood by members of this ethnic group in not so different terms from anthropological models. Specifically, I found that A'uwẽ talked about formal age groups in abstract terms, being fully aware of their patterned or structural features (Graham 1995) and appreciating them as socially beneficial and aesthetically pleasing. They were also conscientious of social practice and its potential divergences from traditionalist notions of proper and good structures and organizations, which they expressed as concern that valued social constructions believed to promote community well-being were at risk of being lost due to changing perspectives among younger people.

In this sense, I would suggest that the A'uwẽ provide a counterexample to the argument by Seeger, DaMatta, and Viveiros de Castro (2019) that in Indigenous South America, the appearance of fluidity and flexibility in social organization can be attributed to lack of concern with social groups and, ultimately, reliance on symbolic notions of "the construction of people and the fabrication of bodies" (698). Although A'uwẽ bodily substance and the construction of personhood contributed to some group formulations, such as exogamous moieties, many examples of group participation were not merely symbolic and did not exhibit notable fluidity or flexibility. Many A'uwẽ social arrangements were highly, often complexly, formalized conceptually in ways that explained apparent exceptions in nuanced structural terms. With their cultural emphasis on perpetuating structurally rigid social relations, perhaps the A'uwẽ were an unusual example among Indigenous groups in lowland South America. For example, the A'uwẽ case was very different from the Wari' in Rondônia, Brazil, for whom "the only social groups with which individuals identified, other than their household and residential community, were [six] kin-based, named, territorial sub-groups" (Conklin 2015, 74).

In my experience, age organization was an explicit and pervasive aspect of the A'uwẽ social experience. In fact, as a "young" (by A'uwẽ social convention) male researcher in an A'uwẽ community, I sometimes felt overwhelmed by the ubiquitousness of the age distinctions people drew. I was age classified early in my first visit and was thereafter expected to adhere to associated social roles sometimes irrespective of whether they affected my ability to conduct research. For the A'uwẽ, age hierarchies were more than abstractions; they were conspicuously and often consciously involved in how people saw and interacted with each other. They were also an important part of how they welcomed and incorporated non-A'uwẽ into their society. In the remainder of this section, I draw on one of my earlier experiences participating in a spiritual

ritual (*wai'a*) to illustrate key features of A'uwẽ age organization: its plurality and contingency.

Incurring the Wrath of Spiritual Guards

In October 2004, shortly before I began my dissertation research in November, I had the opportunity to meet up with then vice-chief Paulo and his A'uwẽ travel companions in Rio de Janeiro. The occasion was a theatrical play featuring performances by this "troupe" from the Pimentel Barbosa community. One evening, sitting with Paulo and some other A'uwẽ actors at an outdoor restaurant along the beach in Copacabana, I ordered a draft beer without a second thought. No one at the table so much as raised an eyebrow, and I did not think about the episode again for about two months.

In late December, back in the community, I participated in a spiritual ritual. In the afternoon, once painted and after the spiritual singers resumed their repetitive and mesmerizing performance of their song, I stood in the middle of the arced line of perhaps forty spiritual initiates around the edge of the circular forest clearing. Like the others, my body was painted mostly red, and my feet were bare. My initiate peers had told me to take off my shoes to avoid angering our spiritual guards.

Beginning this phase of the ritual, two groups of guards, each numbering three or four individuals, stomped passed us, pounding their feet on the ground just in front of ours. These initial sets of guards made notably subdued shows of aggression toward me, stomping their feet a safe distance from mine with almost relaxed demeanors. I did not feel threatened by them. This changed, however, with the next group of five guards, whose demeanor transmitted genuine anger and hostility. These men raised large clouds of dust as they forcefully stomped passed each initiate in turn on their way down the line toward me.

The initiate beside me marveled, "Ooh, they're stepping hard on those guys' feet!" Sure enough, through the plumes of dust I could see some guards' feet landing squarely and forcefully on top of initiates' feet. He continued, "I heard the guards are angry with us today!"

Perplexed and somewhat nervous, I asked, "What did we do to deserve it?"

"I don't know. Maybe someone ate a prohibited food," he answered enigmatically.

Still unsure what transgression was being punished and therefore whether I too was in danger, but at that moment more concerned with the approaching threat than its explanation, I mimicked my A'uwẽ peers, trying to affect an unexpressive stance as I faced the approaching guards. Like them, I rested my weight on my right foot and set my left foot lightly to the side, offering it to be stepped on. I crossed my arms loosely and looked past the formidable guards as though they were not there, feigning indifference. My fears were realized when several of them stomped squarely on my foot not once, but repeatedly and painfully. They passed none too soon, leaving me shamed and with a throbbing forefoot.

The following day, during a trip to the small town of Matinha, just outside the Indigenous land, I bought a can of Coca-Cola at a roadside restaurant. Before I had a chance to put my lips to the opening, an A'uwẽ man grabbed it from my hand, slammed it in a splash on the counter, and began stomping his feet and swinging his arms at me, as the spiritual guards had done during the ritual the day before. Several non-Indigenous customers watched with wide eyes, and the other A'uwẽ men erupted in uncontrolled laughter. Several moments later, the man handed the Coke back to me, kindly put a straw in it, and sat down. Tsuptó came to my side to explain this most unnerving episode. Initiates, he explained, were prohibited from eating certain foods until they were liberated by their guards. Except for alcoholic beverages, most industrialized foods were not prohibited, including soft drinks. The man who feigned stomping on my feet used the can of Coke to pretend he was punishing me for drinking it without authorization, recalling for everyone's amusement the previous days' punishments during the spiritual ritual. "Okay, but why did the guards step on my foot during the spiritual ritual?" I asked. I had no idea when or how I might have violated a dietary prohibition. Tsuptó said he did not know because he was not my guard.

It took me several weeks to discover that my transgression was to have unwittingly consumed that beer in Copacabana in front of one of my spiritual guards, who was in the theater troupe and had observed my transgression. Word that I had consumed a prohibited food was relayed to the other guards in the community. As is appropriate in such matters, even those involving an unwitting newcomer, no one called attention to the prohibition when I ordered the beer, nor after I drank it, and yet the guards administered punishment for it during the next spiritual ritual in which I participated. Clearly, lack of knowledge of the prohibition did not excuse violating it. The experience left me with the somber impression that navigating these food prohibitions would be nearly impossible during daily life inside and outside the community, wherever I was under the gaze of people from the community. Not only was the list of prohibited foods very long and hard to keep track of, but I could never be sure if a guard or someone from the guards' spiritual age set moiety was nearby when I was eating. I feared I would constantly risk painful punishment because, in my ignorance, I could commit dietary transgressions in the wrong company.

Fortunately, that did not turn out to be the case. As I gradually worked out the contours of our guards' dietary prohibitions for my group of spiritual initiates, I found it was less oppressive than I had imagined. Technically, initiates should avoid an extensive list of prohibited foods, mostly wild game and fish, as well as eggs and alcoholic beverages, until these were liberated, one by one, for each spiritual initiate over the course of years, occasionally extending well beyond initiate status. For example, one spiritual post-officiant informed me that as a forty-seven-year-old, he was not yet authorized to eat marsh deer (*Blastocerus dichotomus*) or traira fish (*Hoplias* spp.).

In practice, however, most meals in the communities were made from purchased or nontraditional cultivated foods, which were not prohibited. Also, initiates tended to rely on the goodwill of socially proximate guards, whom they trusted would not punish them or tell other guards about their dietary transgressions. For example, the first two groups of guards in the spiritual ritual I described above, who did not stomp on my feet and made lackluster shows of aggression as they passed me in line, included one of my older adoptive brothers and one of my mentors in the secular age group system. They and the other guards who did not punish my dietary transgression were connected to me by close social relationships outside the spiritual age group system that tempered their interest in punishing me. In fact, were I to violate food restrictions in front of them, these allies might be expected to keep my secret from the other, less forgiving guards. Nevertheless, there were no strict rules that social proximity through kinship or secular mentorship should prevail over the antagonistic vigilance that characterized usual relations between guards and initiates. I found that each guard interpreted for himself the multiple social factors that bore on his relationship with a spiritual initiate. In some cases, even the closest of elder brothers did not afford their younger siblings the confidence of eating without fear of reprisal.

Creative Interpretation of Multiple Points of Reference

These options for creative interpretation of the social framework that characterized relationships between members of adjacent spiritual age sets emerged from the coexistence of multiple social points of reference. In the example above, the antagonistic relationship between guards and initiates could be softened through coexistent bonds of kinship or secular mentorship. Such intersections of plural social orientations contributed to the fabric of A'uwẽ sociality, whereby nobody was merely someone's spiritual guard, or sibling, or mentor. Everyone was connected in countless ways, creating an infinitely varied field of perceptions of social proximity and distance, alliance and opposition, that people drew on as they encountered one another in moments of ceremonial and daily life. This intertwining of equalizing and ranking social statuses was not confusing or incongruent from A'uwẽ points of view. Rather, it was aesthetically pleasing and a proper social component of how people understood their situated positions in society relative to diverse classes of people, both proximate and distant.

The notions of "our side" versus the "other side," developed here in the contexts of the secular and spiritual age set moiety systems, were just some of many dimensions of sociality that textured how people viewed and interacted with one another. Other systems of age organization were similarly ubiquitous aspects of the A'uwẽ experience, providing abundant means to unify certain groups of people as equals and segregate others as unequals. For example, exogamous moiety membership, heritable prerogative ownership, sibling solidarity, and affinal obeisance cast people in additional and unique configurations of proximity and distance. Often, the same two people would find themselves unified as equals in certain social domains while they were divided as unequals in others. A'uwẽ age hierarchies were multiple and interrelated, such that the significance of each was contingent on the totality of any given social dynamic and how the individual actors involved made sense of those relationships. Within that whole, there were no absolute or singular power relationships, as between, for example, younger and older, junior and senior, or subordinate and dominant. Nor was there any uniform equivalence between age equals. Rather, age classifications united and differentiated individuals in multiple conditional ways that influenced their modes of engagement in diverse social settings. Thus, through the simultaneous operating of multiple systems of age ranking and many other social means of evaluating social difference and sameness, social action considered beautiful and good took place. The very plurality of A'uwẽ social organizations linked them to notions of well-being because it created a landscape of human relations contingent on the mutual constitution of inequality and parity. Thus, community wellness depended on people attending to their multiple social statuses, whereby different relations or settings might call for contrasting social attitudes, such as conviviality, modesty, or bravado. These dynamics shaped how people interacted properly with one another during ceremonial activities, at home, while socializing in the plaza, and in the cerrado.

The multiplex hierarchical and oppositional relationships that variously united and separated individuals within A'uwẽ society point to a pervasive feature of sociality—no single fixed point of reference for constructing inclusive and exclusive identity categories. Every outsider was simultaneously an insider. Every equal was also a senior or a junior. Status was not absolute or fixed. It was contingent, transitory, and circumstantial. It was not, though, particularly "fluid" because it was based in highly structured and nuanced social constructions that people navigated in their interpersonal interactions. The A'uwẽ reality was that identity was multiple, that each formulation of identity had its place and time to engage, and that individuals of all ages had the autonomy to construe those formulations as they saw fit.

The congruence of hierarchy and equality as a social theory (Schryer 2001) has made inroads into the social sciences under the label of heterarchy, which is understood in this context to be the multiplicity, heterogeneity, and simultaneity of mixed systems of equality and ranking (Bondarenko 2007; Crumley 2015). In anthropology, heterarchy has proved a useful concept for making sense of the diverse social relations that exist in complex societies (Crumley 1995, 2005; Stark 2001). In the A'uwẽ case, it is also a useful concept because it highlights that plurality of social identity and difference was an intrinsic feature of social structure that was internally congruent and, as such, allowed for highly individualized modes of engaging with other people.

Mutual Constitution of Difference and Similarity

Among the early explanations offered for age set systems throughout humanity was that they facilitated militaristic organization. Some scholars argued that they served as alternate forms of political integration in societies that lacked centralized authority, while others proposed that they provided a standard mode of military recruitment between otherwise unrelated societies (Bernardi 1952; Eisenstadt 1954; Hanson 1988; LeVine and Sangree 1962). Common to each of these proposals was the idea that age sets had a sociopolitically integrative function. They tended to differ regarding the nature of this integrative role. Shmuel Noah Eisenstadt (1954) and Bernardo Bernardi (1952) suggested that age sets organized people vertically through authority, while Robert A. LeVine and Walter H. Sangree (1962) proposed that they organized people horizontally through recruitment. The nature of this association was further specified by a global cross-cultural examination of age set organization. Madeline Lattman Ritter (1980, 102) concluded that "age-set systems serve to integrate societies which are politically uncentralized, lack territorially based descent groups, and engage in frequent warfare. The results are consistent with the interpretation offered here that age-set systems are adaptive in societies where warfare is frequent or a constant threat and where composition of the local group fluctuates, necessitating a society-wide, or major societal division-wide, integrative mechanism." The author illustrated her findings ethnographically with a description of A'uwẽ age group organization, kinship, and history based on Maybury-Lewis (1967) and personal communication with Nancy M. Flowers.

Those functionalist explanations of the occurrence of age sets across cultures illustrate the complex nature of the relationship between social similarity and difference in age organization. Central to the debate featuring these contrasting explanations was the question of whether age sets integrated otherwise fragmented societies vertically through authority or horizontally through a logic of unity between members of autonomous groups. In other words, did age sets operate analogously to political or descent-based hierarchy or through social relations that cross-cut other distinctions to create allies. Based on my reading of A'uwẽ age group organization, I suggest that it did both by joining diverse members of society through age set and age set moiety solidarity while binding others in adversarial ranked relationships through age set moiety opposition. This interpretation leads to the conclusion that the enduring question of how age sets integrate society is based on a false dichotomy.[1]

Another example of the complexity of the nexus of similarity and difference in age organization can be found in how diverse informal and formal A'uwẽ age constructions created a dynamic field of social relationships with important implications for A'uwẽ social identity. As Richard Jenkins (2004) argued, social identity involves both individual and group factors. Those two aspects, however, are not always easily differentiated because both are constructed and engaged through the human social experience. In the context of A'uwẽ age organization, individual identity was not only idiosyncratic, but also informed by a complex intersection of shared social identities, including pertaining to transitory and enduring age-based social organizations, which helped formulate the social field for a given person at a specific time. Thus, A'uwẽ cultural emphasis on group identity in such forms as age sets, age grades, age set subgroups, and age set moieties in aggregate contributed to highly individualized social identities.

The preceding two examples illustrate that A'uwẽ age organization was simultaneously ranking/differentiating and equalizing/unifying. A'uwẽ age formulations might also involve both asymmetrical and symmetrical dimensions, as in the case of age sets organized into age grades and age set moieties. Furthermore, the quality of the asymmetries involved might vary, as in the contrasting examples of rivalry between adjacent age sets and solidarity between alternate age sets, or avoidance behavior between parents-in-law and sons-in-law and intimate joking relationships between siblings-in-law in adjacent secular age sets. The complexities of such mutually constituted pairs as group and individual identity or social similarity and difference were compounded by other dimensions distinct from age in principle, such as gender and exogamous moiety membership. Thus, the multiplex nature of A'uwẽ social organization generated intricate and personalized social landscapes that united and differentiated people in diverse ways between contexts and through time.

I propose that this plurality of similarity and difference was a pervasive aspect of A'uwẽ sociality not by coincidence but because people tended to view similarity and difference as integral parts of the same phenomena, according to a general philosophy that their interdependence was a beautiful configuration most conducive for promoting social well-being. The same might be said of other related sets of principles, including equality and hierarchy, symmetry and asymmetry, inclusion and exclusion, and individuality and collectivity. In each case, A'uwẽ culture deemphasized the apparent antithesis of the pair in favor of a formulation that prioritized their mutuality. I derive this conclusion in part from the observation that the A'uwẽ social experience involved abundant interpersonal arrangements that implicated both similarity and difference in congruent fashion. I also derive it from my experience of A'uwẽ social interaction, which I found presumed and accommodated the multiplicity of social configurations between individuals, a point that I address in greater detail in the final subsection of this chapter. This proposal echoes other scholars' characterizations of A'uwẽ social dualism as congruent with or presupposing asymmetrical structures (e.g., Seeger 1989), but goes further to suggest that each is predicated on the other according to a pervasive social logic of the plurality and simultaneity of similarity and difference.

Unequal age relationships were accompanied by expectations of behavioral conformity and a simultaneous morality of individualism. It was also the case that age status equality concurrently emphasized group and individual identity. Other scholars have emphasized that the earlier phases of age set membership involved a social milieu that prioritized collectivity and conformity among age set peers (Graham 1995; Maybury-Lewis 1967). I suggest in chapter 3 that this morality of collectivity involved a meticulous display of adherence to aesthetic conventions of their status while simultaneously promoting a strong philosophy of individuality. For example, the aesthetics of novitiate adult male song performance not only showcased the collective voice of an age set and its allies but also highlighted the individual voice of each song's public dreamer/leader, who received enduring accolades from spectators who thought his song and performance were exceptional. My reading of social emphasis on the individuality of song dreamers/leaders differs somewhat from Graham's (1995) account, according to which the collectivity of group performance overshadowed the individual aspect, suggesting the possibility of historical change.

In A'uwẽ society, people asserted direct vertical authority in limited circumstances. For example, elderly women often used brooms to scatter playing children from the middle of ritual performances. I observed spiritual guards (*dama'ai'a'wa*) use moderate physical force to effect behavioral compliance by spiritual initiates (*wai'ãra*), including moving them away from fires on cold nights and interrupting horseplay during spiritual rituals. Also, those same guards stomped on the feet of initiates who had eaten prohibited foods (although the initiates voluntarily offered their feet to be stepped on) and enforced initiand participation in initiation rites. Similarly, members of the novitiate adult age grade (*dahí'wa* or *'ritei'wa*) were expected to remain vigilant of their immediate juniors in the preinitiate age grade (*wapté*) and punish serious behavioral transgressions by dishonorably piercing their ears. Except for the first example, however, all those scenarios involved a special antagonistic social relationship between adjacent age sets in opposite age set moieties.

Despite those counterexamples, the A'uwẽ formulation of age hierarchy tended to entail individualism while it emphasized conformity. In asymmetrical age relationships, junior status did not preclude individual autonomy, as expressed through personal decision making or noncompliance with the wishes of seniors. In symmetrical age relationships, emphasis on collectivity and similarity between peers did not preclude concurrent attention being given to the positive individualistic values of being known and gaining prestige as an individual. More succinctly, unequal age status did not usually imply direct control, and equal age status did not usually imply a subordination of individuality.

The simultaneity of similarity and difference was also apparent in certain structural arrangements that cast people as both equal and ranked members of a single age category. In mentioning this aspect, I draw attention to the logic of age hierarchy whereby ranks were subdivided into subranks. Among the A'uwẽ, that logic of rank implied that members of single age categories were simultaneously equals in relation to external points of reference and unequals in relation to one another. Several examples pertaining to the informal and formal age grade systems, the age set system, and genealogical hierarchy illustrate this point.

The informal female age grade wife with child (*ĩ'rarē*) entailed the greater portion of the female's life cycle, from the birth of her first child through late life or death. All married women who had at least one child were considered to have achieved maturity within the informal age grade system and thus had equal status as wives and mothers in their respective nuclear families. Yet, several other aspects of age status further qualified mature womanhood. For example, within the informal female age grade system, elder status differentiated mature women according to whether they had reached menopause. As compared to premenopausal mature women, elders were generally thought to have greater knowledge, wisdom, and respectability. As grandmothers (real and categorical) they commanded the adoration of often large numbers of younger people and thus may have had considerable range of social influence within and beyond their community of residence. Thus, in the case of mature womanhood and elder womanhood, the interaction of two informal age statuses simultaneously identified individuals as similar and different. Also, aspects of the formal age group system might differentiate between otherwise equal members of the mature womanhood. For example, females who were mature women in the informal age grade system might be either novitiate adults (*dahí'wa* or *'ritei'wa*) or mature adults (*iprédu*) in the formal secular age grade system as well as belonging to one of many age sets, all of which carried their own social correlates.

In A'uwẽ discourse, male members of the formal mature adult age grade (*iprédu*) were said to share the right and responsibility to attend the twice daily men's council (*warã*). Doing so was considered a defining aspect of that status. Nevertheless, what it meant to participate varied according to men's relative age statuses. I found that the *warã* seating arrangement reflected age in such a manner as to accentuate elders in the center and marginalize younger men at the periphery. Graham (1995) described the men's council seating arrangement as deriving from the progressive and fixed placement of new members between opposite exogamous moiety members of the next senior age set. As older members died or left the community, gaps and inconsistencies accumulated. As new members were introduced, order was reestablished. It was my observation that most men occupied positions around the council circle that roughly corresponded with the positions of their houses in the community, such that residential neighbors tended to sit near one another. Although some elder men chose to sit next to their opposite-moiety formal friends (*da'amo*), my consultants said that they did not otherwise currently follow any prescribed seating order. This difference between Graham's and my findings appears to be the result of chronological change between the 1980s and 2000s.

As discussed in chapter 3, the spiritual age system similarly involved age categories that were internally distinguished by yet other age categories. For example, each of the younger two spiritual age grades, initiates (*waiãra*) and guards (*damaʼaiʼaʼwa*), were subdivided into junior (*aʼutéʼrene*) and senior (*ipredumrini*) designations that implied differentiated ceremonial roles. The weighty responsibility of carrying sacred cane arrows (*tiʼipê*) belonged only to senior initiates (*waiãra ipredumrini*), who were considered disciplined and resistant enough to do so without risk of failure.

Internal age-based hierarchies among males of a single age set were established while they were preinitiates (*wapté*) and lived in the preinitiate house (*hö*). In the two examples of age set hierarchy in chapter 4, the first ranked them according to the order they were inducted into the preinitiate house, which occurred in a series of three to six staggered groups according to parents' perceptions of their sons' social ages. Induction order not only differentiated them in terms of relative maturity and seniority, but also served as a criterion for selecting age set leaders, an additional ranked category with leadership and ceremonial prerogatives.

The preceding examples of holarchical relationships between rank and sub-rank illustrate that age categories were simultaneously homogeneous and heterogeneous. Considering the additional aspect of age structure multiplicity, the totality of age identity among the Aʼuwẽ might be seen as plurally uniform and dissimilar. Another way of framing that plurality and thereby also the concurrence of similarity and difference in the Aʼuwẽ experience is through the diversity of ways in which individuals progressively came to be included and excluded from assorted configurations throughout the life cycle. Age status transitions were accompanied by transformations in one's social affiliations. In the male and female life cycles, individuals passed through multiple statuses that temporarily associated them with certain groups of people and disassociated them from others. Examples of such transitions during a man's life included temporarily leaving his parents' household to take up residence with his new age set in the preadolescent house, as well as leaving his parents' household once again to join his wife in her household and gradually creating a nuclear family of their own. Important shifts during a woman's life typically included receiving her husband in her parent's household and establishing a nuclear family with him, belonging to a household in which her husband's influence came to replace her father's, and then in one in which her sons-in-law's political associations became dominant. Those limited examples illustrate how each stage of life was accompanied by a different set of social associations. A similar process occurred as peoples' nonresidential associations shifted during the life cycle. In some cases, joining one association implied leaving others, either permanently or temporarily. In this sense, unity may be understood to have derived from separation and vice versa. For example, joining the ranks of initiated adults implied leaving the category of uninitiated adults. On the other hand, joining some associations did not imply disassociating from others. For example, men often left their natal households when they married, but in my experience, this did not imply that their social connection to their natal households diminished. Rather, they became active members in two households instead of one. Thus, one's progressive passage between age statuses during a lifetime might be viewed as a process of identity transformation and multiplication.

A fundamental aspect of the two A'uwẽ age group systems was that their dual symmetrical features (moieties) were inseparable from their hierarchical features (age grades and age sets). That is because both the secular and spiritual age set moieties were generated through the passage of age sets through age grades. In this context, symmetrical moieties and ranked age sets existed through and defined one another. It is my assertion that their mutual constitution engaged A'uwẽ formulations of similarity and difference (also symmetry/asymmetry, equality/inequality, and inclusion/exclusion) as congruent, simultaneous, beautiful, and conducive to the production of good social relations.

The multiplicity of age and dual organizations contributed to a pervasive logic of heterarchy and contingency in social identity, which I argue was close to A'uwẽ perspectives of what were good and beautiful social relations. Hierarchical and dualistic (moiety) age structures were created through one another and were experienced as simultaneous and coherent. In the next section, I explore A'uwẽ life cycles and age organization considering previous literature about linguistically and culturally related Indigenous peoples in Central Brazil.

Gê Ethnological Frameworks

Emergence of a Field of Study

The current formulation of the Gê linguistic family was proposed by Čestmír Loukotka (1935), who distinguished it from the previous and more ample grouping by the same name first proposed by Karl Friedrich Philipp von Martius

(1867) and also known as Tapuya (Brinton 1901; Rivet 1924; Wright 1996). Based on a brief vocabulary comparison, Alden J. Mason (1950) formalized that distinction, renaming the larger and more inclusive grouping Macro-Gê and adjusting the member languages at both levels. In this book, I follow the version summarized by Aryon Dall'Igna Rodrigues (2012), according to which the Gê linguistic family comprises a northern group (Timbira, Mebêngôkre or Kayapó, Panará or Krenakore, and Kisêdjê or Suyá), a central group (A'uwẽ or Xavante, Akwẽ or Xerente, Akroá-Gamella, and Xakriabá), and a southern group (Kaingáng and Laklanõ or Xokleng). According to Julio C. Melatti (2009), the Timbira within the northern group are divided into an eastern subgroup (Parkatejê Gavião, Pykopjê Gavião, Krĩkati, Ramkokamekrá Canela, Apanyekrá Canela, and Krahô) and a western subgroup (Apinayé).

Curt Nimuendajú and Robert H. Lowie suggested that Gê-speaking and other Central Brazilian groups displayed a solid core of derived cultural similarities, thereby defining them as a coherent unit of anthropological study (Lowie 1941; Nimuendajú and Lowie 1937). Among the cultural features identified by those scholars as characteristic of Gê-speaking groups were circular communities, log racing, exogamous moieties, uxorilocal residence, and formal name-giving systems. Nimuendajú and Lowie did not identify age organization as characteristic of Gê groups, but it was a prominent topic in their discussions of specific Gê-speaking groups. Later, Lévi-Strauss (1963) asserted that these groups constituted a single sociocultural complex and that their differences were variations on underlying shared structures. Although the specific Indigenous peoples included in this culture group and the names given to it varied by author (Galvão 1960; Lowie 1946a; Maybury-Lewis 1979b; Murdock 1974), very early on it became a basic unit of analysis in various areas of scholarship. The integrity and distinctiveness of that unit became a primary assumption of Gê and Central Brazilian anthropology and remains a paradigmatic principle in the field.

Reconciling this assumption with ethnographic data has long been a major focus of Gê studies. It is an agenda that crosses theoretical boundaries because it is based on the seemingly uncomplicated presumption that these groups share history and hence ought to exhibit common cultural solutions to similar problems. Cultural materialists found this agenda appealing because the Central Brazilian cerrado landscape was thought to present these groups with cognate ecological challenges that they would have presumably solved in similar ways (e.g., Gross 1979). It was an equally attractive agenda for structuralists, because as divergent as these cultural systems seemed, their differences could easily be imagined as transformations of one another that revolved around universal themes, prominently structural dualism (Lévi-Strauss 1963; Maybury-Lewis 1979b). Structural functionalists also found it to be a compelling agenda because the diverse Gê societies seemed to share similar forms of internal integration. For example, the diversely elaborate Gê social organization seemed to consistently create crosscutting social allegiances that minimized the likelihood that one or another would result in societal cleavages (J. C. Crocker 1979).

One of the earliest concerns of Gê and Central Brazilian studies was the apparent contradiction between these societies' comparatively simple material technology and unexpectedly complex social organization, which challenged previous characterizations of them as "marginal" hunters and gatherers (for example, Carneiro da Cunha 1993; Cooper 1942a, 1942b; Lévi-Strauss 1963; Lowie 1946b, 1946a; Maybury-Lewis 1979d; Schmidt 1942). Initial attempts to reconcile this apparent paradox did not gain widespread or lasting support (Lowie 1941; Nimuendajú and Lowie 1937; Lévi-Strauss 1944; Lowie 1941; Maybury-Lewis 1979e), but the subject remained of interest and led to new investigative approaches to address the relationship between Central Brazilian societies and the physical landscape (Bamberger 1967; Coimbra Jr. et al. 2002; Fisher 2000; Flowers 1983, 1994b; Gross et al. 1979; Posey 1985; Santos et al. 1997). Terence Turner (1979, 1984) responded specifically to the question of complex social organization in combination with predominantly hunter-gatherer subsistence regimes in a manner that prominently featured age relations. He proposed a Marxist structural model, whereby Central Brazilian modes of production and forms of sociocultural organization institutionalized and reinforced social control of youths by elders and of women by men. Turner's model was important especially because it proposed a link between symbolic and materialistic interpretations of Gê and Central Brazilian societies.

Lévi-Strauss strongly affected the course of Gê and Central Brazilian studies by reformulating the relationship between these groups as originally presented by Nimuendajú and Lowie (Lowie 1941; Nimuendajú and Lowie 1937). He proposed that they composed a single sociocultural complex and that the differences observed among them could be attributed to variations on or elaborations of a single, shared underlying structure (Lévi-Strauss 1963). His proposal established new possibilities for the integrated analysis of Central Brazilian sociocultural systems, including the prevalence of age organization, without reference to material dimensions.

Lévi-Strauss's ongoing scholarship (e.g., 1943, 1944, 1963) continued to feature Central Brazilian examples, especially the Nambiquara and Bororo. Ethnographic data from these groups factored importantly in his initial and subsequent formulations of structuralism. More specifically, they contributed to his innovative ideas regarding dual organization that continued to factor importantly into anthropological thought regarding Indigenous lowland South America (Coelho de Souza and Fausto 2004; Viveiros de Castro 1998b). Lévi-Strauss's (1943, 1969) initial formulations of dual organization in Central Brazil were framed in terms of unilineal exogamous moieties linked through marital exchange. Although that idea was recovered later, when Vanessa R. Lea (1992, 1993, 1995a, 1995b) argued that Mebêngôkre (Kayapó) residential units ("Houses") were matrilineal corporate groups that exchanged patrimony in the form of personal names, closer examination of Central Brazilian ethnographic examples with multiple moiety structures but without clear rules of unilineal descent or marriage exchange later caused Lévi-Strauss (1963) to reassess the nature of dual organization. Specifically, he suggested that the apparent binary structures that separated societies into opposing halves masked more fundamental tertiary or concentric structures that entailed unequal relations between those groups with reference to an external point. These ideas and others of Lévi-Strauss regarding the structural analysis of social organization, kinship, and mythology became primary references for an ample body of scholarship regarding Gê and Central Brazilian sociosymbolic organization (Dudley and Welch 2006). They also continued to strongly influence anthropological representations of A'uwẽ social organization.

The Search for an Underlying Model of Gê Social Structure

David Maybury-Lewis, the first anthropologist to work with the A'uwẽ and the author of the seminal ethnography of A'uwẽ society (1967) was unmistakably influenced by Lévi-Strauss's structural model and his proposals regarding dualism. Nevertheless, they also motivated him to dispute the legitimacy of established structural theory and its strict applicability to Gê social organization (Maybury-Lewis 1960, 1970a, 1970b; Sztutman 2002). In contrast to Lévi-Strauss's globalizing approach, Maybury-Lewis sought to understand social organization within comparatively limited social and geographic dimensions, which in this case were the A'uwẽ and other Gê societies of Central Brazil. He rejected the ethnographic veracity of Lévi-Strauss's proposition that dual organization was fundamentally tertiary, arguing instead that dualism was an ideological strategy for seeking social harmony that manifested itself through different social orders, such as kinship, politics, and cosmology (Maybury-Lewis 1967, 1979e; Seeger 1989). He also proposed a relatively modest comparative model of Gê social organization, whereby the presence of strong political factionalism in some but not other groups derived from a particular combination of cultural features: men's houses, patrilineality, and uxorilocality.

Through the Harvard Central Brazil Project, a collaboration with the Museu Nacional in Rio de Janeiro, Maybury-Lewis (1979c) stimulated many other scholars to conduct research about Central Brazilian social organization. Although those scholars shared no single theoretical framework, they were united in continuing to engage Lévi-Strauss's ideas to specify the nature and meaning of dual organization among Central Brazilian societies. Lévi-Strauss's models enabled scholars to imagine how the many sociocultural commonalities observed among Gê and other Central Brazilian societies might be transformations of one another revolving around universal themes, especially dualistic principles (Lévi-Strauss 1963; Maybury-Lewis 1979b). Considerable scholarly attention came to be dedicated to the objective of identifying the underlying dual structures that united all Gê and Central Brazilian societies. Yet, reconciling Lévi-Strauss's proposal of cultural unity with new ethnographic data regarding Gê and Central Brazilian groups proved to be challenging, as many of the early observations regarding social organization were revised, and considerable heterogeneity was encountered (Viveiros de Castro 1988, 1996).

A most striking pattern is that the call for a unified Gê theoretical model resulted in exactly the opposite—a diversity of proposed solutions and little consensus regarding their validity or applicability. Much of Gê scholarship was characterized by theoretical cleavage and multiplication. Although several models gained wider followings than others and continue to influence the field, none has produced the scholarly consensus that the problem seemed to require. Lévi-Strauss's (1969) alliance theory, Maybury-Lewis's (1979e) dialectical approach to dualism, and Turner's (1979) formulation of structural Marxism gained some traction in the field at one time or another.

Some scholars sought to explain dualistic configurations through primary ideological structures or models at other levels of cognition or sociality. For example, Roberto DaMatta (1973, 1979, 1983) argued that the Apinayé social universe was divided between two paradigms, one based on procreative relations (substance) and one based on ceremonial relations (status), that resulted in the sociosymbolic separation of family from ceremonial associations, private from public domains, and community periphery (houses) from community center (plaza). Manuela Carneiro da Cunha (1978, 1981) argued that among the Krahô, the opposition between the living and the dead was the "maximal alterity" and the ideological basis of other oppositions between the self and affines, enemies, and ceremonial counterparts.

Other scholars similarly sought to encounter fundamental dual structures but did so according to the functionalist logic that certain dual organizations, ideologies, or processes contributed to the maintenance of social continuity over time. For example, Jean Carter Lave (1967, 1977, 1979) argued that Krĩkati dual organizations operated in conjunction with name transmission and age sets to create a symbolic basis for the continuity of social identity through time. Melatti (1970, 1978) focused on the multiplicity of Krahô ideological dualisms as mutually negating such that they produced a highly contingent social experience. Joan Bamberger (1974) identified Mebêngôkre name transmission between pairs of opposite-sex siblings as the basis of intergenerational solidarity and access to prestige. J. Christopher Crocker (1979) argued that among the Bororo, numerous asymmetrical dualities counterbalanced one another for the sake of overall social solidarity. Lux B. Vidal (1976, 1977, 1981) proposed that Mebêngôkre age grades were an important structuring principle of social life that shared a historical and functional relationship to social moiety systems.

Some of the themes introduced by the scholars mentioned above may be detected in later scholarship that sought to understand Central Brazilian societies in terms of not only structure but also more recent anthropological concepts regarding personhood, corporality, and agency. For example, Seeger (1981, 1987) focused on how a Kisêdjê ideological opposition between society and nature underlay other levels of perception, such as the ideological opposition between community center and periphery, and was worked out through concepts of personhood and corporality as well as through song. Turner (1980, 1995) also directed his attention to corporality, exploring the Mebêngôkre body as a site of cultural production and social action. Lopes da Silva (1989) argued that name transmission among the A'uwẽ contributed to the symbolic and social construction of personhood and facilitated intergenerational social continuity in an otherwise socially fragmented society. Graham (1995, 2005) initially focused on A'uwẽ song and speech performances as expressive practices by which individuals at different stages of life constructed cultural, social, and spiritual realities beyond their immediate social environment. William H. Fisher (2000, 2001, 2003) approached Mebêngôkre social structure as a heterogeneous framework that contributed to how gendered and feeling actors went about social life. These innovative approaches share an important aspect that deserves special attention because it informs my work. They all demonstrated in Gê contexts the ethnographic importance of the individual as an actor and subject within social contexts.

Marcela Coelho de Souza (2001, 2002, 2004) discussed notions of relatedness among Timbira and other Gê groups, arguing that they elucidate a fundamental similarity between the highly structured and dualistic forms of social organization found in Central Brazil and the ostensibly very different forms found in other South American societies. Similarly, Elizabeth Ewart (2003, 2005) argued that Panará dual organization conformed to Lévi-Strauss's reformulation of concentric dualism and Viveiros de Castro's (2002) notion of "ontological predation" such that dual organization is not oppositional but transformational with reference to external "enemy-others." Gordon (2006) also drew on Viveiros de Castro's notion of ontological predation to assist his interpretation of contemporary formulations of Mebêngôkre consumerism. These examples attest an interesting turn of scholarly events. In the first instance, one Lévi-Straussian model stimulated scholars to treat Gê and Central Brazilian societies as members of a distinct and congruent cultural unit. In the second, another model inspired by Lévi-Strauss encouraged scholars to refute that distinctiveness and argue instead that those groups were fundamentally aligned with lowland South American cultural universalities.

The wider field of scholarship about Indigenous peoples in lowland South America further suggests the merits of considering alternative investigative directions in the study of Gê peoples. Several conceptual frameworks advanced as potentially universal among Indigenous peoples throughout lowland South America have made precious few inroads into scholarship regarding Gê groups. Examples include Seeger, DaMatta, and Viveiros de Castro's conceptualization of personhood and corporality (2019), Viveiros de Castro's models of Amerindian perspectivism and potential affinity (1995, 1998a), Fausto's commensality (2002), and Costa and Fausto's master/owner relational schema (2019). Of particular interest is scholarship asserting that experiences of emotion (e.g., friendship, anger, fear) represent a robust ethnological tool for understanding Indigenous Amazonian social realities (Overing and Passes 2000b; Overing 1999; Santos-Granero 2007). According to this approach, traditional anthropological formulations of kinship and social structure take a back seat to the everyday aesthetics of sociality and emotion. Although such approaches make uncommon appearances in Gê and Central Brazilian scholarship (e.g., Fisher 2003), their relevance has been noted (Santos-Granero 2007). These approaches and my own share the important features of examining the contours and heterogeneity of sociality through the lens of everyday experience and their relationships to notions of well-being, although I also found kinship and social structure to be productive topics of inquiry among the A'uwẽ.

Amid these very complex academic traditions, I purposefully contribute this study of A'uwẽ age organization and community wellness without an a priori theoretical orientation. I do not seek from the outset to subordinate the A'uwẽ to theoretical models based on other ethnic groups or to propose a unified model of Gê or Amerindian social organization because I believe the A'uwẽ were sufficiently different from other Indigenous groups as to make such projects potentially reductive and distortive. Instead, I draw on previous scholarship in ways I believe reinforce or complement A'uwẽ framings of their culture, as I encountered them during my fieldwork.

In the preceding chapters I employ the notion of social experience in counterpoint with social structure. This approach shares certain assumptions with structure and agency theory (e.g., Bourdieu 1977; Giddens 1986) in that it supposes that structure, considered abstractly, gains meaning individually and interpersonally through everyday social interaction. My access to everyday social experience was greatly influenced by my insertion into A'uwẽ social life. Just as A'uwẽ sociality differs for distinct individuals, my exposure to it was different than it might be for others who might assume different social statuses than I did. For example, my presentation of A'uwẽ social life is predicated on my exposure to it as a male researcher who was a member of the Tadpole (*porezaõno*) exogamous moiety, the *êtẽpa* secular age set, and the secular age set moiety associated with the left side of the community. I was also initially classified as a member of the novitiate adult age grade and a spiritual initiate. My full involvement with young secular and spiritual age sets allowed me to perceive, through personal social engagement, nuanced aspects of the secular age group system and spiritual hierarchy that characterized early life (young adulthood). At the same time, those conditions excluded me from other social circles and undoubtedly prevented me from perceiving and therefore addressing in a comparatively precise manner certain other aspects of A'uwẽ age organization. My social status as young and male may have diminished my ability to analyze critically certain aspects of late life and the female experience. Yet, over the years I have benefited from participating in two formal secular age grades (*dahí'wa* or *'ritei'wa* and *iprédu*) and two spiritual age grades (*wai'ãra* and *damaʾaiʾaʾwa*), including the rites of passage between them. I have also come to know preinitiation as a mentor to a group of boys from their inauguration as an age set through their passage into mature adulthood. Such relationships and roles caused me to engage the community from a nexus of social positions that demanded near constant participation in secular age set activities and male spiritual obligations, among other age-related dynamics, that other researchers might not have experienced in the same manner at the same time and place. Those circumstances caused my data to be more empirically robust in certain respects and less so in others. They also may help explain some of the divergences between my account of A'uwẽ social reality and those of other scholars. Accordingly, in this chapter, I seek to remain mindful of my relationship to the data, offering my findings and conclusions not as a whole or single truth, but as a distinctive slice of A'uwẽ social experience at a particular time and place, according to my firsthand examination of it.

Congruence of Dualism and Age Organization

If any common theme can be isolated from the divergent propositions in the literature for principal underlying Gê social structures, it may be that dual social or ideological structures were of particular importance. In fact, within the field of Gê studies, dualism became something of an object of scholarly obsession. Accordingly, a predominant objective of Gê scholarship has been to propose that one or another single fundamental dual structure could explain a particular Gê ethnic group's (or all Gê groups') social organization, ideology, or cosmology. Such dualistic models came in various forms, some reciprocal (e.g., Lea 1992; Lévi-Strauss 1944), some ranked (e.g., Bamberger 1974; Lave 1975; Turner 1984), and some tripartite (e.g., Carneiro da Cunha 1981; DaMatta 1983; Ewart 2003). Commonly, in an attempt to attribute complex social dynamics to singular dualistic root components, age organization was relegated, implicitly or explicitly, to secondary status. Thus, my emphasis on age organization contrasts sharply with prevalent themes in Gê scholarship. This emphasis is not arbitrary. A'uwẽ sociocultural reality, as I encountered it in the Pimentel Barbosa and Etênhiritipá communities, involved a striking number of age-based social configurations that contributed pervasively to the social experience. The same may correctly be said of dual structures, although that point was already well established in the literature. My ethnographic data suggest that the near exclusive attention paid to dual structures that predominates in Gê literature at the expense of age relations is not justified for the A'uwẽ case. As I argue throughout this chapter, dual structures were no more salient in the A'uwẽ experience than age structures.

Maybury-Lewis wrote that the "most immediately striking feature of Gê societies is their proliferation of moiety systems" (1967, 296). Contrary to his perception, my field experience among the A'uwẽ led me to conclude that age structures were at least as proliferous, if not more so, than moiety systems. My initial perception derived from the seemingly constant attention given by A'uwẽ individuals to age in our daily interactions as well as the sheer number of age structures that exist in A'uwẽ society. Nevertheless, I am little interested in assessing the relative importance of dual organization and age organization, because I do not believe one necessarily should be considered more important than the other.

If it is allowed that some but not all societies are fundamentally dualistic, A'uwẽ society certainly qualified as such (cf. Maybury-Lewis 1967). That said, it was also many other things, none of which was necessarily less important or less diagnostic than dualism. For example, it is ethnographically unwarranted to relegate age to secondary status in the A'uwẽ case. In fact, as I argue below, my data suggest that age organization was a defining feature of A'uwẽ social identity. That conclusion derives in part from the evidence discussed in this book of the pervasiveness and prolificacy of age organization in the social experience. It also derives from the circumstances of my field experience.

Despite many scholars emphasizing the importance of dual structures, several previous representations of A'uwẽ society clearly indicate that attention to A'uwẽ age organization is warranted. Although age may have received less attention in prior ethnographic representations of A'uwẽ society, it still factored prominently in some texts, including those written by ethnographers who assumed very different social statuses in their field communities and chose to focus on distinct aspects of A'uwẽ society than I. For example, researchers who focused on such diverse aspects as social structure (Maybury-Lewis 1967), ritual discourse (Graham 1995), body ornamentation (Müller 1992), and subsistence practices (Flowers 1983) also found age to be a conspicuous aspect of A'uwẽ sociality.

I do not rule out the possibility that my finding of age organization as a prominent cultural feature could derive in whole or in part from recent culture change. Nonetheless, A'uwẽ elders' oral accounts of their youth and critical assessment of earlier ethnographic accounts support the interpretation that the age organizations discussed in chapter 3 were present before sustained relations were initiated with the Brazilian government in the 1940s. Inconsistencies in some scholars' treatments of A'uwẽ age grades suggest that they may not have attended to the distinction between informal and formal systems (e.g., Graham 1995; Lopes da Silva 1986; Maybury-Lewis 1967; Müller 1976), which is one of the defining features of age group organization (Bernardi 1985; Prins 1953). That possibility may account for apparent blending of informal and formal age grade sequences and lack of recognition of the spiritual age grade sequence as part of a formal age group system with age set moieties. Additionally, Maybury-Lewis (1967) precisely described some ritual activities that I found to be virtually unchanged and specifically allocated to older members of spiritual cohorts nearly seventy-five years later, suggesting that the spiritual age group system existed at that time.

Although age is recognized as an important aspect of social organization in other Central Brazilian and Gê groups (Gross 1979; Vidal 1976), the proliferation of formal and informal age distinctions among the A'uwẽ appears from the literature to be unique. Secular age sets were clearly distinguished among several other Gê groups, but it is uncertain if they operated in conjunction with formal age grades. The most likely evidence of formal age group systems was found in Eastern Timbira groups. Age sets were intact among the Ramkokamekrá Canela (W. H. Crocker 1990; Lave 1977; Nimuendajú 1946), but were less organized among the Krahô (Melatti 1970; Nimuendajú 1946) and merely remembered among the Krĩkati (Lave 1967, 1979). In these societies, not only was passage between age sets a collective ceremonial affair that operated on a ten-year cycle, but the alternation of those age sets divided them into age set moieties (W. H. Crocker 1990; Lave 1979; Melatti 1978, 1979). That configuration suggests the possibility of formal age grades, even if they might be unnamed. In other Gê societies, age grades and age sets seem to have operated quite differently.

Among the closely related Akwẽ (Xerente), age grades were relevant components of male sociality and may be remnants of a former age group system (Farias 1990, 1994; Lopes da Silva and Farias 1992; Maybury-Lewis 2009). Despite a lack of clarity regarding the details of that system and the apparent absence of age sets, Akwẽ age grades appear to have operated in conjunction with age grade moieties but not through the alternation of age sets (Lowie 1939; Lopes da Silva and Farias 1992). Similarly, the Apinayé had clearly delineated age grades that did not appear to have operated in conjunction with age sets and therefore could not be considered formal (DaMatta 1979; Farias 1990, 1994; Lopes da Silva and Farias 1992; Nimuendajú 1939).

Differently, among Mebêngôkre groups, both males and females belonged to age sets and age grades, although ethnographic descriptions indicated that recruitment into the age grades was not based on collective and simultaneous recruitment of all members of age sets, thus precluding the possibility of a formal age grade sequence (Bamberger 1979; Fisher 1991; Lowie 1943; Turner 1965; Vidal 1976, 1977). Furthermore, whereas A'uwẽ, Akwẽ, and Eastern Timbira age sets were internally structured according to induction sequence or age-based leadership positions, Mebêngôkre age sets appear to lack internal age differentiation (W. H. Crocker 1990; Nimuendajú 1942; Turner 1965).

Until the possibility of formal age group systems among these or other groups is confirmed ethnographically, the A'uwẽ remain the only Gê people documented to have a fully functioning age group system comprising age sets that pass through formal age grades. They are therefore also the only one with two documented age group systems (secular and spiritual).

In contrast, several age constructions that were prevalent among other Gê groups were absent or less prominent among the A'uwẽ. The most striking of these are age hierarchies based on name transmission relationships. Among the A'uwẽ, name transmission was not institutionalized and did not create cohesive social groups or emphasize formal intergenerational relationships. A'uwẽ names might be transmitted by just about any consanguineal relative in ascending generations, typically fathers, bilateral uncles, and grandfathers (Lopes da Silva 1986). A similar situation was described for the Akwẽ (Nimuendajú 1942). In contrast, name transmission among Northern Gê societies tends to be a singularly important basis for one's participation in abundant social groups and relationships (Lave 1967). Among the Timbira, names were passed intergenerationally between senior name givers (mother's brother or father's sister) and junior name receivers (sister's son or brother's daughter), each of which constituted age ranks within name-holding groups that were also arranged in moieties (Lave 1977; Melatti 1979; Nimuendajú and Lowie 1937). Kisêdjê name transmission also occurred along intergenerational lines and determined one's membership in four plaza groups and two ceremonial moieties (Seeger 1981). In some societies, as in the case of the Bororo, name organizations were internally ranked according to age seniority (J. C. Crocker 1979).

Interestingly, the very Northern Gê societies that had institutionalized name-based social organization also tended to have intergenerational formal friend relationships between name givers and name receivers. Formal friendship in these contexts refers to special bonds between somehow structurally opposed individuals that were expressed in ceremonial contexts, among others. Among Eastern and Western Timbira, intergenerational formal friendships were formed between name givers and name receivers (Lave 1967, 1977, 1979; Melatti 1979; Nimuendajú and Lowie 1937). Among those groups, formal friendship was characterized by asymmetrical solidarity and social avoidance between a younger and older partner (Carneiro da Cunha 1978; Melatti 1979). Kisêdjê name transmission also accompanied formal friendship, but, in contrast to the previous examples, was explicitly nonhierarchical as it emphasized absolute symmetrical identity between formal friends despite systematic differences in generation between name givers and receivers (Seeger 1981). Among the Mebêngôkre and Apinayé, formal friendship did not follow name transmission but was characterized by similar relationships of respectful avoidance (DaMatta 1973, 1976, 1979; Vidal 1977).

In much of the Gê literature, formal friends were characterized not only as relationships that connected individuals, but also as symbolic expressions of social distance between symbolic opposites (DaMatta 1976; Carneiro da Cunha 1978; Lea 1995a, 1995b). Some scholars interpreted formal friendship and name transmission in Northern Gê contexts as expressions of the dualistic principles of affinity and reciprocity that were not overtly attested through marriage exchange (Gordon 1996; Lea 1995a; Melatti 1979; Viveiros de Castro 1995). Among the A'uwẽ, formal friendship took somewhat different forms but was always between members of opposing exogamous moieties. Unlike in most of the Gê groups mentioned above, however, it implied extreme social solidarity and intimacy such that connotations of "otherness" or distance were diminished. Among male members of the preinitiate age grade, formal friendship was established between age set peers and was accompanied by constant social partnership. Among older males, formal friendship was usually established between members of different age sets but was similarly characterized by equality, solidarity, and proximity (Lopes da Silva 1986). Whereas formal friends between preinitiates might be temporary, those chosen by mature adults lasted a lifetime. Formal friends might sit together in the men's council, hunt together, bathe together, and otherwise share their time and company.

Individuality and Agency

Although the principle of youth autonomy appears to be prevalent among other lowland South American societies (Tassinari 2014), individualism and individual agency appeared inconsistently in the Gê literature. At one extreme was scholarship explicitly excluding the individual factor (e.g., Carneiro da Cunha 1978). Other scholars allowed for individual agency in conjunction with structural or functional frameworks. For example, Fisher (1991) presented Mebêngôkre (subgroup Xikrin) social structure as complexly contingent, arguing that it provided a nondeterministic ideological framework for social and productive action. In a later publication, he characterized Mebêngôkre rituals as sites of emotional expression and means by which individuals constructed social order (Fisher 2003). Lave (1979) made the historical argument that Krĩkati social organization underwent a process of individualization through the transformation of age set moieties to moieties based on personal name transmission. Lopes da Silva (1986, 1989) developed the idea that in A'uwẽ society, naming practices did not produce social groups, as they did among the Northern Gê, but rather created identity between individuals of different generations and thereby contributed to the maintenance of social continuity over time. The few examples of scholarship that expressly prioritized individual agency followed from theoretical orientations involving performance. Graham (1995) took such an approach in addressing the relationship between ideologies of individuality and collectivity in A'uwẽ discourse. Similarly, Seeger (1987) explored the relationships between the individual and the collective in Kisêdjê song performance.

A'uwẽ men's inclination to speak in the men's council similarly reflected their relative age statuses, such that elder mature men spoke with more frequency and generally did so while standing. In contrast, younger mature men spoke less frequently and usually did so while seated. Such internal age differentiation within the single category of mature adulthood occurred in a wider social context of seniority-based prestige and political influence. Similar observations have been made for other Gê groups, most notably the Xikrin subgroup of the Mebêngôkre. As among the A'uwẽ, Mebêngôkre age grades were ranked internally as well as relative to one another. As Vidal (1976) described, the initiate group was internally stratified for its functioning and education. Also, married men with children made up the politically active age grade, but only its older members availed themselves of the forum and exhibited the adult male ideal of eloquence. Mebêngôkre political process also seems to resemble the A'uwẽ case in that public associations created an impression of collective interest that in fact overlaid less explicit personal interests (Fisher 1991).

Given the importance of age organization in many Gê societies, the process of transition between age categories was necessarily an important aspect of the life cycle. For example, among Northern Gê groups, where name transmission was central to social identity and process, age grade transitions (initiate, mature man, counselor) could run parallel to changes in naming status (name receivers, name givers) (Lave 1979). That plurality of age trajectory mirrors the A'uwẽ case, with its multiple systems of age gradation. Also, according to Fisher (1991, 398), the Mebêngôkre (subgroup Xikrin) life cycle involved the "constant breaking and recasting of relationships," much as I described for the A'uwẽ. Although they are not a focus of this book, similar name transitions occur among the A'uwẽ. As Lopes da Silva described, name changes "indicate the process of living the social experiences and transformations an individual has to go through in order to achieve the necessary attributes of a human being" (1989, 337).

Gê Similarities to A'uwẽ Age Groups

A'uwẽ formal age group organization, involving age sets that pass through a series of formal age grades, may be unique among contemporary Gê groups. Yet, it shared important elements with other groups in this language family. As mentioned above, both the Akwẽ and Apinayé had age grades, although they did not recently correspond with age sets and did not form moieties through an operation of alternation (DaMatta 1979; Farias 1990, 1994; Lopes da Silva and Farias 1992; Nimuendajú 1939). The Mebêngôkre system also differed from that of the A'uwẽ in that recruitment into age grades was not based on collective and simultaneous recruitment of all members of age sets, and adjacent age sets enjoyed close social solidarity rather than rivalry (Bamberger 1979; Fisher 1991; Lowie 1943; Turner 1965; Vidal 1977).

Although the Akwẽ were linguistically and historically most closely related to the A'uwẽ, Eastern Timbira groups resembled it most closely in terms of age set organization (Lave 1979; Melatti 1978, 1979). Although analogous age set organizations were documented for all Eastern Timbira groups, they were most well defined among the Ramkokamekrá Canela (Hornborg 1988). The striking parallel to the A'uwẽ is that Ramkokamekrá Canela age sets formed moieties through their spatial alternation between the east and west (or upper and lower) sides of the community (W. H. Crocker 1990; Nimuendajú and Lowie 1937). As among the A'uwẽ, new age sets were incorporated in alternation on opposing sides of the community. In the Ramkokamekrá Canela case, however, the installation of each new age set in either the northwest or northeast quadrant about every ten years initiated a sequence of displacement, whereby older age sets on the same side moved in counterclockwise or clockwise direction toward the elder men's council in the center of the community (Farias 1994; Nimuendajú 1942). This circular rotation of existing age sets to make room for new ones had no paral-lel among the A'uwẽ. Similarly to A'uwẽ age set organization, Ramkokamekrá Canela age sets and the moieties they formed engaged each other in various activities, including sports, initiations, communal hunting, agricultural work, and warfare raids (W. H. Crocker 1990). Thus, although it appears that Eastern Timbira age sets did not pass through formal or named age grades (cf. Melatti 1970), the overall pattern of age moieties generated through the alternation of ranked age sets was extremely similar to that of the A'uwẽ. One important dif-ference is that Eastern Timbira age set moieties appeared to be associated with political asymmetry (W. H. Crocker 1990).

Age organization seems to be more formally and thoroughly specified among the A'uwẽ than any other Gê group. Nevertheless, numerous scholars have hy-pothesized for other Gê groups that age set organization received more cultural emphasis in the past, which, through a process of historical transformation, was transferred to other social institutions. For example, various authors have proposed for Mebêngôkre groups that age-based moieties were once an import-ant organizing principle of ceremonial life but were transformed through time to meet changing needs of the community, including transfer of emphasis on age competition to junior and senior divisions of other moiety organizations (Turner 1965; Vidal 1976, 1977). DaMatta (1983) similarly interpreted contem-porary emphasis on name-based societies among the Apinayé as historically derived from decreased emphasis being placed on age organization. The hy-pothesis was most thoroughly developed by Lave (1979), who proposed for the Krĩkati that plaza group moieties based on name transmission historically were age set moieties. She accounted for that change as a gradual shift in emphasis from age sets to personal name transmission as a means of ceremonial group recruitment. Importantly, age was central to both configurations, but it was re-configured according to individual naming relationships between formal friends. Whereas in the past men changed status from initiates to mature men and el-ders, under the naming system, they changed from name receivers to name givers. Lave's argument relied on evidence that the Krĩkati terms *kuigatiye* and *harungatiye* were used for moieties that did not currently involve age sets but were previously documented by Nimuendajú to be used for age set moieties (Lave 1979; Nimuendajú 1946).

That historical argument has found support in hypotheses that Northern Gê name transmission and formal friendship were structural cognates of A'uwẽ age set organization (Lopes da Silva 1986; Seeger 1989). That interpretation would seem to gain support from similarities in the social relationships involved in each. Among the Mebêngôkre, naming relationships could establish access to social status and implied paternal social relationships, at least in the ceremonial realm (Bamberger 1974). Among Eastern Timbira groups, these relationships took on an explicitly pedagogical aspect, with age seniors (name givers) explicitly behaving as mentors to their age juniors (name receivers) (Lave 1979). Such mentors of both genders served as guides in ceremonial performances, teachers of lore and singing, athletic trainers, and daily companions. Furthermore, intergenerational formal friendships formed through naming relationships bore a striking resemblance to A'uwẽ mentorship relationships (Lave 1967; Lopes da Silva 1986; Melatti 1979; Nimuendajú and Lowie 1937).

A'uwẽ Pedagogical Model Based on Social Proximity and Distance

Uxorilocal residence became a prominent subject in Gê studies when various scholars affiliated with the Maybury-Lewis's Harvard Central Brazil Project found it to be common to all groups they studied (Melatti 1970). Only among the A'uwẽ, however, and perhaps the Akwẽ, did it coexist with patrilineal descent in the form of exogamous moieties (Maybury-Lewis 1979b; Hornborg 1988). The combination of patrilineal descent with uxorilocal residence has been documented elsewhere in Amazonia (Kracke 1976; Murphy 1956).

Uxorilocal residence tended to disperse male members of patrilines and unite female members of matrilines (Maybury-Lewis 1979a) This pattern might be reinforced by the common A'uwẽ practice of sororal polygyny, whereby two or more sisters married the same man (not all polygyny was sororal, but it was often preferred by wives' parents when relations with their son-in-law were amiable). The typical combination of uxorilocal residence, sororal polygyny, and patrilineal exogamous moieties resulted in a generational alternation of moiety affiliations within a household as young husbands-in-law moved in and eventually became heads of household through the deaths of their fathers-in-law. Maybury-Lewis (1967) provided a detailed account of that cyclical household pattern, but did so strictly in terms of the male experience, characterizing it as a cycle of alternating domestic political dominance based on the assumption of a certain congruence between patrilineal exogamous moiety affiliation and political allegiance.

As the issue was originally framed in androcentric terms by Maybury-Lewis (1967), domestic intergenerational alternation of moiety affiliation generated social distance between coresident adults in adjacent generations. This was only the case for men, however, not coresident women who tended to be close consanguineal kin despite belonging to opposite exogamous moieties in alternate generations. Also, relations between mothers-in-law and sons-in-law were typically characterized by formality and avoidance even though they belonged to the same exogamous moiety. Consequently, belonging to the same or different exogamous moiety did necessarily correlate with social proximity or distance.

Another way of making sense of this residential alternation of generations is by framing the issue not in terms of descent relationships, but rather in terms of knowledge transmission. As I argued elsewhere (Welch 2022b), the social institutions Maybury-Lewis called "lineages" (Maybury-Lewis 1967, 169) are better understood as heritable prerogatives involving transmission of proprietary knowledge ownership between individuals in different generations. Although it was the prerogative of senior owners to pass their guarded knowledge and accompanying prerogatives to whom they saw fit, they tended to do so lineally. Some knowledge ownerships, including those that most attracted the attention of previous scholars (Giaccaria and Heide 1984; Lopes da Silva 1986; Maybury-Lewis 1967), tended to be passed from fathers to sons and thereby assumed a patrilineal aspect. Others, which escaped the attention of previous scholars, tended to be passed from mothers to daughters according to a pattern of matrilineal inheritance. This gender contrast was explicit in A'uwẽ discourse and suggests a preference for parallel inheritance for certain domains of proprietary information. Those patterns may be thought of as patrilines and matrilines in the sense suggested by Lea (1995b), whereby lines were different from lineages in that they exist de facto through repetition and were not necessarily consciously recognized. The intimate transmission of privileged knowledge between parents and their same-gender children may be thought of as the pedagogical inverse of the social distance that separated them from their children-in-law (especially sons-in-law). The former involved familiarity and privilege, while the latter involved formality and tension.

Following a suggestion by Lévi-Strauss that alternation of generations was part of an underlying Gê structure (Lévi-Strauss 1963, 1983), Alf Hornborg proposed that among the A'uwẽ, the "continuous spatial alternation of generations has been recognized by the A'uwẽ themselves, and is probably the structural principle on which much of the ceremonial alternation has been modeled" (1988, 83). I agree with Lévi-Strauss and Hornborg that there may have been an aesthetic parallel between alternation in the residential cycle and in the age group systems. One of the similarities between them was an apparent A'uwẽ sociology of knowledge based on the bifurcation of proximate and distant social relations. Indulgence and information sharing were consistent with proximate relations, while vigilance and secrecy characterized distant relations. Furthermore, encouragement to learn proper information, skills, and behaviors were encouraged by intimacy and camaraderie through proximate relations but by aggression and punishment through distant relations. Importantly, as I was told by one of my A'uwẽ secular moiety elders, both models were expressions of respect, but one expressed respect through permissiveness while the other did so through opposition.

This bifurcation of pedagogical theories was evident in the secular and spiritual age group systems, the exogamous moiety system, and relations between sons-in-law and their parents-in-law. In each of these cases, specific traditionalist formulations of proximate social relations between in-group allies and distant social relations between out-group opponents generated explicit hierarchical dynamics whereby seniors were charged with promoting the betterment of their juniors according to contrastive logics. The mutual constitution of these contrastive arrangements and their corresponding pedagogical methods caused them to be viewed as complementary aspects of the same educational processes, not competing or alternative strategies. This pedagogical model, which was evident in diverse social domains, approximated a traditionalist A'uwẽ aesthetic for the proper cultivation of desirable adult capacities for attending to the well-being of their families, protégés, comrades, and communities.

Plurality and Contingency of Social Orientations

Traditionalism did not imply historical stasis for the A'uwẽ, but rather meant that certain valued cultural modalities were maintained into the present and with attention to the future through their strategic reconciliation with contemporary sociocultural and socioeconomic realities. One of those modalities was the very plurality of social organization and, more specifically, the configurations of age organization that I discuss here. Thus, A'uwẽ exhibited a very high degree of resilience in plural social organizations, which was apparent in their marked persistence of traditionalist configurations of social well-being. This plurality contributed to contemporary A'uwẽ understandings of healthy social lives and the promotion of wellness in communities.

The theme of multiple age and moiety organizations was also ubiquitous in the Gê ethnographic literature. Some scholars respond to that plurality by asserting that some single structure was dominant or causal, thus essentially denying the very plurality that served as a starting point (Carneiro da Cunha 1978; Coelho de Souza 2002; DaMatta 1973, 1979, 1983). Nevertheless, the fact of multidimensionality in Gê social systems is remarkable. For example, although DaMatta attributed multiple Apinayé social structures to a single underlying opposition, he simultaneously made the assessment, "The social world of the Northern Gê is disjointed and its dual ideology permits multiple readings of social reality" (1976, 247). Similarly, although Turner (1965) explained Mebêngôkre social structures in terms of a single underlying socioeconomic and ideological dynamic, he also ascertained the abundance of contingent human relationships and recognized that social organization simultaneously unites and divides society. These examples attest to a theoretical difficulty in reconciling structural plurality and singularity.

The tendency to propose that single motivating structures explained the ethnographic facts of multiple social structures may derive, in part, from the perception by some scholars that plurality and heterogeneity implies contradiction. That possibility was apparent in literature asserting the impossibility of simultaneous social roles. For example, Turner (1965) wrote that in Mebêngôkre society, for a man to become a husband and father, he must cease to be a brother. Similarly, Jackson (1975) identified one way of understanding the variability of Gê social alignments as a "surplus" of memberships, whereby for one to be activated others necessarily must be inactivated. My research suggests that such compartmentalization of social roles was not the only possible strategy for reconciling the multiplicity of social relations that existed between individuals. Another involved their integration by allowing status in one domain to affect status in another. That dynamic was more closely aligned with the theoretical position that the multiplicity of social organization was always simultaneous and plural. Crocker and Crocker (2004) illustrated that position when they accounted for multiple Ramkokamekrá Canela age hierarchies and dual structures as alternative systems that counterbalanced one another for the sake of greater overall social solidarity. Melatti (1970, 1978, 1979) took a similar position in arguing that in Krahô society, multiple social and ideological configurations negated one another, thereby denying social contrast and increasing the overall equality of individuals. An important insight in Melatti's work was his description of the availability of multiple social perspectives: "Krahô rites appear to give individuals the possibility to view social relations and the relations between the elements of the Universe, as they imagine them, from different points of view" (1978, 357).

Gordon took his analysis of Mebêngôkre (subgroup Xikrin) ceremonialism in another direction, asserting the essential importance of differentiation between people: "The final aim of ritual is precisely the reaffirmation of global differentiation between all terms, and segmentation at the heart of the community. These divisions guarantee that life does not drift dangerously close to the limiting state of undifferentiation that threatens the well-being of the whole community" (2016, 222). These theoretical positions are important because they recognize in different ways the irreducibility of multiplex social organization.

Fisher took these ideas even further in describing Mebêngôkre social structure as fundamentally contingent. According to his evaluation, the plurality of social structure was both simultaneous and mutually exclusive such that in the kinship realm, "there is an internal relation between hierarchy, equality, and identity" (1991, 480). According to his view, one could simultaneously assume multiple roles and switch between them in turn, a paradox that contributed to the conditionality of social status and the unpredictability of social action. Such was also the case in A'uwẽ society, where multiple systems for reckoning age in absolute and relative terms contributed to a complex terrain of social unity and differentiation. It was a social landscape that denied the distinctions between such heterogeneous oppositions as hierarchy and equality, separation and integration, individuality and collectivity, and difference and sameness.

The ethnographic literature about Gê peoples illustrates how theoretical trends regarding culture groups with presumed underlying similarities do not always lead to consensus about what unites or differentiates distinct ethnic or linguistic groups. The search for an underlying model of Gê social structure did not result in a unified concept about these groups, although there was a tendency to focus on their dualistic aspects rather than their hierarchical or age-related dimensions. When compared with my findings regarding the A'uwẽ, this body of literature would suggest that the A'uwẽ are unique in their cultural focus on systems of age identity, which are multiple and involve both hierarchical and equalizing aspects. Yet, significant alignment between my reading of A'uwẽ social organization and other scholars' readings of social organization among such groups as the Mebêngôkre suggests that this distinctiveness may be due in part to the theoretical frameworks that informed diverse studies. Although not all Gê literature leads to similar conclusions, there is substantial support for many of the characterizations I present in this book, such as the congruence of dualism and age organization, the importance of individuality and agency, the relevance of contrastive social roles of proximity and distance for promoting youth betterment, and the plurality and contingency of social perspectives. As I argue in this and other chapters, these dimensions of social organization are not merely theoretical but contribute to an understanding of what many A'uwẽ understood to be good and productive social relations that contributed to social well-being and sustain cultural resilience. In my view, anthropological theory is useful insofar as it helps understand or translate a people's viewpoints regarding their own society. In the context of this book, this means that social theory is most pertinent if it illuminates aspects of how A'uwẽ viewed good living in social context.

CHAPTER 6

Life Cycles of Environmental Engagement

Age Organization and Environmental Practice

Since Before There Were Boundaries

Age-related notions of social well-being intersected with the multitude of ways people engaged with the environment, which was a cultural landscape in transformation. In the 1930s and 1940s the Brazilian government pushed to colonize Central Brazil, leading to the formerly autonomous A'uwẽ becoming surrounded by settlers, losing access to vast portions of their former territories, and suffering from disease, hunger, and frontier violence. The eldest living individuals when I began my research in the Pimentel Barbosa community were children and youths during this time of stress, insecurity, and territorial exclusion due to internal colonialism. Some of them were born on trek in locations now occupied by the regional cities Água Boa, Canarana, and Ribeirão Cascalheira. Some lived as small children in the ancestral community Sõrepré before internal conflict drove it to splinter and thus the A'uwẽ people to permanently divide for the first time in approximately a century (Lopes da Silva 1992). They recalled the year 1946, when they were teens and young adults, the year stable contact was first established with the SPI. The late elder Darú recalled learning to smoke tobacco and eat white rice from SPI agents, which he introduced to the rest of the community. Antônio recalled the early years of cultivating rice in family gardens. Hipru remembered the abundant presents received from the SPI, such as machetes, axes, and hoes.

In those times, certain foods understood to promote health and wellness were especially important for use as presents in ceremonial contexts (spiritual rituals, rites of passage, and weddings, among others). These foods were wild root vegetables, maize loaves, macaúba bread, and game meat. Whereas wild root vegetables, macaúba, and game meat were then procured in great quantities, reports indicate that the quantity of maize produced in the small A'uwẽ gardens typical of the early to mid-twentieth century was hardly more than was required for use as ceremonial presents throughout the year (Maybury-Lewis 1967). This contrast is consistent with historical characterizations of the A'uwẽ as primarily collectors, hunters, and fishers, and only secondarily horticulturalists (Flowers 2014; Maybury-Lewis 1967). These foods continued to be produced or collected for use as important ceremonial gifts expressing respect and gratitude toward others and thereby fostering a sense of celebration and cheer throughout the community. Giving these gifts was essential to the performance of these ceremonies, understood to promote social wellness and a sense of connection to the past and ancestors. They provided resources and frameworks for cultural resiliency by enhancing contemporary popularity of traditional self-provisioning knowledge and activities.

The elders I met who were born when early twentieth-century frontier advancement was still a comfortable distance away were raised in times of hardship and transformation. Their transformative experiences as children, youths, adults, and elders were vastly different in some respects from those of their parents and grandparents. While they still went on trek for some decades, by the mid-1950s, their group had relocated to a site adjacent to the SPI attraction post, with its gifts, cattle, horses, tobacco, and rice. When, in the late 1960s and early 1970s, their children were old enough for several to leave the community to attend elementary school in distant cities, they were fraudulently relocated across the Rio das Mortes so their land could be occupied by ranchers who had previously bought it from government representatives (see Graham 1995; Welch, Santos, et al. 2013). In the 1970s and 1980s, much of their subsistence efforts were directed toward the mechanized production of rice, which FUNAI hoped they would come to commercialize and thereby become economically self-sufficient and integrate into rural Central Brazilian society. By the 1990s the rice project had failed, and they came to refocus some of their subsistence efforts from rice production to collecting, hunting, and fishing (see Graham 1995; also Coimbra Jr. et al. 2002; Garfield 2001). Yet, by this time rice had become the basic starchy dietary staple, replacing collected wild root vegetables. Between the 1990s and late 2010s, as they became elders, monetarization of the food economy dramatically increased, providing the means for purchasing most consumed food in regional supermarkets.

Despite these economic transformations, most households continued to secure enough wild root vegetables, maize, macaúba, and game meat for their residents to give as gifts on these important ceremonial occasions. Recently, these three plant foods were consumed almost exclusively during ceremonial occasions, suggesting that their maintenance within the A'uwẽ dietary portfolio and the retention of associated ecological knowledge required for their production (maize) and collection (wild root vegetables and macaúba fruit) was motivated almost exclusively by social and health interests within ceremonial contexts (Welch 2022a). In contrast, game meat continued to be a frequently consumed food in many households in Pimentel Barbosa and Etênhiritipá, in addition to being an important ceremonial gift food.

Thus, the last survivors of this generation of elders experienced qualitatively different life cycles than their ancestors, witnessing the broad transformations of their society from autonomous trekkers without artificial geographic borders to sedentary market consumers on a relatively small bounded land with limited natural resources. Nevertheless, these historical facts did not discourage contemporary A'uwẽ pride of being guardians of tradition and keepers of knowledge they considered essential to their ethnic identity. They saw themselves as traditionalists who maintained patently A'uwẽ social arrangements and configurations, including the forms of age organization widely valued as essential to community well-being. They also believed themselves to be defenders of traditional subsistence techniques integral to the social process of aging, from childhood to adulthood. Although many households came to purchase the greater part of the food they consume, most A'uwẽ continued to practice select food self-provisioning activities considered essential to the performance of ceremonial events that mark key events in traditional A'uwẽ life cycles.

Intergenerational Transmission of Knowledge

One of the most marked dimensions of how age affected environmental engagement was the loss of life of cherished elders who lived in the Pimentel Barbosa and Etênhiritipá communities. The loss of elders is not new, of course. A'uwẽ oral history told of innumerous deceased parents, grandparents, great-grandparents, and so on, who were remembered to this day for their best or worst qualities, depending on who was doing the remembering. For example, some prominent deceased individuals were considered to have been peacekeepers or powerful healers, while others were remembered as self-interested or sorcerous. Connecting with the ancestors through dreams continued to be one of the most potent means of receiving important knowledge, such as songs. Some A'uwẽ asserted that dreaming was the most important means of transmitting traditional culture. In this life, however, the loss of elders was an acute reminder of the importance of intergenerational transmission of knowledge. One of the responsibilities of age among the A'uwẽ was the communication of one's privileged knowledge to a younger relative or other beneficiary so that it might be maintained without interruption into the future and thereby continue to benefit the elder's loved ones (Graham 1995). The content of this kind of guarded information remains opaque to me because of its covert nature.

The intergenerational transmission of traditional knowledge, especially about the environment, also took many other forms. For example, the relationship between mentors and their protégés in the secular age group system was an important formative experience, especially for males. Uniquely, the age difference between the two was not large, as protégés were only two age sets and approximately ten years younger than their mentors. This is to say that mentors were encumbered with teaching their protégés about hunting, fishing, medicinal plants, and many other aspects of environmental engagement when they were in their midtwenties. Nevertheless, this configuration was considered the proper and beautiful format for environmental education of youths. Mentors passed to their protégés privileged ethnobotanical information regarding plants that promoted strength and speed during log races and other competitions. Some of these were rubbed on one's legs while bathing, while others were rubbed into superficial cuts on one's thighs and shins. Other substances of animal origin were used as body adornments to promote running as fast as the animals from which they were derived. Elders pertaining to the same age set moiety might be privy to these information transfers between mentor and protégé age sets, while elders pertaining to the opposite age set moiety considered educating these protégés none of their business. Thus, in this context, elders had little to do with environmental education of youths despite their social recognition as ultimate authorities on the subject because of their vast experience in the cerrado and connection to the past.

Contemporary community leaders also sought opportunities to promote youth education about the environment through projects in collaboration with non-A'uwẽ scholars and indigenists. Several such undertakings had the express objective of exposing youths to elders' traditional ecological knowledge, as well as familiarizing them with the local landscape and its resources. The project I am most familiar with was one my colleagues and I undertook in collaboration with Tsuptó and two young A'uwẽ assistants in the Pimentel Barbosa community, with financing from the Indian Museum (Museu do Índio), FUNAI. Inspiration for the project was a request by Tsuptó to bring youths and elders together at locations outside the community so that the young people could learn their territory and hear elders' stories about the landscape, its plants and animals, and events that had transpired in the cerrado. Although the project was frustrated by financial interruptions, it nevertheless succeeded in several important ways. First, it innovated a workshop-style format for elders to share knowledge with youths and cameramen. We held successful workshops addressing wild root vegetables, cotton preparation and spinning, hunting arrow fabrication, bird feathers, maize, squash, and traditional fire making. In each case, multiple elders demonstrated and delivered speeches about the chosen topic, while children and youths watched, and A'uwẽ cameramen photographed and filmed. These registers remain available to the community in digital format, and preparations are underway to develop a platform for more widespread access in multiple communities and A'uwẽ schoolhouses. This effort continues under collaborative development in new formats, with reimagined goals, and with different institutional affiliations, but its original incarnation illustrates how new forms of engaging youths and elders to transmit ecological knowledge were possible under A'uwẽ supervision in consonance with the cultural preference for such formats of youth education as informal observation and imitation.

Different dimensions of life cycles of environmental engagement illustrate how age and A'uwẽ age organization influenced and, in some cases, structured how people went about using, caring for, and knowing about the local landscape. I continue this chapter with a brief sketch of how historical ecological and territorial change affected different generations at the Pimentel Barbosa and Etênhiritipá communities, focusing on the transition from greater mobility to circumscription and monetarization. I then discuss A'uwẽ concepts of environmental conservation, and how they partially changed through younger generations' involvement with national and international conservation discourse (see Graham 2002). Finally, I present three case studies of the relationship between age organization and environmental engagement: women's collecting excursions, men's age set fishing expeditions, and men's group hunting with fire.

Mobility, Circumscription, and Monetarization

An Era of Liberty

The long colonial legacy of A'uwẽ migrations and engagements with non-Indigenous settlers highlights a central theme about the past, which is that the ancestors of the study population had a high degree of mobility during the trajectory that culminated in their settling in the contemporary communities Pimentel Barbosa and Etênhiritipá (Coimbra Jr. et al. 2002; Garfield 2001; Graham 1995; Lopes da Silva 1999; Welch, Santos, et al. 2013). According to A'uwẽ oral history, part of this story was a history of migration from the Atlantic coast and across the cerrado regions of Central Brazil (Tsa'e'omo'wa 2021; Sereburã et al. 1998). Another part of this story is a pattern of trekking (*zömoni*), whereby small to large family groups left a principal community at different times of the year to travel for weeks or months through the landscape and acquire wild foods and other landscape resources via collecting, hunting, and fishing. Contemporary elders reported that trekking in the past often followed established routes between frequently visited camping sites according to their respective seasonal resources. Although they traveled through diverse landscapes, trekking parties preferred headwaters because of the great diversity of foods and other valued resources found there. Often, women would collect plant foods in and around these headwaters while men would hunt in adjacent grasslands or scrublands. When Maybury-Lewis (1967) conducted research at the Wedezé community, many families spent more time on trek than in the community. When today's elders were younger, trekking was a key aspect of their relationship to the cerrado landscape. It was not only an opportunity to use geographically dispersed wild resources, but also a means to survey the territory and educate youths about the environment and its resources.

The late elder Sereburã was a storyteller, considered to be among the most authoritative voices regarding the past and traditional A'uwẽ values because of his oratory skills and lived experience. For Sereburã, trekking was a different experience when he was younger, when there was more land and less of the pressures related to contemporary life: "I have many memories about trekking, about the people, about hunting. Sometimes I get sad when I talk about that good time, when we didn't worry about returning quickly. Then the worry was to savor the flavor of the meat, every kind of animal that one might kill, not to return quickly. This was a part of my stage of life as a boy, for us to learn the names of the many locations we visited." Sereburã discussed how a decision to go on trek was made:

> The decision to go on trek is always made by the eldest person. He will say that he wants to walk, wants to leave for a bit. Some others that accompany his group will respond, from both clans [exogamous moieties]. For example, they will say that the animals are eating well, that it is good, if you kill them, they are fat and

the flavor is better, but only now in this season. Or there is the gardening season, when everything has been planted, they want to go hunting, go on trek. So, the other clan accepts this proposal, and a large group will leave to go on trek.

According to Sereburã, trekking involved some discomforts:

I'm going to talk about my time, when I was a child. Life for the A'uwẽ people was walking, walking, what we call *zömoni*. The ancestral people would always walk, and also kill animals and eat everything, like palm and other kinds of fruits. There was so much food in that era. These ancestral people didn't even have shoes. They were always barefoot. Everyone felt pain in their feet. Even so, they endured it. Some youths cried because of their laziness to walk. This is how it was in the walking lifestyle of my people. My group, the adolescent boys [preinitiates], always carried rocks, the rocks used to break the shells of palm fruits, and it hurt here in the back. This was the life of the adolescent boys. And we always observed what the men, the hunters, did. And the women also. I observed everything that the adults did. We imitated what the adults did.

While the preinitiate boys suffered carrying rocks, girls in their age set suffered a ritual intended to make them strong walkers: "During a trek, the girls in the same age set as the preinitiate boys were called by the mentors to stand in a line. The mentors decide, or sometimes an elder. Then, the mentors had to hit them with special wooden sticks on their legs to test how much courage the girls had, if they could endure these hard blows. It is also to strengthen their legs, so they didn't get tired while walking."

Trekking also had its pleasures, as when scouts fetched fresh maize from the community and brought it back to the families on trek:

Some of the scouts, called *ĩ'rehí*, stayed in the village, while others came from hunting far away to check on things in the village, to make sure everything was all right, everyone was happy, and no one had become ill. They did this while hiding the whole time, not appearing in the village. At night they approached the men's council to receive news and to tell how things were on trek. At that time, the gardens were not large; they were small, but produced well. The scouts came when the fresh maize was being harvested and brought back maize to the families who were on trek. And when they arrived there, everyone became so happy with the food, with the wonderful smell and taste of fresh corn. This is how things were, how I observed things during my childhood.

Encroachment and Settlement

Sereburã was a child and preinitiate before stable contact was made between his people and the SPI in 1946, during a historical period before large numbers of settlers arrived in the region. Thus, his recollections of trekking as a child were of a time the A'uwẽ were unencumbered by territorial borders, by unfriendly agribusiness landowners, by towns, and by roads. Although the eastern portion of Mato Grosso state was being colonized at the time, the reputation of the A'uwẽ as fearsome kept all but a few settlers out of most of their territory along both margins of the Rio das Mortes and surrounding regions.[1] The group that now lives in the Pimentel Barbosa and Etênhiritipá communities had ample room to trek while avoiding non-Indigenous settlements on the other side of the Araguaia River. It would not be long before this autonomy and freedom would end, as establishing enduring contact with the SPI was part of a colonizing effort by the Brazilian government intended to facilitate the opening of A'uwẽ lands to agricultural settlers. Many other A'uwẽ groups remained out of reach of SPI and missionary contact efforts for a few additional years, only establishing contact with these organizations when localized groups were overwhelmed by the acute hardships of circumscription, disease, and warfare. Just a decade after Sereburã's group established contact with the government, it would relocate its main community to the site called Wedezé, just a kilometer from the SPI Indigenous Attraction Post at São Domingos, and, unbeknownst to them, set into accelerated motion the government's plans to settle the A'uwẽ and develop their territories.

The SPI post at São Domingos was a large enterprise, with cattle production, a school for children of employees, and an electrical generator (Flowers 2014). A service order issued by the SPI exhorted the chief agent at the post to "convince the Xavante to dedicate themselves to agriculture and gradually abandon their nomadic habits. It was hoped that this would result in their concentration inside a more limited territory" (Flowers 2014, 68). Initial efforts to encourage their adoption of rice, manioc, sugar cane, and banana agriculture failed, as the A'uwẽ quickly lost interest and returned to planting just maize (*nozö*), beans (*uhí*), and squash (*uzöné*) (Maybury-Lewis 1967). According to Maybury-Lewis's (1967) account from the 1950s and 1960s, the A'uwẽ had long practiced horticulture but relied on it relatively little compared with gathering and hunting. This author identified maize, beans, and squash as the only food crops historically cultivated by the A'uwẽ, although those residing in other Indigenous lands may cultivate peanuts, and an observation by Johann Emanuel Pohl (1837) in 1819 indicates that they grew peanuts historically. Contemporary oral tradition at the Pimentel Barbosa and Etênhiritipá communities suggests that one introduced variety of sweet manioc (*Manihot esculenta*) was also grown in recent centuries, having been adopted through contact with early non-Indigenous settlers in the region. Because of a lack of adequate land for gardens at Wedezé, the A'uwẽ community near the SPI post at São Domingos initially gardened at Etênhiritipá, about forty kilometers distant, carrying the produce back on foot. After several years, however, they abandoned agriculture altogether for about three years, depending on wild foods complemented by donations from the SPI of manioc meal and rice (Flowers 2014). This seems to have been the first moment of reliance on the government for basic sustenance, although there would be many more in the future. Unlike Sereburã's generation, those who experienced childhood at Wedezé under the influence of the SPI post did not know a time when the community was completely autonomous. Although their subsistence activities remained largely unchanged until after they left Wedezé, they now relied on governmental gifts, including food, gardening tools, and medicine, for their day-to-day well-being. Yet, at that time, they still trekked freely without concern for territorial borders and property lines (Maybury-Lewis 1967; Welch, Santos, et al. 2013). This situation would change rapidly once encroachment and circumscription accelerated in the 1960s.

In 1953, just a few years before Sereburã's group moved its community to Wedezé, the state of Mato Grosso sold large tracts of land on the east margin of the Rio das Mortes, including the community site at Wedezé, to ranchers.[2] Thus, after the community was established at Wedezé in 1956 and the A'uwẽ were no longer viewed as a threat to colonization by the 1960s, immense pressure was placed on the SPI to remove the community so that landowners could occupy their ranches (for example, Graham 1995; Lopes da Silva 1999; Welch, Santos, et al. 2013).

In the early 1960s, the A'uwẽ at Wedezé suffered tremendous population loss due to epidemics and warfare. They also began to fragment as subgroups relocated away from the SPI post at São Domingos, with its incommoding bustle of activity as many non-Indigenous settlers arrived. They relocated to locations such as Ötõ and Pazahöi'wapré on the west side of the Rio das Mortes. By the late 1960s, another subgroup had established itself at Etênhiritipá.

In 1965, the SPI authorized the cessation of the post at São Domingos and its transfer to the other side of the Rio das Mortes in exchange for payment by the landowner of nine head of cattle and 500,000 cruzeiros (US$275), but this move did not occur for another seven years. In the early 1970s, after age set initiation rites were held at Pazahöi'wapré, these other splinter groups also began to relocate to Etênhiritipá. From 1969 to 1973, the entire group that formerly resided at Wedezé took up residence at Etênhiritipá. The SPI moved the post there in 1973 to attend to the A'uwẽ population and to allow the ranchers to develop the parcels they had bought in 1953.

According to A'uwẽ who participated in these moves, they did not understand that their relocation to the west side of the Rio das Mortes was to be permanent because they were not yet informed about the concepts or practices of land ownership and sale. Nor did they know that their new residence was to be located within a bounded land that they would be discouraged from leaving for trekking or other reasons. They were accustomed to moving community sites frequently, having lived at such locations as Wedezé and Etênhiritipá multiple times in their history. Consequently, they had understood the move to be convenient at the time but not definitive. Unfortunately, the doors were figuratively slammed behind them.

By the 1970s, now permanently settled at Pimentel Barbosa, also known as the Etênhiritipá community, circumstances had changed dramatically. From 1969 to 1975, their land was reduced in size from 816,500 to 204,000 hectares and came to be bounded on all sides by ranches, which encroached from the west so far into their former territory that the Etênhiritipá community was separated from them by just a few kilometers of cerrado, cutting off the A'uwẽ from former gardening, collecting, hunting, fishing, and trekking areas.[3] According to my interlocutors, the federal police were at times posted at the border between the nearest ranch and the community to prevent armed conflicts (see Graham 1995 for firsthand reports and a fascinating discussion of the land conflicts that occurred in the 1970s and 1980s). Following A'uwẽ political mobilization to increase their land size, by 1980 the current boundaries were established with 328,966 hectares. Removing all ranchers and squatters, however, took until the late 1980s.

The SPI, which had lost interest in providing so many gifts now that the A'uwẽ were no longer a threat to colonization, was replaced by FUNAI in 1967. In the late 1970s, FUNAI began its mega rice project with the A'uwẽ, aimed at transforming them into economically independent commercial rice producers and integrating them into Central Brazilian society. Although the project eventually failed and was gradually defunded in the mid-1980s, it had important lasting effects (Coimbra Jr. et al. 2002; Garfield 2001; Graham 1987, 1995).

Major consequences of the rice project were increased sedentism, a new phase of community fissions, and new strategies of political activism. With subsistence and economic attention focused on rice production and people accustomed to receiving health and other services from the FUNAI post, family trekking was reduced in the 1970s and was effectively discontinued in the 1990s, when only a few families still practiced extended treks, and most excursions were limited to just a few days or less. Thus, younger generations had fewer opportunities to familiarize themselves with the cerrado landscape and its resources. A new phase of community fissions began with the enlargement of the Caçula community in 1980, followed by the establishment of Tanguro in 1983. According to Graham, part of the motivation for establishing new communities was the reproduction of FUNAI investments, including salaried employment positions (Graham 1995). Other reasons were internal political conflict and population increase. Political activism also increased during the rice project, as A'uwẽ leaders sought to secure FUNAI financial support for their communities, as well as resources such as trucks (see Graham 1995). Although the intensity of their political engagement reduced with the end of the rice project, they inherited from this era new strategies of political activism based on the lesson that FUNAI and other governmental organizations could be manipulated using traditional techniques of intimidation and persuasion.

Monetarization of Communities

Children raised in Pimentel Barbosa in the 1970s and 1980s knew a very different reality than that of their elders. Theirs was a childhood rooted in community life, reliance on the FUNAI post with its health services, and rice-based agricultural subsistence. It was the first time substantial political attention was focused outside the A'uwẽ community, as they had become dependent on inputs, decisions, and policies from the federal government. New value was placed on males attending formal schooling and learning Portuguese. For females, emphasis was placed on learning homecare, childcare, and gardening. Although some individuals took interest in traditional subsistence techniques and knowledge, many did not, preferring to remain in the community than leave to collect or hunt. Some people learned these skills later in life than their elders had. Thus, many people learned about the landscape and its resources as young adults, whereas their elders had done so as children and preinitiates.

The transitional 1990s were a time of recovery from the rice project and economic reorientation. One of the most notable shifts was a proportional increase in traditional wild food provisioning as compared to the 1970s, which other scholars have attributed to the failure of the rice project, A'uwẽ's relative success at having their territorial boundaries expanded in 1979 and 1980, their undegraded landscape within the Pimentel Barbosa Indigenous Land, and financial inflows from government salaries and social security pensions (Coimbra Jr. et al. 2002; Santos et al. 1997). Despite this change, the increase in average household income also contributed to the A'uwẽ at Pimentel Barbosa becoming market consumers, purchasing food, clothing, tobacco, and other sundry items. This period represents the maturation of the "hybrid economy," involving Indigenous production, market participation, and government inputs (Altman 2009; Altman, Buchanan, and Biddle 2006). With the return to collecting, hunting, and fishing in conjunction with the introduction of social security pensions and other social benefits, the balance of the hybrid economy stabilized for the first time since the start of the monetarization process that had begun with the rice project. This is how I would describe circumstances when I first visited the A'uwẽ in 2004, although they subsequently changed in favor of even greater market participation and government inputs.

Part of the monetarization process involved the emergence in the 1980s of internal differentiation between households, whereby some households had more or less income than others in the same community. As a result, it became increasingly difficult to generalize about household economies, even within a single community. In recent years, sources of monetary income were more diverse and accessible than in the past but remained quite low in absolute terms (in 2019, 90.1 percent of adults in the Etênhiritipá community earned less than R$1,000 per month, which was equivalent to US$250). In addition to social security pensions for the elderly, parents of young children became eligible for the cash transfer program known as Auxílio Brasil (Brazil Assistance), formerly Bolsa Família, and maternity financial assistance (*salário maternidade*). Salaries were also paid to health and sanitation agents and school employees (such as teachers, director and vice-director, cook, janitor, and guard). Although several households had no source of income, the vast majority had at least one source and usually more sources of income. Differently from what I encountered in 2004, when all but one household maintained a swidden garden, in 2019 about a quarter of households did not have swidden gardens, maintaining only small home gardens with limited food plants. According to interviewees in such households, the younger generations did not like to procure or eat traditional foods and opted to discontinue gardening, collecting, and hunting in favor of purchased foods.

Although trekking was largely discontinued by the 1990s, during my studies with the A'uwẽ, there were a few events I would characterize as trekking or trekking adjacent, although they did not closely resemble Sereburã's accounts. Men's treks (*hömono*) continued to be held almost exclusively about every five years in anticipation of secular age set initiation rites (Welch 2015). "Family" treks (*zömoni*), which included women and children, occurred less frequently. The most recent family treks I am aware of were undertaken by the Pimentel Barbosa community in 2003 and 2020. The 2003 trek was held to obtain meat for a wedding. The 2020 trek was an effort to isolate to reduce the risk of contracting COVID-19.

A'uwẽ Concepts of Environmental Conservation

One criterion for labeling Indigenous subsistence practices as conservationist stipulates that they be designed to have conservation effects (Smith and Wishnie 2000). A challenge in applying this principle is that conservation effects may apply to multiple subjects, which are not necessarily congruent with one another. For example, conserving forest cover may come at the expense of reducing grasslands. Furthermore, the A'uwẽ were a heterogeneous group of people, to which a single motivation or set of motivations could not be attributed, especially for something as complex as environmental conservation. To approach the question of A'uwẽ concepts of environmental conservation, I recall traditionalist narratives criticizing youths for wanting to emulate non-Indigenous behaviors and abandon A'uwẽ modes of living. Additionally, I identify several examples of thinking and behaving that illustrate how environmental conservationism was contemplated by A'uwẽ cultural traditionalism. Furthermore, I explore some emergent contemporary ways of understanding environmental conservation that were more in line with national and international conservation discourse.

Youthful Agents of Change
One of the poignant criticisms I heard from elder men at the Pimentel Barbosa community was that young men had lost interest in hunting or had learned to hunt at relatively older ages. According to some elders, this lack of hunting

interest by younger generations was a primary reason there was so much game available in the Indigenous land (they considered it underhunted). Indeed, according to elders in 2005, they never remembered a time when there was so much game so close to the community. Among the most valued and abundant animals they cited was white-lipped peccary, which occasionally passed close to communities in large bands. Yet, this prevalent observation contradicted some A'uwẽ narratives in other communities that white-lipped peccary was locally threatened and required immediate measures to research and protect its diminishing population. Similarly, some A'uwẽ discourse mirrors that of non-A'uwẽ who claimed that the traditional use of fire to flush out game during group hunts was causing deforestation and environmental degradation and therefore should be reduced significantly or discontinued. My interlocutors argued, however, that they worked very hard to use burning regimes that were appropriate to specific local landscapes, allowing for vegetative regrowth and controlling excessive accumulation of fuel. A study by a research team I participated in showed that they were largely successful, maintaining deforestation at 0.6 percent from 1973 to 2010 and allowing for vegetative recuperation in areas formerly occupied by cattle ranches (Welch, Brondízio, et al. 2013).

Similar criticism was expressed by elder women regarding younger women's lack of interest in collecting wild root vegetables. They justifiably characterized themselves as members of the last generations to actively seek these food resources, which were dispersed throughout the landscape and required significant walking to obtain if community vehicles were unavailable. This generational change in enthusiasm for collecting was often characterized as a danger for the maintenance of women's traditional environmental knowledge, as many younger women today were not gaining the complex skills necessary to locate and excavate these valuable botanical resources. It was also described as a cause of reduced health and well-being, as these foods were understood to prevent and cure many diseases. Furthermore, these foods were highly valued by men as healthful ceremonial gifts during spiritual rituals. Their cultural conservation depended not only on the continued transfer of knowledge between generations, but also on the preservation and maintenance of access to the lands on which they grew. These wild root vegetables grew in diverse types of soils and vegetation, including riparian areas and dry upland forests, with some preferring ecotones and disturbed soils. According to elder women, their current limited Indigenous land included precious few good collecting grounds for many highly valued taxa. Thus, their continued use required stewardship of existing collecting areas within the land and additional access to lands not included within its current boundaries. Thus, women's formulations of environmental conservation interfaced with political priorities for federal recognition of more of their traditional territories.

According to the late elder Barbosa, during his youth, hunters ignited cerrado vegetation for hunting whenever they wished, recognizing that each place had its own correct burning season and frequency. These were practical concerns to ensure ground fuel was sufficient to allow the fire to sustain itself throughout the hunt but not so abundant that the fire burned too hot, creating danger for the hunters. Burns were therefore spaced temporally to allow for a sufficient but not excessive amount of accumulated dry vegetative fuel, according to A'uwẽ standards. With ample access to a large territory in the past, however, they could use fire for hunting with total liberty, easily moving while on trek to locations that had not been burned recently. A'uwẽ group hunting with fire remained very popular, and hunters struggled to observe appropriate anthropogenic fire regimes for specific environments, as understood through their traditional ecological knowledge. With their circumscription by ranches and fixation within a much smaller territory in the 1970s, A'uwẽ found it difficult to distribute hunting fires in such a manner as to promote effective, nondestructive, and safe fires. This conscientiousness motivated the Pimentel Barbosa community in 1990 to seek a collaboration with ecologist Frans Leeuwenberg, who helped analyze their hunting practices and facilitated the community recommendation that hunting be rotated within the land to allow for adequate recuperation of vegetative and animal resources (Leeuwenberg 1995; Leeuwenberg and Robinson 2000).

Occasionally a hunting ground was burned before its proper time. I have observed the consequences of such inappropriate burns initiated by groups of younger men, which were followed by ample discussion by elders in the men's council to educate younger hunters and prevent similar errors in the future. Among the arguments they raised were that insufficient ground fuel caused the fire to burn too cool and intermittently to effectively flush out game, thus causing the hunt to be less than successful. Also, with limited access to hunting grounds within the Indigenous land, early burning of prime hunting grounds would make it difficult to find appropriate locations with adequate ground fuel for wedding and rite-of-passage hunts planned for subsequent years. These discussions were considered of extreme importance for maintaining the tradition of group hunting with fire under contemporary circumstances of limited territory and high demand for ceremonial game meat. This hunting technique was preferred as the most effective means of acquiring the large quantities of game meat necessary to generate desirable community enthusiasm for meat distributions associated with weddings and rites of passage. Also, this form of hunting and its associated gifts and distributions of game meat were considered patently A'uwẽ and therefore contributed importantly to people's sense of ethnic identity. I am aware of one attempt to replace a ritual group hunt with a fishing trip at the conclusion of secular rites of passage into adulthood. This innovation was intended to conserve vegetation and game populations but was resoundingly criticized by other communities for corrupting proper ceremonial form and thus diminishing the rites. Prevalent A'uwẽ perspectives regarding appropriate hunting with fire explicitly prioritized the conservation of game populations and vegetation cover, goals considered inherently congruent with such practical concerns as safe fires and hunting success.

Traditionalism and Conservation: Maize

Among the A'uwẽ, environmental conservation could not be disarticulated from the transmission of traditional ecological knowledge, appropriate landscape use, sociocultural conservation, and the maintenance of ethnic identity. The previous example of hunting with fire illustrates these connections. Another example can be found in the traditional garden plants maize, beans, and squash. Traditional maize production presented a special challenge for the communities because people said that over the years, their stock had lost is vigor, producing smaller ears with fewer kernels. A'uwẽ maize was cultivated mainly as a ceremonial food, although it was also eaten fresh from the stalk during the harvest season (Maybury-Lewis 1967; Welch, Santos, et al. 2013). The quantity of maize produced on annually was relatively small, being dried (figure 35) and saved mainly for ceremonial occasions that called for gifts of maize loaves, such as spiritual rituals and the ceremony in which a mother's brother formalizes his ceremonial parenthood by painting his sister's daughters and sons. Maize loaves were also used to formalize wedding agreements between parents of future spouses. Additionally, maize was considered to be a particularly healthful food, providing nutrition and force beyond what is found in most other foods. Thus, this food was an important dimension of A'uwẽ traditionalism, being connected to spiritualism and the joining of families through marriage (Welch 2022a). In the past, before the adoption of cultivating rice for home consumption, household garden plots were much smaller than they were more recently. Besides dried maize saved for ceremonial occasions throughout the year, limited garden

Figure 35 Traditional A'uwẽ maize (*nozö*) drying in the sun, 2006.

produce of fresh maize, beans, and squash was consumed only seasonally. The harvest season was a happy occasion to return from trek and participate in such festive activities as log races and singing around the community.

With the introduction of rice to household gardens, the size of cultivated areas increased substantially, causing greater demand for areas of gallery forest appropriate for swidden agriculture. Felling trees, burning, and planting in larger plots put pressure on people to choose between opening gardens at greater distances from the community or planting before a previously used location had adequate fallow time. In some cases, people chose to plant at greater distances, as exemplified by the population residing at Wedezé in the 1960s planting as far away as Etênhiritipá, some forty kilometers away. During my research, many households cultivated gardens as far as twelve kilometers from the community, opting to build garden houses that they occupied full time during the planting and harvesting seasons. Others experimented with reducing fallow time to just a few years, which they considered inadequate for promoting desirable growth of most cultivated food plants. As one gardener told me, since they started planting nontraditional foods, they continued to experiment with what worked best in terms of soils and fallow times. Most notably, they observed that their production of traditional strains of maize seemed to suffer, producing fewer and smaller ears with sparce and underdeveloped kernels. Recognizing that they did not understand all the reasons for these undesirable traits, some people suggested possible explanations, including overtaxing the soil, hybridization with nontraditional commercial strains, and discontinuation of traditional forms of strain specialization by growers. The A'uwẽ distinguish six different kinds of maize, identified by the coloration of their kernels. In the past, women specialized in growing one or another type of maize, trading undesired kernels for those of her desired color pattern, thereby purifying them for future planting. Discontinuation of this practice was considered by some women to be an oversight that had contributed to strain impurity and potentially loss of vigor. Overall, the problems with maize were viewed by many as an indicator that garden cultivation was no longer being practiced in accordance with traditional knowledge and that this form of landscape use had suffered from contemporary alterations. This concern motivated leaders at the Pimentel Barbosa community to seek help from agronomists, but to my knowledge this assistance has not yet happened.

Contemporary Strategies

Seeking scientific collaborations with ecologists to produce knowledge about the Pimentel Barbosa Indigenous Land and ascertain measures that could be taken to protect it was a key A'uwẽ conservation strategy (Welch 2014). This was especially true for hunting with fire. Since at least the 1990s, local ranchers and journalists have directed public attention to the presumed negative environmental impacts of A'uwẽ hunting with fire. This coupled with exposure to national and international discourse about concern for the environmental consequences of their hunting activities within a small reservation raised awareness within the Pimentel Barbosa community of the need to assess what these impacts were, if any, and ascertain what measures might be taken to mitigate them. As a result, they collaborated with numerous researchers to study the ecological effects of hunting with fire and develop scientifically informed conservation strategies (Briani et al. 2004; Fragoso, Silvius, and VillaLobos 2000; Graham 2000; Leeuwenberg and Robinson 2000; Leite 2007; Prada and Marinho-Filho 2004; VillaLobos 2002; Welch, Brondízio, et al. 2013). These studies found no measurable negative environmental impacts from hunting after the early 1990s, despite the community's continually growing population during the same period.

Another central strategy was political organization and advocacy to ensure that adequate portions of their territory were federally recognized as A'uwẽ Indigenous lands. As I mention above, from 1950 to the early 1970s, the size of the land set aside for the A'uwẽ of Pimentel Barbosa was progressively reduced to a small fraction of its former size (Coimbra Jr. et al. 2002; Graham 1995; Welch, Santos, et al. 2013). In 1979 the population at Pimentel Barbosa mounted a political action campaign that called on A'uwẽ from other lands to reinforce them as they orchestrated a nonsanctioned revision to their land borders by clearing the vegetation along lines they considered fair (Graham 1995). The government responded to resulting pressure by expanding the land by approximately 125,000 hectares in 1979 and 1980. Similarly, political engagement by the A'uwẽ was responsible for the identification of a new Indigenous land on the east side of the Rio das Mortes, which included the historical community of Wedezé. The identification of this area began in 2001, after an A'uwẽ contingent occupied a location near the farmhouse that was constructed on the site of the old SPI post at São Domingos. Since the A'uwẽ moved to Etênhiritipá in the late 1960s and early 1970s, this land had been occupied by ranches but continually used by the A'uwẽ for hunting, fishing, collecting, and visits to ancestral burial sites. After a decade of activism and collaboration with FUNAI, the new Wedezé Indigenous Land was finally identified (a preliminary stage in the process of recognition) in 2011 (Welch, Santos, et al. 2013). Unfortunately, in 2022 it continues in a state of limbo in the justice system, which prevents it from continuing along the steps required for full recognition as a homologated land.

Historical and contemporary A'uwẽ territorial activism was central to A'uwẽ conservationist efforts because they recognized that lands under their control were preserved or recuperated, in stark contrast to those under non-A'uwẽ control, which were deforested, degraded, and poisoned with chemical fertilizers and pesticides. They continued to seek federal recognition of historically important territories that provided them with sustenance, were ecologically important for the reproduction of game animals, supported renewable landscape resources such as foods and ceremonial items that were scarce within their current Indigenous lands, and held sentimental importance as locations where their ancestors had lived and died. A'uwẽ political priorities to recognize, recuperate, and sustainably use constitutionally guaranteed lands were congruent with scientific literature affirming the key role of Indigenous lands for promoting environmental conservation efforts in Brazil. Not only were Indigenous lands among the best protection vehicles for conserving vegetation and wildlife, but they also did more than their equal share (by area) in mitigating climate change (Carranza et al. 2014; Le Tourneau 2015; Nolte et al. 2013; Pfaff et al. 2015; Soares-Filho et al. 2010). Often described as "green islands" within otherwise degraded and deforested landscapes, the conservation role of Indigenous lands was ever more evident with the extensive conversion of cerrado and Amazonian rainforest vegetation to monoculture crops such as soy, maize, and eucalyptus.

These few examples of A'uwẽ environmental conservationism demonstrate that traditionalism and conservationism were compatible modes of thinking and priorities for action under current circumstances. This is true despite the presumption that some older people tended to be more culturally traditionalist, while some younger people advocated for more environmental conservationist positions. Indeed, sometimes these two orientations conflicted when younger peoples' notions of ecological conservation were at odds with elders' values regarding the proper execution of traditional ceremonies and rites. In my experience, however, such incongruities were rare and resolved without undue difficulty through public conversation and debate. The main driver of conservationist consensus in the communities was recognition that the most valued dimensions of traditional subsistence, which are most universally considered to be those involved in ceremonial life and rites of passage, require an ample and healthy landscape. According to A'uwẽ scholar Michael Rã'wa Tsa'ẽomo'wa (2021), "We value our territory because the spirit provides us with the hunt, traditional remedies, water that sustains our people, and for this reason we do not practice deforestation. Without our territory and its natural riches, we could not realize secular initiation rites." Ecological degradation and circumscription resulting from encroachment by neighboring ranches, which degraded vegetation and polluted waterways, and proposed development projects (navigable waterways, train corridors, and rural road pavement) were among the main threats to the integrity of the land. On the other hand, traditional A'uwẽ subsistence practices had minimal negative impacts such as deforestation (Welch, Brondízio, et al. 2013). Thus, to the degree that these two communities continued to practice and preserve knowledge about their subsistence traditions, they would support the reciprocal link between cultural traditionalism and environmental conservation.

In my observation, people of diverse ages enjoyed some but not all traditional subsistence activities. Many young women told me that they did not collect heart of palm because the trunks were covered with painful sharp thorns. Many young men reported that they did not hunt because the sun was too hot, and the brush scratched their legs and arms. Nevertheless, some activities generated special interest among youths, prompting them to join their elders out in the cerrado despite the thorns, sun, and brush. These were activities that involved large groups of people and generated animated social settings between people with close affective relationships. These events effectively leveraged social relationships to generate enthusiasm for participating in otherwise (potentially) undesirable subsistence activities. In the remainder of this chapter, I discuss three examples of such subsistence activities that generated the necessary enthusiasm for large groups of younger people to participate. I interpret them as subsistence anchors mitigating the recent tendency for youths to not participate in some subsistence activities and therefore not learn them by observation and imitation. They were therefore also mechanisms for resilience and for young people to learn about their landscape and its diverse food and nonfood resources.

Women's Collecting Excursion

In June 2016, I organized a group interview with elder women at the Pimentel Barbosa community to ask that they share recollections about food collecting when they were younger and how it had changed through time, to the present. I had already interviewed individual women about this and similar questions, and my intention with this group interview was to hear more voices in a setting where they could interact by complementing one another's statements or assisting with one another's memories. By their choice, such group interviews among the A'uwẽ were usually self-organized by interviewees, who stood in turn to deliver speeches addressing the proposed question. This interview did not go as I had hoped. Responses focused exclusively on why elder women no longer collected in the present rather than addressing how they collected in the past. Each woman who spoke emphasized a somewhat different dimension, but the general themes expressed were that the wild foods they desired to collect, especially wild root vegetables, were located very far from the community, that their advanced age made it difficult to walk to productive collecting grounds, and that they lacked motorized transportation to reach these places. They did not answer my questions about collecting when they were younger. By the end of this first meeting, not all women who wished to speak had had the opportunity, so we returned the next day to continue the conversation. At the beginning of this second day's group interview, all women who spoke emphasized the narrower dimension that they currently lacked a means of transportation to reach collecting grounds—they did not have access to a truck or money for fuel. Finally, one woman stood up to speak and stated her concerns in a more direct manner than the others. She told me that they would like to collect wild root vegetables the following day and asked that I pay for a freight truck to take them (the community did not own a truck at the time). It became evident that they had been working toward expressing this request in coordinated fashion since the day before by not answering my interview questions directly and instead focusing on the importance of having access to a truck for collecting wild foods at that moment in time. Now fully cognizant of their desired outcome of the group interview, which was not to inform me about their recollections of the past, I suggested we interrupt the interview and organize a group collecting expedition instead. I was well accustomed to such expressions of interviewee agency among elder A'uwẽ, who typically discussed what they felt was important for me to hear rather than answering the questions asked of them. Therefore, I was pleased to accommodate their desire to go collecting rather than talk about it.

The sedentarization of A'uwẽ communities in recent decades, due in part to their increased reliance on schools, health posts, and electrification (see chapter 7), had contributed to the monetarization of wild food acquisition by transforming travel into an extremely expensive component of subsistence excursions. Reaching distant collecting grounds and returning with ample loads of collected foods and other resources was now constrained by elder women's limited access to motorized vehicles, which enabled them to leave after coordinating morning visits to the primary healthcare unit for routine medical attention and return the same day to prepare evening meals for their coresident family members. Also, in advanced age, carrying heavy loads for long distances in a single day was painful and prohibitive.

Like the snowmobile in the artic (Pelto 1973) and the pickup truck among the Diné (Navajo) (Chisholm 1981), access to flatbed trucks revolutionized transportation for residents of the Pimentel Barbosa Indigenous Land. They now brought people to regional towns to conduct all sorts of routine business, including withdrawing salaries and social service benefits at banks and purchasing food in supermarkets. They also carried large groups to hunt, fish, and collect at distant locations within the Indigenous land and in neighboring territories. Trucks with large beds were preferred because they could accommodate greater numbers of people with larger volumes of produce or groceries. In recent years, motorcycle ownership had become somewhat common, and several individuals had purchased private cars. These private low-capacity vehicles afforded some people increased mobility even in the absence of community trucks but were not usually used to transport women to collecting grounds. The advantages of access to flatbed trucks for the maintenance of traditional group subsistence activities were many, making it a key facilitator of cultural and social resilience. Having visited most corners of the Indigenous land during subsistence excursions and ecological and territorial research projects, I found it was crisscrossed by well-known but sometimes barely visible truck routes that permitted passage to most areas. Reportedly, some of these tracks were plotted in the early 1990s during collaborative projects coordinated by Leeuwenberg to facilitate the spatial distribution of hunting with fire (Graham 2000; Leeuwenberg and Robinson 2000). Collecting, hunting, and fishing excursions to remote regions of the land could now be held in a single day or over a weekend without need to miss school or skip scheduled visits to primary healthcare services. Flatbed trucks made virtually the entire Indigenous land accessible for group subsistence activities in a manner entirely compatible with contemporary community life.

Traveling by truck was not cheap. If a community owned a truck, large volumes of diesel were purchased in advance so refueling could be done in the community. When community trucks broke temporarily or permanently, residents without access to private motorcycles or cars were forced to pay for expensive freight services based in nearby towns. Prices were quite elevated, costing more for a round-trip service than nine in ten adults earned in a month. When no anthropologist or other outsider was available to subsidize the cost of fuel or freight for subsistence excursions within the Indigenous land, participants each paid a portion of the cost. For trips to the city, the cost per person was predetermined according to a sliding income-based scale.

According to the group of women I interviewed about their collecting experiences, men dominated access to trucks, using them almost exclusively for travel to town and for their hunting and fishing excursions. These women rebutted male criticism that they did not collect enough wild root vegetables by asserting that they would do so if the men would provide women with a truck. Eager to attend to their eloquently communicated desire to organize a group collecting excursion the next day, I arranged to contract a freight truck that would take us from the community to their preferred collecting grounds in the morning and return us in the later afternoon.

I was pleased to see that a sizable group of women gathered the next morning to ride in the truck to the gathering grounds, although I had participated in better attended collecting excursions in the past. The sixteen participants included not only elders, but also individuals of a wide variety of ages. Most elder women were accompanied by a younger companion, which I found encouraging considering their often-repeated fear that younger generations of women were not learning important collecting skills. Such age diversity among participants of women's collecting excursions was typical in my observation, as was the cheer and excitement they expressed as they gathered to leave the community. Women arrived prepared with collecting baskets containing ditch bank blade digging sticks, axes, machetes, and knives. They wore sun hats, T-shirts, skirts, and flip-flops. When the truck was turned on, signaling departure was imminent, they climbed into the back, nearly filling it to capacity (figure 36).

Women laughed and smiled during the half-hour drive to their intended collecting area, which was known as a preferred habitat for several highly desirable wild root vegetables and many other resources. As soon as the driver turned off the motor, the passengers climbed out of the truck and dispersed without delay in small groups following different routes into the cerrado. Most of these collecting groups numbered three or four women, often including real or classificatory sisters and their younger daughters, daughters-in-law, grand-

Figure 36 Women in back of truck, departing the community on group collecting excursion, 2016.

daughters, or granddaughters-in-law. I accompanied one such group of women as they slipped through the vegetation following a barely visible trail. Although this and other such excursions I accompanied were explicitly motivated by the desire to excavate wild root vegetables, this principal goal did not limit women's enthusiasm for collecting whatever else they encountered along the way, such as heart of palm, palm fiber and thatch, honey and bee larvae, and babassu (*Attalea speciosa*) nuts (figure 37).

On this specific occasion, the first resource we encountered was a young palm tree, presenting the opportunity to remove the heart of palm. The eldest woman began removing its large fronds with a machete until only the trunk remained. Another woman then began reducing the trunk by cutting into and removing its thick leaf scars until she reached the succulent interior. She skillfully reduced it to a long and narrow bundle that was easily strapped to her carrying basket.

We then moved on to an area known for plentiful wild root vegetables of two specific types. I was allowed to observe how they identified the plant stems and located their hidden wild root vegetables to further my understanding of A'uwẽ collecting activities but was informed that this knowledge was carefully guarded and may not be shared with the public. Although obscure publications exist that purport to identify the botanical species of these sacred food plants,

Figure 37 Women returning from collecting excursion with full baskets, 2016.

they do not appear to have benefited from professional botanical inspection. I do not cite these sources here to discourage the public dissemination of this privileged information. I was impressed by the efficiency and stamina of women of all ages as they dug for these concealed underground foods. Each time they located the aboveground stem of a desirable wild root vegetable, they dug a precisely located deep hole in a flurry of activity until its edible underground part was exposed. The women spread out into the brush, digging everywhere they found indications of buried wild root vegetables. While they worked, they joked with one another that those in adjacent and opposite-moiety secular age sets were lazy (*wa'a di*) and weak (*sib'uware*). After about an hour of work, they exhausted that collecting location, loaded their carrying baskets with their yields, and continued walking single file through the cerrado.

Our next stop was a beehive. Whereas introduced honeybees (*Apis* spp.) have stingers, native bees in the Brazilian cerrado (Tribe Meliponini) do not.[4] This was a nonnative beehive in a fallen tree trunk, which required laborious and dangerous work to smoke out the bees and expose the hive. With clothing wrapped around their heads, the women burned dried palm fronds at the base of the trunk and directed smoke into the beehive until most of the bees had dispersed. They then removed and divided the honeycombs, which in fact contained very little honey and many larvae. Each woman in our small group enthusiastically removed the larvae, accumulating them in depressions in their skirts, before eating them with a great deal of satisfaction. In my experience, cerrado "honey" of most types (the A'uwẽ recognized seven kinds of bees in the family Apidae and one kind of wasp in the family Vespidae that were valued for their honey) had proportionally very little honey and much more larvae, which many individuals cherished as a delicacy.

The excursion continued until everyone's baskets were full of diverse collected goods. The women's good humor and exuberant demeanor despite their apparent fatigue made an impression on me, as I felt considerably more exhausted than they appeared even though they had done all the strenuous work while I observed and took photographs. Especially when everyone gathered at the truck at the end of the day, exchanging stories while laughing, it was apparent to me that the social dimension of the trip rivaled the food procurement aspect in importance. I was reminded of the comments I had heard in other contexts that suffering for the benefit of your community, kin, or protégés is good and should be undertaken with responsibility, thus contributing to other people's and one's own well-being. My impression of the importance of the social aspect of the trip was amplified when we returned to the community, and large numbers of cheerful children, women, and men from households represented on the outing came to help carry the collected foods and materials back to their houses. The mood was electric, with the women who went on the excursion at the center of attention for bringing back baskets overflowing with such delights as hearts of palm and wild root vegetables, as well as necessities including babassu nuts (producing oil used for grooming) and buriti leaves (used for basketry and house thatching). This was an unusual and uplifting moment, when women of diverse ages received an overflow of public appreciation for provisioning their households (as well as other kin and neighbors through gifts of reciprocity) with ever less procured cerrado foods and resources. Their good-spirited suffering throughout the day of hard work collecting was transformed into collective joy as their healthful and useful bounty was ushered to their houses, where women would oversee its distribution, preparation, and consumption. Nearly everyone in the community would receive a taste of heart of palm or wild root vegetables collected by those sixteen women who were discontented with an anthropologist's efforts to talk about collecting in the community rather than going collecting in the cerrado.

Secular Age Set Fishing Expedition

As preinitiates and novitiate men, male protégés required ample time to rehearse their songs before presenting them publicly in the community. According to my age set peers, they only presented songs once.[5] Thus, each singing occasion required members of age sets at these stages of life to learn an entire set of newly dreamed songs, which could number close to forty for longer presentations, such as daytime protégé singing and dance performances (*rowete danho're*). Also, because they were expected to maintain the transparent fiction for members of the opposite secular age set moiety that they had learned the songs to perfection without rehearsing, they scheduled rehearsals with their mentors while alone at distant locations in the cerrado. The most common excuse they used to legitimize their absences during song rehearsals was to go fishing. My interviewees indicated that in the past, it was more common to go hunting. This excuse enabled them to secure transportation, such as a community truck, with the cost of fuel being shared between all members of the age set. Usually in attendance were a substantial portion of their mentors, perhaps several of their mentors' mentors (*dahi'rada*), and sometimes elder members of their age set moiety. Occasionally, rehearsals were scheduled during collecting expeditions for materials used for ceremonial accoutrements or in the middle of the night in locations all participants could reach on foot, bicycle, or motorcycle.

Fishing during group expeditions may be done with line and hooks or, when water levels were low at the end of the dry season, long fishing nets stretched across a lagoon and slowly walked by wading protégés toward the closed end, where fish had no escape route (figure 38). Once encircled with nets, fish were dispatched one by one with a crack of a stick or a firm bite on the back of the head. In the past, fishing was accomplished with bows and arrows often in conjunction with fish-stupefying plants. The most recent age set fishing expedition I attended was in June 2016, when my age set (*êtẽpa*) attended as mentors while our novitiate adult protégés (*nozö'u* age set) participated as fishers. In previous years I attended as a novitiate adult fisher accompanied by our mentors (*hötörã* age set) and as a mentor when our protégés were preinitiates. In 2016, the fishing trip lasted two days, as was usual for weekend trips involving students. The first day's entire catch was given as a gift to accompanying mentors, while the second day's catch was retained by protégés for their own households, which at that time were mostly their intended parents-in-law's houses because they were

Figure 38 Novitiate adult protégés fishing in a lagoon with nets, 2016.

close to marriage if not already married. Through this arrangement, protégés expressed their social values of respect and gratitude for their secular mentors and parents-in-law.

After each day's fishing was complete, the yields were meticulously divided into equal piles for each of the participants or beneficiaries (figure 39). This division was overseen by several protégés to ensure that the portions were fair despite the diversity of types and sizes of fish. The equity of the distribution reflected protégés' desire that each recipient deliver an adequate quantity of fish to the women of his household to satisfy all residents and permit some sharing with members of other households.

This fishing trip was a festive occasion, an opportunity for protégés and mentors to reunite several years after leaving the preinitiate house. The affective bonds between protégés and mentors that developed during their years in the preinitiate house were deep and enduring, but the opportunities to indulge them as a group became increasingly scarce as they grew older. The age set fishing expedition was one such opportunity for them to rekindle these bonds and enjoy each other's company. The mood was light, joking was constant, and mentors

Figure 39 Novitiate adult protégés distributing fish in piles for mentors to take home to the women of their households, 2016.

treated their protégés with the usual permissiveness that distinguished their relationships. The gifts of fish from protégés to mentors acknowledged mentors' ongoing dedication and fidelity and the specific service of accompanying them on this fishing excursion. In A'uwẽ society, giving a gift of food is a means of expressing respect, appreciation, and remembrance.

Mentors continued to dedicate themselves to the well-being of their protégés long after the latter left the preinitiate house. For example, protégé singing and dance performances (*rowete danho're*) were a grueling chore lasting from sunrise to sunset and sometimes later. During these performances, protégés sang each song in their new repertoire in front of houses as they worked their way around the community from one end to the other. A single song was performed multiple times during each round, which could take up to approximately forty-five minutes in the blazing sun. In between songs, protégés had just precious moments to rest, as the next song began immediately after finishing the previous round. With repertoires ranging from twenty to close to forty songs (longer repertoires were often pared down in the late afternoon so that the ceremony need not continue late into the night), these performances were extremely straining on protégés. Consequently, their mentors diligently participated from start to finish to bolster the less experienced protégés and provide them with good examples of resolute dedication while suffering and thereby promote their future capacities to serve as responsible and competent mentors to their own protégés. Sometimes older members of their age set moiety would join in as well. Whereas in the past, only male mentors joined their protégés, more recently female mentors and protégés also participated because of their desire to share these responsibilities with their male age set peers.

Male mentors participated in the preparations for these singing and dance performances. In the cerrado, under the guise of the age set fishing expedition, protégés rehearsed their songs numerous times, often late into the night. Mentors critiqued their singing techniques and helped them decide how to order the songs for greater appeal. After many back-to-back rehearsals, everyone knew their part and mastered every song. The result was astounding, with the final rehearsals moving quickly and seamlessly, without even the slightest gap between songs.

Age set fishing expeditions were well-attended subsistence events providing healthful sustenance to families of protégés and mentors and promoting traditional ecological knowledge among youths. In my evaluation, they were well attended because protégés value the song rehearsals that occurred during these expeditions and the opportunity to spend social time with their fellow protégés and mentors. Well-executed public singing performances were great sources of pride for protégés, as they would be talked about for months or years to come. When novitiate adult protégés organized such an excursion, spending pleasurable social time with their age set peers and mentors provided an opportunity to ensure that the groups remained close and cohesive even as adults. Thus, social motivations served as impetuses for the continuance and resilience of certain traditional subsistence practices, social relationships, and ceremonial activities. In this case, these were group fishing, protégé and mentor solidarity, providing sustenance to parents-in-law, and age set singing performances.

The dimensions of such forms of resilience were evidently subject to transformation as participants reevaluated their compatibility with contemporary life. For example, it appeared that delivering flawless singing performances in the community was as important as ever for preinitiates, novitiate adults, and their mentors, but the kinds of subsistence activities they chose to participate in to disguise their rehearsals from the opposite secular age set moiety changed from mostly hunting to mostly fishing. Maintaining certain subsistence activities and associated traditional ecological knowledge because they play important roles in cherished social activities exemplifies interconnections between the persistence of well-being, beautiful social relations, and beneficial engagement with the environment. In the next section, I discuss another popular group subsistence activity that captures especially well this contemporary nexus of social and environmental well-being.

Group Hunting with Fire

Early historical accounts described A'uwẽ in Central Brazil using fire to facilitate group hunting in the cerrado. An excellent example was recorded by Austrian naturalist Johannes Emanuel Pohl (1837, 149), who made the following observation in 1819 while traveling along the Rio Maranhão, in Goiás state: "We could see grasslands on fire from afar, burned by the Indians, who frequently abandon their communities in the dry season and live along the river, in groups of 40 to 50 men, with women and children, and practice a type of circular hunt. They set fire to the fields and form a large circle in opposite direction at a convenient distance. They wait for the frightened animals, which flee the flames, and kill them with their portfolios of arrows." This account captured with succinct specificity the A'uwẽ practice of hunting with fire during trekking excursions. The circular form of A'uwẽ hunting fires Pohl described is unmistakable evidence that some symbolic and organizational principles distinguishing contemporary A'uwẽ ritual hunting were also evident in the early nineteenth century.

Ample gifts of game meat were given during weddings (*dabasa*), secular rites of initiation (*danhono*), and spiritual initiation rituals (*darini*). Group hunting with fire provided an expedient and environmentally sound means of obtaining adequate quantities of meat in short periods. Traditionalist A'uwẽ values associated the procurement and consumption of all wild foods and traditional crops with healthfulness, environmental proficiency, and participation in proper social relations. Sacred foods given as ceremonial gifts, including game meat, were considered especially beneficial to individuals and communities. They were iconically "strengthening" (*danhiptetezé*) because procuring and eating them was considered to promote exceptional well-being, including physical and spiritual strength. Game animals preferred as ceremonial gifts included tapir, white-lipped peccary, collared peccary (*Pecari tajacu*), marsh deer, pampas deer (*Ozotoceros bezoarticus*), gray brocket deer, red brocket deer (*Mazama americana*), and giant anteater (*Myrmecophaga tridactyla*).

Group hunting was most often done in advance of weddings in the 2000s and 2010s. Whereas wedding hunts used to be held over several days to weeks, today they more frequently lasted a single day.[6] The last wedding hunt I am aware of that lasted several days to a week was in 2003. Most of the adult men in a community participated in these single-day hunts irrespective of whether they belonged to the bride's or groom's family, although the groom should not kill animals lest it cause harm to an unborn or infant child.[7] Participation by so many of the men in the community made the acquisition of wedding meat (*adabasa*) a community affair. It was not the sole responsibility of the groom and his family to obtain this gift of meat on their own. Hunters participated in wedding hunts even if they were not avid hunters because they were festive occasions, men wanted to contribute to the bride's and groom's well-being, and they liked participating in what would ultimately be a distribution of highly desired food throughout the community. As I explore below, the game meat was not just given by the groom to the bride's family, but from there was given to others and eventually distributed to the whole community. These gifts were a form of reciprocity that began with a collective hunting effort and ended with the pleasure of giving and receiving meat that everyone would enjoy. Participating in hunts was therefore an expression of respectful appreciation of others and the desire for everyone to participate in the cheerfulness of the occasion.

Figure 40 Groom carrying wedding meat (*adabasa*) suspended with improvised tumplines to his bride's house, 2004.

Delivery of game meat by a groom to his future parents-in-law initiated his wedding ceremonies and was the first stage of wedding meat distribution. Whole or dismembered carcasses were bound by their feet or placed in a large basket and suspended from the groom's forehead by a tumpline to the maximum weight he could support on his back.[8] He then ran across the community plaza, often with some help from his real or categorical brothers, and deposited the meat in a pile at his bride's doorstep (figure 40). The groom presented this gift in the spirit of demonstrating respect for and commitment to his parents-in-law. Participants viewed his gift as one among several links in a cycle of mutually respectful gestures by different segments of the community for the sake of a festive wedding event that was enjoyed by all. As receivers of wedding meat, the bride's family did not possess it for more than a few moments because they immediately relayed it to the house of the bride's ceremonial parents. This transfer demonstrated respect and gratitude for their contributions to her upbringing, including their presents of cotton necklaces and maize loaves during a ceremonial event when she was a child. Thus, often within just a few short minutes, the wedding meat was transferred from the hunting party to the groom, to the groom's parents-in-law, and then to the bride's ceremonial parents. At the ceremonial parents' household, the meat was smoked or slowly roasted, if not done in the field (which was usually the case for single-day hunts), and reapportioned for distribution throughout the community (figure 41). Usually the next morning, representatives from most households came to collect a piece. Thus, ultimately, the entire community received gifts of wedding meat, including members of the households of hunters who participated in the group hunt, thereby sharing in the experience of cheer and wellness following a wedding.

Figure 41 Roasted and smoked wedding meat (*adabasa*) being reapportioned by women of the family of the bride's ceremonial father (*danhorebzu'wa*) for communitywide distribution, 2004.

Considering the large size of some A'uwẽ communities, this final disposition implied a need for large quantities of meat so that everyone in the community felt included and therefore shared in the sense of goodwill of the occasion. The relay of gifts of meat between multiple givers and receivers before their distribution to the entire community contributed to widespread concern with and enjoyment of well-apportioned distributions. In this sense, large group hunts undertaken to obtain wedding meat were partly motivated by shared community interest in well-received gift exchanges. Moreover, they were opportunities for participants to express positive social values and sentiments toward one another. Furthermore, initiating weddings with gifts of game meat was proudly considered a mark of A'uwẽ cultural distinctiveness that should be maintained in contemporary times. For all these reasons, there was widespread support for continuing to practice group hunts sustainably within the limited Indigenous land now available to them.

Group hunts were also held in conjunction with other ceremonial occasions, such as approximately quinquennial rites of passage into novitiate adulthood. About one year before the beginning of these ceremonies, essentially all preinitiate boys and adults in a community participated in an extended hunting expedition (*uiwede zada'rã*) (Welch 2015). The game meat acquired by all hunters was distributed to the preinitiates' male mentors for the benefit of their families. I was told by hunters on many occasions that this hunt was the first opportunity available to contemporary boys to learn the skills involved in hunting animals in groups. My interviews with these preinitiates revealed it to be their first opportunity to learn about any kind of hunt, as they told me that they had never accompanied men in the cerrado during even individual or small group hunts. Men therefore valued this hunting expedition as an educational opportunity for preinitiates, who would come, within a few short years, to rely on hunting as a means to fulfill the masculine duty of providing parents-in-law with food.

This hunt involved a unique competitive arrangement that pitted age set members against one another in their hunting success, while game sharing was practiced among members of diverse age sets. Four hunting teams were selected, comprising preinitiates and men from younger to older age sets. These teams slept together and maintained their own cooking fires in their respective sections of the camp circle. The goal was for each team to compete with the others by acquiring more game more quickly than the others (usually within two or three weeks). At the hunt's conclusion, each team's meat was distributed among its mentors to the preinitiates, while any less desirable or excess cuts were given to the team's novitiate adults. These men would provide these large quantities of meat to their coresident female in-laws to manage and redistribute to kin in other households and neighbors.

Another form of ceremonial hunting occurred about sixteen months later during the final stages of age set initiation rites. These hunts (*īmanadö*) comprised four hunting teams, two of which hunted on behalf of *pahöri'wa* ceremonial designees and two on behalf of *tebé* designees. All four of these designees belonged to the age set that was in the process of being initiated to novitiate adulthood. At the conclusion of the hunt, which could last weeks, each team's yields were assembled separately in the community plaza before being ceremoniously carried to the houses of the *pahöri'wa* and *tebé* designees. From there the meat was forwarded to its ultimate recipients. The *tebé* meat was sent to all elder owners of the *tepé'tede'wa* heritable prerogative, while the *pahöri'wa* meat was sent to all female mentors of the secular age set who were in the process of being initiated into novitiate adulthood.

Group hunts could be held all year long, but those employing burning cerrado vegetation to flush out game (*du*) were held only during the dry season (see Maybury-Lewis 1967).[9] During the early dry season, when the ground was still moist and vegetation lush, usually from May into June, open grasslands were the preferred settings for hunting with fire because they had sufficient dry surface fuel to sustain an effective burn (Welch 2014). These fires were ignited late in the morning after the sun had dried the dew from the blades of grass and leaves of taller plants. Fires set in grasslands at this time of year were relatively cool, low, and patchy (Warming 1892). They were not destructive to the vegetation and usually died out from one day to the next when they reached moist vegetation and waterways. I found it striking how quickly the burn scars were replaced with lush vegetative growth, with almost all visual evidence of grassland fires disappearing within a few short weeks (Welch, Santos, et al. 2013).

By the late dry season, usually July to October, taller forms of vegetation such as scrublands and dry upland forests were exceedingly dry and therefore capable of sustaining hunting fires in more diverse forms of vegetation. Unlike early season grassland fires, late season burns could consume the leaves of trees in great bursts of hot flames and might continue overnight as a result of an abundance of surface fuel. Cerrado trees and other forms of plants are evolutionally resistant to fire damage, being capable of surviving most such fires and regrowing with the return of rain around November (Simon et al. 2009). My collaborative research has shown that this burning regime did not cause deforestation (Welch,

Brondízio, et al. 2013). Many A'uwẽ hunters were concerned with the impacts of such uncontrolled fires, while others did not believe they were damaging to the environment if elders' guidance regarding proper burning techniques was followed. These elders promoted the perspective that each and every location in the landscape had its own proper burning frequency and season. By respecting elders, the environment was conserved. This kind of respect was understood to be an expression of proper social relations that conformed to A'uwẽ cultural notions of the transmission and reproduction of traditional ecological knowledge between generations, especially between mentors and their protégés and other members of their secular age set moiety.

Igniting hunting fires was always performed according to a ritualized format involving two real or categorical brothers from opposite exogamous moieties and preferably adversarial adjacent secular age sets. These competitive men set fire to the vegetation as they raced against one another by running along opposing semicircular paths to a predetermined finishing place some five to six kilometers away. Thus, these hunts were opportunities for hunters to express the good-humored morality of rivalry according to traditionalist formulations of social organization involving secular age groups and exogamous moieties.

Most group hunts employing fire other than the mentor's hunting expedition involving four teams involved collaboration between independent hunters who sought to acquire ample game for their families, unless it was to be used for a marriage or other ceremonial purpose. While some men followed the lead racers along their semicircular paths while igniting the vegetation, many walked into the center of the emerging ring of fire to ignite vegetation sporadically. On windy days, the lead racers could follow serpentine paths that burned more effectively under such conditions. Either burning strategy produced a large circle of patchy fire that burned inward from the perimeter and outward from many ignition points. The view from inside the fire perimeter was of patchy combustion creating a mosaic burn pattern where the complete gradient from scorched land to unburned green vegetation was visible. The hunting strategy relied on this mosaic burn pattern to expose hiding game animals and direct them through open areas toward unburned vegetative cover. As they ran through clearings opened by the fire, they were more easily dispatched with hunting arms (usually firearms and, until recently, bows and arrows). With visual communication and common speech disrupted by vegetation, flames, and smoke, men used loud hunting calls to advise one another of their locations, the presence of game animals, and needed coordination (Welch 2020). As the fire and moving hunters motivated animals to flee through clearings, multiple men coordinated to block their paths and thereby dispatch them, assisted by modifications to the physical environment caused by fire.

Out of concern for the safety and performance of contemporary male youths, who were ill-prepared to hunt autonomously, lacking experience compared to elders when they had been similarly aged, the youths were advised to begin to hunt gradually and in the company of more experienced hunters (Welch 2015). When they first began to accompany group hunting expeditions, preinitiate males and novitiate men frequently gathered firewood and tended cooking fires in the campsite. Sometimes they chose to follow their experienced mentors, fathers, grandfathers, or other hunters and thereby observe how hunting was accomplished. They also occasionally ventured into hunting grounds in groups without elder supervision. Novitiates did so carrying clubs rather than fire-arms, while preinitiates were unarmed. Although they almost always observed or fooled around rather than actively hunting, they were called on by their elders at the end of the day to carry game carcasses back to camp or to the truck. Back in camp, some novitiate men butchered animals, which was a difficult and consequential task because A'uwẽ cuts are very specific and unique to each type of animal. They did so under supervision until they demonstrated mastery of the technique for all animals.

Although preinitiate boys and novitiate men were relatively constrained in their participation in hunting activities, hunters informed me that tending to camp and observing hunters were necessary steps in learning to hunt effectively. They were expected to respectfully support their elders while gradually learning the terrain and basic self-reliance skills. During this phase of the process, they were to demonstrate discipline and responsibility, necessary characteristics for adulthood. By learning to exhibit respect for their elders during group hunts, they were thought to practice observation and imitation, the proper methods of learning, which would cause the whole learning process to occur with minimal effort. In this manner, older men believed group hunts were opportune events for youths to incorporate skills, behaviors, and morals necessary for becoming conscientious mature men and hunters.

These youths were engaged with large group hunts despite their more typical disinterest in individual and small group hunts because they cared about their social outcomes, which were often weddings of people they cared for or activities related to rites of passage. The celebratory mood of these events motivated youths to join group hunts with enthusiasm and thereby inadvertently learn hunting principles and deportment. These young males faced dilemmas as they considered their economic roles in contemporary social life, often deciding they preferred nontraditionalist productive activities. These tendencies highlighted the perspectives of many elders that collective hunts were important not only for preparing young males to provide for their families with self-provisioning skills, but also for preparing them to assume the social responsibilities of mature adulthood. Consequently, hunting as an ongoing factor in cultural and economic resilience depended on the contemporary relevance of group hunting, which was motivated by celebrating cherished social relations with beautifully ample gifts of game meat during ceremonies marking important life events.

Each of the three examples of environmental practices presented in this chapter, women's collecting excursion, secular age set fishing expedition, and group hunting with fire, show how contemporary subsistence activities understood by A'uwẽ to be traditional involved innumerous reconfigurations to make them relevant and congruent for younger people today. They were enthusiastically attended by younger people despite contemporary preferences for purchased foods because they involved desirable social interactions and met their responsible desires to provide others with appreciated healthful foods. These experiences also familiarized younger people with valuable cultural knowledge of self-provisioning activities in an era when such opportunities were less common than they were when their parents and grandparents were younger. They show how age organization contributed to the promotion of cultural resilience even among some people who were not particularly inclined toward traditionalist values of some forms of cultural conservation. Furthermore, they illustrate how youth who lived in monetized stationary communities learned about responsible resource extraction within a circumscribed territory through the customary A'uwẽ method of observation and imitation of their elders. In these ways, these activities contributed to intergenerational social well-being in ways that involved connection to "country" in contemporary context.

CHAPTER 7

Dimensions of Community Well-Being Today

Contemporary Contexts

Continuity between traditionalist recollections of the past and age organization today served as one of many facilitators of A'uwẽ resilience amid abundant sociocultural, environmental, and economic change. Age organization and all its associated rites, relationships, and activities grounded A'uwẽ social and ethnic identity in ways that permitted a sense of cultural stasis during a whirlwind of contemporary transformations in life circumstances. A'uwẽ children today continued to learn from older people through observation and imitation, exercising the autonomy to reproduce the behaviors and endeavors they found appealing and rewarding. Often as not, what they reproduced were distinctly A'uwẽ ways of going about life even if they also appropriated non-A'uwẽ dimensions, setting in motion their own historically situated life cycles, which would differ substantially from those of their parents, grandparents, great-grandparents, and great-great-grandparents. These life cycles and the age organization, rites of passage, and privileged social relations they entailed contributed to resiliency of identity—what it meant to be A'uwẽ today. Furthermore, they provided a social and cultural basis for engaging socially in ways that were understood to be good, responsible, and to promote well-being for oneself and others.

In this chapter, I discuss three selected arenas of well-being to illustrate in greater depth how contemporary circumstances and A'uwẽ agency affected wellness and concepts of living well. The first is food security, considered by many scholars to be a key dimension of well-being, and reciprocity, a hunger mitigation strategy that nearly eliminated the most severe form of food insecurity in the study communities. The second is how health posts, schoolhouses, and electrification of communities contributed to sedentism. This section addresses how sedentarization in three forms (reduced trekking, community movements, and physical activity) affected community well-being both positively and negatively, according to diverse A'uwẽ perspectives. The third is the camaraderie that characterized privileged relationships among preinitiates of each secular age set, and between them and their age set mentors and age set moiety members. This section highlights some of the most intimate data I collected as a male member of the *êtẽpa* age set, including its journey from novitiate to mature adulthood, participation in the secular age group system as protégés and mentors, and dedication to enduring strife and hardship for the sake of others, meeting traditionalist expectations in ways that contributed to good living as understood today.

Food Security and Reciprocity

Historical Context

Historically, hunger, food security, food production, and economic self-sufficiency were recurrent themes in the Brazilian indigenist literature, associated with the process of "pacification," which involved the attraction and fixation of an Indigenous group to an indigenist post or religious mission, and, subsequently, opening their original territories for developmentalist projects (Lima 1995; Ramos 1998).[1] This policy, based in now antiquated notions of assimilation, was a primary orienting principle of the Brazilian indigenist agency (SPI followed by FUNAI), which always aligned with government aspirations to develop and incorporate Indigenous peoples into the market economy (Davis 1977; Oliveira 1998; Ramos 1998, 1984). In seeking to make Indigenous people economically self-sufficient, the government intervened in Indigenous economies by means of top-down agricultural and extractive community projects. This boom-and-bust governmental approach to Indigenous people's economies and food security prevailed throughout the twentieth century and continues in different forms in present times (Welch and Coimbra Jr. 2022).

In the 1950s, when Maybury-Lewis (1967) undertook anthropological research among the A'uwẽ who today live in the Pimentel Barbosa Indigenous Land, agriculture was viewed as a secondary activity to collecting, hunting, and fishing. Between the time Maybury-Lewis conducted his research and anthropologist Flowers (1983) initiated her studies in the same population twenty years later, important economic, political, and environmental changes had occurred in Mato Grosso, with notable consequences for A'uwẽ well-being.

In the 1970s and 1980s, the governmental goal of integrating Indigenous peoples into the national economy, especially ethnic groups located in regions considered "empty" or "underdeveloped" like the cerrado, was accompanied by spending enormous sums of money to stimulate mechanized agriculture (Coimbra Jr. et al. 2002; Graham 1995; Garfield 2001; Santos et al. 1997; Welch, Santos, et al. 2013). The A'uwẽ were in the crosshairs of the government's developmental policy, seen for their potential as rural labor to transform Indigenous lands and their residents into large commercial producers of grain and cattle.

FUNAI inaugurated its mechanized rice-producing initiative, called the Xavante Project, in A'uwẽ lands to a euphoric reception in communities. Anthropologists who conducted fieldwork among the A'uwẽ in the 1970s and 1980s commented on its "colossal" scale (Graham 1995, 44) and "extremely high investments" (Lopes da Silva 1992, 376). According to Maybury-Lewis, who visited A'uwẽ territories at the apex of the project, "The Shavante Project is undoubtedly the most ambitious development project which has been undertaken in recent years by FUNAI on behalf of any single group of Indians" (1978, 77). Despite initial enthusiasm, the Xavante Project dwindled and failed quickly, as did so many other similar development initiatives. Generous initial investments were discontinued, and agricultural machines and trucks were abandoned in the cerrado where they broke (see Graham 1995).

What remained for the A'uwẽ from this experiment was the rice, which today makes up an overwhelmingly important part of the daily diet in practically all communities. Grown in traditional swidden gardens, bought in local markets, or received through basic food baskets or other donations, rice became a convenient substitute for the many traditional varieties of wild root vegetables. From a nutritional point of view, the introduction of rice as the primary caloric staple was deleterious for the A'uwẽ because it was a main trigger of the accelerated nutritional transition underway in practically all communities and the fast-growing prevalence of obesity and diabetes mellitus type II in most communities (Coimbra Jr. et al. 2002; DalFabbro et al. 2014; Vieira-Filho 1996; Welch et al. 2009).

Markets and Foodways

Another important inheritance of the Xavante Project was the beginnings of monetarization of domestic and community economies. During this project, the first A'uwẽ began receiving governmental salaries (Graham 1995). Young A'uwẽ men were contracted by FUNAI for positions as tractor operators, truck drivers, and other jobs necessary for the functioning of the agricultural project. After the project ended, many of these employees remained in public service and continued to receive salaries and pensions until the present. At about the same time, some other young men were given temporary work for neighboring mines, ranches, and farms, especially during agricultural harvest season, when rural labor was scarce. Thus, in the 1970s, money came to circulate in A'uwẽ communities (Flowers 2014).

Indigenous peoples in Brazil were not characterized as "poor" or victims of "hunger" for most official purposes until the implementation of large-scale public policies of social inclusion in the early 2000s (Soares 2011). These designations prompted FUNAI and other federal agencies to direct diverse social and economic programs to Indigenous populations, including the A'uwẽ. These programs sought to alleviate poverty by injecting money and resources into households and communities by means of salaries, retirement pensions, basic food baskets (*cestas básicas de alimentos*), school meal programs, maternity financial assistance (*salário maternidade*), and cash transfer programs (originally Bolsa Família, reconfigured as Auxílio Brasil in 2022).

Under current circumstances, the Pimentel Barbosa and Etênhiritipá communities also benefited from various salaries that became available over the last two to three decades. The primary healthcare unit offered at least two paid jobs for each community (Indigenous health agent and Indigenous sanitation agent). The educational system also contributed to community economies where elementary schools were present, such as in the Pimentel Barbosa and Etênhiritipá communities. Schools employed teachers and a full administrative and support staff, now exclusively Indigenous residents, providing a significant direct influx of steady income into many household budgets and indirectly into extended families and whole communities.

The Pimentel Barbosa and Etênhiritipá communities engaged in a "hybrid economy" (Altman 2009; Altman, Buchanan, and Biddle 2006), involving Indigenous food production, market participation, and government inputs. Residents of both communities had direct or indirect access to financial resources to purchase foods and continued to benefit from garden and cerrado food resources. Furthermore, different households had unequal direct access to garden, cerrado, and market foods associated with an emergent process of socioeconomic differentiation inside A'uwẽ communities (Coimbra Jr. et al. 2002; Welch et al. 2009). These differences predisposed some households to depend to greater or lesser degrees on Indigenous production, including gardening, collecting, fishing, and hunting. Households with greater access to monetary resources had more capacity to purchase food and therefore more options regarding their degree of investment in food self-provisioning activities. Also, some people had divergent preferences unrelated to income availability regarding whether to invest in these activities. In this kind of mixed food economy, differences between households deserve attention to avoid overgeneralization about how members of the same ethnic group or community provided food for their domestic groups.

A'uwẽ at Pimentel Barbosa and Etênhiritipá purchased market foods in three types of commercial outlets: regional market centers, roadside restaurants and stores, and traveling automobile vendors. Many people traveled to main regional market centers, including Água Boa, Canarana, and Ribeirão Cascalheira, at least once per month to withdraw their income at banks and purchase food, clothes, and other necessities. Food was usually purchased at supermarkets, often in big containers for such staples as rice and beans. Clothing and sundry items were often purchased in stores catering to the A'uwẽ and the Indigenous population from the Upper Xingu.

Hunger Mitigation

In 2019, colleagues and I undertook a study that included all households and adult residents in three A'uwẽ communities in the Pimentel Barbosa Indigenous Land (Pimentel Barbosa, Etênhiritipá, and Paraíso), with the objective of analyzing how people used and understood public policies of social inclusion, as well as evaluating their perceptions of food security. The results of this survey helped elucidate relationships between Indigenous agency, social organization, public policies, and food security. The perception of hunger and food insecurity involved cultural, situational, and individual dimensions. I focus here on the first two, where the main cultural aspect is reciprocity and food sharing between family members and neighbors, and the situational aspect is linked to the increasing monetarization of domestic economies through government programs. In the study communities, social programs did little to mitigate mild and moderate forms of food insecurity, but the complex network of A'uwẽ food reciprocity was a fundamental element that successfully mitigated the most serious form of food insecurity—not eating.

The household food security portion of the questionnaire consisted of a series of three questions, each representing a more severe level of food insecurity than the prior question: (1) did you feel concerned that the staple/important food in your home could run out before you could get more?; (2) was there a day when you or someone else at home was hungry but ate little because there was not enough food?; and (3) did you or someone else in the household go a full day without eating because you did not have any food? The three questions were applied twice, once in reference to the prior month and once for the prior year.

According to the results of these food security questions, fewer people reported that someone in the household worried in the prior month that food would run out before they could get more (69.0 percent) than reported that someone in the household felt hungry (83.3 percent). Far fewer people reported that someone in the household spent a whole day without eating in the prior month (7.1 percent). The results of the same questions referring to the prior year show a similar pattern with somewhat more expressive values: 78.6 percent reported that someone at home worried that food would run out before they could get more, 85.7 percent reported that someone in the household felt hungry, and only 19.0 percent reported that someone in the household spent a whole day without eating. Thus, feeling hungry was more common than worrying that food would run out before more could be obtained, while it was comparatively unusual for someone to go a whole day without eating.

In our semistructured interviews, a recurrent theme was that many members of younger generations no longer appreciated or were not interested in traditional or locally produced A'uwẽ foods. Many interviewees, both young and old, highlighted the preference of younger individuals to eat food purchased in the city. Many young mothers reported exclusively purchasing food in town rather than participating in local subsistence activities to produce or collect food within the Indigenous land, despite the high prices in supermarkets. From the perspective of a young mother, "for food on a daily basis, I shop in the city, right, it's not here in the Indigenous land, but I buy sometimes in the city." Another young mother reinforced the pattern: "I only buy in the city. I'm the new generation, you know, I don't produce on Indigenous land now. Now I buy food out there." The preference for market foods was maintained despite many individuals reporting that in their opinions, purchased foods brought diseases that could be avoided with a traditional diet. One man explained, "White people's food is good, but it brings disease, many diseases."

Both men and women reported participating in the management of household financial resources, with a tendency for women to indicate that they had autonomy to decide how money was spent in town. According to an elderly mother, "I'm the one who decides, because only I have a retirement pension here. I do the shopping." A younger mother emphasized the important role women played in managing household financial resources: "I decide to buy clothes for the children. Here men don't run things; it is the woman who decides." A younger father characterized financial management in his household as a collaboration between himself and his two wives. Yet another young father explained how he purchased the food, but the women of the household told him what to purchase: "I receive R$180 from Bolsa Família. I spend this money buying food for the family, but who decides are the women." Similar statements were recurrent in our interviews.

These responses reflected cultural patterns involving the themes of individual and collective property, as well as the influential roles of women in making spending decisions. Traditionally, when women collected food, they did so on their own without input from their husbands. When men hunted or fished, they also did so according to their own priorities, without interference from their wives. Spending money seems to occupy an intermediate position between these two cultural models, since the decision of what to buy may be retained by women even when men earn the money or do the shopping.

Most women considered decisions to share food with other households their domain, although some men reported participating. An older woman explained that she distributed purchased and garden foods to her sons' households as well as to houses in other communities because financial resources and garden produce were more abundant in her household. Her son provided a complementary statement, explaining that because he earned very little money, the food in his house disappeared quickly. In these moments, his mother helped, as she did for her other sons. He also mentioned that at other times, when he had the money to purchase food, it was shared with other houses in need. One young woman reported that the decision to share food was hers alone, as well as the decision to ask for food from other households when hers had run out. Her discourse was punctuated with the unhappy observation that there were many mouths to feed, such as her father-in-law, who eats at her house, leaving her unsatisfied with the quantity of food in her household.

One woman characterized the new trend of eating primarily market foods, rather than replenishable traditional foods, as connected to what she characterized as the increasing necessity of routinely asking for food from other households. Similarly, an elder man reported that in his evaluation, worrying about lack of food, or feeling lack of food, could be attributed to increased reliance on market foods: "As for the food in my house, I am satisfied. This despite being worried at the end of the month because everything starts to run out. The 'whites' taught us all the things that make us suffer. . . . Before, I didn't miss city food. Before, we ate fish, game, didn't worry about anything. Now, we must buy things from the market, like rice and beans, soy oil . . . now we buy these things, but there's not enough money." Satisfaction with one's household food conditions was often attributed to the happiness of one's children when food is plentiful. For example, one man reported. "I am satisfied when there is a lot of food at home. The children are happy with the food. They are going to celebrate, play, that's when I am very satisfied."

Dissatisfaction with one's household's food was also a common theme, often mixed with comments or complaints that certain relatives deplete food reserves by eating at their house. A recurrent statement was that immediately after shopping in the market, when the house was full of food, people were content with their household food situation. After relatives visited and ate their food or took food as gifts, however, the reserves became depleted, and people became dissatisfied with their household food conditions. The theme of satisfaction upon purchasing ample foods and dissatisfaction upon their depletion through sharing with relatives and neighbors was reported by multiple young women and demonstrates that reciprocity and food sharing can be accompanied by dissatisfaction. I am aware of an acute ambiguity between the importance for well-being (hunger mitigation) of asking or receiving food from others and the discontentment that resulted from exhausting food resources by sharing and attending to others' requests.

According to some interviewees, when food ran out at home, they looked to traditional subsistence activities to meet households demands. This was a recurrent but less common response. For example, according to a young mother, "when the food runs out, I'll go to the cerrado to get traditional food to sustain the children." Similarly, a young man described hunting with his elders when market food ran out and sharing the resulting game meat with others. These final reports show that reciprocity was common but not the only hunger mitigation strategy for some households in the study communities.

The food security profile reported above was discouraging, with large majorities of households reporting worrying that food would run out and feeling hunger. These results showed that public policies aimed at mitigating food insecurity had little success in these A'uwẽ communities. In contrast, however, very few respondent households reported that someone in the household went without food for an entire day. Based on our qualitative interviews, we conclude that A'uwẽ strategies for mitigating hunger, especially traditional forms of food reciprocity, provided residents of most households means to obtain food before a full day passed without eating. Reciprocity was practiced with market foods in addition to traditional or garden foods. In fact, it may have been even more common to give or receive market foods because their economic prominence and perpetual scarcity was reported by interviewees to stimulate need.

Recent literature regarding Australian Aborigines has focused on demonstrating that hybrid economies are "more than merely transitional to capitalist incorporation" (Buchanan 2014, 12). Research among the A'uwẽ at the Pimentel Barbosa community is consistent with this orientation, showing that after the Xavante Project was defunded and people's time investment in rice agriculture decreased, they reemphasized collecting, hunting, and fishing accompanied by small-scale family gardening (Coimbra Jr. et al. 2002; Santos et al. 1997). These events demonstrate A'uwẽ resilience to dramatic transformations in the availability of external government inputs. The contemporary public policies of social inclusion accessed by residents of the study communities, which included Bolsa Família, retirement pensions, school meal programs, basic food baskets, and maternity financial assistance, should be understood as products of a specific moment in the country's political history that might not endure. With a long history of boom-and-bust economies driven by unstable government inputs, the A'uwẽ at Pimentel Barbosa and Etênhiritipá will likely experience future episodes of rebalancing of the hybrid economy, potentially in favor of subsistence food production.

Other factors may also affect the scales of the hybrid economy. For example, A'uwẽ communities and the rest of the world have recently been faced with the need to protect themselves during the COVID-19 pandemic. The Pimentel Barbosa community reacted with the innovative solution of going on trek in the cerrado to reduce their risk of exposure. A large portion of the community relocated to the Rio das Mortes, some forty kilometers distant, for about five months in 2020, where they collected, fished, and hunted for food. Although participants referred to this trip as a family trek, they remained at a single base camp rather than traveling between camp sites.

They had the benefit of on-hand transportation (truck and motorcycles) to return to the community should need arise, such as to visit the primary health-care unit. It was not an attempt at total isolation. Some people also left camp to go to town for political meetings and to conduct other kinds of business. Some salaried individuals and social benefit recipients may have gone to town to collect their money and purchase foods. I interpret this family trek as an adjustment of a traditional subsistence mode to contemporary circumstances, prompted by concern about the pandemic. It provides insight into what was currently considered a trek, with motorized vehicles and continued reliance on governmental services. It demonstrates a high potential for food sovereignty despite an apparent generational gap in traditional food knowledge transmission to some younger people. It also suggests that the transition from household food production to purchasing was not unilinear, just as the end of the rice project resulted in a return to food collecting, hunting, and fishing. This family trek was an opportunity for youths to comprehend some benefits of continuing traditional subsistence practices and learning about the landscape resources available to them despite the dominance of market foods in their contemporary food economy.

Bridging Generational Gaps

The current situation at the Pimentel Barbosa and Etênhiritipá communities involved a pervasive generational bifurcation. Many elders valued traditional foods and wished their younger relatives would come to appreciate them and learn how to procure them. Many youths and young adults had little interest in them and preferred to rely on market foods. Yet, neither elders nor younger people consumed traditional foods with notable frequency. In these communities, there had not yet occurred a generalized resurgence in interest in traditional foods or amplified discourse about food sovereignty motivated by health concerns or interest in preserving cultural food heritage. Nevertheless, some younger people showed great interest in collecting or hunting, having the potential to bridge the generational gap by retaining traditional ecological knowledge without interruption.

Participation by A'uwē of the Pimentel Barbosa Indigenous Land in Brazilian national society brought enormous transformations over the seventy-five years since stable contact was established with the SPI. However impactful these changes may have been on foodways, they were mediated by A'uwē cultural resilience, strongly informed by highly salient traditionalist social constructions of reciprocity understood to promote community well-being. A'uwē foods were not only about nutrition, but also involved strong identity markers that were lavishly displayed during community distributions of game meat during wedding and initiation rites, as well as gifts of maize loaves and roasted wild root vegetables during spiritual rituals and other ceremonial occasions. These ceremonies and their significance for social relations, ethnic identity, and well-being invigorated community interest in traditional foodways independently of the abundant economic changes currently underway. Thus, regardless of the future direction of the country's public policies that bear on diets and food economies, there is a good chance A'uwẽ society will be sufficiently flexible within its nonstatic hybrid economy to maintain culturally relevant traditional ecological knowledge of cerrado foods and thereby exhibit greater resilience in the face of changing circumstances of monetarization and food security.

Sedentism, Healthcare Units, Schoolhouses, and Electrification

The A'uwẽ were a highly mobile people until the late 1970s through the early 1990s, about the time the Xavante Project was underway. Their mobility took three main forms: trekking for substantial portions of the year, moving community sites relatively frequently, and being regularly physically active. Even when, according to their oral history, they lived as a single people, undivided, at Sõrepré community for several decades, there were many satellite communities, and people tended to move about using Sõrepré as a main community of reference. They continued to be highly mobile even for decades after establishing enduring relations with the SPI. The first A'uwẽ group to engage amicably with this government agency was one that currently occupies the Pimentel Barbosa Indigenous Land. They eventually relocated to a site near the SPI post at São Domingos, but it took them a decade, from 1946 to 1956, relocating from the Arobonhipo'opá community to the Etênhiritipá community (the same location that is now occupied by the Pimentel Barbosa and Etênhiritipá communities) and then to Wedezé community, near the SPI post. Elders described those years as characterized by "total liberty" and "freedom" to do as people pleased, including trekking wherever family groups chose. While conducting ethnographic fieldwork at Wedezé in 1958 and 1962, Maybury-Lewis (1967) observed that most households spent more time on trek than they did in the community. As settler activity increased near the post, several subgroups left Wedezé in the late 1950s and early 1960s, relocating to other community sites. Only between about 1969 to 1973 did everyone reunite in residence at Etênhiritipá in the community now known as Pimentel Barbosa. In 1973, the post, then run by FUNAI, was relocated to the site beside the Pimentel Barbosa community where the current primary healthcare unit is located (Graham 1995; Welch, Santos, et al. 2013).

Aside from community divisions, which were responsible for the multiplication of communities within the current boundaries of the Pimentel Barbosa Indigenous Land from one to twenty as of the writing of this book (establishment of just one of these communities, Belém, was due to immigration from a different Indigenous land), the population at the Pimentel Barbosa community remained residentially sedentary since it first moved there about fifty years ago. As I discussed in chapter 6, the A'uwẽ did not consider the original move from Wedezé and its satellite communities to the Pimentel Barbosa community to be permanent at the time. They subsequently discovered that their previous territories had been sold to ranchers except within a drastically reduced parcel that would soon become the Pimentel Barbosa Indigenous Land. Thus, limited to a small officially recognized territory circumscribed by agribusiness, they were forced to modify their mobile lifestyle to fit within these new boundaries and limit visits to traditional territories outside the Indigenous land to avoid aggravating disagreeable ranchers (some ranchers were more welcoming and allowed A'uwẽ from Pimentel Barbosa and subsequently established communities to visit for hunting, collecting, and to pay their respects at ancestors' burial sites). Communities no longer relocated temporarily, and trekking was constrained to few campsites until it was largely discontinued in the 1990s. Residential mobility, which was a key social and subsistence modality strongly associated with ethnic identity (many A'uwẽ refer to themselves as historically nomadic), was drastically impeded, thereby contributing to a sense of constraint and loss of tradition among elders I interviewed. Whereas many of these elders viewed this residential immobilization as a cause of reduced community well-being, some younger parents expressed preference for the present sedentary lifestyle with its diverse benefits, many of which are described in the remainder of this chapter, as well as its compatibility with having desirably larger families, especially numerous children and grandchildren.

Established communities rarely relocated in recent years, for several reasons, even though they continued to fission. There were no longer such ample and immediate benefits to opening new communities as there were during the Xavante Project in the 1970s and 1980s, which included reproduction of governmental salaries and other financial inputs, but there were a series of public investments that, once realized, tended to encourage communities to stay put. Unlike in the past, many of these benefits were hard won through political advocacy by community leaders. The first of these were primary healthcare units and schoolhouses.

Primary Healthcare Units

Contrary to the large SPI operation at São Domingos, the modest FUNAI post at Pimentel Barbosa in the 1970s and 1980s was typical of the era, with several buildings constructed to house a small staff and a school. The miniscule primary healthcare unit operated out of a door behind the schoolhouse, was intermittently staffed by a nursing assistant (secondary education preparation), and contained insufficient supplies of basic medicines, such as aspirin, antibiotics, and antimalarials, as well as oversupplies of medicines of no use for the A'uwẽ, such as those to treat high blood pressure, with which the A'uwẽ were not yet afflicted in the 1970s (Flowers 1983).

Over the years, however, the Indigenous primary healthcare unit developed and became more important in the lives of people residing in the Pimentel Barbosa community and, after its foundation in 2006, the Etênhiritipá community. The healthcare unit's benefits, such as significantly reducing child mortality, expressively affected A'uwẽ notions of how to properly care for children to improve their bodily wellness. It also illustrates how the healthcare unit's intercultural dynamic contributed to the emergence of new notions of appropriate therapeutic itineraries, which now included reliance on traditional A'uwẽ ethnobiological and spiritual medical practices in combination with biomedicine accessed through governmental health services (medical pluralism).

Although not all communities had their own primary healthcare units, the Pimentel Barbosa community had had one since soon after FUNAI became responsible for Indigenous people's primary healthcare in 1967. In 1999, following creation of the Unified Health System (Sistema Unico de Saude), the Indigenous Healthcare Subsystem (Subsistema de Atenção à Saúde Indígena, or SASI) was established to provide differentiated healthcare, which was conceived as primary healthcare that functions in consonance with Indigenous communities, thereby ensuring that Indigenous knowledge and practices were respected, and culturally appropriate care was provided. Responsibility for executing the Indigenous Healthcare Subsystem changed hands twice since the Pimentel Barbosa community was established (for a review of the history of public health policy for Indigenous peoples in Brazil, see Cardoso et al. 2013).

With the creation of the subsystem, Indigenous health services were transferred from FUNAI to the National Health Foundation (Fundação Nacional de Saúde—FUNASA), Ministry of Health. As a result, a new primary healthcare unit was established in a small building constructed by a European nongovernmental association near the old Pimentel Barbosa community schoolhouse, and

FUNASA staffed it with a full-time nurse technician and two salaried Indigenous health agents, supported by a nurse who traveled between communities. This was the first time the Pimentel Barbosa population had access to reliable, if still deficient, health services. Primary care nurses played a strategic role in the routine functioning of the primary healthcare unit, being responsible for maintaining updated vaccination schedules, conducting prenatal consultations, dispensing prescribed medications, monitoring chronic diseases (e.g., diabetes, hypertension), among many other important tasks. Very often, the nurse was the only health professional with higher education at the primary healthcare unit, usually assisted by at least one bilingual Indigenous health agent, who was essential to the workflow because many members of the community did not speak Portuguese and had culturally distinct understandings of health and illness processes.

Following implementation of the SASI, which remained in effect through the present, several major healthcare improvements occurred that directly affected well-being among resident A'uwẽ. One was the beginning of scheduled childhood vaccinations for measles and polio, which had been major causes of death and illness among the A'uwẽ in previous decades. Another example was the furnishing of supervised tuberculosis chemotherapy, which practically eliminated this disease from the population. Also, regular prenatal consultations, which did not exist beforehand, became available to all expectant mothers. These interventions alone were responsible for drastically improving the survival of A'uwẽ children. Many parents and grandparents I spoke with were enormously pleased with the large sizes of their families, which they indicated was not possible in earlier decades because of higher child mortality and greater interbirth spacing. Finally, another benefit of the Indigenous Healthcare Subsystem was access by referral to secondary and tertiary services such as cataract, orthopedic, and congenital heart defect surgeries. These newly available services dramatically improved A'uwẽ physical wellness even though the Indigenous Healthcare Subsystem was justifiably criticized for diverse ongoing deficiencies, including mismanagement of financial resources, unavailability of needed medications and supplies, lack of qualified health professionals, and deficient intercultural sensitivity and accommodations, among others.

By 2004, when I first visited, standing in the morning line at the FUNASA primary healthcare unit was a regular, even daily, habit for many mothers with children and people taking overseen medications. As more people came to suffer from chronic noncommunicable diseases such as diabetes and hypertension, and others contracted infectious diseases requiring antibiotics, visits to the healthcare unit came to be a regular occurrence for many people. Besides dispensing medications, the healthcare unit served as a front-line resource for children and adults with illnesses or injuries. If the health technician judged a case to require additional professional attention, transportation was arranged to take patients to the nearest public hospital of reference, about a hundred kilometers distant. Additionally, the health services were responsible for maintaining water wells and tanks with treated potable water for every community, although it can take many years for these to be constructed in newly established communities, thus seriously compromising health, especially of young children vulnerable to diarrhea and collateral effects.

The presence of a (relatively) well-functioning healthcare unit came to motivate people to remain in their community or to live close by to easily access its services daily. It also caused many individuals to avoid leaving the community temporarily to go on trek, as was common in the past, for fear of being isolated from valued health services in the event of unexpected injury or illness. This remained especially true for parents of young children, who often expressed to me their desire to stay close to the healthcare unit in case their children needed its services. My A'uwẽ interlocutors told me and demonstrated by their actions that the healthcare unit was a key resource, and they valued its proximity to such a degree that they opted to modify their residential and subsistence activities. When Etênhiritipá separated from Pimentel Barbosa, it relocated such a short distance away in part to benefit from the local presence of the primary healthcare unit. The benefits of having a healthcare unit in proximity to one's community were significant and included improved access to emergency care, transport to hospitals, facility in obtaining routine consultations, and local administration of controlled and maintenance medications. Smaller and newer communities tended not to receive healthcare units of their own, being serviced by those located in larger nearby communities, with obvious disadvantages. Larger and older communities with local healthcare units, such as Etênhiritipá and Pimentel Barbosa, had considerable motivation to remain in their existing locations. Thus, community healthcare units served as a first major pillar of contemporary sedentarization.

In 2010, amid accusations that FUNASA mismanaged resources and was plagued by corruption, the Indigenous Healthcare Subsystem was transferred to the Special Secretariat for Indigenous Health (Secretaria Especial de Saúde Indígena—SESAI), which implemented a higher standard of health services than had previously existed. Several years after SESAI assumed responsibility for healthcare at the Pimentel Barbosa and Etênhiritipá communities, a new primary healthcare unit was constructed that conformed to upgraded national standards, with a reception desk; nursing, medical, and dentistry consultation rooms; and adequate staff housing in a separate building to the back. The entire primary healthcare unit was surrounded by a wall with barbed wire, with room for two SESAI vehicles within the gate. Although SESAI was rightfully criticized by A'uwẽ health service users as understaffed, underfunded, and lacking in basic supplies, the current service standard was higher than it had been under FUNASA. In the first place, there were now full-time nurses on staff at the healthcare unit, not just nurse assistants or technicians, who continued to be assisted by Indigenous health agents. Additionally, health professionals including doctors and dentists now frequented the healthcare unit to offer additional services without requiring that A'uwẽ patients travel to the nearest hospital in town. Access to doctors was greatly improved beginning in 2013 by the More Doctors (Mais Médicos) program that initially contracted Cuban doctors under a bilateral agreement to improve access to doctors nationally, and subsequently employed Brazilian doctors to work in underserved communities, including Indigenous lands. Dentists, who rotated through multiple A'uwẽ healthcare units, maintained regular calendars to attend to the oral health needs of the population. Before SESAI, no oral health services were offered to the A'uwẽ residing in the Pimentel Barbosa Indigenous Land. Improved infrastructure, more professional staff, and more comfortable clinical spaces continued to reinforce the importance of the primary healthcare unit in the lives of Pimentel and Etênhiritipá community residents.

Most illnesses currently treated at the healthcare unit were not present before the A'uwẽ interacted directly or indirectly with people of European descent. Although such diseases as some chronic viral infections (e.g., hepatitis B and herpes), intestinal parasites, gastroenteritis, cutaneous leishmaniosis, and routine injuries are known to have been present in precolonial times (Coimbra Jr. and Santos 2004; Merbs 1992; Salzano and Callegari-Jacques 1988), many of the other reasons people sought medical attention in recent years are historically derived from the colonial experience. For example, A'uwẽ continued to suffer from tuberculosis (in greatly reduced numbers), influenza, and pneumonia (malaria was eradicated from the region that includes the A'uwẽ territories between the late 1970s and the early 1990s). Additionally, they increasingly suffered from chronic noncommunicable diseases, such as cancer, and those associated with transformations in the dietary economy and physical inactivity, such as diabetes and cardiovascular diseases. With the introduction and widespread acquisition of motorized vehicles, there was now an unprecedentedly high frequency of vehicular accidents besides increased physical inactivity resulting from reduced walking. Here we see the rub of the primary healthcare unit's contribution to A'uwẽ sedentism—in anchoring people to a fixed community and thereby reducing physical activity, limiting access to arable land for agriculture, and reducing access to local wild food resources, it contributed to some of the very illnesses it sought to address. This apparent irony was complex and not reducible to the sole role of primary healthcare. There are multiple reasons the A'uwẽ are now more sedentary than they were in the past, and the ramifications of this transformation are not simple.

Schoolhouses

A second pillar of the transformation to sedentarism since the 1990s was local community primary education schools. The first such school was opened by FUNAI after it relocated to the Pimentel Barbosa community in 1973 and was abandoned for a time in 1976 as a result of disinterest by the A'uwẽ. It operated intermittently through the 1980s when teachers were available (Laura R. Graham, personal communication, 2021). Responsibility for schoolhouses was decentralized between state secretariates of education and federally funded municipal secretariats of education in 1991. The Pimentel Barbosa Municipal Primary Education School was opened in 1992. The number of enrolled students boomed after 1998, mainly because it converted to bilingual (A'uwẽ/Portuguese) teaching in 1997 (Russo 2005). This major shift in educational logic was brought about by a 1996 national law establishing bilingual teaching and interculturality as basic principles of Indigenous education, which was an important move to implement the 1988 constitutional right of Indigenous peoples to use their own languages and learning processes.

Bilingualism implied hiring A'uwẽ teachers. The teaching staff was mostly A'uwẽ by 2004, when I arrived, and soon thereafter became exclusively A'uwẽ after implementation of a 2001 law providing for the autonomy of Indigenous schools and higher education of Indigenous professors. These changes stimulated community schoolhouses to become more consistently important features of community life. Students enrolled in much greater numbers with the educational experience then under the responsibility of mostly A'uwẽ teachers. Although the national school curriculum did not change, the indigenization of the teaching staff transformed the school into an A'uwẽ space, where the curriculum was taught in a language students understood and culturally interpreted to make it more relevant and intelligible.

When I first visited the Pimentel Barbosa community in 2004, numerous classes were attended by male students of diverse ages, covering the first eight years of primary education. For a time, classes for women were held in a separate building within the community, not in the schoolhouse at the post adjacent to the community. Some years later, the first female A'uwẽ teacher was hired to teach girls in a classroom in the main schoolhouse. More recently, there were two female A'uwẽ teachers at this school, from whom many of the community's girls took classes.

When the Etênhiritipá community separated from the Pimentel Barbosa community in 2006 and moved just a half kilometer away, both continued to share the existing primary healthcare unit, but Etênhiritipá decided to construct its own new schoolhouse within the community. Whereas the Pimentel Barbosa school was municipal, the A'uwẽ at Etênhiritipá sought a state school, a project that took more than two years to formalize, during which no classes were held. Thereafter, for many years, school operation was funded by the state of Mato Grosso, but no resources were allocated for the construction of a schoolhouse. The school operated out of a long palm-thatched structure built with unfinished wooden poles by the community residents. Only later did the state pay for the construction of a provisional school with cement block walls, although the roofing continued to be made of palm thatch installed and maintained by the community. The last time I visited, plans were underway to improve the permanence of the structure and facilities.

Recently, both schools were fully functioning, offering all eight years of primary education. The Pimentel Barbosa school had also received state funding to complement the municipal school budget and thereby offer more comprehensive educational services. Development of the Pimentel Barbosa and Etênhiritipá schools contributed to their becoming considered virtually mandatory for all children. Part of this change occurred through the federal cash transfer program Bolsa Família, initiated in 2003, which provided monthly assistance payments to mothers or, in the case of underage mothers, fathers, if they met a series of conditionalities, which included children's minimum school attendance and being measured, weighed, and vaccinated regularly at the primary healthcare unit. Unsatisfactory school attendance could cause suspension of a mother's monthly benefit. The Bolsa Família program was therefore a major factor in stimulating contemporary sedentism (it is still too early to tell how the replacement cash transfer program, Brazil Assistance, will affect this trend).

Also, the perspectives of A'uwẽ parents changed substantially in the intervening years after the FUNAI school fell into intermittent use after 1976. There was now widespread recognition that learning to speak Portuguese and gaining knowledge about the non-A'uwẽ world benefited individuals and their communities. Formerly, this kind of intercultural education was only available by sending children away to study in distant cities while living with non-Indigenous host families. Now, children could attend their community's school and gain important knowledge to prepare them for engaging with the outside world, especially Brazilian society but also people from foreign countries, such as myself (I was once asked to sing along while my age set peers performed "Twinkle, Twinkle, Little Star" in broken English, which they had learned from the school's English curriculum).

Schooling recently became widely valued as a means to continue to higher education, as evidenced by the first generation of students who were currently studying at or had recently graduated from regional universities. Given the rapid pace of A'uwẽ entrance into university programs, I expect the educational landscape to change noticeably by the time this book goes to print. Schooling was also valued as a step toward accessing employment. Until recently, most advanced students sought employment as teachers at their community's schools, while many others sought work in support positions at these schools, such as cooks and custodial staff, or as community health agents at the primary healthcare unit. Nonetheless, recently, some individuals were looking beyond their communities for employment, which had not occurred since the 1970s, when some A'uwẽ worked for nearby mines, farms, and ranches, or for FUNAI. For example, in 2019, my younger adoptive brother Hernan passed the qualification process for hire as a municipal police officer. The last time I visited, he was taking classes in preparation for this job. Thus, schooling was a relatively new means to meet cultural expectations that a young A'uwẽ man provide for his wife, children, parents-in-law, and other kin. Through employment made possible by schooling, young women and men could purchase food and other supplies for their households and, through mostly female-coordinated reciprocity, contribute to other households as well.

Another way of looking at formal education as an emergent cultural value is through its potential power to engage and reorder the ongoing legacy of colonial relationships. Education was viewed by many A'uwẽ as a means to operate in a non-A'uwẽ world more competently and therefore to become less vulnerable to racially based inequality. By learning about the colonizers, one became able to engage them without sacrificing one's cultural values and beliefs. I was told by several of the first A'uwẽ to receive formal education outside their communities in the 1970s and 1980s that they were refused service at some local restaurants despite constitutional law prohibiting racial discrimination. They told me that based on their education about their rights to equal treatment, they formulated a peaceful strategy for combating this form of discrimination. As they recalled, they began sitting down in local restaurants that had previously treated them poorly or refused them service rather than avoiding such establishments. They ignored disrespectful treatment by staff and customers, maintaining respectful composure or politely informing people of their right to receive equal service. As they reported to me, by persisting with this strategy, A'uwẽ customers were eventually treated more respectfully by these restaurants. When I arrived in 2004 and continuing to this day, A'uwẽ received stares and occasional disrespectful comments by some restaurant customers but no longer experienced unequal service. This example illustrates how some A'uwẽ valued education as a means to resist oppression and take steps to unburden themselves of the colonial inheritance of their contemporary social environments. Thus, schooling was valued by the A'uwẽ not only as a mechanism to facilitate receiving government assistance and obtaining salaried employment, but also for improving their broader intercultural circumstances in a region of Brazil where internal colonialism is recent and ongoing, associated with abundant racism and other dehumanizing experiences involving prejudice. I can attest to examples, such as my discovery in 2014 that a regional public hospital reserved two rooms near the garbage bins at the back exit with no furnishings other than old mattresses on the floor for A'uwẽ patients and their companions to rest and sleep. This arrangement was described to me by an A'uwẽ leader as a humiliating experience that was made worse when he overheard health professionals discussing who would do the undesirable chore of attending to A'uwẽ patients housed in these disheveled rooms. He said he knew he had a right to a clean bed elevated from the floor but was too shamed by this treatment to register a complaint, although he intended to in the future. Having been educated about legal guarantees against such discrimination, he considered it his right and duty to make it known that he did not accept it.

School attendance affected many of the events and practices associated with age organization discussed in previous chapters. The schools at Pimentel Barbosa and Etênhiritipá generally followed the same calendars as their urban counterparts, with five days of classes per week, two-day weekends, and predetermined holidays and vacation periods. Unfortunately, these calendars were rarely congruent with the many rites and ceremonies associated with the A'uwẽ life cycle. For example, in 2005 my novitiate adult peers were all taking night classes, which started roughly at the same time they were expected to congregate in their novitiate adult council meeting in the community plaza and sing around the community after sunset. This conflict was resolved in two ways. First, the community forgave their absence in the community when they had class. Second, when they were on vacation, they made exemplary efforts to hold their meetings and to sing every night, and thereby reestablish their traditionalist routine and contribute to a cheerful mood in the community.

Other adaptations were also made to reconcile the ceremonial and school calendars. Sometimes, a school director sought permission from school secretariates to alter the class calendar to accommodate important rites and ceremonies that would otherwise create scheduling conflicts. For example, in 2011, special permission was obtained for the Pimentel Barbosa community school to close during key segments of the ceremonial events associated with the preinitiates' initiation into novitiate adulthood. Thus, that year the boys could participate fully in all the capacities expected of them during the ceremonial calendar. In 2019, however, a different strategy was used to accommodate the next cycle of secular initiation rites in the Pimentel Barbosa community. The ceremonies that year, which had been delayed three years because of several deaths of important ceremonial officiants and spiritual initiation rites held in 2018, were consolidated from the usual span of approximately six months to a single month to coincide with the standard July school vacation. In consultation with elders, the rites were abbreviated to compact all the important ceremonial events into this four-week period and thereby retain the municipal school calendar unaltered.

These examples illustrate how important school attendance had become and show that even the ritual calendar had been modified to ensure boys and girls could continue to attend both school and their important rites of passage. Framed in terms of well-being, they demonstrated that considerable attention was dedicated to ensuring the ongoing viability of both traditionalist cultural values expressed through A'uwẽ age organization, which was considered integral to the proper social construction of adults from children, and emergent values of the importance of formal schooling for the wellness of young people and the whole community. It appears that neither was understood to be more important than the other. Rather, they were considered equally worthy of youth participation and community accommodation, such as when they came into scheduling conflict. Consequently, community schoolhouses provided a reason for youths in all households to remain close to their community for most of the calendar year, decreasing opportunities for these young people to participate in multiple-day excursions, such as treks, except on weekends and during official holidays and vacations.

A final factor encouraged residential permanence to retain access to established schools. Under the current decentralized organizational structure that delegates responsibility for Indigenous schools to states and municipalities, construction of new schoolhouses in recently established rural Indigenous communities was not automatic, and their residents had to advocate for allocation of state or municipal funds for schools to provide their children with local access to primary education. Once established, however, a schoolhouse was a powerful motivator for a community to remain where it was. The uncertainty of moving to a new location, where it may take years to regain access to local schooling, was an imposing deterrent to relocating a community.

Electrification

The third and final major pillar of sedentarization was more recent than the first two. Indigenous health posts and schoolhouses were first established for the Pimentel Barbosa community in the 1970s, or even earlier if one considers their former occupation of Wedezé in the 1950s near the SPI post at São Domingos. In contrast, electrification of A'uwẽ communities including Pimentel Barbosa and Etênhiritipá did not occur until 2011. Before that year, the drinking water well at the Pimentel Barbosa community had a diesel generator donated by a European nonprofit organization to power a pump. A few people diverted energy from this generator to their houses to run televisions intermittently.

Initiated in 2003, Brazil's progressive rural electrification initiative Light for All (Luz para Todos) aimed to promote socioeconomic development and improve quality of life by providing universal subsidized domestic access to the electrical grid. Although this program sought to benefit all rural Brazilian households, special priority was given to the country's diverse Indigenous population, as well as to other traditional communities who wished to participate. Over the course of a year beginning in 2010, multiple community meetings with representatives of all nine communities then present in the Pimentel Barbosa Indigenous Land were held to determine whether consent should be given to install electrical lines within the land. Debate touched on the many benefits of having access to illumination, refrigerators or freezers, and televisions within the home, as well as potential negative consequences of these changes, including cultural change through excessive television watching and alterations to food-ways through the introduction of refrigerators and freezers. Elders expressed concern that younger people would further lose interest in traditional foods and fail to learn how to gather and hunt wild foods because kitchen appliances would allow perishable food from supermarkets to be stored and accessed throughout the month following payday. Most people expressed to me that they welcomed the benefits of electricity in their homes while expecting its introduction to provoke some changes. The final decision to allow installation of power lines was eventually made through consensus by almost all communities. Many families began saving money months in advance to buy appliances. Some retail stores sent sales representatives to communities to offer appliances on credit.

Installation of power lines from the nearest highway to the communities was accomplished quickly in late 2011 by the local electricity distribution company. Each house received an electrical meter, which was read monthly by the power company. The corresponding batch of bills were picked up in town by a community representative, who distributed them to households. According to this representative in one community, a large portion of the bills each month were past due, and many people paid only when disconnection was imminent. Virtually all households came to have a refrigerator or freezer, as well as a television and electrical lighting. The near universality of televisions was an incremental change, considering that before the electrification project, about five households had televisions powered by the intermittent water well generator in the Pimentel Barbosa community, where relatives and neighbors gathered to watch the news, novelas, and movies on rented DVDs (see Graham 2016).

Implementation of this national infrastructure program contributed to recent changes in the local A'uwẽ food economy, with repercussions for the community's food diversity and social relations of resource sharing. Freezers and refrigerators improved storage of foods and led to increased purchasing of industrialized perishables. For example, beef, chicken, and fish came to be purchased more frequently and in larger quantities. Wild game and fish no longer needed to be consumed or shared immediately. Although A'uwẽ cultural protocols for sharing wild and purchased meats and fish with extended family members and neighbors continued to be practiced, these new storage technologies, some of which incidentally hid food stores from sight during visits by members of other households, permitted greater retention within the household. With households purchasing more perishable foods after 2011, within-community sale of foods began to occur for the first time alongside traditional reciprocity and exchange. Increased reliance on purchased industrialized foods, which was also attributable to the general process of monetarization of community and household economies underway at the same time, discouraged physical activities associated with traditional food procurement, especially among youths. For similar reasons, comparing 2011 and 2019, household gardens came to be less common, smaller, and located closer to the community. These factors suggest decreased food sovereignty with potential health consequences.

Before connection to the grid, the presence of a television at home was shown to be associated with physical inactivity (Lucena et al. 2016). After 2011, most households had televisions that were often left on day and night. With the ability to recharge devices and the installation of internet access at local schoolhouses, many students and teachers acquired smartphones and came to access social media regularly. Use of Bluetooth facilitated file exchange, even in the absence of internet. Exposure to idealizations of consumerism and other forms of media expression became nearly constant via such avenues as advertisements, television programs, and social media platforms. Child play and games seemed to reflect traditional subsistence and homemaking themes less than they had previously, although I did not investigate this dimension thoroughly.

Some households with less access to income appeared to be increasingly marginalized, unable to participate in the emergent food economy. Several households that did not purchase foods regularly for lack of income also reported having very little access to locally produced and acquired foods, perhaps due to the absence of knowledgeable residents, such as elders, who could procure these foods for the household. Emergence of socioeconomic differentiation between households in the same community and between communities was noticed in public health literature (Arantes et al. 2018; Welch et al. 2009). These studies showed that contrasts in income and industrialized household goods (as a measure of wealth) were associated with such health outcomes as dental caries and excess weight.

Since installation of the first electrical lines, the power company did not respond to requests for additional installations. Consequently, new houses tended to be positioned close to houses with an electrical meter so improvised lines could be run between them. New houses without this kind of access must go without in-home electricity but often stored foods in relatives' freezers. Also, since the lines' installation, eleven new communities were established within the land by splinter groups leaving other communities. This traditionally A'uwẽ demographic pattern continued despite new communities lacking access to grid connection. Residents in such communities expressed their hopes that power lines would soon reach them. Independently of their impacts, freezers, refrigerators, and televisions were desirable conveniences that contributed to the motivation to remain in an established community. Given the bureaucracy and delays in bringing electricity to a new community site, relocating a community, as was so common in the past, would introduce a great deal of uncertainty as to when these services and goods could be reacquired. Combined with the uncertainty of access to a primary healthcare unit and schooling, the impediments to relocation derived from stationary access to government services and policies were formidable.

Reflections on Contemporary Mobility

The multiplication of communities despite lack of access to electricity, schoolhouses, and health posts after relocation suggests these services were not significant factors in discouraging community divisions. They were, however, ample motivation for an existing community to remain where it was rather than following the historical pattern of moving community locations frequently and temporarily. This scenario led to a historically novel situation where communities continued to split but once established were not abandoned. In the past, community locations could be occupied for relatively short periods (as little as a few years) and, when unoccupied, served as trekking camps. For example, the Pimentel Barbosa community, which had given rise to eighteen derivative communities through successive divisions, continued to occupy the same location since it was (re)occupied in the late 1960s to early 1970s (it was previously occupied in the late 1940s to late 1950s) (Welch, Santos, et al. 2013). When the Etênhiritipá community split from Pimentel Barbosa in 2006, there was a cutting dispute over which faction would remain in the established community location and which would leave and open a new community elsewhere. This argument was resolved by the dissenting faction constructing its new community very close by and staking claim to the A'uwẽ language name for the site on which both communities—new and old—were located (Etênhiritipá). Not only did the new community wish to retain access to the primary healthcare unit, but it wanted to retain the reputation of being the traditionalist mother community that gave rise to many other newer communities within the land. The current

(2021–2022) division of the Etênhiritipá community faced a similarly tense dispute, with both factions refusing to leave and thereby relinquish control of its infrastructure and services, as well as its historically valuable name.

Community sedentism had several benefits that were appreciated by many A'uwẽ. Many younger people preferred the new lifestyle and the security it offered, including the ability to raise larger, healthier families and enjoy perceptions of decreased hardship. Indeed, with sedentarization and monetarization of the local economy (in part promoted through the presence of a primary healthcare unit and schoolhouse salaries), younger people had greater liberty to abstain from strenuous subsistence activities including collecting, hunting, fishing, and gardening. With access to primary healthcare units and decreased mobility, elders reported that shorter interbirth spacing was possible, and infant mortality was greatly reduced. Women who so desire might therefore have more children during their lifetimes. In 2011 the total fertility rate of women in the Pimentel Barbosa Indigenous Land was 8.2, which was very high but represented a decrease from a maximum of 10.2 in 1999–2004 (according to the 2010 national census, the Brazilian total fertility rate was 1.9) (Bibiani 2018; L. G. Souza 2008). Men with jobs were no longer expected to provide food for their families by hunting and gardening if they now had the means to purchase industrialized and ultraprocessed foods, which were preferred by many people today despite their potential negative health consequences.

Sedentism within a circumscribed Indigenous land also had potential undesirable implications. Among these were loss of traditional environmental knowledge, diminishment of bodily and spiritual force, environmental overuse, and potential for social conflict. The current trends of economic emphasis on maximizing financial income and consuming foods purchased at supermarkets at the expense of products of traditional collecting, hunting, fishing, and gardening activities in the cerrado landscape contributed to a partial generational gap in traditional environmental knowledge. With many elders reducing the frequency of their self-provisioning activities outside their communities, and many younger people disinterested in learning A'uwẽ subsistence activities that take place in the cerrado, continuous knowledge transmission was concentrated in fewer young people than it had been just a decade ago. Should this pattern continue, it would likely have unfavorable impacts on traditional environmental knowledge viability as it transforms from general to specialized knowledge.

According to contemporary male common knowledge, physical stamina was required for acquiring bodily and spiritual force. Bodily force was achieved by

walking and performing subsistence activities in the cerrado, as well as participating in strenuous ceremonial activities and competitions. Having participated
in dialogue with public health researchers for years and increasingly observed
the consequences of nutrition transition, A'uwẽ understood that not participating in these physical activities caused the body to lack strength, promoted accumulation of body fat, and facilitated development of cardiovascular diseases,
which in turn discouraged participation in healthful strenuous activities. This
catch-22 of physical inactivity also affected one's capacity for developing spiritual force, which was gained by demonstrating resolute endurance and stamina
during spiritual initiations and rituals. Lack of physical force due to sedentism
could lead to lack of spiritual capability and therefore to lower capacity for healing one's kin when they were afflicted by ailments or sorcery.

Unbeknownst to the A'uwẽ at the time, the historical move from Wedezé and
other communities to the Pimentel Barbosa community was a first step in ced-
ing much of their traditional territory to private interests and restricting themselves to a small land circumscribed by agribusiness. Nevertheless, residents of
the Pimentel Barbosa Indigenous Land were fortunate in that they continued
to have the smallest population density of any A'uwẽ land. This fact is largely
the result of A'uwẽ political activism, which had significant success increasing
the area of their land from 204,000 hectares in 1975 to 328,966 hectares in 1980.
Also, continual A'uwẽ political activism from 2000 through 2010 resulted in
identification of the nearby Wedezé Indigenous Land of 145,881 hectares, which
currently remains contested in the courts. The population continued to grow at
a fast pace, however, making it likely that their land could become inadequate,
as illustrated by current challenges faced by hunters when planning appropriate
hunting fires in the cerrado. Also, the dynamic of communities' hybrid economies (Altman 2007) should not be presumed to be a unilinear course toward
greater market participation. Should the current phase of increased access to
financial resources prove to be yet another boom-and-bust economic cycle, economic resilience might be required to transition from acquisition of traditional
foods mainly for limited ceremonial uses to daily consumption. Such a transformation would potentially place new strains on the restricted land available
to them, especially near sedentary communities.

Another negative consequence of sedentarization for well-being was the potential for exacerbated political conflict. The most well-known historical community to be inhabited for many decades was Sõrepré, thought to have been
continuously occupied from about 1890 to 1920 by the entirety of the A'uwẽ

population (Lopes da Silva 1992). Sõrepré was also famous in A'uwẽ oral history for its acute interfamily conflicts and accusations of sorcery, which ultimately caused the population to permanently divide into about seven subgroups that never reunited, except for occasional isolated marriages and minor relocations of individuals and small families. Similarly, today the centrifugal forces of health posts, schools, and electrification that disincentivized residential relocation may lead to exaggerated conflicts, which might have been dissipated were communities more mobile. The ability to go on trek for months at a time with just one's extended family may have provided a social escape valve that helped diffuse arguments before they became too intense (Maybury-Lewis 1967). Similarly, the flexibility of community subgroups to establish new, often temporary, communities may have contributed to checking disagreements before they grew overt and caused irreconcilable factional separations. This hypothesis is supported by A'uwẽ oral history, according to which communities often split and then rejoined several years later, rather than suffering from permanent ruptures. With the current pattern of sedentism, however, whereby people are motivated to reside continually in existing communities and trekking has been largely discontinued, tensions could escalate to dangerous levels before a subgroup or faction decided to establish a new community elsewhere. Thus, people embroiled in grave disputes potentially continued to occupy the same community for many months or years before splitting, during which resentment, distrust, and anger could grow.

One recent example suggests that the historical pattern of residential mobility did not become entirely obsolete. Wederã community left the Pimentel Barbosa community in 1996 in a storm of political tensions that continue to sour their relationship today. Some people who remained at Pimentel Barbosa, however, were close kin and friends of the group that relocated to Wederã, maintaining close ties with them over the years. When Pimentel Barbosa split again in 2006, many of these allies of Wederã moved to the Etênhiritipá community. Over the next few years, many households relocated from Wederã to Etênhiritipá, thereby reuniting extended families that had been ruptured by the 1996 split. This example suggests residential mobility in the form of temporary community divisions followed by amicable reunions remained a possibility under appropriate contemporary circumstances.

In closing this section, I would also like to call attention to the importance of recognizing that decreased residential mobility and trekking did not imply that all forms of mobility, some rooted in historical cultural values and practices, disappeared or lost their significance in recent times. Of the Mebêngôkre (Kayapó), Laura Zanotti (2014, 121) wrote, "Over the past 200 years, Kayapó communities have undergone a dramatic change from savannah-based semi-nomadism to living in villages in a federally protected reserve. Where these changes have been described as increased sedentism and decreased trekking, I suggest that such depictions of current Kayapó livelihoods conceal the fact that movement and mobility, in different ways, still play a role in everyday practices." Similarly, contemporary A'uwẽ moved from place to place on foot, by bicycle, riding motorcycles, in cars, by truck, aboard buses, and on airplanes. They circulated between community, river, schoolhouse, primary healthcare unit, gardens, song rehearsal hideouts, collecting areas, fishing spots, hunting grounds, regional towns, universities, distant Brazilian cities, and foreign countries (see Graham 1995). During these travels they continued to procure valued resources to support their kin, ceremonial groups, and communities, although sometimes these benefits were immaterial. When they left the Indigenous land, it might have been to access bank accounts, register for social services, seek medical treatment, take classes, make political demands, visit kin, renew friendships with allies, participate in cultural presentations, or contribute to media products. Although their routes and modes of transportation changed, they continued to seek dispersed resources of benefit to their people while moving throughout their present-day landscape.

Camaraderie

I discussed some formal aspects of the secular age group system in chapter 3, including the special proximate relationships among mentors and protégés (also Graham 1995; Lopes da Silva 1986; Maybury-Lewis 1967). In this section I delve into a particular social dimension deriving from mentorship relations and the preinitiate experience—camaraderie—that had important implications for social well-being throughout society.[2] The camaraderie of the mentor/protégé relationship produced individualized biographies of reconceptualized collectivity, which was communicated to outsiders through performance of strong intergenerational social conformity. This display of cultural traditionalism served as a beautiful shroud of secrecy covering a youthful morality of individuality among comrades through self-discovery, identity play, and freedom of expression. To be A'uwẽ, and thereby transmit the valued appearance of timeless and precise cultural consistency, required that individuals discover and assume this shared identity of their own accord. Through the catalyst of camaraderie, this discovery occurred quite uniformly if not effortlessly, because learning to think like an adult under the guidance of one's mentors involved constant tests of dedication, challenge, resistance, and endurance according to traditionalist formulations. These discomforts were understood as examples of suffering for the sake of well-being within privileged social relationships.

Camaraderie among secular age set peers, mentors, and age set moiety members was cherished by women and men alike. For many men, however, living in the preinitiate house with their age set peers and singing with their mentors were remembered as among life's most valued events (also Graham 1995; Maybury-Lewis 1967). As an emotive experience, age set camaraderie was the milieu through which individualized youths came together in friendship and commitment to represent themselves to society as respectful, uniform, and beautiful. It was through their dedication to one another that they gained such pleasure from hiding internal aspects of their age set camaraderie from outsiders, such as opposite age set moiety members. This dynamic created a scenario of distinction that placed high moral value on certain kinds of lies, trickery, and deceit, which were also considered part of living well.

Camaraderie in the Preinitiate House

Among the most fundamental of social bonds that develop while boys live in the preinitiate house were the ones that united age set mates. Each cohort of boys, especially the first staggered groups to be inducted, became something of a second family to one another. On arrival, the boys were largely unknown to one another, except those who happened to be close relatives or neighbors. Promptly, however, any initial fears or inhibitions were shed, being replaced by fraternal joviality and eventually intimate camaraderie. Coresident preinitiates developed the kinds of friendships that only occur through living together, playing together, sleeping together, and passing trials together for an extended period. The living quarters were close, with the entire age set occupying a single-room structure with no partitions of any kind (figure 42). Much of what they did for up to four years, from the most mundane of activities to the most defining of formative experiences, was as a cohesive group.

The social collectivity of the preinitiate house both comprised and was parsed by a special bond that linked pairs of boys in a most intimate formulation of companionship. Before boys were inaugurated into the preinitiate house, their fathers selected one or two formal friends (*da'amo*) for each, who would be their

Figure 42 Typical daytime scene in the preinitiate house (hö) in the Pimentel Barbosa community, 2005.

closest comrades at least until their initiation into novitiate adulthood, when they might select an additional formal friend. Formal friends were a typical but nonuniform Gê idea that strongly affected one's social life among the A'uwẽ and other groups (e.g., Carneiro da Cunha 1978; W. H. Crocker 1990; Lave 1979; Lopes da Silva 1986). In all A'uwẽ cases, formal friends belonged to opposite exogamous moieties, which lent them an aspect of balance and reciprocity, as well as symbolically differentiating them into actors (Tadpole moiety) and co-adjutants (Big Water moiety). These boys were not only close peers in formal or ceremonial settings, as described by Maybury-Lewis (1967), but also the closest of mates in daily life. They held hands during ceremonial song performances, often slept next to each other, shared food, and generally spent a great deal of time in each other's company. It was a relationship of uninhibited jocularity and social interdependence. Although Lopes da Silva (1986) indicated that the familiarity of preinitiate formal friendships was systematically transformed into more distant relations of affinity as boys reached adulthood and married, my data show that those first formal friendships might be maintained for a lifetime should the individuals involved choose to do so. Formal friends were another dimension of social organization that promoted social well-being through their contribution to people's sense of belonging, companionship, and support.

Not to be overshadowed by its communality, the fraternal milieu of the preinitiate house was also the social environment that enabled boys to come into their own as individuals. Under the gentle camaraderie of their mentors, preinitiate coresidents began the work of learning who they were to be as adults. Previously known outside their families by generic terms for child or adolescent (*a'uté, watebremí*, or *ai'repudu*), preinitiate coresidents bestowed on one another nicknames as each boy became known for his unique personality, quirks, capabilities, and shortcomings. The informality of these names was marked by frequent use of comical Portuguese language words, not proper A'uwẽ names. Beyond the social realm of age set peers and mentors, preinitiate boys came to be known as individuals by the whole community as they increasingly participated in public events. Through song performances, club fights (*oi'o*), wrestling matches, and soccer games, each boy was placed in public view and thereby became known for his unique composition. As Tsuptó told me, "Ceremonial contests are how we get to know what each boy is made of, what are his strengths and weaknesses." Some of these trials involved suffering or pain, which was believed to strengthen the boy and, through his exposure, contribute to his social wellness throughout life.

Another more explicit way preinitiate individuality was recognized was through a series of age set leadership positions that were bestowed on some coresident peers, but not all, according to certain personal and genealogical characteristics. A first example of preinitiate age set leadership occurred early in the coresident experience, when several of the oldest (first to be inducted) boys were selected by mature men with certain heritable prerogatives to have their ears pierced years before the rest of their age set peers, who would do so as part of the age set initiation rites that marked their passage to the novitiate adult age grade. These boys, called *aihööboni*, composed a public class of age set seniors for the remainder of their term as preinitiates. They were considered elder representatives of their age set and were afforded the responsibilities of repeating their mentors' lessons to reinforce them among younger age set members, speaking for their group, and intervening when their age set peers acted inappropriately. They thereby contributed to the betterment of the entire age set.

Another example of age set leaders, selected by elders as both the eldest and strongest of their age set, were *ĩmurĩ'rada*. They did not have a formally differentiated social role but assumed a somewhat informal status as senior members of the age set and leaders of ceremonial processions and competitions. Whereas the senior statuses of *aihöoboni* and *ĩmurĩ'rada* leaders endured only while they remained in the preinitiate house, two other ceremonial designations within an age set distinguished individuals for the remainder of their lives. *Pahöri'wa* were designated by certain mature adult men who were owners of the heritable prerogative *pahöri'wa'tede'wa*, usually chosen from among their patrilineal descendants. Two such *pahöri'wa* leaders were selected from among the eldest (first to be inducted) preinitiates, reflecting the elders' positive evaluation of their commitment to singing and competing in log races, as well as their physical strength and beauty (face, body shape, and musculature). Two *tebé* were similarly selected by elders from among the younger ranks of *tepé'tede'wa* heritable prerogative owners. Two *pahöri'wa* and two *tebé* leaders, four in total, were pierced a short time before the rest of their age set mates and expected to always conduct themselves in an exemplary manner.[3] They held honored ceremonial roles in the age set initiation rites that marked their passage into novitiate manhood, and, thereafter, as adults, they retained permanent usage of the honorary titles *pahöri'wa* and *tebé* instead of usual kinship terms. These distinctions bestowed on just a few of the preinitiates were considered part of the beauty of the preinitiate experience and thereby expressions of good living through social differentiation within the unity of the group.

In addition to the intimate bonds that developed between age set peers while living in the preinitiate house, profound social relationships also developed between the boys and their mentors. The term *danhohui'wa* referred to all members of an age set that collectively mentor another age set, irrespective of any other, more specific bonds that might exist between them (the age set peers that collectively were protégés of their mentors were called *hö'wa nõri*). Another term, *danimiwanho*, referred to an individual boy's personal mentor, chosen from among his age set mentors by his father, who gave him special attention, care, and guidance (this individual mentor's personal protégé was termed *hö'wa*) (cf. Giaccaria and Heide 1984; Lopes da Silva 1986; Maybury-Lewis 1967). Contrary to my cultural expectations that mentoring relationships would be more about proctorship and tutelage, I found the relationship between mentors (*danhohui'wa* and *danimiwanho*) and their protégés (*hö'wa nõri* and *hö'wa*) to be much more about intimate comradeship and sponsorship, what Lopes da Silva (1986) characterized as another type of formal friendship, albeit, in this case, an unequal one. For the A'uwẽ, these feelings of friendship were bound up in the term *īnhimnhōhu*, often used reciprocally between protégés and mentors after the younger of the two had married and had children.

Mentors sometimes discussed with their protégés how to behave responsibly but did so in such a way that it came across as kind advice rather than an order or demand. A mentor might expound on the virtues of keeping their voices down, sticking together as a group, minding their own business, keeping the preinitiate house tidy, playing out of the way of others, treating elders with respect, and not responding to women's calls. Yet, such guidance was not accompanied by a threat of policing or punishment, and the boys knew this. A mentor's presence was not met by his protégés with notable deference and did not necessarily encourage good behavior. In fact, the quality of the relationships between them was notably horizontal despite their inherently asymmetrical positions in the secular age set system. In practice, mentors were extremely permissive and seemed to care more about their mutual reputation in the community than about how their protégés behaved while out of sight of the public. Mentors and protégés were equally vulnerable to community disapproval, and together they strove to put on a good show for others. Both mentors and protégés were bound to one another as comrades, and mentors did not seek to be the bosses of their protégés.

At the heart of this relationship was trust—to share, to lend a hand, to keep a secret. Even after they married and had children of their own, young males were expected to be providers to their mentors. In the preinitiate house, boys shared with their mentors the food their families sent them. In the event a young age set went fishing as a group, which was most common in the years immediately preceding and following their graduation from the preinitiate house, it was expected that protégés give a substantial portion of the yield to accompanying mentors. Mentors offered protégés guidance, interest, and confidence. Often, an individual mentor would bring his specific protégé a gift of food, accompany him to the river to take a bath, or instruct him on how to prepare his body to become strong. Mentors shared with their protégés privileged ethnobotanical knowledge about remedies that made one grow strong and run fast in inter-age-set competitions (figure 43). These remedies were known only to members of their own secular age set moiety, being passed down between successive generations of mentors and protégés. Such gestures implied mutual solidarity and allegiance between mentors and protégés.

I found that preinitiate coresidents were rarely left alone because their mentors took turns away from their families to look after them. Mentoring preiniti-

Figure 43 Preinitiate (*wapté*) washing his legs with a privileged plant remedy known by his mentors (*danhohui'wa*) to
cause one to become a fast runner, 2006.

ates required around-the-clock coordinated presence, guidance, and companionship. A greater portion of the day-to-day responsibility fell on unmarried
mentors, who had more available time and less competing responsibilities than
their married peers. Yet, all mentors attended their protégés' most important
events, such as ceremonial presentations. New mature adult mentors were not
alone in this effort, as they continued to be benevolently guided and encouraged

by their mentors and other members of their age set moiety (their mentors' mentors and so on). This chain of mentorship was what transformed the preinitiate experience into a social institution that transcended many generations and united allied age sets with a sense of common purpose and interest through intimate bonds of camaraderie.

The allegiance between mentors and protégés was nowhere as apparent as in the code of secrecy between them. The two were on the same side in all senses of the phrase. To be on one's side had both literal and figurative meanings that I discussed in detail in chapter 3. In the present context of camaraderie, it is important to understand sidedness (pertaining to the same secular age set moiety) in terms of the fraternal bond between mentors and protégés. Importantly, they shared each other's abundant secrets, many of them personal and many pertaining to ritual activities. They shared a presumption that when in the company of age set mates and mentors, self-expression and reasonable rule breaking was allowed. Absent were the tensions of hierarchy implied by authoritarian models. In the case of A'uwẽ mentorship, age asymmetry was not entangled with vigilance. Mentors and protégés indulged one another and kept it to themselves. This was their socially proper technique for promoting learning of expected adult behaviors and responsibilities among their protégés.

Perhaps the most cherished public symbol of the bonds between mentors and protégés was their joint song performances (*danho're*). Graham explored in rich detail how group singing publicized the special relationship between protégés and their mentors (Graham 1994, 1995). She highlighted the individual and collective nature of these performances, arguing that song acquisition and performance were highly personal creative endeavors, while performances also emphasized group unity (Graham 1986). Mentors taught song repertoires to their young protégés, thereby informing them about appropriate song forms and performance techniques, so they might subsequently produce and perform songs on their own and, in turn, teach their protégés to sing. According to Graham, songs were initially owned by individuals but through their unified performance came to be owned by their age set collectively. Additionally, their songs came to be associated with their protégés, mentors, and the entire ensuing sequence of alternate age sets (Graham 1995). My evidence also shows singing to have individual and collective dimensions.

For the A'uwẽ, songs were learned by hearing them in dreams followed by imitation and practice. Novitiate adult males were generally thought to dream songs more prolifically than men of other ages (Graham 1995), but some dreamed more than others, and a few did not dream at all. Nevertheless, during song performances, all members of the age set were expected by the community to lead a song or two they dreamed, partly to contribute to the age set morality of sharing responsibility and participating equally and partly because admiration as a singer is earned by lead performances. The idea of everyone contributing as song leaders was connected to the acute need for abundant new songs that my age set peers reported were only presented publicly once, and performance opportunities were frequent.

In my age set, the most prolific dreamers gave songs to those who did not dream to perform as their own. We maintained the public lie that they had dreamed the songs they led in performance, but within the group everyone knew who its true dreamer was. Because I never dreamed a song, I always led songs others had dreamed. Hidden in the cerrado outside the community, the dreamer and I rehearsed the song together until I could sing it on my own. We then practiced it as an age set. As was customary for song dreamers, when I led, I began singing alone for a few seconds before the others joined in (Graham 1995). After the performance, I would sometimes be provoked by older members of the opposite secular age set moiety, who wanted me to confirm if I had dreamed my song. When I said I had, they often expressed disbelief. The lie was implausible, and no one believed me, but my age set peers insisted I maintain the fib to protect our reputation. People became known for their lead performances of songs they were believed to have dreamed, demonstrating that singing as an age set was an expression of both group solidarity and individual beauty.

Age Set Solidarity During Adulthood

The close bonds between mentors and protégés continued long after the boys left the preinitiate house. I experienced this when my age set (*êtẽpa*) was in novitiate adulthood. Several of our mentors (belonging to the *hötörã* age set) always accompanied us when we left the community as a group to fish, sing, or collect materials in the cerrado. On one such excursion to the other side of the Indigenous land to collect the inner bark of a special tree to make ceremonial ankle bands, we were joined by four of our mentors, who led us to the collecting location, organized the harvesting of some additional privileged ritual materials, and oversaw a song rehearsal. Being the most ignorant of our group about collecting this inner bark but expected to do so along with my age set peers, I needed special guidance. One of our mentors noticed this and made a point of keeping tabs on me. He showed me how to identify the proper tree, demonstrated how to cut a young sapling, strip its bark, clean the sinuous inner bark of its crisp outer bark, wash it in the river, and wrap it into a neat bundle for carrying. He did not force this lesson on me but asked if I wanted to learn. He showed me once, then discreetly watched from nearby as I did it on my own several times. Once he was satisfied I was on the right track, he drifted farther away without a word. I found this unimposing but thoughtful guidance style typical of mentors. To me it signaled a special attitude of respect, responsibility, and intimacy toward their protégés.

Similarly, in certain ritual contexts, mentors continued to guide their protégés long after they had graduated from the preinitiate house. For example, in May 2005 when we were novitiate adults, at the beginning of a large group multiday hunt, we were accompanied by the late Ronaldo, one of our age set mentors, into the cerrado to rehearse a song repertoire (figure 44). He took the opportunity to lecture us in his gentle manner, softly encouraging us to behave ourselves during the hunt, keep quiet, do our share of the camp chores, obey the wishes of elders, and not gossip about anyone. Finally, he said he did not want to hear later from members of competitive age sets that we had behaved poorly.

Figure 44 Novitiate adults (*'ritei'wa*) rehearsing song repertoire at hidden location in the cerrado, 2005.

In another instance, our novitiate adult age set covertly went to a location in the cerrado for a song rehearsal. We were accompanied by a large contingent of older men in our age set moiety, including five of our mentors, two of our mentors' mentors (from the *sada'ro* age set), and one of their mentors (from the *nozö'u* age set). Thus, four alternate age sets united by a continual series of mentor-protégé bonds were present and involved in ensuring that the youngest among them were prepared to give a flawless performance. During the rehearsal we were directly guided by our mentors, but on several occasions, they consulted with or were corrected by their mentors. The eldest man present looked on from a cool spot in the shade of a tree and did not give direct input. This sort of encouraging oversight by members of multiple same-side age sets was typical. It illustrates that the special relationship between mentors and protégés transcended the preinitiate house experience, continuing throughout life and leading to a sense of unity and mutual dedication among members of a secular age set moiety.

Other scholars have correctly noted that these age sets tended to act less cohesively later in life, as family and political concerns took priority (Maybury-Lewis 1967; Graham 1995). Nevertheless, the bonds between age set mates lasted a lifetime. I became acutely aware of this in the aftermath of a sad episode in which Raimundo Serezabdi, a member of one of the oldest secular age sets with living members at the Pimentel Barbosa community (*ai'rere'rada*), died at a hospital in Brasília. According to my A'uwẽ consultants, FUNASA representatives failed to inform the community of the death in a timely manner, performed unacceptable postmortem (autopsy) procedures on his body without permission, and delayed transport of his body to the community. The A'uwẽ viewed these as gross violations of their cultural and moral rights. When the body was finally delivered and inspected, and the funeral rites were complete, the four living members of Raimundo's age set, including women and men, met to assess the offense and determine a course of action. I was not present for that meeting but was told that under such grave circumstances as these, surviving age set mates had the right and responsibility to begin deliberating a course of action. Subsequently, the affair became the business of the entire community, being discussed in the men's council. This example of the continuation of secular age set solidarity from approximately adolescence to old age was a testament to the camaraderie that bound them throughout life.

I mention in chapter 1 that I heard apparently contradictory comments by elders that the preinitiate house experience was unchanged since ancestral times and yet also irreparably misconfigured such that its value had diminished. I interpreted these expressions in terms of a contrast whereby mentorship and preinitiate coresidence were viewed as irreproachable social arrangements rooted in "our traditions, our culture" (*wahöimanazé*) but to the extent the preinitiate house was a collection of fallible young individuals (i.e., preinitiates and mentors), it was a constant reminder of the inevitability and undesirability of change. From my point of view as an outsider, I perceived continuity in the protégé/mentor relationship, affirmation that there was truth in elders' characterizations of it as similar to ancestral times and integral to the construction of their resilient identity as A'uwẽ Uptabi (The True People) despite the magnitude of sociocultural, economic, and environmental change that had occurred over the prior seventy-five years. I participated in lengthy and exhausting ceremonial activities all day in the hot sun during which mentors seemingly tested their physical limits to demonstrate strength in the face of hardship for their protégés to emulate, as well as to invigorate the boys with their supportive presence. I passed entire nights hidden in the cerrado, assisting our protégés with their song rehearsals, accompanied by several of our mentors and several of theirs. I accompanied age set fishing expeditions during which adult protégés labored cheerfully to provide sustenance for their mentors. These activities were sure to have suffered change over the decades because cultural resilience involves modification, but the age set activities I experienced were thought of as traditional, as were the special enduring social relations between mentors and protégés. In this sense, camaraderie among age set peers and between mentors and protégés, as well as the rites, ceremonies, and activities they entail, continued to provide an avenue for the promotion of male unity of purpose and duty to society in contemporary times. My recognition of these examples of cultural continuity is not for the sake of nostalgia but to identify how some activities thought to be traditional by A'uwẽ involve resilience of social identity and relations (see Graham 1995, 2005). Camaraderie, sometimes expressed through willingly suffering together, bound these groups of people together for life.

The movement to protect Indigenous knowledge provides the insight that what makes knowledge traditional is not its antiquity, but rather the culturally specific social process of sharing and learning it (Battiste and Henderson 2000). This point applies equally well to the social identity processes discussed here. A'uwẽ elders seemed to share this point of view regarding manhood, mentorship, and camaraderie, and by extension the construction of A'uwẽ ethnic identity among young males. I would elaborate on this point by reemphasizing that a man's commitment to his protégés, his mentors, and his age set moiety was mirrored by his dedication to watching vigil over younger members of the opposite age set moiety and fulfilling one's duties as a husband, son-in-law, and father. The former implied the latter. Considered together, it became apparent that manhood involved service to all of society through proximate and distant respect relationships that sought to contribute to the betterment of others.

This optimistic note does not imply that the A'uwẽ were free of conflict and dissent. To the contrary, political factionalism is one of their most famous anthropological features (Maybury-Lewis 1967). Yet, the mentorship relationship and sense of camaraderie derived through the preinitiate house experience were not the source of the problem and might have helped mitigate against it. When I participated in exhausting and painful spiritual rites of initiation (*darini*) in the Pimentel Barbosa community over several weeks in 2018, one of my secular age set mates who had moved to the Etênhiritipá community during the division in 2006 returned to dance with us to help reinforce our endurance. I believe it was the first time he had returned in twelve years, but he was received as a comrade as though he had never left. The bond that united our age set was, in that moment, stronger than the smoldering conflict between adversarial communities.

Mentorship and Rivalry as Service

A final point to close this discussion of camaraderie and well-being is the evident association between mentorship and suffering. Protégés service to their secular mentors was extremely physically challenging, just as mentoring as a service to one's protégés was a demanding role. Preparations for and execution of such ceremonial activities as daylong song performances were an example, requiring sleepless nights and feats of physical endurance in the hot sun for many hours without rest. As one older man explained to me, sharing challenges and suffering with one's protégés supported them, increased their ability to endure hardship, and provided them with a behavioral example of what was expected of them now and when they became mentors to their own protégés. Sacrifices based in affection and duty promoted endurance and force, which were important for one's age set moiety. Service to one's protégés furthered the interests of their age set moiety and society at large. Thus, this form of suffering was positively valued in A'uwẽ society as an important instrument in the proper construction of adults and should therefore be considered a dimension of well-being rather than unwellness. This was increasingly the case for women as well, because they recently sought to begin holding some women's secular age set ceremonies, one of which included daytime singing performances by mentors and their protégés. The last time they did so, in late 2021, they invited men of the same age grades to join them to build solidarity between them and help support the protégé women in enduring the physical challenge.

Not all suffering was associated with positive A'uwẽ cultural values and well-being. Also, the meanings attached to different kinds of suffering were undergoing changes. For example, young A'uwẽ women today would be unlikely to suffer their shins being beaten with sticks by men while on trek to test their stamina and promote strength in their legs. According to Serebur̃a, this was a typical occurrence for generations that was thought to promote well-being but was recently no longer understood in those terms. Similarly, the women's naming ceremony was discontinued around the same time because it involved activities no longer thought to promote wellness. Specifically, it could entail extramarital sex between young women, some who were already mothers, and men in the elder adjacent secular age set. This practice was recast by a new generation of women and men as involving undue suffering by women and their husbands. Thus, the kinds of suffering thought to be associated with good living had and would continue to change as A'uwẽ people gained exposure to non-A'uwẽ social values and as formerly muted segments of society sought new social spaces to be heard and to express agency. In the case of mentors' challenging services to their protégés motivated by a shared sense of camaraderie, it is my impression that the association between suffering and well-being was as strong as ever, being freely maintained by new generations of female (who recently assumed these roles of their own initiative) and male mentors.

The camaraderie enjoyed by male secular age set peers, their mentors, and members of their age set moiety transcended other kinds of intimacy and friendship associated with kinship, formal friendship, and other sodalities. It emerged from secular coresident age set fraternity and extended to the entire sequence of alternate age sets that composed an age set moiety through intergenerational bonds of mentorship. Thus, it divided male society into two halves, each with its own interests and privileged knowledge and practices. Relationships between the two age set moieties was rivalrous and competitive. Both moieties, however, worked toward the same goals of bettering all youths through respect relationships with contrasting logics. Whereas intramoiety relations were permissive and intimate, intermoiety relations were antagonistic. Yet, both types of relations entailed strategies to encourage youths and younger people to learn, behave themselves, and represent their age set moiety well to the rest of the community. In this sense, the two moieties were united in their objectives to promote the construction of responsible men from children of both moieties.

This logic of service for the betterment of subordinates through respectful antagonism was apparent in other contexts, independent of the secular age group system. For example, the two exogamous moieties Tadpole (*porezaʼõno*) and Big Water (*öwawe*) had a complementary relationship with one another imbued with competitiveness and a moderate dose of antagonism. They were hierarchically ranked, with members of the Tadpole moiety usually being community leaders and initiators of action, and members of the Big Water moiety being voices of dissent or approval and the executers of action. Consequently, they were often cast in opposing roles whereby, for example, Tadpole members wanted to act quickly while Big Water members preferred to pause to think and discuss first. According to some Tadpole members, Big Water members were argumentative and hesitant. According to some Big Water members, Tadpole members were prone to cause blunders that the Big Water moiety must clean up. Nevertheless, their unequal and rivalrous relations were understood according to traditionalist viewpoints as proper social relations that benefited society through their oppositional complementarity. Thus, when a Tadpole member spoke in the men's council, a Big Water member often responded. When a Tadpole member proposed action, a Big Water member likely voiced agreement or disagreement. Their interdependent strategies were equally motivated by the desire to treat one another with respect and reach the best decisions for the sake of the whole community.

Competitive relations also existed in the spiritual age group system, with certain age sets in opposing spiritual moieties treating one another with considerable antagonism. Specifically, adjacent age sets (those that were initiated immediately before or after one another) partook in highly adversarial relations, whereby the older adjacent age set exercised authority to police the younger, control its food consumption, require it to undergo suffering, and punish its transgressions. The younger adjacent age set sought to conceal its transgressions from the older to escape punishment. These contrastive roles were most apparent during spiritual initiations and rituals, when their antagonism was performed publicly. During these events, it became apparent that their opposition entailed great sacrifices by the elder age set for the benefit of the younger, to encourage their spiritual vigor and development. Behind shows of antagonism was an underlying intentionality to promote well-being among their subordinates. Their expressions of hostility were a cultural formulation of respect that was executed with near militaristic severity for the ultimate goal of promoting betterment among youths in the form of acquisition of spiritual force.

Social distance was also a characteristic of traditionalist relations between parents-in-law and sons-in-law. When two young people were promised in marriage after the approximately quinquennial secular age set rites of initiation (*danhono*), their parents, often good friends, began to treat each other with a new form of respect whereby they stopped visiting one another at home and avoided direct communication. For example, a mentor whose daughter was promised to one of his protégés would cease to act as a socially proximate mentor to that specific protégé. Two men who arranged a marriage between their children would express their mutual respect by avoiding speaking directly against one other in the men's council. According to traditionalist expectations that were changing among some younger people, when a new husband moved into his parents-in-law's house, he must avoid speaking directly to them or even looking at them to show them respect (Graham 1995). Eyes cast down or turning his back to his parents-in-law to avoid meeting their glance embodied his respectful subordination in the relationship. A son-in-law gained the esteem and support of his parents-in-law, and perhaps eventually relaxation of these expectations of social distance, by providing them with food and performing his husbandly and fatherly duties well. Thus, the expectation of social distance between sons-in-law and their parents-in-law encouraged responsible behavior by young husbands and fathers, benefiting his wife, children, and the whole residential unit.

These select examples of competitive, antagonistic, and distant social relations shared the feature of contributing to the well-being of the community. A'uwẽ society did not expect that good social relations be amicable, at least not all the time. It also did not expect that all people with close social ties would treat one another affectionately. Sometimes A'uwẽ traditionalism called for other kinds of respect relationships, characterized by rivalrous interactions, for the sake of one another's betterment. These examples elaborate on the special camaraderie relations highlighted in this section. Whereas camaraderie was fraternal and friendly, many other interrelated and mutually constituted forms of proper social relations were not.

Social well-being among the A'uwẽ involved diverse forms of relating to other people, some affectionate and some oppositional, depending on multiple culturally celebrated forms of difference paired with equality that placed value on social contingencies with the potential to inflect the options available for interactions between creative social actors. Good social living involved caring for one's comrades while adopting authoritative postures toward one's rivals, embracing as congruent contextual shifts that recast one's juniors as seniors and one's masters as subordinates, just as they provoked a trading of places between equals and unequals or allies and competitors. It also involved individuals' liberty to creatively interpret these multiple configurations in ways that promoted mutual respect and best contributed to other's social wellness, even if they did so in ways that generated discomfort or suffering. These cultural expectations for healthy adult social relations in service to community demanded skillful alternation between appropriate social stances of meekness and boldness or gentleness and callousness, which was learned and practiced at early ages through observation and imitation of one's seniors and practice as young participants of formal age group systems.

Postscript

As I conclude the writing of this book in 2022, I am struck by how long it has been since I visited the Pimentel Barbosa and Etênhiritipá communities due to the COVID-19 pandemic. I went in June 2019 to conduct a survey of A'uwẽ perspectives regarding public policies of social inclusion and have not been able to return since. FUNAI has prohibited all access by researchers to Indigenous lands since March 2020. When I can return, more of the young children I met in 2004 will have grown seemingly so rapidly that I will have difficulty recognizing them. Most of them will be married, and some young men will have taken additional wives and have more children. My secular age set peers will reintroduce me to their now large families, perhaps ask me about the universities they are considering applying to, and in a few cases discuss with me their new responsibilities as executives of their Indigenous associations. My secular mentors' mentors, who are about my chronological age, will be showing the first signs of approaching young eldership (īhire), while my once spry adoptive father may be walking with a cane.

It is impossible to track all the changes that have occurred and will occur in these A'uwẽ communities as the years pass, but it is necessary to ensure my ethnographic data are current. My notebooks are full of recent updates to and elaborations on notations I made as many as eighteen years ago, which I have rigorously digested and confirmed are consistently incorporated into this book. I have yet to unravel all the interconnections and implications of ethnographic details I offer in this book and can only guess how their meanings may change in the future. As I ponder these possibilities, A'uwẽ perspectives about social and environmental wellness are rapidly transforming in consonance with changing circumstances in the Pimentel Barbosa and Etênhiritipá communities.

Change is a constant for contemporary and historical A'uwẽ people, as others have noted (e.g., Graham 1995, 2002, 2005, 2014, 2016). Their oral history recounts a long series of migrations, many provoked by interactions with non-

Indigenous colonists. They also tell of ancestral times when the population enjoyed greater liberty and happiness than they do today. Their experience of engagement with Brazilian society since the 1940s is rife with disagreeable stories of constriction and confinement associated with untrustworthy actors and government representatives. It is also full of conquests through political action, rethinking of old ideas in light of new circumstances, and acquisition of favorable technologies such as trucks, water wells, and textbooks.

Their cerrado territory has been invaded and reduced, with small and not so small cities growing where living elders remember camping on trek just over a half century ago. Yet, their land is well stewarded, with extremely low deforestation and anecdotal evidence of healthy plant and animal populations. Their social spheres have grown, with unwelcome exposure to racial discrimination and institutional dishonesty alongside close affective relationships with non-A'uwẽ friends who have taken them into their homes while they were away from their communities to study, advocated for their environmental rights with the government, and developed with them long-lasting research collaborations. Personally, I have been treated by A'uwẽ as kin, trusted with privileged information, and called on to perform my responsibilities as a member of secular and spiritual age sets. Undoubtedly, I have affected the lives of many of the A'uwẽ I have met and thereby contributed to change, but I hope it has been in ways that promoted the values of interculturalism through dialogue and transparent interaction.

While change is pervasive, some social constructions tether A'uwẽ society to traditionalist concepts of community well-being in ways that enhance resilience. The A'uwẽ life cycle is marked by abundant cherished social moments, many formalized through ritual, which ground contemporary change in tangible concepts of how a good life should be lived. Standing out among these moments are those involving age organization, including informal age grades and secular and spiritual age group systems. Leadership styles, kinship relations, and heritable prerogative ownerships are similarly responsible for orienting people toward good and proper social relations throughout the life cycle. Some subsistence activities, traditional ecological knowledge, and forms of environmental conservation are foci of community attention because of their importance for social activities popularly viewed as traditional and important for the promotion of community wellness today. These dimensions illustrate how social and environmental well-being intersect in contemporary A'uwẽ life.

Reflecting on the process of writing this book, I am drawn to recall how A'uwẽ sociality strikes me as complex and involving some demanding ideas about how to live a good life. Living well in communities is not only about having hedonic experiences. It is also about diligently participating in channeled expressions of confidence, rivalry, endurance, and respect. Multiple configurations of age hierarchy counterbalance rivalrous vigilance with intimate permissiveness in contrasting yet collaborating A'uwẽ models for promoting wellness among others. The plural and mutual construction of difference and equality is based in rigid not fluid formulations of social organization but affords individuals the liberty to view and interact socially with one another in their own creative and boundless ways. A key to understanding social well-being among A'uwẽ at the Pimentel and Etênhiritipá communities is recognizing that unrelenting service to one's allies and adversaries sets the stage for a life well lived. Knitting these ideas together is a powerful expression of interpersonal solidarity, camaraderie, which upholds individuals within intergenerational blocs of mutual commitment, indulgence, and support. Through camaraderie, people learn to use and care for the cerrado landscape in ways that facilitate the persistence of well-being. These were some of the most memorable themes that emerged from the process of writing this book, which motivated me to scrutinize my notes and recollections of contemporary A'uwẽ social lives as I experienced and observed them from my unique vantage point. In the spirit of camaraderie between students of A'uwẽ culture, which increasingly include Indigenous A'uwẽ scholars, I look forward to future publications that draw on different perspectives to complement and critique the ethnographic representations I present in this book.

GLOSSARY OF A'UWẼ TERMS

aba Hunt; individual or small group hunt.

abare Pequi fruit (*Caryocar brasiliense*).

abare'u Secular age set name (may derive from *abare*).

abarudu Wrist and ankle straps (used in spiritual rituals).

abaze pra'rí Tracking animals during hunts.

abzé Sorcery. Also see *simi'ö*.

adabá Married woman without child ("childless wife"), young bride (informal female age grade).

adabasa Wedding meat (game meat given by a groom to the family of his bride).

aibö Male, man. Also initiated adult male (age-graded kinship term).

aihö'oboni Age set leadership position.

aimana Term of address for a ceremonial father. See *danhorebzu'wa*.

ai'repudu Male adolescent (informal male age grade).

ai'rere Secular age set name. Also guariroba palm (*Syagrus oleracea*).

ai'rere'rada Secular age set name (distinguished from a junior age set with the same name, *ai'rere*).

anhana Feces.

anhanarowa Secular age set name (may derive from *anhana*).

anhanarowa'rada Secular age set name (distinguished from a junior age set with the same name, *anhanarowa*).

araté Married woman with child (informal age grade, infrequently used). Also see *i'raré*.

asada Puma (*Puma concolor*).

a'uté Infant, child, fetus (informal male and female age grade).

a'uté'manhãri'wa A heritable prerogative ownership (women's naming ceremony coordinator, or "baby maker," "baby organizer").

a'utépré Infant (diminutive); small infant, newborn.

a'uté'rene   Junior category within younger spiritual age grades.

a'utézo rõmhöri   "Baby work," whereby a father wore special painted ear plugs to stimulate pregnancy and influence the trajectory of the child's physical development toward maleness or femaleness.

azarudu   Adolescent girl (informal female age grade).

ba'õno   Female child, girl (informal female age grade).

ba'õtõre   Female child (diminutive), young/small girl.

barana si'iné   Nighttime visits by a young man to the house of his future wife ("to walk only at night" or "to visit only at night").

bödi   Grandson (kinship term). Also uninitiated male (age-graded kinship term).

da'amo   Formal friend, third person (ceremonial comrade in the opposite exogamous moiety).

dabasa   Marriage ceremony.

dabasa ĩsemere   Formal wedding ceremony ("meat basket wedding").

dabasa ĩserere   Informal, abbreviated wedding ceremony.

dahi'rada   Members of the fourth older secular age set; mentor's mentors, third person.

dahí'wa   Novitiate adult, young adult (formal age grade). Also see *'ritei'wa*.

dama'ai'a'wa   Guard, soldier (spiritual age grade).

dama'dö'ö'wa   Chief, formal community leadership position.

damaprewa   Parents-in-law, third person.

damro   Spouse (wife or husband).

danhim'apito   Traditionalist form of community leaders whose status derives from a combination of genealogy, seniority, personal capacity, and prestige. Also see *danhim'höa*.

danhimi'e   Left, left side (may refer to left side of the community and its associated age set moiety).

danhim'hö'a   Traditionalist form of community leaders whose status derives from a combination of genealogy, seniority, personal capacity, and prestige. Also see *danhim'apito*.

danhimire   Right, right side (may refer to right side of the community and its associated age set moiety).

danhiptede   Strong, vigorous. Also see *siptede*.

danhiptetezé   Healthful, strengthening (especially foods).

danhisé   Modesty, shame, respect.

danhizu   Imitation (may refer to learning through imitation).

danhohui'wa   Mentor to the age set whose male members occupy the preinitiate house, third person.

danhono   Secular age set initiation rites (mark passage into novitiate adulthood).

danho're   Collective singing and dancing performances, performed around the community in front of residences, with participants joined with clasped hands in a circle.

danho'rebzu'a   Cotton necktie knotted in front and affixed with an ethnobiological insert in back.

danhorebzu'wa   Ceremonial father (a mother's brother who assumes certain ceremonial responsibilities for a sister's children).

danimiwanho   An individual boy's personal mentor, chosen by the boy's father from among his age set's mentors (*danhohui'wa*), third person.

daporezapú   Boys' ear-piercing ceremony marking impending advancement to novitiate adulthood.

daporezapu'u'wa   Ceremonial ear piercer.

daporezapu'u'wa'tede'wa   A heritable prerogative ownership (master of ear piercers).

da'rã si sãmra dahã   "Opening your mind" (to adult ways of thinking), a goal for preinitiates while residing in the preinitiate house.

darini   Quindecinnial spiritual initiation rites.

dasai'pe   Dietary restrictions observed by parents during and soon after pregnancy to protect their child from ill effects, including sickness and death.

dasiré   Together with, joined.

dasi'sanho   To set an example for young people to learn through observation and imitation.

dasiwaté   Part of *danhono* initiation rites; an endurance exercise involving boys vigorously splashing water in the river.

dasi'tó   Initiation rites marking transition from novitiate adulthood to mature adulthood, held separately for women and men.

dasiwẽ   Girlfriend or fiancée, a girl whose future husband visits her at night.

dati'ö   Mother, categorical mother (vocative kinship term).

da'usú za'ra   Secular age set.

dawapru   Blood.

dawawa   Mourning song.

dawawa'ĩrõ   Second staggered induction group into an age set ("middle penis sheath").

dazada'ro   Breath, bad breath.

dazahihöri   Age set inauguration ceremony.

dazani'wa   Daughter-in-law.

daza'õmo   Son-in-law.

du   Group hunt employing fire to flush out game animals.

êtẽpa   Secular age set name. Also, "scarce stone," used as mortar or hammer stone.

êtẽpa'rada   Secular age set name (distinguished from a junior age set with the same name, *êtẽpa*).

heroi'wa   Ceremonial stage and minor formal age grade during secular age set initiation rites (*danhono*).

hö   Preinitiate house (residence of preinitiates under supervision of their mentors), located just beyond ring of residences and in symbolic isolation from community.

hö'amoniwĩmhã   The other secular age set moiety; people in the other secular age set moiety.

hödawa'u'hã   Fourth staggered induction group into a secular age set.

höimana'u'ö   "Descendants of the first creators" (Graham 1995, 19).

hömono   A men's trek, without the participation of women, usually undertaken for the primary purpose of hunting.

hötörã   Secular age set name. Also oscar fish (*Astronotus* spp.).

hö'wa   Coresident of the preinitiate house (*hö*); a specific protégé to a specific mentor (*danimiwanho*). Also age-graded kinship term.

hö'wa nõri   Preinitiate protégés (members of the *wapté* formal age grade under the guidance of *danhohui'wa* mentors).

ĩ'amo   Formal friend, first person (ceremonial comrade in the opposite exogamous moiety).

ĩdub'rada   Older same-gender sibling (kinship term).

ĩhi   Elder (informal male and female age grade).

ĩhídiba   Sister, categorical sister (kinship term for male speakers).

ĩhire   Elder (diminutive), young elder.

ĩhíteb're   Brother, categorical brother (kinship term).

ĩhi'wa   Members of one's next oldest age set (used until the speaker's age set has attained mature adulthood).

ĩhöiba'rada   Old person ("old life/body").

ĩhöibaté   Young person ("young life/body").

ĩmama   Father, categorical father (kinship term).

ĩmama'amo   Father's brother, categorical father's brother (referential kinship term).

ĩmamawapté   Mother's brother, categorical mother's brother (referential kinship term).

ĩmanadö   Extended ceremonial hunt held during the final stages of secular age set initiation rites for the benefit of *pahöri'wa* and *tebé* ceremonial designees.

ĩmaprewa   Parents-in-law, first person.

ĩmawapté   Mother's brother, categorical mother's brother (vocative kinship term).

ĩmurĩ'rada   Age set leadership position.

ĩna   Mother, categorical mother (referential kinship term).

ĩnawapté   Mother's sister, categorical mother's sister (referential kinship term).

ĩnhimnhõhu   Term used reciprocally throughout life between protégés and mentors in the secular age group system.

ĩno   Younger same-gender sibling (kinship term).

iprédu   Mature adult (formal age grade).

ipredumrini   Elder category within younger spiritual age grades.

ĩpredupté   "Young animal" or "new growth."

ĩ'rada   Grandparent (kinship term).

ĩrapté   Male and female children of categorical sisters (vocative kinship term).

ĩ'raré   Married woman with child (informal age grade). Also see *araté*.

ĩ'rehí   Scout (male member of *dahí'wa* or *'ritei'wa* age grade or first age set in *iprédu* age grade who has been trained for territorial surveillance.)

ĩrõ   Penis sheath (precontact article of clothing).

ĩrõ'rada   First staggered induction group into an age set ("first penis sheath").

ĩrõ'té   Third staggered induction group into an age set ("last penis sheath").

ĩsidána   Brother's wife and wife's sister (vocative kinship term).

ĩtebe   Father's sister, categorical father's sister (kinship term).

ĩwe   Beautiful, good.

noni   Ceremonial mantle made of buriti leaves, worn by *tebé* age set ceremonial leaders while leading sprinting races across the community plaza during the initial stages of quinquennial rites of initiation into novitiate adulthood (*danhono*).

nozö   Traditional (A'uwẽ) maize (*Zea mays*).

nozö'u   Secular age set name (may derive from *nozö*).

ōhã hö'abaniwimhã   "People on their side" (may be used for age set moieties, exogamous moieties, and other instances of sidedness).

oi'o   Ceremonial club fight.

ōniwimhã   "Their side" (may be used for age set moieties, exogamous moieties, and other instances of sidedness).

otí   Granddaughter (kinship term). Also girl (age-graded kinship term).

öwawe   Exogamous moiety name (Big Water).

pahöri'wa   Age set ceremonial position and associated ceremony.

pahöri'wa'tede'wa   A heritable prerogative ownership (owner of *pahöri'wa*).

pi'ŏ   Female, woman. Also married female with child (age-graded kinship term).

pi'ŏsiwe   Boyfriend or fiancé, a young man who visits his future wife at night.

poreza'ŏno   Exogamous moiety name (Tadpole).

-'rada   First, old (used as suffix with secular age set names to distinguish senior from junior age sets).

'repudu   Male adolescent (used for certain consanguineal kin, usually categorical sons, in the first descending generation of vocative kinship terminology).

'ri   House.

'ritei'wa   Novitiate adult, young adult (formal age grade). Also see *dahí'wa*.

rowaihu   To learn, to understand.

rowete danho're   A daytime singing ceremony sponsored by female and/or male mentors for their protégés.

sada'ro   Secular age set name (may derive from *dazada'ro*).

sa'uri   Ceremonial foot race marking transition from novitiate to mature adulthood during *dasi'tó* rites of passage.

sib'uware   Weak, lacking fortitude.

simana   Mature ceremonial child.

simi'ö   Sorcery. Also see *abzé*.

simi'ö'tede'wa   A heritable prerogative ownership (owners of sorcery).

sinhŏ'ra   Members of one's next youngest age set (used until the referent age set has attained mature adulthood).

siptede   Strong, vigorous. Also see *danhiptede*.

soimbá   Married female without child (age-graded kinship term).

sorebzu'wa   Term used by fathers for their children's ceremonial parents.

ta'rebzu   Ceremonial child (a sister's child for whom a man performs certain rituals).

tebé   Age set ceremonial leaders appointed for secular age set initiation rites (*danhono*) by elder owners of the *tepé'tede'wa* heritable prerogative.

tepé'tede'wa   A heritable prerogative ownership (owner of *tebé*).

tepezo   Fishing.

ti   Arrow.

ti'a   Tick (parasitic arachnid).

ti'ipê   Sacred cane arrows (used in certain spiritual rituals).

tirowa   Secular age set name (may derive from *ti* or *ti'a*).

tirowa'rada   Secular age set name (distinguished from a junior age set with the same name, *tirowa*).

topdató   A circular mark on the face used by *a'uté'manhāri'wa* heritable prerogative owners (Face Circle).

ubranhowahā   Final and solitary inductee into the preinitiate house.

uhí   Traditional (A'uwẽ) beans (*Phaseolus* spp.).

uhö'tede'wa   A heritable prerogative ownership (white-lipped peccary owner).

uiwede   Ceremonial log race.

uiwede zada'rā   Ceremonial mentor's group hunt.

umrẽ'tede'wa   Spiritual moiety name (rattle owners).

uptabi   True, genuine.

uzöné   Traditional (A'uwẽ) squash (*Cucurbita* spp.).

wa'a di   Lazy.

wa'i   Ceremonial wrestling match.

wahi'wa   Members of one's next oldest age set (used until the referent age set has attained mature adulthood).

wahöiba niwĩmhā   "People on our side" (may be used for age set moieties, exogamous moieties, and other instances of sidedness).

wahöimanazé   Traditions, customs, culture.

wai'a   A complex of male spiritual rituals that involve male spiritual age group organization.

wai'a amo   "People on the other spiritual side" (spiritual age set moiety).

wai'āra   Spiritual initiate (spiritual age grade).

wai'āra a'uté'rene   Junior spiritual initiate.

wai'a'rada   Spiritual post-officiant (spiritual age grade).

wai'ãra ipredumrini   Senior spiritual initiate.

wai'a sipi'õ   Women who were admitted into men's spiritual rituals following punishment for spiritual transgressions, discontinued in the present.

wamarĩzu'tede'wa   A heritable prerogative ownership (owner of "peace-keeper" sacred powder).

wamnhono   Ceremonial masks, worn during one of the final stages of initiation rites into novitiate adulthood (*danhono*).

waniwĩmhã   "Our side" or "people on our side" (may be used for age set moieties and exogamous moieties).

wapté   Preinitiate (formal secular age grade).

wapté rõiwĩhã   Preinitiate induction rites.

warã   Men's council.

warazu   Non-Indigenous people, "white" people.

warazu'tede'wa   A heritable prerogative ownership (owner of non-Indigenous people).

wasi'höiba   Close bilateral kin (one's close same-moiety kin and one's first-degree cross-cousins).

wasiní   Term of respect used reciprocally by real and categorical fathers of a bride and groom.

wasiréhã   Any group of three people; a person who is "with us" (may be used for age set moieties, exogamous moieties, and other instances of sidedness).

wasi're'wa   "Separated from us" or "people separated from us" (may be used for age set moieties, exogamous moieties, and other instances of sidedness).

wasiré wai'a   "People on our spiritual side" (spiritual age set moiety).

wasirewarõ   Members of one's age set that are in the same exogamous moiety or that one considers particularly intimate friends.

wasirewãhõno   Members of one's age set who are also in one's exogamous moiety, one's first-degree cousins, or socially very close.

wasisinawa   One's genealogically close same-moiety categorical siblings.

wasiwadí   One's genealogically distant categorical siblings or distant members of one's exogamous moiety.

watebremí   Boy, male child (informal age grade).

watebremire   Boy (diminutive), male child (diminutive), young/small boy.

watei'wa   Ceremonial stage during secular age set initiation rites (*danhono*), characterized by water-splashing exercises.

wautoptu Spiritual preinitiate.

waza'runiwĩmhã "Our secular age set moiety" or "people in our secular age set moiety."

wedehöri'wa Spiritual moiety name (wood owners).

wedehu Men's wooden ear plugs.

wedi Good, well.

zarudu Adolescent girl (used for certain consanguineal kin in first descending generation of vocative kinship terminology).

zömoni Trekking, walking, going on excursions outside the community with entire families.

zö'ra'si'wa Singer (spiritual age grade).

NOTES

Chapter 1

1. See Welch (2021a) for a preliminary published version of the first section of this chapter. It is adapted here with permission from the editor and per the funding statement in the article, according to which a CC BY open access license was applied to the Author-Accepted Manuscript.

2. The A'uwẽ were first mentioned in the historical literature in 1751, identified on a map as the "Xavante Heathen" in the Província de Goyaz to the east of the Ilha do Bananal, roughly six hundred kilometers northeast of their present location (Chaim 1974; Maybury-Lewis 1967; Ravagnani 1991). According to other historical sources, they also inhabited territories as far to the northeast as the Província do Maranhão, on the east side of the Tocantins River (Lopes da Silva 1992; Nimuendajú 2017). By 1780, the A'uwẽ were the most populous of the few Indigenous groups who continued to maintain hostile relations with settlers in the region, having forced some ranchers to abandon their cattle ranches and disrupted mining camps by raiding their food crops. In 1784, Governor Tristão de Menezes transmitted an offer of peace accompanied by a threat of additional attacks by settlers and their Mebêngôkre associates. This offer was accepted, and the A'uwẽ agreed to be settled (Freire 1951). In advance of their arrival, the settlement Carretão was prepared near the capital Vila Boa, and crops were planted to sustain its A'uwẽ residents. An unexpected two thousand A'uwẽ arrived in Carretão after six months of slow travel on foot. Having successfully maneuvered so many A'uwẽ to relocate from territories they had previously defended from incursions by settlers, it became possible for the first time for miners to advance westward and prospect for gold. Many A'uwẽ fled Carretão when an onset of disease killed more than one hundred people, but the settlement was initially deemed a success. Its A'uwẽ residents reportedly dedicated greater time and effort to agriculture, thereby producing ample food for their sustenance. By the end of the century, however, pervasive disease, hunger, and "other disgraces," caused the near abandonment of Carretão, as most A'uwẽ left to live in cerrado regions that remained unoccupied by settlers (Baldus 1948; Ravagnani 1991). A'uwẽ migration toward the east in the nineteenth century, into the region of the Rio das Mortes, where many remain today, appears to have been an effort to distance themselves from frontier expansion from the east

(e.g., Coimbra et al. 2002; Graham 1995; Lopes da Silva 1992; Maybury-Lewis 1965a, 1965b; Nimuendajú 1942, 2017; Ravagnani 1991).

3. A'uwẽ oral historians identified the location of the first permanent community to be occupied for many years after migrating from the east as Wedezé, on the eastern margin of the Rio das Mortes, just outside the current eastern limit of the Pimentel Barbosa Indigenous Land. A'uwẽ oral history identified two primary periods of extended settlement at the Wedezé site. The first, mentioned above, was long before sustained contact was established with the Brazilian government in the 1940s. The second, which occurred in the 1950s, was the primary A'uwẽ field site of anthropologist Maybury-Lewis (1967). Additionally, a third occurred from 2009 into the 2010s when a group relocated there from the Caçula community, reaffirming their ongoing reliance on Wedezé as an essential part of their contemporary territory. Elders reported that even when no permanent community resided at Wedezé, the location was visited continually during seasonal treks to make use of its rich landscape resources and to visit ancestral burial sites.

The A'uwẽ departure from Wedezé after its first occupation in the nineteenth century was provoked by disagreeable engagements with non-Indigenous settlers (Welch, Santos, et al. 2013). According to oral history, at first, when the settlers arrived, relations were amicable, with both groups exchanging presents in a friendly manner. In one case, however, a non-Indigenous man became interested in a married A'uwẽ woman, giving her many gifts to gain her attention. She came to visit him in his house, and they began to have sexual relations. Then came a day when he visited her house while she was cooking, and they had sexual relations in front of her husband and children. Her kin and the rest of the community were surprised and offended by this disrespectful behavior. They left Wedezé to distance themselves from these settlers, crossing the Rio das Mortes and continuing to the headwaters of a small river, just to the north of the present-day Pimentel Barbosa Indigenous Land. The woman's husband relocated with the rest of the community, leaving his wife with her non-Indigenous lover. Only her two brothers, Pareupsewawe and Serezaduté, stayed behind to try to convince their sister to join the rest of the population at the new community, which was called Sõrepré. Eventually, they gave up, leaving their sister behind and joining the others at the new community. Sõrepré became the second A'uwẽ community to be inhabited for many years (probably from the end of the nineteenth century to the late 1920s) since they crossed the Araguaia River and migrated to the west. Contemporary elders called Sõrepré the ancestral home of the A'uwẽ people because it was remembered as an exalted time of cultural flourishing and the final era of A'uwẽ political unity. The accounts I heard echoed oral histories from other A'uwẽ communities, who also considered Sõrepré to be a high moment in A'uwẽ history and a focal point of ethnic identity and pride (Lopes da Silva 1992; Graham 1995). The cultural significance of Sõrepré was summarized by Paulo Supreteprã Xavante (2015, 102), who wrote, "This village is where the creation of culture, the creation of dance began. It was in Sõrepré. It was there that began spiritual initiation, power, and the revelation of our people's spiritual secrets. Many things were created while our ancestors lived in the village Sõrepré. . . . It is the spiritual reference of my people."

4. The A'uwẽ are iconic in the literature on Indigenous lowland South American anthropology and public health and prominent in such diverse fields as genetics, ecology, demography, history, and linguistics (Dent 2017; Santos, Coimbra, and Welch 2013; Welch and Coimbra 2014). Inspired by Maybury-Lewis's ethnographic research at Wedezé, early researchers addressing human biology, demography, and health sought the A'uwẽ as a scientifically valid proxy for "unacculturated" Indigenous groups (Dent 2017; Neel et al. 1964; Santos, Coimbra, and Radin 2020). Later anthropological studies by Flowers (1994a, 2014; Flowers et al. 1982), Graham (1995; also, for example, 2000, 2005), and Coimbra et al. (2002) presented rigorous evidence from the same community, after it had relocated to Pimentel Barbosa, of sociocultural, economic, and health transformations that had occurred over previous decades. These anthropologists' works also had the effect of consolidating the reputation of the Pimentel Barbosa community as the paradigmatic ethnographic example of A'uwẽ society. As a result of the depth and breadth of scientific literature already produced about them, the A'uwẽ are an example of an intensively studied Indigenous ethnic group that continues to offer important opportunities to understand social and other kinds of processes involving the nexus of traditionalism and change in contemporary context. A'uwẽ at Pimentel Barbosa Indigenous Land did not consider themselves overstudied but rather wished to expand their relationships with scholars from diverse disciplines to ensure they were accurately and rigorously knowable by the public (Welch and Coimbra 2014).

Chapter 2

1. Although not all younger spouses continued to accept extramarital sexual relations, there was a prevalent historical and traditionalist perspective that sexual relations between certain kinds of affinal kin were not only acceptable, but often desirable provided they occurred consensually. For example, a person could have relations with their real and categorical siblings-in-law pertaining to the opposite exogamous moiety. For men, extramarital sexual relations were encouraged only with a wife's sister or an older brother's wife. I do not have data regarding such a restriction according to the relative age for sisters. Now that some younger individuals did not support such relations, it was not uncommon for them to happen anyway, without a sibling's knowledge, but usually following the traditionalist pattern sanctioning relations between real or categorical siblings-in-law.

2. What Maybury-Lewis called exogamous "clans" were, in their recent formulation at the Pimentel Barbosa and Etênhiritipá communities, exogamous moieties (Welch 2022b). According to Maybury-Lewis's model of three A'uwẽ clans, Face Circle (*topdató*; his orthography) complicates the otherwise reciprocal exogamy between the Tadpole (*tpereya'óno*) and Big Water (*ę wawẽ*). He resolved this problem by uniting Face Circle and Big Water under the umbrella of an unnamed exogamous moiety, such that both Face Circle and Big Water individuals marry Tadpole indi-

viduals and do not marry each other. According to Maybury-Lewis (1967), naming ceremony coordinator (*a'uté'manhāri'wa*; my orthography) was one of two lineages in the Face Circle clan. According to the current senior naming ceremony coordinator at the Pimentel Barbosa community, however, Face Circle is and was the name for a graphic symbol painted on the face by naming ceremony coordinators, not a "clan." Furthermore, he asserted that Face Circle has no relationship to the Tadpole and Big Water moieties other than that it so happens that at Pimentel Barbosa, all naming ceremony coordinators are members of the Big Water exogamous moiety, which is not the case in all communities. Additionally, he explicitly denied that there is any proscription against naming ceremony coordinators in the Tadpole moiety marrying members of the Big Water exogamous moiety. Recent Indigenous anthropological scholarship addressing ceremonialism at São Marcos Indigenous Land identified two opposing "clans" that operate in a manner consistent with the anthropological notion of exogamous moieties (Tsàe'omo'wa 2021).

3. Parental food proscriptions during the fragile fetal/newborn phase included alcoholic beverages, which were understood to cause poisoning and stillbirth; greater rhea (*Rhea americana*) and seriema (*Cariama cristata*), which prevented the child from growing tall; yellow-spotted Amazon river turtle (*Podocnemis unifilis*) and South American river turtle (*Podocnemis expansa*), which caused child vomiting; white-lipped peccary, which caused incessant crying, sleeplessness, and short stature; intestines of all game animals, which caused diarrhea and could kill the fetus/child; and brains of all game animals, which could cause mental disabilities. Parental dietary prescriptions included tapir, deer, and piau fish (*Leporinus* spp.).

4. Maybury-Lewis's (1967, 339) model of the female life cycle consisted of a continuous series of six female age grades from infancy to old age: "not babies" (*adzẹrudu*; his orthography), "girls" (*baono*), "girls whose husbands brought meat" (*soimba*), "women with children" (*arate*), "named women" (*adaba*), and "mature women" (*piö*). He asserted that women passed between these age grades synchronously with males, whose age grades were analogous despite mostly being designated with distinct terms. In a major revision to Maybury-Lewis's model, drawing on a brief account by Müller (1976), Lopes da Silva (1986) accepted Maybury-Lewis's basic model of distinct male and female age grade sequences but rejected his assumption that they operate synchronously according to similar logics. According to her account, female age grade membership was based on individualistic criteria while male age grade membership was defined through participation in ceremonial rites of passage by groups of males as age sets. Notably, she asserted that females did not belong to these age sets and associated formal age grades, which were exclusively male.

5. Previous scholars proposed that males passed through a single sequence of four to eight discrete and consecutive age grades from birth to death (Graham 1995; Lopes da Silva 1986; Maybury-Lewis 1967; Müller 1976). These included, variously according to author, infant (*a'uté*), boy (*watebremí*), older boy (*ai'repudu*), adolescent (*wapté*), young man ('*ritei'wa*), new mature man (*ïpredupté*), mature man

(*iprédu*), and elder (*īhi*). I found the term *īpredupté* used not as an age grade term, but rather to signify "young animal" or "new growth."

6. The term *piŏ* also signified *female* (all ages), just as *aibö* also meant *male* (all ages).

7. Maybury-Lewis (1967, 339) considered the entire span of female childhood to be entailed by the term *baono* ("children [girls]"; his orthography). In contrast, Lopes da Silva identified the additional term *aiuté* (her orthography) and defined it as "recently born girls (and boys) until children from one to one and a half years of age" (1986, 133). She also designated female infancy (*aiuté*) and girlhood (*baŏnŏ*) to be mutually exclusive and sequential categories, with the transition between them occurring when a girl is no longer a "baby."

8. According to Maybury-Lewis, the term *adzęrudu* (his orthography) might be used optionally and according to no specific criteria for older members ("not babies") of the *baono* age grade (Maybury-Lewis 1967, 150). Lopes da Silva, however, characterized *adzarudu* (her orthography) as a separate and subsequent age grade to *baŏnŏ*, with the transition between them marked by the initial development of a girl's breasts during adolescence (Lopes da Silva 1986, 133).

9. According to Maybury-Lewis (1967), *ai'repudu* ("not babies"; his orthography) was a subcategory of *watębremī*, the primary boyhood age grade. Some subsequent scholars, however, seem to have considered these discrete and sequential age grades (e.g., Graham 1995; Lopes da Silva 1986).

10. Maybury-Lewis (1967) indicated that elder status corresponded with the eldest four living age sets. Lopes da Silva (1986) suggested that one became an elder when one had grown grandchildren. Graham wrote that a man became an elder by the time he "has many grandchildren and several age sets have joined the ranks of fully mature men" (Graham 1995, 97) and mentioned that elders no longer participated in certain religious ceremonies.

11. According to Graham (1995), the final stage of the human life cycle was an approximation to deceased ancestors, which elders expect to become in the afterlife.

Chapter 3

1. Portions of this section were adapted from Welch (2021b).

2. The distinction between the classificatory informality of male childhood (*a'uté*), boyhood (*watebremí*), and male adolescence (*ai'repudu*) and the formality of preinitiation (*wapté*) not only was theoretical but also reflected the explicit A'uwê recognition that preinitiate status is predicated on participation in public rites of passage as a member of an age set, independent of one's prior stage of personal development.

3. Graham (1990) provided a provocative example of women engaging in typically male forms of ritual singing for the sake of demonstrating their own collectivity and independence.

4. Mentors could also be called *danhimnhohu* or *simnhohu* (see Graham 1995).

5. Central to Maybury-Lewis's (1967) model of A'uwê cognitive dualism was the term *waniwihā* (his orthography). He claimed that it had the specific connotation of

exogamous moiety membership, and that it extended symbolically to other associations, including factions, close kin, and lineage members.

6.   According to Maybury-Lewis (1967), mature manhood began when novitiate adults
     participated in the sequence of age set initiation rites that simultaneously marked
     the passage of preinitiates into the novitiate adult age grade and the inauguration of
     a new age set. According to some scholars, an additional age grade (*ipredúpte*, new
     mature adult, or *danhohui'wa*, mentor) occupied an intermediate position between
     young manhood (*ritei'wa*) and mature manhood (*iprédu*) (Graham 1995; Lopes da
     Silva 1986; Müller 1976). That age grade was described as corresponding precisely
     with the third most recently inaugurated age set, that is, the age set serving as men-
     tors to preinitiates. According to that account, young mature adulthood (*ipredúpte*
     or *danhohui'wa*) was distinct from and preceded mature adulthood (*iprédu*). I did
     not find the term *ipredúpte* to be used for any individuals, including those in the
     third most recently inaugurated age set.

7.   The framework of new houses was built by the husband with assistance from his
     real and categorical brothers and fathers while the wife installed palm thatch roof-
     ing and walls with the assistance of her real and categorical sisters and mothers.

8.   The practice of shouting decisions from the men's council for women to hear, re-
     ported by Graham (1993, 1995), seems to have diminished or been discontinued,
     as I never witnessed it during my fieldwork.

9.   Portions of the section that follows were adapted from Welch (2010).

10. I also did not record such privileged spiritual knowledge and practices in my field-
     notes to protect them from potentially being accessed by people who have not been
     initiated into the spiritual age group system. As an additional layer of protection
     to prevent privileged information inadvertently registered in my fieldnotes, I keep
     only encrypted electronic copies with two-factor authentication and do not share
     the password with anyone. In the event of their eventual donation to a repository,
     they will be meticulously redacted.

Chapter 4

1.   One of the consequences of the dispersal from Sõrepré was subsequent socio-
     cultural differentiation of now geographically dispersed A'uwẽ communities.
     Maybury-Lewis made the important observation that as early as the 1950s and
     1960s, there were basic differences in language and social organization between
     what he termed the Eastern and Western Xavante, which he attributed to both
     sociocultural disjuncture and different postcontact experiences (Maybury-Lewis
     1967). The Eastern Xavante included communities in the Pimentel Barbosa In-
     digenous Land and others that remained in the region near the ancestral Sõrepré
     community. The Western Xavante included communities that moved to more dis-
     tant territories to the south and west. Lopes da Silva proposed another model,
     with three A'uwẽ subgroups characterized by different degrees of intercommunity
     contact, territorial continuity, and contact experience (Lopes da Silva 1986). Lopes
     da Silva and other scholars characterized the communities that moved farther from

the vicinity of Sõrepré as less traditional, in part because of increased involvement with missionaries and inadequate access to natural resources (Coimbra et al. 2002; Graham 1995; Gugelmin and Santos 2001; Lopes da Silva 1986; Maybury-Lewis 1967).

2. Central to Maybury-Lewis's analysis of A'uwẽ factionalism was a symbolic congruence between heritable prerogative ownership ("lineage"), exogamous moiety ("clan"), and political faction. He proposed a fundamental cognitive opposition between two categories, "our people" (*waniwihã*; his orthography) and "other people" (*wasi're'wa*), which he described as the logic behind the emic formulation of exogamous moiety ("clan") membership (Maybury-Lewis 1967, 169). Thus, fellow moiety members were assumed to be potential factional allies, and opposite-moiety members were assumed to be likely factional opponents. An important aspect of his model was that a pervasive we/they distinction formally indicates moiety membership but was also construed according to a nested series of we/they categories in decreasing order of inclusiveness: "my people" or "my moiety" (*waniwihã*), "my faction" (*wasiwadí*), "my close kin" (*wasisẽnẽwẽ*), and "my lineage" (*ĩ-hitebre* for males and *ĩ-hidibá* for females). *Waniwĩmhã* (my orthography), however, was not semantically opposed by the term *wasi're'wa*, as given by Maybury-Lewis. The appropriate antonym to *waniwĩmhã* was *õniwimhã* ("their side"), which has the same liberty of applicability to any scenario involving sidedness. Two such sets of oppositional terms, with much the same semantic applicability as *waniwĩmhã* and *õniwimhã* were *wahöiba niwĩmhã* ("people on our side") and *õhã höabaniwimhã* ("people on their side"). Also, *wasiréhã* might be used to indicate any group of three people who are or any person who is "with us" in any sense, whether it be as members of the same exogamous moiety, age set moiety, team, workgroup, or any other conjunction of individuals. According to my data, the term *wasiwadí* was recently understood to mean "distant categorical sibling" or "distant member of our moiety." The terms Maybury-Lewis gave for "my lineage" (*ĩ-hitebre* for males and *ĩ-hidibá* for females; his orthography) were kinship terms denoting not lineage members, but rather opposite-sex siblings (real and categorical). Thus, *ĩhídiba* (my orthography) was used by male speakers for female siblings (real and categorical) and *ĩhíteb're* was used by female speakers for male siblings (real and categorical). According to the logic of Maybury-Lewis's model, members of one's own moiety were potentially one's factional allies, one's factional allies were thought of as close kin, and one's close kin were most concretely traced through lineages. According to his viewpoint, in the kinship terminology, "my people" terms were not used for one's same moiety members unless they were members of one's political faction, that being a condition for considering them one's people. Similarly, "my people" kin terms might, optionally, be used for members of one's faction but were always used for one's close kin and, even more axiomatically, members of one's patrilineal lineage. Lineages, then, were the most restricted formulation of "my people" and, unlike exogamous moieties, which were mere classes of people, operated in the political arena as corporate groups. Thus, according to Maybury-Lewis, political

opposition operated socially through lineages but came to be expressed symbolically in the exogamous moiety dichotomy.

3. According to Maybury-Lewis (1967, 165–71), A'uwẽ "lineages" were relatively static
    corporate descent groups associated with one of the three patrilineal "clans." As the
    smallest unit of patrilineal membership, lineages formed the ideological basis of
    the political system, which, according to Maybury-Lewis, operated according to a
    symbolic equivalence between lineages, clans, and political factions (cf. Lopes da
    Silva 1986).

4. In contrast to distant relationships between parents-in-law and sons-in-law,
    siblings-in-law enjoyed close joking relationships. This was especially the case be-
    tween siblings-in-law in adjacent secular age sets, relationships in which the jokes
    could take sexual overtones.

Chapter 5

1. I also argue that the necessary association with warfare proposed by the authors
    cited in this discussion does not seem to hold true, as the A'uwẽ continued to re-
    invest their social attentions on age group organization and ceremonial activities
    despite an absence of warfare for about seventy-five years.

Chapter 6

1. In the 1930s and early 1940s, the A'uwẽ were considered a most fearsome group
    that impeded Brazilian efforts to colonize the interior of Brazil, specifically the
    region west of the Araguaia River on both sides of the Rio das Mortes. At that
    time, the A'uwẽ were considered "uncontacted" despite their long history of inter-
    actions with non-Indigenous settlers since the eighteenth century. The Brazilian
    government expanded its colonization efforts in 1938 with the March into the West,
    a colonization effort that began with the Roncador-Xingu Expedition, which in-
    cluded the settlement of the Rio das Mortes by two hundred families who were to
    become cattle ranchers (e.g., Coimbra et al. 2002; Garfield 2001). In 1944, as the
    expedition planned to cross A'uwẽ territory, the SPI formalized its effort to "pacify"
    this formidable Indigenous group.

2. The government issued false declarations that the land on the east side of the river
    was unoccupied by Indigenous populations to legalize the sale of large parcels
    (Welch, Santos, et al. 2013).

3. These ranches altered the cerrado ecology so much that half-century-old vegeta-
    tion scars are apparent in satellite imagery today (Welch, Brondízio, et al. 2013).
    Beef cattle productivity was maximized through mechanized vegetation clearing
    and planted pasture grasses. Clearing of pastures and fields was accomplished by
    chaining, which involves uprooting trees and shrubs by slowly pulling a long thick
    chain suspended between two tractors. This method of clearing cerrado vegetation
    dramatically impedes regrowth. Jaragua grass (*Hyparrhenia rufa*), molasses grass
    (*Melinis minutiflora*), gamba grass (*Andropogon gayanus*), guinea grass (*Megathyr-
    sus maximus*), and signalgrass (*Urochloa* spp.) were the most invasive of the forages

planted for pasture in the 1970s and in subsequent decades (Welch and Coimbra 2021). These grasses, mostly introduced from Africa, create a dense blanket of highly flammable vegetation, which is essentially impervious to native understory regrowth. These grasses continue to grow where they were planted and result in light tan patches surrounded by green in current satellite imagery.

4. Honey-producing wasps (family Vespidae) known to the A'uwẽ do have stingers (Welch, Santos, et al. 2013).

5. According to Graham (1995), protégés sang their mentors' songs more than once, continuing to present them on occasion and thereby keeping them in circulation.

6. Single-day group hunts were still exceedingly rare in 1991 (Laura R. Graham, personal communication, 2021).

7. Whereas Graham (personal communication, 2021) reported that extended (multiple-day) wedding hunts were attended only by the groom's extended family members, I observed in the 2000s and 2010s that all adult men including the bride's extended family members participated in single-day wedding hunts, which were then most common.

8. There were two types of wedding ceremonies among the A'uwẽ, "meat-basket weddings" (*dabasa īsemere*) and "quick weddings" (*dabasa īserere*). For meat-basket weddings, the hunting excursion lasted days or weeks until a satisfactory quantity of meat was accumulated. At that point, the hunters headed back toward the community, stopping several kilometers away to make final ceremonial preparations in secret. There, one of the groom's elder relatives wove an enormous basket from fresh buriti palm fronds, and the groom's father painted him with urucum and charcoal pigments. With everything in order and the wedding meat loaded into the buriti basket, the hunting party returned on foot to the community. Beginning from a central location in the plaza, the groom, assisted by his real or classificatory brothers, ran with the basket of meat supported by a tumpline against his back to the front of his bride's house. He dropped the heavy basket in a heap at her door and walked away nonchalantly. In contrast, for quick weddings, the final decision to hold them was usually made just hours beforehand, at the conclusion of a successful hunt. Before returning to the community after such a hunt, men gathered to discuss whether the quantity of animals killed was sufficient to satisfy the intended brides' parents. Occasionally, a hunt was so productive that additional unplanned weddings were held. After identifying which brides and grooms were to marry after a particular hunt, the carcasses were taken back to the community plaza and bound with improvised tumplines. There, they were unceremoniously slung onto the groom's back, without the use of a large wedding basket, to the maximum weight he could support. He then ran across the community plaza, often with some help from his real or categorical brothers, and deposited the meat in a pile at his bride's doorstep.

9. According to Graham (personal communication, 2021), special songs were sung by groups of people in the morning on days group hunts with fire were held. During my fieldwork, I did not witness these songs being performed.

Chapter 7

1. Portions of this section were adapted from Welch and Coimbra (2022).
2. Portions of this section were adapted from Welch (2021b).
3. At the Pimentel Barbosa and Etênhiritipá communities during my fieldwork, the *pahöri'wa'tede'wa* and *tepé'tede'wa* heritable prerogative owners pertained to different exogamous moieties (*porezaõno* and *öwawe*, respectively). I was informed, however, that they need not be and indeed may not be in some other A'uwẽ communities in different Indigenous lands.

REFERENCES

Abelson, Philip H., and James W. Rowe. 1987. "A New Agricultural Frontier." *Science* 235 (4795): 1450–51. https://doi.org/10.1126/science.235.4795.1450.

Acosta, Alberto. 2018. *O Bem Viver: Uma Oportunidade para Imaginar Outros Mundos.* São Paulo: Autonomia Literária.

Adelson, Naomi. 2000. *"Being Alive Well": Health and the Politics of Cree Well-Being.* Toronto: University of Toronto Press.

Alfonso, Amanda, Francisco Zorondo-Rodríguez, and Javier A. Simonetti. 2017. "Perceived Changes in Environmental Degradation and Loss of Ecosystem Services, and Their Implications in Human Well-Being." *International Journal of Sustainable Development and World Ecology* 24 (6): 561–74. https://doi.org/10.1080/13504509.2016.1255674.

Almedom, Astier M., Evelyn A. Brensinger, and Gordon M. Adam. 2010. "Identifying the 'Resilience Factor': An Emerging Counter Narrative to the Traditional Discourse of 'Vulnerability' in 'Social Suffering.'" In *Global Perspectives on War, Gender and Health*, edited by Hannah Bradby and Gillian L. Hundt, 127–45. Farnham, UK: Routledge.

Altman, Jon. 2007. "Alleviating Poverty in Remote Indigenous Australia: The Role of the Hybrid Economy." *Development Bulletin* 72:47–51.

Altman, Jon. 2009. "The Hybrid Economy and Anthropological Engagements with Policy Discourse: A Brief Reflection." *Australian Journal of Anthropology* 20 (3): 318–29. https://doi.org/10.1111/j.1757-6547.2009.00039.x.

Altman, Jon, Geoff Buchanan, and Nicholas Biddle. 2006. "The Real 'Real' Economy in Remote Australia." In *Assessing the Evidence on Indigenous Socioeconomic Outcomes*, edited by B. H. Hunter, 139–52. Canberra: ANU Press.

Alvares, Clayton Alcarde, José Luiz Stape, Paulo Cesar Sentelhas, José Leonardo de Moraes Gonçalves, and Gerd Sparovek. 2013. "Köppen's Climate Classification Map for Brazil." *Meteorologische Zeitschrift* 22 (6): 711–28. https://doi.org/10.1127/0941-2948/2013/0507.

Anderson, Ian. 1999. "Aboriginal Well-Being." In *Health in Australia: Sociological Concepts and Issues*, edited by Carol Grbich, 53–73. Toronto: University of Toronto Press.

Arantes, Rui, James R. Welch, Felipe Guimarães Tavares, Aline Alves Ferreira, Mario Vianna Vettore, and Carlos E. A. Coimbra Jr. 2018. "Human Ecological and Social Determinants of Dental Caries among the Xavante Indigenous People in Central Brazil." *PLOS ONE* 13 (12): e0208312. https://doi.org/10.1371/journal.pone.0208312.

Azzopardi, Peter S., Susan M. Sawyer, John B. Carlin, Louisa Degenhardt, Ngiare Brown, Alex D. Brown, and George C. Patton. 2018. "Health and Wellbeing of Indigenous Adolescents in Australia: A Systematic Synthesis of Population Data." *Lancet* 391 (10122): 766–82. https://doi.org/10.1016/S0140-6736(17)32141-4.

Baldus, Herbert. 1948. "Tribos da Bacia do Araguaia e o Serviço de Proteção aos Índios." *Revista do Museu Paulista* 2:137–68.

Bamberger, Joan. 1967. "Environment and Cultural Classification: A Study of the Northern Kayapó." PhD diss., Harvard University, Cambridge, Massachusetts.

Bamberger, Joan. 1974. "Naming and the Transmission of Status in a Central Brazilian Society." *Ethnology* 13 (4): 363–78. https://doi.org/10.2307/3773052.

Bamberger, Joan. 1979. "Exit and Voice in Central Brazil: The Politics of Flight in Kayapó Society." In *Dialectical Societies: The Gê and Bororo of Central Brazil*, edited by David Maybury-Lewis, 130–46. Cambridge, Mass.: Harvard University Press.

Barletti, Juan Pablo Sarmiento. 2016. "The Angry Earth: Wellbeing, Place and Extractivism in the Amazon." *Anthropology in Action* 23 (3): 43–53. https://doi.org/10.3167/aia.2016.230305.

Basso, Keith H. 1996. *Wisdom Sits in Places: Landscape and Language among the Western Apache*. Albuquerque: University of New Mexico Press.

Battiste, Marie, and James Youngblood (Sa'ke'j) Henderson. 2000. *Protecting Indigenous Knowledge and Heritage: A Global Challenge*. Saskatoon: Purich.

Beckerman, Stephen, and Paul Valentine. 2002. "Introduction: The Concept of Partible Paternity among Native South Americans." In *Cultures of Multiple Fathers: The Theory and Practice of Partible Paternity in Lowland South America*, edited by Stephen Beckerman and Paul Valentine, 1–13. Gainesville: University Press of Florida.

Bell, Sarah L., Michael Westley, Rebecca Lovell, and Benedict W. Wheeler. 2018. "Everyday Green Space and Experienced Well-Being: The Significance of Wildlife Encounters." *Landscape Research* 43 (1): 8–19. https://doi.org/10.1080/01426397.2016.1267721.

Bernardi, Bernardo. 1952. "The Age-System of the Nilo-Hamitic Peoples: A Critical Evaluation." *Africa: Journal of the International African Institute* 22 (4): 316–32. https://doi.org/10.2307/1156916.

Bernardi, Bernardo. 1985. *Age Class Systems: Social Institutions and Politics Based on Age*. Cambridge: Cambridge University Press.

Bibiani, Caio. 2018. "Mudanças Demográficas nas Terras Indígenas Xavante de Pimentel Barbosa e Wedezé." Master's thesis, Centro de Planejamento e Desenvolvimento Regional, Universidade Federal de Minas Gerais, Belo Horizonte, Brazil.

Bieling, Claudia, Tobias Plieninger, Heidemarie Pirker, and Christian R. Vogl. 2014. "Linkages between Landscapes and Human Well-Being: An Empirical Exploration with Short Interviews." *Ecological Economics* 105:19–30. https://doi.org/10.1016/j.ecolecon.2014.05.013.

Bignante, Elisa. 2015. "Therapeutic Landscapes of Traditional Healing: Building Spaces of Well-Being with the Traditional Healer in St. Louis, Senegal." *Social and Cultural Geography* 16 (6): 698–713. https://doi.org/10.1080/14649365.2015.1009852.

Billiot, S., and F. M. Mitchell. 2019. "Conceptual Interdisciplinary Model of Exposure to Environmental Changes to Address Indigenous Health and Well-Being." *Public Health* 176:142–48. https://doi.org/10.1016/j.puhe.2018.08.011.

Bondarenko, Dmitri. 2007. "What Is There in a Word? Heterarchy, Homoarchy and the Difference in Understanding Complexity in the Social Sciences and Complexity Studies." In *Explorations in Complexity Thinking: Pre-Proceedings of the 3rd International Workshop on Complexity and Philosophy*, edited by Kurt A. Richardson and Paul Cilliers, 35–48. Mansfield, Mass.: ISCE.

Bourdieu, Pierre. 1977. *Outline of a Theory of Practice*. Translated by Richard Nice. Cambridge: Cambridge University Press.

Briani, Denis C., Alexandre R. T. Palma, Emerson M. Vieira, and Raimundo P. B. Henriques. 2004. "Post-Fire Succession of Small Mammals in the Cerrado of Central Brazil." *Biodiversity and Conservation* 13 (5): 1023–37. https://doi.org/10.1023/B:BIOC .0000014467.27138.0b.

Brinton, Daniel G. 1901. *The American Race: A Linguistic Classification and Ethnographic Description of the Native Tribes of North and South America*. Philadelphia, Pa.: David McKay.

Brulé, Gaël, and Christian Suter. 2019. "Why Wealth Matters More than Income for Subjective Well-Being?" In *Wealth(s) and Subjective Well-Being*, edited by Gaël Brulé and Christian Suter, 1–13. Social Indicators Research Series. Cham: Springer International.

Buchanan, Geoff. 2014. "Hybrid Economy Research in Remote Indigenous Australia: Seeing and Supporting the Customary in Community Food Economies." *Local Environment* 19 (1): 10–32. https://doi.org/10.1080/13549839.2013.787973.

Burnette, Catherine E., Caro B. Clark, and Christopher B. Rodning. 2018. "'Living off the Land': How Subsistence Promotes Well-Being and Resilience among Indigenous Peoples of the Southeastern United States." *Social Service Review* 92 (3): 369–400. https://doi.org/10.1086/699287.

Busija, Lucy, Renata Cinelli, Maree R. Toombs, Caitlin Easton, Ron Hampton, Kristen Holdsworth, Ashley Macleod, et al. 2020. "The Role of Elders in the Wellbeing of a Contemporary Australian Indigenous Community." *Gerontologist* 60 (3): 513–24. https://doi.org/10.1093/geront/gny140.

Butler, Tamara L., Kate Anderson, Gail Garvey, Joan Cunningham, Julie Ratcliffe, Allison Tong, Lisa J. Whop, Alan Cass, Michelle Dickson, and Kirsten Howard. 2019. "Aboriginal and Torres Strait Islander People's Domains of Wellbeing: A Comprehensive Literature Review." *Social Science and Medicine* 233:138–57. https://doi.org/10.1016/j .socscimed.2019.06.004.

Cardoso, Andrey Moreira, Ricardo Ventura Santos, Luiza Garnelo, Carlos E. A. Coimbra Jr., and Maria B. Garcia Chaves. 2013. "Políticas Públicas de Saúde para os Povos Indígenas." In *Políticas e Sistemas de Saúde no Brasil*, edited by Lígia Giovanella, Sarah Escorel, Lenaura V. C. Lobato, José Carvalho de Noronha, and Antonio Ivo de Carvalho, 911–32. 2nd ed. Rio de Janeiro: Editora FIOCRUZ.

Carlisle, Sandra, and Phil Hanlon. 2008. "'Well-Being' as a Focus for Public Health? A Critique and Defense." *Critical Public Health* 18 (3): 263–70. https://doi.org/10.1080 /09581590802277358.

Carneiro da Cunha, Manuela. 1978. *Os Mortos e os Outros: Uma Análise do Sistema Fu-nerário e da Noção de Pessôa entre os Índios Krahó*. São Paulo: HUCITEC.

Carneiro da Cunha, Manuela. 1981. "Eschatology among the Krahó: Reflection upon Society, Free Field of Fabulation." In *Mortality and Immortality: The Anthropology and Archaeology of Death*, edited by Sally C. Humphreys and Helen King, 161–74. London: Academic Press.

Carneiro da Cunha, Manuela. 1993. "Les Études Gé." *L'Homme* 33 (2–4): 77–93.

Carranza, Tharsila, Andrew Balmford, Valerie Kapos, and Andrea Manica. 2014. "Pro-tected Area Effectiveness in Reducing Conversion in a Rapidly Vanishing Ecosystem: The Brazilian Cerrado." *Conservation Letters* 7 (3): 216–23. https://doi.org/10.1111/conl .12049.

Carrara, Eduardo. 2002. "Um Pouco da Educação Ambiental Xavante." In *Crianças In-dígenas: Ensaios Antropológicos*, edited by Aracy Lopes da Silva, Angela Nunes, and Ana Vera Lopes da Silva Macedo, 100–116. São Paulo: Global Editora.

Castro, Elmar Andrade, and J. Boone Kauffman. 1998. "Ecosystem Structure in the Bra-zilian Cerrado: A Vegetation Gradient of Aboveground Biomass, Root Mass and Consumption by Fire." *Journal of Tropical Ecology* 14 (3): 263–83. https://doi.org/10 .1017/S0266467498000212.

Chaim, Marivone Matos. 1974. *Os Aldeamentos Indígenas na Capitania de Goiás: Sua Importância na Política do Povoamento (1749–1811)*. Goiânia, Brazil: Oriente.

Chisholm, James S. 1981. "Social and Economic Change among the Navajo: Residence Patterns and the Pickup Truck." *Journal of Anthropological Research* 37 (2): 148–57. https://doi.org/10.1086/jar.37.2.3629706.

Coelho de Souza, Marcela. 2001. "Nós os Vivos: Construção da Pessoa e 'Construção do Parentesco' entre Alguns Grupos Jê." *Revista Brasileira de Ciências Sociais* 16 (46): 69–96. https://doi.org/10.1590/S0102-69092001000200004.

Coelho de Souza, Marcela. 2002. "O Traço e o Círculo: O Conceito de Parentesco entre os Jê e seus Antropólogos." PhD diss., Museu Nacional, Universidade Federal do Rio de Janeiro.

Coelho de Souza, Marcela. 2004. "Parentes de Sangue: Incesto, Substância e Relação no Pensamento Timbira." *Mana* 10 (1): 25–60. https://doi.org/10.1590/S0104-93132004 000100002.

Coelho de Souza, Marcela, and Carlos Fausto. 2004. "Reconquistando o Campo Perdido: O que Lévi-Strauss deve aos Ameríndios." *Revista de Antropologia* 47 (1): 87–131. https://doi.org/10.1590/S0034-77012004000100003.

Cohn, Clarice. 2002. "A Criança, o Aprendizado e a Socialização na Antropologia." In *Crianças Indígenas: Ensaios Antropológicos*, edited by Aracy Lopes da Silva, Angela Nunes, and Ana Vera L. S. Macedo, 213–35. São Paulo: Global.

Coimbra Jr., Carlos E. A., Nancy M. Flowers, Francisco M. Salzano, and Ricardo Ven-tura Santos. 2002. *The Xavánte in Transition: Health, Ecology, and Bioanthropology in Central Brazil*. Ann Arbor: University of Michigan Press.

Coimbra Jr., Carlos E. A., and Ricardo Ventura Santos. 2004. "Emerging Health Needs and Epidemiological Research in Indigenous Peoples in Brazil." In *Lost Paradise and the Ethics of Research and Publication*, edited by Francisco M. Salzano and A. Magdalena Hurtado, 89–109. Oxford: Oxford University Press.

Conklin, Beth A. 2015. "Biopolitics of Health as Wealth in the Original Risk Society." In *Images of Public Wealth or the Anatomy of Well-Being in Indigenous Amazonia*, edited by Fernando Santos-Granero, 60–88. Tucson: University of Arizona Press.

Cooper, John M. 1942a. "Areal and Temporal Aspects of Aboriginal South American Culture." *Primitive Man* 15 (1–2): 1–38. https://doi.org/10.2307/3316342.

Cooper, John M. 1942b. "The South American Marginal Cultures." In *Proceedings of the Eighth American Scientific Congress*. Vol. 2, *Anthropological Sciences*, 147–60. Washington, D.C.: Department of State.

Costa, Luiz, and Carlos Fausto. 2019. "The Enemy, the Unwilling Guest and the Jaguar Host. An Amazonian Story." *L'Homme* 231–32:195–226. https://doi.org/10.4000/lhomme.35579.

Coutinho, Leopoldo Magno. 1990. "Fire in the Ecology of the Brazilian Cerrado." In *Fire in the Tropical Biota: Ecosystem Processes and Global Challenges*, edited by J. G. Goldammer, 82–105. Berlin: Springer-Verlag.

Crocker, J. Christopher. 1979. "Selves and Alters among the Eastern Bororo." In *Dialectical Societies: The Gê and Bororo of Central Brazil*, edited by David Maybury-Lewis, 249–300. Cambridge, Mass.: Harvard University Press.

Crocker, William H. 1990. *The Canela (Eastern Timbira), I: An Ethnographic Introduction*. Smithsonian Contributions to Anthropology, vol. 33. Washington, D.C.: Smithsonian Institution Press.

Crocker, William H., and Jean G. Crocker. 2004. *The Canela: Kinship, Ritual, and Sex in an Amazonian Tribe*. 2nd ed. Belmont, Calif.: Wadsworth.

Crumley, Carole L. 1995. "Heterarchy and the Analysis of Complex Societies." In *Heterarchy and the Analysis of Complex Societies*, edited by Robert M. Ehrenreich, Carole L. Crumley, and Janet E. Levy. Archaeological Papers of the American Anthropological Association, no. 6, 1–5. Arlington, Va.: American Anthropological Association.

Crumley, Carole L. 2005. "Remember How to Organize: Heterarchy across Disciplines." In *Nonlinear Models for Archaeology and Anthropology: Continuing the Revolution*, edited by Christopher S. Beekman and William W. Baden. Burlington, Vt.: Ashgate.

Crumley, Carole L. 2015. "Heterarchy." In *Emerging Trends in the Social and Behavioral Sciences: An Interdisciplinary, Searchable, and Linkable Resource*, edited by Robert A. Scott, Marlis C. Buchmann, and Stephen M. Kosslyn, 1–14. Hoboken, N.J.: Wiley.

DalFabbro, Amaury L., Laércio J. Franco, Anderson S. Silva, Daniela S. Sartorelli, Luana P. Soares, Luciana F. Franco, Patrícia C. Kuhn, et al. 2014. "High Prevalence of Type 2 Diabetes Mellitus in Xavante Indians from Mato Grosso, Brazil." *Ethnicity and Disease* 24 (1): 35–40.

Dallimer, Martin, Katherine N. Irvine, Andrew M. J. Skinner, Zoe G. Davies, James R. Rouquette, Lorraine L. Maltby, Philip H. Warren, Paul R. Armsworth, and Kevin J. Gaston. 2012. "Biodiversity and the Feel-Good Factor: Understanding Associations between Self-Reported Human Well-Being and Species Richness." *BioScience* 62 (1): 47–55. https://doi.org/10.1525/bio.2012.62.1.9.

DaMatta, Roberto. 1973. "A Reconsideration of Apinayé Social Morphology." In *Peoples and Cultures of Native South America*, edited by Daniel R. Gross, 277–91. Garden City, N.Y.: Doubleday.

DaMatta, Roberto. 1976. *Um Mundo Dividido: A Estrutura Social dos Índios Apinayé*. Petrópolis, Brazil: Vozes.

DaMatta, Roberto. 1979. "The Apinayé Relationship System: Terminology and Ideology." In *Dialectical Societies: The Gê and Bororo of Central Brazil*, edited by David Maybury-Lewis, 83–127. Cambridge, Mass.: Harvard University Press.

DaMatta, Roberto. 1983. *A Divided World: Apinaye Social Structure*. Translated by Alan Campbell. Cambridge, Mass.: Harvard University Press.

Dasgupta, Partha. 2001. *Human Well-Being and the Natural Environment*. Oxford: Oxford University Press.

Davidson, Eric A., Alessandro C. de Araújo, Paulo Artaxo, Jennifer K. Balch, I. Foster Brown, Mercedes M. C. Bustamante, Michael T. Coe, et al. 2012. "The Amazon Basin in Transition." *Nature* 481 (7381): 321–28. https://doi.org/10.1038/nature10717.

Davis, Shelton H. 1977. *Victims of the Miracle: Development of the Indians in Brazil*. Cambridge: Cambridge University Press.

Deci, Edward L., and Richard M. Ryan. 2008. "Hedonia, Eudaimonia, and Well-Being: An Introduction." *Journal of Happiness Studies* 9 (1): 1–11. https://doi.org/10.1007/s10902-006-9018-1.

Dent, Rosanna. 2016. "Invisible Infrastructures: Xavante Strategies to Enrol and Manage Warazú Researchers." In *Invisibility and Labour in The Human Sciences*, edited by Jenny Bangham and Judith Kaplan, 65–73. Berlin: Max Planck Institute for the History of Science.

Dent, Rosanna. 2017. "Studying Indigenous Brazil: The Xavante and the Human Sciences 1958–2015." PhD diss. University of Pennsylvania, Philadelphia.

Dent, Rosanna. 2020. "Subject 01: Exemplary Indigenous Masculinity in Cold War Genetics." *British Journal for the History of Science* 53 (3): 311–32. https://doi.org/10.1017/S000708742000031X.

Diener, Ed, Marissa Diener, and Carol Diener. 2009. "Factors Predicting the Subjective Well-Being of Nations." In *Culture and Well-Being: The Collected Works of Ed Diener*, edited by Ed Diener, 43–70. Social Indicators Research Series. Dordrecht: Springer Netherlands.

Diener, Ed, Richard Lucas, John F. Helliwell, Ulrich Schimmack, and John Helliwell. 2009. *Well-Being for Public Policy*. Oxford: Oxford University Press.

Dockery, Alfred Michael. 2010. "Culture and Wellbeing: The Case of Indigenous Australians." *Social Indicators Research* 99 (2): 315–32. https://doi.org/10.1007/s11205-010-9582-y.

Dole, Gertrude E. 1969. "Generation Kinship Nomenclature as an Adaptation to Endogamy." *Southwestern Journal of Anthropology* 25 (2): 105–23. https://doi.org/10.1086/soutjanth.25.2.3629197.

Dudley, Meredith, and James R. Welch. 2006. "Amazonia." In *Encyclopedia of Anthropology*, edited by H. James Birx, 56–65. Thousand Oaks, Calif.: Sage.

Earls, Felton, and Mary Carlson. 2001. "The Social Ecology of Child Health and Well-Being." *Annual Review of Public Health* 22 (1): 143–66. https://doi.org/10.1146/annu rev.publhealth.22.1.143.

Eckersley, Richard. 2011. "A New Narrative of Young People's Health and Well-Being." *Journal of Youth Studies* 14 (5): 627–38. https://doi.org/10.1080/13676261.2011.565043.

Eisenstadt, Shmuel Noah. 1954. "African Age Groups: A Comparative Study." *Africa: Journal of the International African Institute* 24 (2): 100–113. https://doi.org/10.2307 /1156134.

Eiten, George. 1972. "The Cerrado Vegetation of Brazil." *Botanical Review* 38 (2): 201–341. https://doi.org/10.1007/BF02859158.

Eiten, George. 1975. "The Vegetation of the Serra do Roncador." *Biotropica* 7 (2): 112–35. https://doi.org/10.2307/2989754.

Ewart, Elizabeth. 2003. "Lines and Circles: Images of Time in a Panará Village." *Journal of the Royal Anthropological Institute* 9 (2): 261–79. https://doi.org/10.1111/1467-9655 .00149.

Ewart, Elizabeth. 2005. "Fazendo Pessoas e Fazendo Roças Entre os Panará do Brasil Central." *Revista de Antropologia* 48 (1): 9–35. https://doi.org/10.1590/S0034-77012 005000100001.

Fache, Elodie, and Bernard Moizo. 2015. "Do Burning Practices Contribute to Caring for Country? Contemporary Uses of Fire for Conservation Purposes in Indigenous Australia." *Journal of Ethnobiology* 35 (1): 163–82. https://doi.org/10.2993/0278-0771 -35.1.163.

Fargione, Joseph, Jason Hill, David Tilman, Stephen Polasky, and Peter Hawthorne. 2008. "Land Clearing and the Biofuel Carbon Debt." *Science* 319 (5867): 1235–38. https:// doi.org/10.1126/science.1152747.

Farias, Agenor José T. P. 1990. "Fluxos Sociais Xerente: Organização Social e Dinâmica das Relações Entre Aldeias." Master's thesis, Universidade de São Paulo.

Farias, Agenor José T. P. 1994. "Ritual e Parentesco na Sociedade Xerente Contemporânea." *Revista de Antropologia* 37:309–31.

Fausto, Carlos. 2002. "Banquete de Gente: Comensalidade e Canibalismo na Amazônia." *Mana* 8 (2): 7–44. https://doi.org/10.1590/S0104-93132002000200001.

Fausto, Carlos. 2008. "Donos Demais: Maestria e Domínio na Amazônia." *Mana* 14 (2): 329–66. https://doi.org/10.1590/S0104-93132008000200003.

Ferreira, Aline A., James R. Welch, Ricardo Ventura Santos, Silvia A. Gugelmin, and Carlos E. A. Coimbra Jr. 2012. "Nutritional Status and Growth of Indigenous Xavante Children, Central Brazil." *Nutrition Journal* 11:3. https://doi.org/10.1186/1475-2891-11-3.

Ferreira, Mariana Kawall Leal. 2015. *Mapping Time, Space and the Body: Indigenous Knowledge and Mathematical Thinking in Brazil*. Rotterdam: Sense.

Ferri, Mário Guimarães, ed. 1976. *IV Simpósio Sobre o Cerrado: Bases para Utilização Agropecuária*. São Paulo: Editora da Universidade de São Paulo.

Firth, Raymond. 1951. *Elements of Social Organization*. London: Watts.

Fischer, Edward F. 2014. *The Good Life: Aspiration, Dignity, and the Anthropology of Well-being*. Stanford, Calif.: Stanford University Press.

Fischer, Michael M. J. 2018. *Anthropology in the Meantime: Experimental Ethnography, Theory, and Method for the Twenty-First Century*. Experimental Futures: Technological Lives, Scientific Arts, Anthropological Voices. Durham, N.C.: Duke University Press.

Fisher, William H. 1991. "Dualism and Its Discontents: Social Organization and Village Fissioning among the Xikrin-Kayapó of Central Brazil." PhD diss., Cornell University, Ithaca, New York.

Fisher, William H. 2000. *Rain Forest Exchanges: Industry and Community on an Amazonian Frontier*. Washington, D.C.: Smithsonian Institution Press.

Fisher, William H. 2001. "Age-Based Genders among the Kayapó." In *Gender in Amazonia and Melanesia: An Exploration of the Comparative Method*, edited by Thomas A. Gregor and Donald Tuzin, 115–40. Berkeley: University of California Press.

Fisher, William H. 2003. "Name Rituals and Acts of Feeling among the Kayapó (Mebengokre)." *Journal of the Royal Anthropological Institute* 9 (1): 117–35. https://doi.org/10.1111/1467-9655.t01-2-00007.

Fleming, John, and Robert J. Ledogar. 2008. "Resilience, an Evolving Concept: A Review of Literature Relevant to Aboriginal Research." *Pimatisiwin* 6 (2): 7–23.

Flint, Courtney G., Ewan S. Robinson, Joshua Kellogg, Gary Ferguson, Lama BouFajreldin, Mallory Dolan, Ilya Raskin, and Mary Ann Lila. 2011. "Promoting Wellness in Alaskan Villages: Integrating Traditional Knowledge and Science of Wild Berries." *EcoHealth* 8 (2): 199–209. https://doi.org/10.1007/s10393-011-0707-9.

Flória, Cristina, dir. 2009. *Piõ Höimanazé: A Mulher Xavante em Sua Arte*. São Paulo: A 2.0 Produções Artísticas. DVD.

Flowers, Nancy M. 1983. "Forager-Farmers: The Xavante Indians of Central Brazil." PhD diss., City University of New York.

Flowers, Nancy M. 1994a. "Demographic Crisis and Recovery: A Case Study of the Xavante of Pimentel Barbosa." In *The Demography of Small-Scale Societies: Case Studies from Lowland South America*, edited by Kathleen Adams and David Price, 18–36. South American Indian Studies 4. Bennington, Vt.: Bennington College.

Flowers, Nancy M. 1994b. "Subsistence Strategy, Social Organization, and Warfare in Central Brazil in the Context of European Penetration." In *Amazonian Indians from Prehistory to the Present*, edited by Anna Curtenius Roosevelt, 249–69. Tucson: University of Arizona Press.

Flowers, Nancy M. 2014. "Economia, Subsistência e Trabalho: Sistema em Mudança." In *Antropologia e História Xavante em Perspectiva*, edited by Carlos E. A. Coimbra Jr and James R. Welch, 67–86. Rio de Janeiro, Brazil: Museu do Índio/FUNAI.

Flowers, Nancy M., Daniel R. Gross, Madeline L. Ritter, and Dennis W. Werner. 1982. "Variation in Swidden Practices in Four Central Brazilian Indian Societies." *Human Ecology* 10 (2): 203–17. https://doi.org/10.1007/BF01531241.

Fortes, Meyer. 1959. *Oedipus and Job in West African Religion*. Cambridge: Cambridge University Press.

Fortes, Meyer. 1961. "Pietas in Ancestor Worship." *Journal of the Royal Anthropological Institute* 91 (2): 166–91. https://doi.org/10.2307/2844412.

Fragoso, José Manuel V., Kirsten M. Silvius, and Manrique Prada. 2000. *Manejo de Fauna na Reserva Xavante Rio das Mortes, MT: Cultura Indígena e Método Científico Integrados para a Conservação*. WWF Brasil, Série Técnica, Vol. 4. Brasília, Brazil: World Wildlife Fund.

Franca, Belisário, dir. 2007. *Estratégia Xavante*. São Paulo: Instituto das Tradições Indígenas (IDETI) and Giros Filmes. DVD.

Freire, José Rodrigues. 1951. *Relação da Conquista do Gentio Xavante*. 2nd ed. Coleção Textos e Documentos, vol. 1. São Paulo: Faculdade de Filosofia, Ciências e Letras, Universidade de São Paulo.

Fuchs, Stephan. 2001. "Beyond Agency." *Sociological Theory* 19 (1): 24–40. https://doi.org /10.1111/0735-2751.00126.

Galvão, Eduardo. 1960. "Áreas Culturais Indígenas do Brasil, 1900–1959." *Boletim do Museu Paraense Emilio Goeldi (Antropologia, Nova Serie)* 8:1–41.

Garfield, Seth. 2001. *Indigenous Struggle at the Heart of Brazil: State Policy, Frontier Expansion, and the Xavante Indians, 1937–1988*. Durham, N.C.: Duke University Press.

Georgescu, Matei, David B. Lobell, Christopher B. Field, and Alex Mahalov. 2013. "Simulated Hydroclimatic Impacts of Projected Brazilian Sugarcane Expansion." *Geophysical Research Letters* 40 (5): 972–77. https://doi.org/10.1002/grl.50206.

Giaccaria, Bartolomeu, and Adalberto Heide. 1984. *Xavante: Auwẽ Uptabi, Povo Autêntico*. São Paulo: Editora Salesiana Dom Bosco.

Giddens, Anthony. 1979. *Central Problems in Social Theory: Action, Structure and Contradiction in Social Analysis*. Cambridge: Cambridge University Press.

Giddens, Anthony. 1986. *The Constitution of Society*. Berkeley, Calif.: University of California Press.

Gleibs, Ilka H., Thomas A. Morton, Anna Rabinovich, S. Alexander Haslam, and John F. Helliwell. 2013. "Unpacking the Hedonic Paradox: A Dynamic Analysis of the Relationships between Financial Capital, Social Capital and Life Satisfaction." *British Journal of Social Psychology* 52 (1): 25–43. https://doi.org/10.1111/j.2044-8309.2011.02035.x.

Godoy, Ricardo, Victoria Reyes-García, Elizabeth Byron, William R. Leonard, and Vincent Vadez. 2005. "The Effect of Market Economies on the Well-Being of Indigenous Peoples and on Their Use of Renewable Natural Resources." *Annual Review of Anthropology* 34:121–38. https://doi.org/10/dqc7m5.

Gordon, Cesar C. 1996. "Aspectos da Organização Social Jê: De Nimuendajú à Decada de 90." Master's thesis, Universidade Federal do Rio de Janeiro/Museu Nacional.

Gordon, Cesar C. 2006. *Economia Selvagem: Ritual e Mercadoria entre os Índios Xikrin-Mebengokre*. São Paulo: Editora UNESP.

Gordon, Cesar C. 2016. "Ownership and Well-Being among the Mebêngôkre-Xikrin Differentiation and Ritual Crisis." In *Ownership and Nurture: Studies in Native Amazonian Property Relations*, edited by Marc Brightman, Carlos Fausto, and Vanessa Grotti, 209–31. New York: Berghahn Books.

Graham, Laura R. 1986. "Three Modes of Xavante Vocal Expression: Wailing, Collective Singing, and Political Oratory." In *Native South American Discourse*, edited by Joel Sherzer and Greg Urban, 83–118. Berlin: Mouton de Gruyter.

Graham, Laura R. 1987. "Uma Aldeia por um 'Projeto.'" In *Povos Indígenas no Brasil 85/86: Aconteceu Especial 17*, 348–30. São Paulo: Centro Ecumênico de Documentação e Informação.

Graham, Laura R. 1990. "The Always Living: Discourse and the Male Lifecycle of the Xavante Indians of Central Brazil." PhD diss., Austin: University of Texas.

Graham, Laura R. 1993. "A Public Sphere in Amazonia? The Depersonalized Collaborative Construction of Discourse in Xavante." *American Ethnologist* 20 (4): 717–41. https://doi.org/10.1525/ae.1993.20.4.02a00030.

Graham, Laura R. 1994. "Dialogic Dreams: Creative Selves Coming into Life in the Flow of Time." *American Ethnologist* 21 (4): 723–45. https://doi.org/10.1525/ae.1994.21.4.02a00040.

Graham, Laura R. 1995. *Performing Dreams: Discourses of Immortality among the Xavante of Central Brazil*. Austin: University of Texas Press.

Graham, Laura R. 2000. "Lessons in Collaboration: The Xavante/WWF Wildlife Management Project in Central Brazil." In *Indigenous Peoples and Conservation Organization: Experiences in Collaboration*, edited by R. Weber, J. Butler, and P. Larson, 47–71. Washington, D.C.: World Wildlife Fund.

Graham, Laura R. 2002. "How Should an Indian Speak? Amazonian Indians and the Symbolic Politics of Language in the Global Public Sphere." In *Indigenous Movements, Self-Representation, and the State in Latin America*, edited by Kay B. Warren and Jean E. Jackson, 181–228. Austin: University of Texas Press.

Graham, Laura R. 2005. "Image and Instrumentality in a Xavante Politics of Existential Recognition: The Public Outreach Work of Eténhiritipa Pimentel Barbosa." *American Ethnologist* 32 (4): 622–41. https://doi.org/10.1525/ae.2005.32.4.622.

Graham, Laura R. 2014. "Genders of Xavante Ethnographic Spectacle: Cultural Politics of Inclusion and Exclusion in Brazil." In *Performing Indigeneity: Global Histories and Contemporary Experiences*, edited by Laura R. Graham and H. Glenn Penny, 305–50. Lincoln: University of Nebraska Press.

Graham, Laura R. 2016. "Toward Representational Sovereignty: Rewards and Challenges of Indigenous Media in the A'uwẽ-Xavante Communities of Eténhiritipa-Pimentel Barbosa." *Media and Communication* 4 (2): 13–32. https://doi.org/10.17645/mac.v4i2.438.

Graham, Laura R., David Hernandez Palmer, and Caimi Waiásse, dirs. 2009. *Owners of the Water: Conflict and Collaboration over Rivers*. Watertown, Mass.: Documentary Educational Resources. DVD.

Green, Donna, and Liz Minchin. 2014. "Living on Climate-Changed Country: Indigenous Health, Well-Being and Climate Change in Remote Australian Communities." *EcoHealth* 11 (2): 263–72. https://doi.org/10.1007/s10393-013-0892-9.

Gross, Daniel R. 1979. "A New Approach to Central Brazilian Social Organization." In *Brazil, Anthropological Perspectives: Essays in Honor of Charles Wagley*, edited by Maxine L. Margolis and William Carter, 321–435. New York: Columbia University Press.

Gross, Daniel R., George Eiten, Nancy M. Flowers, Francisca M. Leoi, Madeline L. Ritter, and Dennis W. Werner. 1979. "Ecology and Acculturation among Native Peoples of Central Brazil." *Science* 206 (4422): 1043–50. https://doi.org/10.1126/science.206.4422.1043.

Gugelmin, Sílvia A., and Ricardo Ventura Santos. 2001. "Ecologia Humana e Antropometria Nutricional de Adultos Xavánte, Mato Grosso, Brasil." *Cadernos de Saúde Pública* 17 (2): 313–22. https://doi.org/10.1590/S0102-311X2001000200006.

Hall, Joan, Ruth Alice McLeod, and Valerie Mitchell. 1987. *Pequeno Dicionário Xavante-Português Português-Xavante.* Brasília: Summer Institute of Linguistics.

Hamilton, Kirk, John F. Helliwell, and Michael Woolcock. 2016. "Social Capital, Trust and Well-Being in the Evaluation of Wealth." Working Paper 22556. Cambridge, Mass.: National Bureau of Economic Research.

Hanson, Jeffery R. 1988. "Age-Set Theory and Plains Indian Age-Grading: A Critical Review and Revision." *American Ethnologist* 15 (2): 349–64. https://doi.org/10.1525/ae.1988.15.2.02a00090.

Harris, Grace G. 1989. "Concepts of Individual, Self, and Person in Description and Analysis." *American Anthropologist* 91 (3): 599–612. https://doi.org/10.1525/aa.1989.91.3.02a00040.

Haworth, John T., and Graham Hart. 2007. *Well-Being: Individual, Community and Social Perspectives.* Basingstoke: Palgrave Macmillan.

Heil, Daniela. 2009. "Embodied Selves and Social Selves: Aboriginal Well-Being in Rural New South Wales, Australia." In *Pursuits of Happiness: Well-Being in Anthropological Perspective*, edited by Gordon Mathews and Carolina Izquierdo, 89–108. New York: Berghahn Books.

Herbert, Steve. 2000. "For Ethnography." *Progress in Human Geography* 24 (4): 550–68. https://doi.org/10.1191/030913200100189102.

Holt, Flora Lu. 2005. "The Catch-22 of Conservation: Indigenous Peoples, Biologists, and Cultural Change." *Human Ecology* 33 (2): 199–215. https://doi.org/10.1007/s10745-005-2432-X.

Hornborg, Alf. 1988. *Dualism and Hierarchy in Lowland South America.* Uppsala, Sweden: Acta Universitatis Upsaliensis.

Idioriê, Severiá Maria. 2019. "Crianças A'uwẽ Uptabi/Xavante-MT: Ser e Estar no Mundo." *Revista Antropologia da UFSCAR* 11 (1): 162–82.

Izquierdo, Carolina. 2005. "When 'Health' Is Not Enough: Societal, Individual and Biomedical Assessments of Well-Being among the Matsigenka of the Peruvian Amazon." *Social Science and Medicine* 61 (4): 767–83. https://doi.org/10.1016/j.socscimed.2004.08.045.

Izquierdo, Carolina. 2009. "Well-Being among the Matsigenka of the Peruvian Amazon: Health, Missions, Oil, and 'Progress.'" In *Pursuits of Happiness: Well-Being in Anthropological Perspective*, edited by Gordon Mathews and Carolina Izquierdo, 67–87. New York: Berghahn Books.

Jackson, Jean E. 1975. "Recent Ethnography of Indigenous Northern Lowland South America." *Annual Review of Anthropology* 4:307–40.

Jenaro, Christina, Miguel A. Verdugo, Cristina Caballo, Giulia Balboni, Yves Lachapelle, Wojciech Otrebski, and Robert L. Schalock. 2005. "Cross-Cultural Study of Person-Centred Quality of Life Domains and Indicators: A Replication." *Journal of Intellectual Disability Research* 49 (10): 734–39. https://doi.org/10.1111/j.1365-2788.2005.00742.x.

Jenkins, Richard. 2004. *Social Identity*. London: Routledge.

Johnson, Leslie Main, ed. 2017. *Wisdom Engaged: Traditional Knowledge for Northern Community Well-Being*. Edmonton: University of Alberta.

Keck, Markus, and Patrick Sakdapolrak. 2013. "What Is Social Resilience? Lessons Learned and Ways Forward." *Erdkunde* 67 (1): 5–19. https://doi.org/10.3112/erdkunde.2013.01.02.

Klink, Carlos A., and Ricardo B. Machado. 2005. "Conservation of the Brazilian Cerrado." *Conservation Biology* 19 (3): 707–13. https://doi.org/10.1111/j.1523-1739.2005.00702.x.

Kracke, Waud H. 1976. "Uxorilocality in Patriliny: Kagwahiv Filial Separation." *Ethos* 4 (3): 295–310. https://doi.org/10.1525/eth.1976.4.3.02a00020.

Lachnitt, Jorge. 2003. *Dicionário Xavante/Português: Romnhitsi'ubumro A'uwẽ Mreme— Waradzu Mreme*. 2nd ed. Campo Grande, Brazil: Missão Selesiana de Mato Grosso, Universidade Católica Dom Bosco.

Laird, Shelby Gull, Angela Wardell-Johnson, and Angela T. Ragusaf. 2014. "Exploring the Human-Environment Connection: Rurality, Ecology and Social Well-Being." *Rural Society* 23 (2): 114–17.

Lave, Jean Carter. 1967. "Social Taxonomy among the Krikati (Gê) of Central Brazil." PhD diss., Harvard University Press, Cambridge, Massachusetts.

Lave, Jean Carter. 1975. *Inter-Moiety Systems: A Structural Explanation of the Proliferation of Ramkokamekra Ceremonial Associations*. Social Science Working Papers. Irvine: University of California, Irvine.

Lave, Jean Carter. 1977. "Eastern Timbira Moiety Systems in Time and Space: A Complex Structure." In *Actes du XLII Congrès International des Américanistes II*, edited by B. Alberti, A. Castel, and M. Guyot, 309–21. Paris : Société des Américanistes.

Lave, Jean Carter. 1979. "Cycles and Trends in Krikatí Naming Practices." In *Dialectical Societies: The Gê and Bororo of Central Brazil*, edited by David Maybury-Lewis, 16–44. Cambridge, Mass.: Harvard University Press.

Lea, Vanessa R. 1992. "Mebengokre (Kayapó) Onomastics: A Facet of Houses as Total Social Facts in Central Brazil." *Man*, n.s., 27 (1): 129–53. https://doi.org/10.2307/2803598.

Lea, Vanessa R. 1993. "Casas e Casas Mebengokre (Jê)." In *Amazônia: Etnologia e História Indígena*, edited by Eduardo Viveiros de Castro and Manuela Carneiro da Cunha, 265–82. São Paulo: Universidade de São Paulo.

Lea, Vanessa R. 1995a. "Casa-Se do Outro Lado: Um Modelo Simulado da Aliança Mebengokre (Jê)." In *Antropologia de Parentesco: Estudos Ameríndios*, edited by Eduardo Viveiros de Castro, 321–59. Rio de Janeiro: Universidade Federal de Rio de Janeiro.

Lea, Vanessa R. 1995b. "The Houses of the Mẽbêngôkre (Kayapó) of Central Brazil: A New Door to Their Social Organization." In *About the House: Lévi-Strauss and Beyond*, edited by Janet Carsten and Stephen Hugh-Jones, 206–25. Cambridge: Cambridge University Press.

Ledru, Marie-Pierre. 2002. "Late Quaternary History and Evolution of the Cerrados as Revealed by Palynological Records." In *The Cerrados of Brazil: Ecology and Natural History of a Neotropical Savanna*, edited by Paulo S. Oliveira and Robert J. Marquis, 33–50. New York: Columbia University Press.

Leeuwenberg, Frans J. 1995. *Diagnóstico de Caça e Manejo da Fauna Cinegética com os Índios Xavante, Aldeia Etenhiritipá.* Brasília: World Wildlife Fund.

Leeuwenberg, Frans J., and John G. Robinson. 2000. "Traditional Management of Hunting by a Xavante Community in Central Brazil: The Search for Sustainability." In *Hunting for Sustainability in Tropical Forests,* edited by John G. Robinson and Elizabeth L. Bennett, 375–94. New York: Columbia University Press.

Leite, Davi Lima Pantoja. 2007. "Efeitos do Fogo Sobre a Taxocenose de Lagartos em Áreas de Cerrado Sensu Stricto no Brasil Central." Master's thesis, Universidade de Brasília.

Le Tourneau, François-Michel. 2015. "The Sustainability Challenges of Indigenous Territories in Brazil's Amazonia." *Current Opinion in Environmental Sustainability* 14:213–20. https://doi.org/10.1016/j.cosust.2015.07.017.

LeVine, Robert A., and Walter H. Sangree. 1962. "The Diffusion of Age Group Organization in East Africa: A Controlled Comparison." *Africa: Journal of the International African Institute* 32: 97–110. https://doi.org/10.2307/1158178.

Lévi-Strauss, Claude. 1943. "The Social Use of Kinship Terms among Brazilian Indians." *American Anthropologist* 45 (3): 398–409.

Lévi-Strauss, Claude. 1944. "On Dual Organization in South America." *América Indígena* 4 :37–47.

Lévi-Strauss, Claude. 1955. *Tristes Tropiques.* Paris : Plon.

Lévi-Strauss, Claude. 1963. *Structural Anthropology.* New York: Basic Books.

Lévi-Strauss, Claude. 1965. "The Future of Kinship Studies." *Proceedings of the Royal Anthropological Institute of Great Britain and Ireland,* no. 1965: 13–22. https://doi.org/10.2307/3031752.

Lévi-Strauss, Claude. 1969. *The Elementary Structures of Kinship.* Translated by James Harle Bell and John Richard von Sturmer. Boston, Mass.: Beacon Press.

Lévi-Strauss, Claude. 1983. *Structural Anthropology.* Vol. 2. Translated by Monique Layton. Chicago: University of Chicago Press.

Lévi-Strauss, Claude. 1984. *Paroles Données.* Paris: Plon.

Lima, Antonio Carlos de Souza. 1995. *Um Grande Cerco de Paz: Poder Tutelar, Indianidade e Formação do Estado no Brasil.* Petrópolis, Brazil: Editora Vozes.

Lopes da Silva, Aracy. 1986. *Nomes e Amigos: Da Prática Xavante à uma Reflexão sobre os Jê.* Antropologia 6. São Paulo: Faculdade de Filosofia, Letras e Ciências Humanas, Universidade de São Paulo.

Lopes da Silva, Aracy. 1989. "Social Practice and Ontology in Akwe-Xavante Naming and Myth." *Ethnology* 28 (4): 331–41. https://doi.org/10.2307/3773538.

Lopes da Silva, Aracy. 1992. "Dois Séculos e Meio de História Xavante." In *História dos Índios no Brasil,* edited by Manuela Carneiro da Cunha, 357–78. São Paulo: Companhia das Letras.

Lopes da Silva, Aracy. 1999. "The Akwe-Xavante in History at the End of the 20th Century." *Journal of Latin American Anthropology* 4 (2): 212–37. https://doi.org/10.1525/jlca.1999.4.2.212.

Lopes da Silva, Aracy, and Agenor José T. P. Farias. 1992. "Pintura Corporal e Sociedade, Os Partidos Xerente." In *Grafísmo Indígena: Estudos de Antropologia Estética*, edited by Lux B. Vidal, 89–116. São Paulo: Studio Nobel, Editora de Universidade de São Paulo, FAPESP.

Lopes da Silva, Aracy, and Angela Nunes. 2002. "Introdução." In *Crianças Indígenas: Ensaios Antropológicos*, edited by Aracy Lopes da Silva, Angela Nunes, and Ana Vera L. S. Macedo, 64–99. São Paulo: Global.

Loukotka, Čestmír. 1935. *Clasificación de las Lenguas Sudamericanas*. Prague: Tipografía Josef Bartl.

Lowie, Robert H. 1939. "The Associations of the Šerénte." *American Anthropologist* 41 (3): 408–15.

Lowie, Robert H. 1941. "A Note on the Northern Gê Tribes of Brazil." *American Anthropologist* 43 (2): 188–96.

Lowie, Robert H. 1943. "A Note on the Social Life of the Northern Kayapó." *American Anthropologist* 45 (4): 633–35.

Lowie, Robert H. 1946a. "The Northwestern and Central Gê." In *Handbook of South American Indians*. Vol. 1, *The Marginal Tribes*, edited by Julian H. Steward, 477–517. Washington, D.C.: Bureau of American Ethnology, U.S. Government Printing Office.

Lowie, Robert H. 1946b. "The 'Tapuya.'" In *Handbook of South American Indians*. Vol. 1, *The Marginal Tribes*, edited by Julian H. Steward, 553–56. Washington, D.C.: Bureau of American Ethnology, U.S. Government Printing Office.

Lucena, J. Rodolfo M., Carlos E. A. Coimbra Jr., Cosme M. F. Passos Silva, and James R. Welch. 2016. "Prevalence of Physical Inactivity and Associated Socioeconomic Indicators in Indigenous Xavante Communities in Central Brazil." *BMC Nutrition* 2:37. https://doi.org/10.1186/s40795-016-0076-4.

Luck, Gary W., Penny Davidson, Dianne Boxall, and Lisa Smallbone. 2011. "Relations between Urban Bird and Plant Communities and Human Well-Being and Connection to Nature." *Conservation Biology* 25 (4): 816–26. https://doi.org/10.1111/j.1523-1739.2011.01685.x.

Maine, Sir Henry S. 1931. *Ancient Law*. London: Oxford University Press.

Manning, Matthew, and Christopher Fleming. 2019a. "The Complexity of Measuring Indigenous Wellbeing." In *Routledge Handbook of Indigenous Wellbeing*, edited by Christopher Fleming and Matthew Manning, 1–2. Routledge International Handbooks. London: Routledge.

Manning, Matthew, and Christopher Fleming. 2019b. "Understanding Wellbeing." In *Routledge Handbook of Indigenous Wellbeing*, edited by Christopher Fleming and Matthew Manning, 3–10. Routledge International Handbooks. London: Routledge.

MapBiomas. 2021. "Land Cover/Use Data Base." Version 6.0. MapBiomas Brasil, August 2021. https://mapbiomas.org/estatisticas.

Mason, Alden J. 1950. "The Languages of South American Indians." In *Handbook of South American Indians*. Vol. 5, *Physical Anthropology, Linguistics and Cultural Geography of South American Indians*, edited by Julian H. Steward, 157–317. Washington, D.C.: Bureau of American Ethnology, U.S. Government Printing Office.

Mathews, Gordon, and Carolina Izquierdo. 2009a. "Anthropology, Happiness, and Well-Being." In *Pursuits of Happiness: Well-Being in Anthropological Perspective*, edited by Gordon Mathews and Carolina Izquierdo, 1–19. New York: Berghahn Books.

Mathews, Gordon, and Carolina Izquierdo, eds. 2009b. *Pursuits of Happiness: Well-Being in Anthropological Perspective*. New York: Berghahn Books.

Maybury-Lewis, David. 1960. "The Analysis of Dual Organizations: A Methodological Critique." *Bijdragen tot de Taal-, Land- en Volkenkunde* 116 (1): 2–44.

Maybury-Lewis, David. 1965a. "On Martius' Distinction between Shavante and Sherente." *Revista do Museu Paulista* 16:263–88.

Maybury-Lewis, David. 1965b. "Some Crucial Distinctions in Central Brazilian Ethnology." *Anthropos* 60:340–58.

Maybury-Lewis, David. 1967. *Akwẽ-Shavante Society*. Oxford: Clarendon Press.

Maybury-Lewis, David. 1970a. "Science by Association." In *Claude Lévi-Strauss: The Anthropologist as Hero*, edited by E. Nelson Hayes and Tanya Hayes, 133–39. Cambridge, Mass.: MIT Press.

Maybury-Lewis, David. 1970b. "Science or Bricolage?" In *Claude Lévi-Strauss: The Anthropologist as Hero*, edited by E. Nelson Hayes and Tanya Hayes, 150–63. Cambridge, Mass.: MIT Press.

Maybury-Lewis, David. 1978. "Brazilian Indianist Policy: Some Lessons from the Shavante Project." In *Native Peoples and Economic Development: Six Case Studies from Latin America*, edited by T. MacDonald, 75–86. Cambridge, Mass.: Cultural Survival.

Maybury-Lewis, David. 1979a. "Conclusion: Kinship, Ideology, and Culture." In *Dialectical Societies: The Gê and Bororo of Central Brazil*, edited by David Maybury-Lewis, 301–12. Cambridge, Mass.: Harvard University Press.

Maybury-Lewis, David. 1979b. "Cultural Categories of the Central Gê." In *Dialectical Societies: The Gê and Bororo of Central Brazil*, edited by David Maybury-Lewis, 218–48. Cambridge, Mass.: Harvard University Press.

Maybury-Lewis, David, ed. 1979c. *Dialectical Societies: The Gê and Bororo of Central Brazil*. Cambridge, Mass.: Harvard University Press.

Maybury-Lewis, David. 1979d. "Introduction." In *Dialectical Societies: The Gê and Bororo of Central Brazil*, edited by David Maybury-Lewis, 1–13. Cambridge, Mass.: Harvard University Press.

Maybury-Lewis, David. 1979e. "Kinship, Ideology, and Culture." In *Dialectical Societies: The Gê and Bororo of Central Brazil*, edited by David Maybury-Lewis, 301–12. Cambridge, Mass.: Harvard University Press.

Maybury-Lewis, David. 2009. "Indigenous Theories, Anthropological Ideas: A View from Lowland South America." *Anthropological Quarterly* 82 (4): 897–927. https://doi.org/10.1353/anq.0.0088.

McGillivray, Mark. 2007. *Human Well-Being: Concept and Measurement*. Basingstoke: Palgrave Macmillan.

Melatti, Julio C. 1970. "O Sistema Social Krahó." PhD diss., Universidade de São Paulo.

Melatti, Julio C. 1978. *Ritos de Uma Tribo Timbira*. São Paulo: Ática.

Melatti, Julio C. 1979. "The Relationship System of the Krahó." In *Dialectical Societies: The Gê and Bororo of Central Brazil*, edited by David Maybury-Lewis, 46–82. Cambridge, Mass.: Harvard University Press.

Melatti, Julio C. 2009. *O Messianismo Craô*. Brasília: Printed by the author.

Menezes, Claudia. 1999. "Missionários e Guerreiros: O Apostolado Salesiano Entre os Xavante." In *Transformando os Deuses: Os Múltiplos Sentidos da Conversão Entre os Povos Indígenas no Brasil*, edited by Robin M. Wright, 309–42. Campinas, Brazil: Editora UNICAMP.

Merbs, Charles F. 1992. "A New World of Infectious Disease." *American Journal of Physical Anthropology* 35 (S15): 3–42. https://doi.org/10.1002/ajpa.1330350603.

Miranda, Heloisa S., Mercedes M. C. Bustamante, and Antonio C. Miranda. 2002. "The Fire Factor." In *The Cerrados of Brazil: Ecology and Natural History of a Neotropical Savannah*, edited by Paulo S. Oliveira and Robert J. Marquis, 51–68. New York: Columbia University Press.

Müller, Regina Aparecida Polo. 1976. "A Pintura do Corpo e os Ornamentos Xavantes: Arte Visual e Comunicação Social." Master's thesis, Universidade Estadual de Campinas, Brazil.

Müller, Regina Aparecida Polo. 1992. "Mensagens Visuais na Ornamentação Corporal Xavante." In *Grafismo Indígena: Estudos de Antropologia Estética*, edited by Lux B. Vidal, 133–42. São Paulo: Studio Nobel, Editora de Universidade de São Paulo, FAPESP.

Murdock, George P. 1974. "South American Culture Areas." In *Native South Americans*, edited by Patricia J. Lyon, 22–39. Prospect Heights, Ill.: Waveland Press.

Murphy, Robert F. 1956. "Matrilocality and Patrilineality in Mundurucú Society." *American Anthropologist* 58:414–34.

Myers, Norman, Russell A. Mittermeier, Cristina G. Mittermeier, Gustavo A. B. Fonseca, and Jennifer Kent. 2000. "Biodiversity Hotspots for Conservation Priorities." *Nature* 403 (6772): 853–58. https://doi.org/10.1038/35002501.

Neel, James V., Francisco M. Salzano, F. Keiter, David Maybury-Lewis, and P. C. C. Junqueira. 1964. "Studies on the Xavante Indians of the Brazilian Mato Grosso." *American Journal of Human Genetics* 16 (1): 52–140.

Nimuendajú, Curt. 1939. *The Apinayé*. Washington, D.C.: Catholic University of America Press.

Nimuendajú, Curt. 1942. *The Šerente*. Los Angeles: Frederick Webb Hodge Anniversary Publication Fund.

Nimuendajú, Curt. 1946. *The Eastern Timbira*. Berkeley: University of California Press.

Nimuendajú, Curt. 2017. *Mapa Etno-histórico de Curt Nimuendajú*. 2nd ed. Brasília: Instituto do Patrimônio Histórico e Artístico Nacional, Instituto Brasileiro de Geografia e Estatística.

Nimuendajú, Curt, and Robert H. Lowie. 1937. "The Dual Organization of the Ramko'kamekra (Canella) of Northern Brazil." *American Anthropologist* 39 (4): 565–82. https://doi.org/10.1525/aa.1937.39.4.02a00020.

Nolte, Christoph, Arun Agrawal, Kirsten M. Silvius, and Britaldo S. Soares-Filho. 2013. "Governance Regime and Location Influence Avoided Deforestation Success of Protected Areas in the Brazilian Amazon." *Proceedings of the National Academy of Sciences of the United States of America* 110 (13): 4956–61. https://doi.org/10.1073/pnas.1214786110.

Nunes, Angela. 2002. "No Tempo e no Espaço: Brincadeiras das Crianças A'uwẽ-Xavante." In *Crianças Indígenas: Ensaios Antropológicos*, edited by Aracy Lopes da Silva, Angela Nunes, and Ana Vera L. S. Macedo, 64–99. São Paulo: Global.

Nunes, Angela. 2011. "A Sociedade das Crianças A'uwe—Xavante: Revisitando um Estudo Antropológico sobre a Infância." *Poiésis—Revista do Programa de Pós-Graduação em Educação* 4 (8): 342–59. https://doi.org/10.19177/prppge.v4e82011342-359.

Oliveira, João Pacheco de. 1998. "Terras Indígenas, Economia de Mercado e Desenvolvimento Rural." In *Indigenismo e Territorializaçõ: Poderes, Rotinas e Saberes Coloniais no Brasil Contemporâneo*, edited by João Pacheco de Oliveira, 43–68. Rio de Janeiro: Contra Capa.

Oliveira, Paulo S., and Robert J. Marquis, eds. 2002. *The Cerrados of Brazil: Ecology and Natural History of a Neotropical Savanna*. New York: Columbia University Press.

Oliveira-Filho, Ary T., and James A. Ratter. 2002. "Vegetation Physiognomies and Woody Flora of the Cerrado Biome." In *The Cerrados of Brazil: Ecology and Natural History of a Neotropical Savanna*, edited by Paulo S. Oliveira and Robert J. Marquis, 91–120. New York: Columbia University Press.

Ortner, Sherry B. 1984. "Theory in Anthropology since the Sixties." *Comparative Studies in Society and History* 26 (1): 126–66. https://doi.org/10.1017/S0010417500010811.

Overing, Joanna. 1999. "Elogio do Cotidiano: A Confiança e a Arte da Vida Social em uma Comunidade Amazônica." *Mana* 5 (1): 81–107. https://doi.org/10.1590/S0104-93131999000100004.

Overing, Joanna, and Alan Passes, eds. 2000a. *The Anthropology of Love and Anger: The Aesthetics of Conviviality in Native Amazonia*. London: Routledge.

Overing, Joanna, and Alan Passes. 2000b. "Introduction: Conviviality and the Opening Up of Amazonian Anthropology." In *The Anthropology of Love and Anger: The Aesthetics of Conviviality in Native Amazonia*, edited by Joanna Overing and Alan Passes, 1–30. London: Routledge.

Panelli, Ruth, and Gail Tipa. 2009. "Beyond Foodscapes: Considering Geographies of Indigenous Well-Being." *Health and Place* 15 (2): 455–65. https://doi.org/10.1016/j.healthplace.2008.08.005.

Panter-Brick, Catherine. 2014. "Health, Risk, and Resilience: Interdisciplinary Concepts and Applications." *Annual Review of Anthropology* 43:431–48. https://doi.org/10.1146/annurev-anthro-102313-025944.

Parsons, Talcott. 1951. *The Social System*. New York: Free Press.

Pelto, Pertti J. 1973. *The Snowmobile Revolution: Technology and Social Change in the Arctic*. Menlo Park, Calif.: Cummings.

Peredo, Ana Maria. 2019. "El Buen Vivir: Notions of Wellbeing among Indigenous Peoples of South America." In *Routledge Handbook of Indigenous Wellbeing*, edited by Christopher Fleming and Matthew Manning, 156–69. Routledge International Handbooks. London: Routledge.

Pfaff, Alexander, Juan Robalino, Catalina Sandoval, and Diego Herrera. 2015. "Protected Area Types, Strategies and Impacts in Brazil's Amazon: Public Protected Area Strategies Do Not Yield a Consistent Ranking of Protected Area Types by Impact." *Philosophical Transactions of the Royal Society B: Biological Sciences* 370 (1681): 20140273. https://doi.org/10.1098/rstb.2014.0273.

Pohl, Johann Emanuel. 1837. *Reise im Innern von Brasilien*. Vol. 2. Vienna: Anton Strauss.

Popkin, Barry M., Camila Corvalan, and Laurence M. Grummer-Strawn. 2020. "Dynamics of the Double Burden of Malnutrition and the Changing Nutrition Reality." *Lancet* 395 (10217): 65–74. https://doi.org/10.1016/S0140-6736(19)32497-3.

Posey, Darrell A. 1985. "Indigenous Management of Tropical Forest Ecosystems: The Case of the Kayapó Indians of the Brazilian Amazon." *Agroforestry Systems* 3 (2): 139–58. https://doi.org/10.1007/BF00122640.

Prada, Manrique. 2002. "Efeito do Fogo e da Caça na Abundância de Mamíferos na Reserva Xavante do Rio das Mortes, MT, Brasil." PhD diss., Universidade de Brasília.

Prada, Manrique, and Jader Marinho-Filho. 2004. "Effects of Fire on the Abundance of Xenarthrans in Mato Grosso, Brazil." *Austral Ecology* 29 (5): 568–73. https://doi.org/10.1111/j.1442-9993.2004.01391.x.

Prilleltensky, Isaac, and Ora Prilleltensky. 2007. "Webs of Well-Being: The Interdependence of Personal, Relational, Organizational and Communal Well-Being." In *Well-Being: Individual, Community and Social Perspectives*, edited by John T. Haworth and Graham Hart, 57–74. Basingstoke: Palgrave Macmillan.

Prins, Adriaan Hendrik Johan. 1953. *East African Age-Class Systems*. Groningen, Netherlands: Wolters.

Putnam, Robert D. 2000. *Bowling Alone: The Collapse and Revival of American Community*. New York: Simon and Schuster.

Radcliffe-Brown, Alfred R. 1929. "Age Organization-Terminology." *Man* 29:21.

Radcliffe-Brown, Alfred R. 1935. "Patrilineal and Matrilineal Succession." *Iowa Law Review* 20 (2): 286–303.

Radcliffe-Brown, Alfred R. 1940. "On Social Structure." *Journal of the Royal Anthropological Institute of Great Britain and Ireland* 70 (1): 1–12. https://doi.org/10.2307/2844197.

Radcliffe-Brown, Alfred R. 1952. *Structure and Function in Primitive Society: Essays and Addresses*. London: Cohen and West.

Ramos, Alcida R. 1984. "Frontier Expansion and Indian Peoples in the Brazilian Amazon." In *Frontier Expansion in Amazonia*, edited by Marianne Schmink and Charles H. Wood, 83–104. Gainesville: University of Florida Press.

Ramos, Alcida R. 1998. *Indigenism: Ethnic Politics in Brazil*. Madison: University of Wisconsin Press.

Ramos, Alcida R. 2012. "The Politics of Perspectivism." *Annual Review of Anthropology* 41:481–94. https://doi.org/10.1146/annurev-anthro-092611-145950.

Ramos-Neto, Mário Barroso, and Vânia Regina Pivello. 2000. "Lightning Fires in a Brazilian Savanna National Park: Rethinking Management Strategies." *Environmental Management* 26 (6): 675–84. https://doi.org/10.1007/s002670010124.

Ratter, James A., José Felipe Ribeiro, and Samuel Bridgewater. 1997. "The Brazilian Cerrado Vegetation and Threats to Its Biodiversity." *Annals of Botany* 80 (3): 223–30. https://doi.org/10.1006/anbo.1997.0469.

Ratter, James A., Paul W. Richards, George Argent, and David R. Gifford. 1973. "Observations on the Vegetation of Northeastern Mato Grosso: I. The Woody Vegetation Types of the Xavantina-Cachimbo Expedition Area." *Philosophical Transactions of the Royal Society of London B: Biological Sciences* 266 (880): 449–92. https://doi.org/10.1098/rstb.1973.0053.

Ravagnani, Oswaldo Martins. 1991. *A Experiência Xavânte com o Mundo dos Brancos*. Araraquara, Brazil: Universidade Estadual Paulista.

Richmond, Chantelle, Susan J. Elliott, Ralph Matthews, and B. Elliott. 2005. "The Political Ecology of Health: Perceptions of Environment, Economy, Health and Well-Being among 'Namgis First Nation." *Health and Place* 11 (4): 349–65. https://doi.org/10.1016/j.healthplace.2004.04.003.

Ringold, Paul L., James Boyd, Dixon Landers, and Matt Weber. 2013. "What Data Should We Collect? A Framework for Identifying Indicators of Ecosystem Contributions to Human Well-Being." *Frontiers in Ecology and the Environment* 11 (2): 98–105. https://doi.org/10.1890/110156.

Ritter, Madeline Lattman. 1980. "The Conditions Favoring Age-Set Organization." *Journal of Anthropological Research* 36 (1): 87–104. https://doi.org/10.1086/jar.36.1.3629554.

Rival, Laura. 2012. "The Materiality of Life: Revisiting the Anthropology of Nature in Amazonia." *Indiana* 29 :127–43. https ://doi.org/10.18441/ind.v29i0.127-143.

Rivet, Paul. 1924. "Langues Américaines." In *Les Langues du Monde*, edited by A. Meillet and Marcel Cohen. Collection Linguistique Publiée par la Société de Linguistique de Paris, vol. 16, 639–712. Paris: Champion.

Rodrigues, Aryon Dall'Igna. 2012. "Flexão Relacional no Tronco Linguístico Macro-Jê." *Revista Brasileira de Linguística Antropológica* 4 (2): 267–77. https://doi.org/10.26512/rbla.v4i2.20691.

Russell, Roly, Anne D. Guerry, Patricia Balvanera, Rachelle K. Gould, Xavier Basurto, Kai M. A. Chan, Sarah Klain, Jordan Levine, and Jordan Tam. 2013. "Humans and Nature: How Knowing and Experiencing Nature Affect Well-Being." *Annual Review of Environment and Resources* 38:473–502. https://doi.org/10.1146/annurev-environ-012312-110838.

Russo, Kelly. 2005. "O Povo Xavante e a Formação dos 'Novos Guerreiros': O Sistema Educativo e a Educação Escolar Indígena no Brasil." Master's thesis, Faculdade Latino-Americana de Ciências Sociais, Buenos Aires, Argentina.

Sahlins, Marshall D. 1968. "Notes on the Original Affluent Society." In *Man the Hunter*, edited by Richard B. Lee and Irven DeVore, 858–59. Chicago, Ill.: Aldine.

Salzano, Francisco M., and Sidia M. Callegari-Jacques. 1988. *South American Indians: A Case Study in Evolution*. Oxford: Clarendon Press.

Sangha, Kamaljit K., Andrew Le Brocque, Robert Costanza, and Yvonne Cadet-James. 2015. "Ecosystems and Indigenous Well-Being: An Integrated Framework." *Global Ecology and Conservation* 4:197–206. https://doi.org/10.1016/j.gecco.2015.06.008.

Santos, Ricardo Ventura, Carlos E. A. Coimbra Jr., and Joanna Radin. 2020. "'Why Did They Die?': Biomedical Narratives of Epidemics and Mortality among Amazonian Indigenous Populations in Sociohistorical and Anthropological Contexts." *Current Anthropology* 61 (4): 441–70. https://doi.org/10.1086/710079.

Santos, Ricardo Ventura, Carlos E. A. Coimbra Jr., and James R. Welch. 2013. "A Half-Century Portrait: Health Transition in the Xavante Indians from Central Brazil." In *Human-Environment Interactions*, edited by Eduardo S. Brondízio and Emilio F. Moran, 29–52. Dordrecht: Springer Netherlands.

Santos, Ricardo Ventura, Nancy M. Flowers, Carlos E. A. Coimbra Jr., and Silvia A. Gugelmin. 1997. "Tapirs, Tractors, and Tapes: The Changing Economy and Ecology of the Xavánte Indians of Central Brazil." *Human Ecology* 25 (4): 545–66. https://doi.org/10.1023/A:1021881823603.

Santos-Granero, Fernando. 2007. "Of Fear and Friendship: Amazonian Sociality beyond Kinship and Affinity." *Journal of the Royal Anthropological Institute* 13 (1): 1–18. https://doi.org/10.1111/j.1467-9655.2007.00410.x.

Santos-Granero, Fernando, ed. 2015a. *Images of Public Wealth or the Anatomy of Well-Being in Indigenous Amazonia*. Tucson: University of Arizona Press.

Santos-Granero, Fernando. 2015b. "Introduction." In *Images of Public Wealth or the Anatomy of Well-Being in Indigenous Amazonia*, edited by Fernando Santos-Granero, 3–34. Tucson: University of Arizona Press.

Schaden, Egon. 1945. "Educação e Magia nas Cerimônias de Iniciação." *Revista Brasileira de Estudos Pedagógicos* 3 (8): 271–74.

Schalock, Robert L., Miguel A. Verdugo, Christina Jenaro, Mian Wang, Mike Wehmeyer, Xu Jiancheng, and Yves Lachapelle. 2005. "Cross-Cultural Study of Quality of Life Indicators." Edited by David Felce. *American Journal on Mental Retardation* 110 (4): 298–311. https://doi.org/10.1352/0895-8017(2005)110[298:CSOQOL]2.0.CO;2.

Schmidt, Wilhelm. 1942. *Ethnologia Sul-Americana*. São Paulo: Companhia Editora Nacional.

Schryer, Frans J. 2001. "Multiple Hierarchies and the Duplex Nature of Groups." *Journal of the Royal Anthropological Institute* 7 (4): 705–21. https://doi.org/10.1111/1467-9655.00085.

Seeger, Anthony. 1981. *Nature and Society in Central Brazil: The Suyá Indians of Mato Grosso*. Cambridge, Mass.: Harvard University Press.

Seeger, Anthony. 1987. *Why Suyá Sing: A Musical Anthropology of an Amazonian People*. Cambridge Studies in Ethnomusicology. Cambridge: Cambridge University Press.

Seeger, Anthony. 1989. "Dualism: Fuzzy Thinking or Fuzzy Sets?" In *The Attraction of Opposites: Thought and Society in the Dualistic Mode*, edited by David Maybury-Lewis, 191–208. Ann Arbor: University of Michigan Press.

Seeger, Anthony. 2015. "It's Ear-y and Euphoric: Amazonian Music and the Performance of Public Wealth among the Suyá/Kïsêdjê." In *Images of Public Wealth or the Anatomy of Well-Being in Indigenous Amazonia*, edited by Fernando Santos-Granero, 37–59. Tucson: University of Arizona Press.

Seeger, Anthony, Roberto DaMatta, and Eduardo B. Viveiros de Castro. 2019. "The Construction of the Person in Indigenous Brazilian Societies." *HAU: Journal of Ethnographic Theory* 9 (3): 694–703. https://doi.org/10.1086/706805.

Sereburã, Hipru, Rupawê, Serezabdi, and Sereñimirãmi. 1998. *Wamrêmê Za'ra—Nossa Palavra: Mito e História do Povo Xavante*. São Paulo: SENAC.

Serewaõmowê, Valmir. 2014. "Warazu Wasu'u: História do Warazu." In *Aihö Ubuni Wasu'u: O Lobo Guará e Outras Histórias do Povo Xavante*, edited by Povo A'uwẽ Uptabi da Aldeia Etenhiritipá, Angela Pappiani, and Maíra P. Lacerda, 69–79. São Paulo: Ikorẽ.

Silva, Hilton P., Odara H. Boscolo, Graziela Nascimento, Flávio Obermüller, and Fernanda Strelow. 2005. "Biodiversity Conservation and Human Well-Being: Challenges for the Populations and Protected Areas of the Brazilian Atlantic Forest." *EcoHealth* 2 (4): 333–42. https://doi.org/10.1007/s10393-005-8361-8.

Simon, Marcelo F., Rosaura Grether, Luciano P. de Queiroz, Cynthia Skema, R. Toby Pennington, and Colin E. Hughes. 2009. "Recent Assembly of the Cerrado, a Neotropical Plant Diversity Hotspot, by in Situ Evolution of Adaptations to Fire." *Proceedings of the National Academy of Sciences* 106 (48): 20359–64. https://doi.org/10.1073/pnas.0903410106.

Six, Perri. 2007. "Sense and Solidarities: Politics and Human Well-Being." In *Well-Being: Individual, Community and Social Perspectives*, edited by John T. Haworth and Graham Hart, 127–45. Basingstoke: Palgrave Macmillan.

Sixsmith, Judith, and Margaret Boneham. 2007. "Health, Well-Being and Social Capital." In *Well-Being: Individual, Community and Social Perspectives*, edited by John T. Haworth and Graham Hart, 75–92. Basingstoke: Palgrave Macmillan.

Smith, Eric Alden, and Mark Wishnie. 2000. "Conservation and Subsistence in Small-Scale Societies." *Annual Review of Anthropology* 29:493–524. https://doi.org/10.1146/annurev.anthro.29.1.493.

Soares, Fabio V. 2011. "Brazil's Bolsa Família: A Review." *Economic and Political Weekly* 46 (21): 55–60.

Soares-Filho, Britaldo S., P. Moutinho, D. Nepstad, A. Anderson, H. Rodrigues, R. Garcia, L. Dietzsch, et al. 2010. "Role of Brazilian Amazon Protected Areas in Climate Change Mitigation." *Proceedings of the National Academy of Sciences* 107 (24): 10821–26. https://doi.org/10.1073/pnas.0913048107.

Souza, Lincoln. 1953. *Os Xavantes e a Civilização (Ensaio Histórico)*. Rio de Janeiro, Brazil: Serviço Gráfico do Instituto Brasileiro de Geografia e Estatística.

Souza, Luciene Guimarães. 2008. "Demografia e Saúde dos Índios Xavante do Brasil Central." PhD diss., Escola Nacional de Saúde Pública Sergio Arouca, Fundação Oswaldo Cruz, Rio de Janeiro, Brazil.

Spier, Leslie. 1925. "The Distribution of Kinship Systems in North America." *University of Washington Publications in Anthropology* 1 (2): 71–88.

Stark, David. 2001. "Heterarchy: Exploiting Ambiguity and Organizing Diversity." *Brazilian Journal of Political Economy* 21 (1): 21–39. https://doi.org/10.1590/0101-31572001-1248.

Steckel, Richard H. 2016. "Biological Measures of Well-Being." In *The Oxford Handbook of Economics and Human Biology*, edited by John Komlos and Inas R. Kelly, 31–51. Oxford: Oxford University Press.

Stewart, Frank Henderson. 1977. *Fundamentals of Age-Group Systems*. New York: Academic Press.

Strassburg, Bernardo B. N., Thomas Brooks, Rafael Feltran-Barbieri, Alvaro Iribarrem, Renato Crouzeilles, Rafael Loyola, Agnieszka E. Latawiec, et al. 2017. "Moment of Truth for the Cerrado Hotspot." *Nature Ecology and Evolution* 1 (4): 1–3. https://doi.org/10.1038/s41559-017-0099.

Sumner, L. Wayne. 1996. *Welfare, Happiness, and Ethics*. Oxford: Clarendon Press.

Supretaprã Xavante, Paulo. 2015. "Paulo Supretaprã Xavante." In *Memórias Sertanistas: Cem Anos de Indigenismo no Brasil*, edited by Felipe Milanez, 98–109. São Paulo: Edições SESC.

Szaffka, Tihamér. 1942. "Sôbre Construções Navais duma Tribo de Índios Desconhecidos do Rio das Mortes." *Revista do Arquivo Municipal (São Paulo)* 87:171–81.

Sztutman, Renato. 2002. "Do Dois ao Múltiplo na Terra do Um: A Experiência Antropológica de David Maybury-Lewis." *Revista de Antropologia* 45 (2): 443–76. https://doi.org/10.1590/S0034-77012002000200006.

Tassinari, Antonella. 2014. "Concepções Indígenas de Infância no Brasil." *Tellus* 7 (13): 11–25.

Tesch-Römer, Clemens, Andreas Motel-Klingebiel, and Martin J. Tomasik. 2008. "Gender Differences in Subjective Well-Being: Comparing Societies with Respect to Gender Equality." *Social Indicators Research* 85 (2): 329–49. https://doi.org/10.1007/s11205-007-9133-3.

Thin, Neil. 2009. "Why Anthropology Can Ill Afford to Ignore Well-Being." In *Pursuits of Happiness: Well-Being in Anthropological Perspective*, edited by Gordon Mathews and Carolina Izquierdo, 23–44. New York: Berghahn Books.

Thomas, Elizabeth M. 1959. *Harmless People*. London: Secker and Warburg.

Trautmann, Thomas R. 1981. *Dravidian Kinship*. Cambridge Studies in Social Anthropology, vol. 36. Cambridge: Cambridge University Press.

Tsa'e'omo'wa, Michael Rã'wa. 2021. "Danhônô: Ritual de Passagem A'uwê Uptabi (Xavante)." Master's thesis, Universidade Federal de Goiás, Goiânia, Brazil.

Turnbull, Colin M. 1961. *The Forest People*. London: Chatto and Windus.

Turner, Terence S. 1965. "Social Structure and Political Organization among the Northern Cayapó." PhD diss., Harvard University, Cambridge, Massachusetts.

Turner, Terence S. 1979. "The Gê and Bororo Societies as Dialectical Systems: A General Model." In *Dialectical Societies: The Gê and Bororo of Central Brazil*, edited by David Maybury-Lewis, 147–78. Cambridge, Mass.: Harvard University Press.

Turner, Terence S. 1980. "The Social Skin." In *Not Work Alone: A Cross-Cultural View of Activities Superfluous to Survival*, edited by Jeremy Cherfas and Roger Lewin, 112–40. London: Temple Smith.

Turner, Terence S. 1984. "Dual Opposition, Hierarchy, and Value: Moiety Structure and Symbolic Polarity in Central Brazil and Elsewhere." In *Différences Valeurs, Hiérarchie, Textes Offerts à Louis Dumont*, edited by J. C. Galey, 335–70. Paris: École des Hautes Études en Sciences Sociales.

Turner, Terence S. 1995. "Social Body and Embodied Subject: Bodiliness, Subjectivity and Sociality among the Kayapó." *Cultural Anthropology* 10 (2): 143–70.

Valentine, Paul. 2017. *The Anthropology of Marriage in Lowland South America: Bending and Breaking the Rules*. Gainesville: University Press of Florida.

Vanhulst, Julien, and Adrian E. Beling. 2013. "Buen Vivir: La Irrupción de América Latina en el Campo Gravitacional del Desarrollo Sostenible." *Revista Iberoamericana de Economía Ecológica* 21:1–14.

Verdon, Michel, and Paul Jorion. 1981. "The Hordes of Discord: Australian Aboriginal Social Organisation Reconsidered." *Man* 16 (1): 90–107.

Vidal, Lux B. 1976. "As Categorias de Idade Como Sistema de Classificação e Controle Demográfico de Grupos Entre os Xikrin do Cateté e de Como São Manipulados em Diferentes Contextos." *Revista do Museu Paulista*, n.s., 23:129–42.

Vidal, Lux B. 1977. *Morte e Vida de Uma Sociedade Indígena Brasileira: Os Kayapó-Xikrin do Rio Cateté*. São Paulo: Hucitec.

Vidal, Lux B. 1981. "Contribution to the Concepts of Person and Self in Lowland South American Societies: Body Painting among the Kayapó-Xikrin." In *Contribuições à Antropologia em Homenagem ao Professor Egon Schaden*, edited by Tekla Hartmann and Vera Penteado Coelho, 291–304. São Paulo: Museu Paulista.

Vieira-Filho, João Paulo B. 1996. "Emergência do Diabetes Melito Tipo II entre os Xavantes." *Revista da Associação Médica Brasileira* 42 (1): 61.

Viveiros de Castro, Eduardo. 1988. "O Teatro Ontológico Bororo." *Anuário Antropológico* 86:227–45.

Viveiros de Castro, Eduardo. 1993. "Alguns Aspectos da Afinidade no Dravidianato Amazônico." In *Amazônia: Etnologia e História Indígena*, edited by Eduardo Viveiros de Castro and Manuela Carneiro da Cunha, 150–210. São Paulo: NHII-Universidade de São Paulo, FAPESP.

Viveiros de Castro, Eduardo. 1995. "Pensando o Parentesco Ameríndio." In *Antropologia do Parentesco*, edited by Eduardo Viveiros de Castro, 7–24. Rio de Janeiro: Editora UFRJ.

Viveiros de Castro, Eduardo. 1996. "Images of Nature and Society in Amazonian Ethnology." *Annual Review of Anthropology* 25:179–200. https://doi.org/10.1146/annurev.anthro.25.1.179.

Viveiros de Castro, Eduardo. 1998a. "Cosmological Deixis and Amerindian Perspectivism." *Journal of the Royal Anthropological Institute* 4:469–88. https://doi.org/10.2307/3034157.

Viveiros de Castro, Eduardo. 1998b. "Lévi-Strauss nos 90: A Antropologia de Cabeça Para Baixo." *Mana* 4 (2): 119–26. https://doi.org/10.1590/S0104-93131998000200006.

Viveiros de Castro, Eduardo. 2002. *A Inconstância da Alma Selvagem*. São Paulo: Cosac and Naify.

von Martius, Karl Friedrich Philipp. 1867. *Beiträge zur Ethnographie und Sprachenkunde Amerika's Zumal Brasiliens*. Vol. 2, *Glossaria Linguarum Brasiliensium*. Leipzig: Friedrich Fleischer.

Warming, Eugen. 1892. *Lagoa Santa: Et Bidrag til den biologiske Plantegeografi*. Copenhagen: Bianco Luno.

Watson, Alan E. 2013. "The Role of Wilderness Protection and Societal Engagement as Indicators of Well-Being: An Examination of Change at the Boundary Waters Canoe Area Wilderness." *Social Indicators Research* 110 (2): 597–611. https://doi.org/10.1007/s11205-011-9947-x.

Welch, James R. 2010. "Hierarchy, Symmetry, and the Xavante Spiritual Life Cycle." *Horizontes Antropológicos* 16 (34): 235–59. https://doi.org/10.1590/S0104-71832010000200011.

Welch, James R. 2014. "Xavante Ritual Hunting: Anthropogenic Fire, Reciprocity, and Collective Landscape Management in the Brazilian Cerrado." *Human Ecology* 42 (1): 47–59. https://doi.org/10.1007/s10745-013-9637-1.

Welch, James R. 2015. "Learning to Hunt by Tending the Fire: Xavante Youth, Ethnoecology, and Ceremony in Central Brazil." *Journal of Ethnobiology* 35 (1): 183–208. https://doi.org/10.2993/0278-0771-35.1.183.

Welch, James R. 2020. "A'uwẽ (Xavante) Hunting Calls: A Vocal Repertoire for Ethnozoological Communication and Coordination in the Brazilian Cerrado." *Ethnobiology Letters* 11 (1): 38–44. https://doi.org/10.14237/ebl.11.1.2020.1688.

Welch, James R. 2021a. "A'uwẽ (Xavante) Social Constructions of Well-Being in Central Brazil." *Medical Anthropology* 40 (8): 799–814. https://doi.org/10.1080/01459740.2021.1961247.

Welch, James R. 2021b. "Camaraderie, Mentorship, and Manhood: Contemporary Indigenous Identities among the A'uwẽ (Xavante) of Central Brazil." *SocArXiv*, August 20, 1–26. Preprint. https://doi.org/10.31235/osf.io/b74fg.

Welch, James R. 2022a. "A'uwẽ (Xavante) Sacred Food Plants: Maize and Wild Root Vegetables." *Anthropology of Consciousness* 33 (2): 202–28. https://doi.org/10.1111/anoc.12152.

Welch, James R. 2022b. "Heritable Prerogatives and Non-Lineages: Proprietary Knowledge Ownership among the A'uwẽ (Xavante) in Central Brazil." *Journal of the Royal Anthropological Institute* 28 (3): 807–27. https://doi.org/10.1111/1467-9655.13775.

Welch, James R., Eduardo S. Brondizio, and Carlos E. A. Coimbra Jr. 2022. "Remote Spatial Analysis Lacking Ethnographic Grounding Mischaracterizes Sustainability of Indigenous Burning Regime." *Biota Neotropica* 22 (1): e20211220. https://doi.org/10.1590/1676-0611-bn-2021-1220.

Welch, James R., Eduardo S. Brondízio, Scott S. Hetrick, and Carlos E. A. Coimbra Jr. 2013. "Indigenous Burning as Conservation Practice: Neotropical Savanna Recovery amid Agribusiness Deforestation in Central Brazil." *PLOS ONE* 8 (12): e81226. https://doi.org/10.1371/journal.pone.0081226.

Welch, James R., and Carlos E. A. Coimbra Jr. 2014. "Os Xavante e Seus Etnógrafos." In *Antropologia e História Xavante em Perspectiva*, edited by Carlos E. A. Coimbra Jr. and James R. Welch, 1–15. Rio de Janeiro: Museu do Índio/FUNAI.

Welch, James R., and Carlos E. A. Coimbra Jr. 2021. "Indigenous Fire Ecologies, Restoration, and Territorial Sovereignty in the Brazilian Cerrado: The Case of Two Xavante Reserves." *Land Use Policy* 104:104055. https://doi.org/10.1016/j.landusepol.2019.104055.

Welch, James R., and Carlos E. A. Coimbra Jr. 2022. "A'uwẽ (Xavante) Views of Food Security in a Context of Monetarization of an Indigenous Economy in Central Brazil." *PLOS ONE* 17 (2): e0264525. https://doi.org/10.1371/journal.pone.0264525.

Welch, James R., Aline A. Ferreira, Ricardo Ventura Santos, Silvia A. Gugelmin, Guilherme L. Werneck, and Carlos E. A. Coimbra Jr. 2009. "Nutrition Transition, Socioeconomic Differentiation, and Gender among Adult Xavante Indians, Brazilian Amazon." *Human Ecology* 37 (1): 13–26. https://doi.org/10.1007/s10745-009-9216-7.

Welch, James R., Aline A. Ferreira, Felipe G. Tavares, J. Rodolfo M. Lucena, Maurício V. Gomes de Oliveira, Ricardo Ventura Santos, and Carlos E. A. Coimbra Jr. 2020. "The Xavante Longitudinal Health Study in Brazil: Objectives, Design, and Key Results." *American Journal of Human Biology* 32 (2): e23339. https://doi.org/10.1002/ajhb.23339.

Welch, James R., Ricardo Ventura Santos, Nancy M. Flowers, and Carlos E. A. Coimbra Jr. 2013. *Na Primeira Margem do Rio: Território e Ecologia do Povo Xavante de Wedezé*. Rio de Janeiro: Museu do Índio.

Werner, Dennis. 1981. "Are Some People More Equal than Others? Status Inequality among the Mekranoti Indians of Central Brazil." *Journal of Anthropological Research* 37 (4): 360–73. https://doi.org/10.1086/jar.37.4.3629833.

White, Mathew P., Ian Alcock, James Grellier, Benedict W. Wheeler, Terry Hartig, Sara L. Warber, Angie Bone, Michael H. Depledge, and Lora E. Fleming. 2019. "Spending at Least 120 Minutes a Week in Nature Is Associated with Good Health and Wellbeing." *Scientific Reports* 9 (1): 1–11. https://doi.org/10.1038/s41598-019-44097-3.

WHO. 1948. "Preamble to the Constitution of the World Health Organization as Adopted by the International Health Conference, New York, 19–22 June 1946." Geneva: World Health Organization.

Wolf, Lukas J., Sophus zu Ermgassen, Andrew Balmford, Mathew White, and Netta Weinstein. 2017. "Is Variety the Spice of Life? An Experimental Investigation into the Effects of Species Richness on Self-Reported Mental Well-Being." *PLOS ONE* 12 (1): e0170225. https://doi.org/10.1371/journal.pone.0170225.

Wolsko, Christopher, Cecile Lardon, Scarlett Hopkins, and Elizabeth Ruppert. 2006. "Conceptions of Wellness among the Yup'ik of the Yukon–Kuskokwim Delta: The Vitality of Social and Natural Connection." *Ethnicity and Health* 11 (4): 345–63. https://doi.org/10.1080/13557850600824005.

Wright, Robin M. 1996. "Destruction, Resistance, and Transformation: Southern Coastal, and Northern Brazil (1850–1890)." In *The Cambridge History of the Native Peoples of the Americas*. Vol. 3, *South America, Part 2*, edited by Bruce G. Trigger, Wilcomb E. Washburn, and Richard E. W. Adam, 287–381. Cambridge: Cambridge University Press.

Zanotti, Laura. 2014. "Political Ecology of Movement: Trekking and Territoriality among the Kayapó." *Journal of Political Ecology* 21 (1): 108–126. https://doi.org/10.2458/v21i1.21127.

Zoia, Alceu, and Odimar J. Peripolli. 2010. "Infância Indígena e Outras Infâncias." *Espaço Ameríndio* 4 (2): 9–24.

INDEX

Note: Page numbers in *italics* denote figures.

ABOUT THE AUTHOR

James R. Welch, PhD, is senior researcher at the National School of Public Health, Oswaldo Cruz Foundation (FIOCRUZ), Rio de Janeiro, Brazil. From 2011 to 2018 he served as co-editor of *Ethnobiology Letters*, a journal of the Society of Ethnobiology. His primary research focuses on Indigenous people's social organization, health and well-being, fire ecology, environmental knowledge, territorial rights, and digital sovereignty. He works closely with the A'uwẽ (Xavante) on land disputes and multimedia cultural documentation.